ECONOGUIDE® CRUISES 2004

Help Us Keep This Guide Up to Date

Every effort has been made by the author and editors to make this guide as accurate and useful as possible. However, many things can change after a guide is published—itineraries and regulations change, ships are removed from service, facilities come under new management, etc.

We would love to hear from you concerning your experiences with this guide and how you feel it could be improved and kept up to date. While we may not be able to respond to all comments and suggestions, we'll take them to heart and we'll also make certain to share them with the author. Please send your comments and suggestions to the following address:

The Globe Pequot Press
Reader Response/Editorial Department
P.O. Box 480
Guilford, CT 06437

Or you may e-mail us at:

editorial@GlobePequot.com

Thanks for your input, and happy travels!

ECONOGUIDE® SERIES

ECONOGUIDE® CRUISES 2004

Cruising the Caribbean, Hawaii, New England, Alaska, and Europe

COREY SANDLER

GUILFORD, CONNECTICUT

The prices and rates listed in this guidebook were confirmed
at press time. We recommend, however, that you call establishments
to obtain current information before traveling.

Text design by Lesley Weissman-Cook

ISBN 0-7627-2751-9
ISSN 1529-9015

Manufactured in the United States of America
Second Globe Pequot Press Edition/First Printing

To Janice, who keeps me on course

CONTENTS

ACKNOWLEDGMENTS

AS ALWAYS, dozens of hardworking and creative people helped move my words from the keyboard to the book you hold in your hands.

Among the many to thank are Jeff Serena and Mary Luders Norris of The Globe Pequot Press; we look forward to many years of partnership. Thanks, too, to the editorial and production staff at Globe Pequot, including Gillian Belnap and Melissa Evarts.

Gene Brissie has been a believer for a decade, and the feeling is mutual.

My appreciation extends to the cruise lines and public relations staffs who helped me assemble the massive stack of specifications, itineraries, and prices and wrangle them into manageable shape.

As always, thanks to Janice Keefe for running the office and putting up with me, a pair of major assignments. Thanks also to Econoguide staffers Michael Lawrence and Maureen Moriarty.

And thanks to you for buying this book. We all hope you find it of value; please let us know how we can improve the book in future editions. (Enclose a stamped envelope if you'd like a reply; no phone calls, please.)

Corey Sandler
Econoguide Travel Books
P.O. Box 2779
Nantucket, MA 02584

You can also consult our Web page at
www.econoguide.com

I hope you'll also consider the other books in the Econoguide series. You can find them at bookstores, or ask your bookseller to order them. All are written by Corey Sandler.

Econoguide Walt Disney World® 2004
Econoguide Disneyland® Resort, Universal Studios Hollywood® 2004
Econoguide Las Vegas 2004
Econoguide Buying or Leasing a Car
Econoguide Buying and Selling a Home
Also by Corey Sandler:
Fix Your Own PC, Seventh Edition

INTRODUCTION

WELCOME ABOARD for a journey between the covers of the 2004 edition.

During the past few years, I've floated from one stunning horizon to the next on a series of journeys that have taken me from my home in one of the rugged harbors of New England to the iridescent waters of the Caribbean, the wild geological stew of geysers and glaciers in Iceland, the wondrous ice-carved canyons of Alaska's Inside Passage, the fire-born islands of Hawaii and the South Pacific, and through the man-made wonder of the Panama Canal. I crossed the "pond" from England to the New World, and I played tag with three hurricanes. For two magical weeks we cruised from one magnificent Mediterranean port to another, and on another trip we circled the British Isles from Dover to Ireland to Scotland.

Some of the highlights of my recent career at sea:

- Ten days afloat from Iceland to New York in sybaritic luxury in a three-room luxury suite on a ship where the champagne flowed like water.
- Crossing the Gulf of Mexico for an exploration of Mayan Central America on the fastest cruise ship afloat, speedy enough to tow a brave water-skier.
- Making a nighttime journey past an erupting volcano on the island of Stromboli in the Tyrrhenian Sea.
- Living the pampered life aboard the world's largest private sailing yacht, while visiting some obscure corners of the Caribbean like Îles des Saintes, Carriacou, and Bequia.
- Enjoying culinary theater in a dining room decorated with century-old paneling from a classic liner, within a high-tech modern ship powered by jet turbines.
- Floating into Skagway, Alaska, to retrace the path of the Gold Rushers on the White Pass and Yukon Railroad.
- Watching the horizon at dawn as a distant Christmas tree slowly revealed itself to be an oil rig standing in the icy Atlantic a few hundred miles off the coast of Newfoundland, the first sign of human civilization other than our own ship after nearly a week on a transatlantic crossing from England to Boston, Massachusetts.
- Seeing the wonder in the eyes of a child on a nearly untouched South Pacific atoll where we had been deposited by a modern cruise ship; we felt like friendly visitors from another planet.
- Sharing a lyrical journey with a grand old lady, in the company of an affable band of jazz lovers on a Caribbean theme cruise aboard the world's longest passenger ship, and one of the oldest afloat.
- Cruising between the hulls of a huge catamaran at anchor off the remote island of San Andrés, a northern outpost of Colombia in the Caribbean Sea. The pilot of our tender drove between the pontoons of the one-of-a-kind twin-hull luxury cruise ship, transporting us through a 400-foot-long white tunnel floating on an azure sea.

■ Thrilling to a midnight fireworks salute offshore a Bahamian island as a cruise ship on her maiden voyage had a rendezvous with her twin sister.

■ Seeing the unreal baby blue hues of South Sawyer Glacier at the end of Tracy Arm in Alaska, as a classic steamship made a slow turnabout in the deep pool at the face of the river of frozen water. We watched squads of seals pass by on ice floes and were in turn tailed by pods of whales in the Inside Passage.

■ Passing by a gigantic megaship docked in New York City, looking, in the pre-dawn darkness, like a floating horizontal version of the Manhattan skyscrapers behind her.

Those were some of the places we went. And then there were the amazing sights onboard the cruise ships that took us there. Things such as:

■ The jaw-dropping decadence of an all-chocolate midnight buffet.

■ A full-scale musical production on a stage that had more technical facilities than many a Broadway theater. And we were moving at 23 knots, a hundred miles off the coast of Florida at the time!

■ Day after day of gourmet food, presented with artistry and attentive service at breakfast, brunch, lunch, midafternoon snack, dinner, and midnight. My children, on the other hand, loved the all-hours room service, ice-cream stand, and pizza parlor.

■ The incomparable beauty of a Caribbean sunset, glimpsed from a deck chair on the private veranda outside our stateroom.

■ The unimaginable heat and bone-rattling rumble of the engine room of a cruise ship moving at full speed through the Pacific. Up above, guests were pampered in air-conditioning and elegant luxury, completely insulated and hidden from the stygian scene down below.

■ The calming vista of endless sea, with no signs of land or life for nearly three days, while traveling south from Honolulu into the South Pacific.

DEAR READER: A CONFESSION

As a travel writer, I love the excitement of an expedition off the beaten track in an unusual place. I like nothing better than "going native" anywhere I visit: renting a car to drive on the wrong side of the road in the United Kingdom or Tortola; riding the subways of Seoul, Tokyo, or Barcelona; heading out with a guide across the top of a mountain in Vermont or Utah, and generally choosing my own schedule and itinerary.

Put another way, there is nothing I dislike more than a regimented trip where everything is arranged: when and where to eat, entertainment, and minute-by-minute calendars of activities. I want to know everything there is to know about the places I visit—before I go there—and then I want to wander off.

And so I fully expected that I would find cruising an intolerably confining and overorganized experience. What if I didn't like the ship? What if the cabin was unappealing? What if the food was awful? What if I didn't like the other people on the ship?

Well, with a bit of careful research before I booked passage, I was able to choose ships that ranged from well-kept old dowagers to a brand-new classic in the making. I knew more about the cabin I had booked than any travel agent did. I knew the details of the ship's cuisine in gourmet detail. And I found ways to shield myself from unwanted company when it suited me.

To my surprise, I found that I greatly enjoyed going on a cruise. During my seasons at sea, I learned the wonderful sense of peace and relaxation that comes from putting yourself in the hands of a capable cruise staff on a well-run cruise ship.

I discovered that I truly enjoyed staying put while the ship kept moving. My "hotel" traveled with me from port to port, along with a cabin steward and restaurant staff who, at least for the week or so I spent with them, treated me as if I were a combination of their benevolent employer and a best friend.

I found that, for a change, I enjoyed leaving the driving and the scheduling to someone else. I concentrated on relaxing.

Each day the ship arrived in a new port, I was among the first to clamber into the tender or charge down the gangplank. Based on research I had done before the trip, my wife and I took an occasional organized shore excursion, rented a car to head away from the tourist section of the port and explore for the day, or embarked on our own shore parties, far from the cruise crowd.

I always intend to do more than my share of off-the-cuff, unplanned travel at almost every opportunity. I will still chafe at any suggestion that someone else plan my trips, and I'll happily clamber aboard a cruise ship headed for unusual ports and high adventure.

WE ARE NOT ALONE

I suppose I should not have been surprised to find myself becoming a cruise convert. It turns out that I'm in very good company. In 1970 about half a million Americans took cruises; in 2003 an estimated eight million of us were expected to go to sea.

Here are some more cruise industry facts:

- Cruise lines aimed at North Americans expected to book about $10 billion in business in 2003.
- About 87 percent of U.S. adults have never cruised.
- The states producing the most cruise passengers are Florida, California, Texas, Massachusetts, New York, Pennsylvania, New Jersey, Illinois, Ohio, and Georgia.
- More than 90 percent of all cruise passengers book through travel agents, and cruise sales account for more than half of agents' vacation sales.
- Cruising has begun to shed its image as a vacation choice of seniors. Although millions of older persons enjoy the stress-free pampered life aboard ship, the average age of cruise passengers has dropped from fifty-six to fifty over the past decade.

The rapid pace of expansion among major cruise lines continued in 2003. Among significant changes to the fleet:

Carnival Cruise Lines. The 2,974-passenger *Carnival Glory* arrived in the summer with plans for year-round seven-day Caribbean service from Port Canaveral. In 2004 the line will add another sister, the 2,974-passenger *Carnival Valor,* as well as the 2,124-passenger *Carnival Miracle.*

Costa Cruises. The line's new flagship, the 2,154-passenger *Costa-Mediterranea,* entered the fleet in the summer, joined by the even larger, 2,720-passenger *CostaFortuna* late in the year.

Crystal Cruises: The ultraluxury 1,080-passenger *Crystal Serenity* arrived in the summer.

Cunard: The *Queen Mary 2,* scheduled to be delivered in early 2004, is both the longest and tallest passenger ship in the world, with capacity for 2,620 passengers.

Holland America Line. The 1,848-passenger *Oosterdam* arrived in the summer, joining sister ship *Zuiderdam,* which arrived at the end of 2002. A third sister, *Westerdam,* is due in 2004.

MSC Italian Cruises. The 1,600-passenger *MSC Lirica,* the first new-build for the line, arrived in the spring.

Norwegian Cruise Line. The 2,224-passenger *Norwegian Dawn* sailed its first season in 2003 in the Caribbean, moving north to sail year-round from New York later in the year. The line also welcomed back from Orient Lines the venerable *Norwegian Crown.* In 2004 the first U.S.-flagged ship in Project America is due to arrive, a 1,900-passenger ship for the Hawaiian Islands.

Oceania Cruises. *Insignia* and *Regatta,* both relaunched ships from the former Renaissance Cruises fleet, began service for this new cruise line.

Princess Cruises. The 88,000-ton *Island Princess* debuted in the spring, joining its sister ship *Coral Princess.* The relaunched 680-passenger *Tahitian Princess* and *Pacific Princess*—both formerly in the Renaissance Cruises fleet—began service in 2003. The 2,675-passenger *Caribbean Princess* is due in 2004.

Radisson Seven Seas Cruises. The all-balcony, all-suite, 700-guest *Seven Seas Voyager* arrived in the spring.

Royal Caribbean International. Two new ships joined the fleet in 2003: the 2,100-passenger *Serenade of the Seas* and the massive 3,114-passenger *Mariner of the Seas.*

Swan Hellenic. The 694-passenger *Minerva II,* which had previously sailed as Renaissance Cruises' *R8,* debuted in the spring.

According to the Cruise Lines International Association (CLIA), in 2003 there were about 214,854 berths on major cruise lines. The average cruise duration is just under seven days; itineraries are growing at both ends of the spectrum, with an increase in three- and four-day trips as well as voyages of ten days or more in exotic places around the world. Even with the tremendous increase in capacity in recent years, many cruise lines are operating at greater than 100 percent capacity on many trips. (A ship's capacity is calculated on the basis of double occupancy; a full ship with children or other family members in extra bunks brings a ship beyond its stated capacity.)

In 2002 the Caribbean continued as the leading destination for cruises. In the face of terror threats, there were declines in trips to the Mediterranean and increases in nearby waters of the Caribbean, Mexico, and Alaska. Here are the CLIA estimates of the breakdown of passengers:

- Caribbean, 42 percent
- Europe, 21 percent (Mediterranean, 10.2 percent; Northern Europe, 10.9 percent)
- Alaska, 8 percent
- Pacific Mexico, 5.3 percent
- Bahamas, 4.5 percent
- Panama Canal, 3.3 percent
- Hawaii, 3 percent
- South America, 2.2 percent
- Bermuda, 2 percent
- Canada and New England, 1.8 percent
- Transatlantic, 1.6 percent
- Orient, Southeast Asia, and Africa, 1.5 percent
- South Pacific, 1.3 percent
- Other areas, including Transpacific and Antarctica, 2 percent

Cruising continues as mainly an American product, with more than 70 percent of cruisegoers hailing from the United States. The next most popular market is the United Kingdom, representing approximately 10 percent of cruise passengers. The percentage of British and European travelers is expected to rise in coming years as some of the megaships expand their presence in the Mediterranean and Asian areas.

More huge new cruise ships are being built in shipyards around the world than ever before. As a result, cruise lines are becoming increasingly competitive. Although berths on holiday and peak-season sailings will remain at a premium, you can expect to see some fabulous deals at other times of the year from every major cruise line.

GONE FROM THE FLEET

Although the number of cruise ships in the global fleet continues to grow, and more and more people discover the joys of a vacation at sea, not all cruise companies are an economic success. One principal reason is the tremendous power of the two largest (and most profitable) companies: Carnival and Royal Caribbean.

In 2003 Carnival completed its unfriendly takeover of Princess, breaking up a planned friendly merger between Princess and Royal Caribbean. Princess will continue to operate as a semiautonomous company with its own ships, policies, and identity.

With the acquisition, Carnival now owns nearly 60 percent of the U.S. cruise market. Royal Caribbean is in distant second place, with about 25 percent of the market. Third place belongs to Singapore's Star Cruises, the parent company of Norwegian Cruise Line.

In late 2001 well-respected Renaissance Cruises fell victim to intense competition and changing economic conditions. The company's fleet of eight upscale destination-oriented ships were dispersed to other lines, including Princess Cruises and Swan Hellenic. A start-up company, Oceania Cruises has taken two of the ships for a new line that closely resembles the former Renaissance operation.

World Explorer Cruises, which operated the venerable *Universe Explorer* in Alaska and Central America with a well-respected curriculum of lectures and enrichment activities, suspended operations in early 2003 when it lost the lease on its vessel. The company hopes to resume cruising in the future.

Regal Cruises went under in April 2003 when its entire fleet, the half-century-old *Regal Empress,* was attached by a creditor. The ship was purchased by Imperial Majesty Cruises.

The Delta Queen Steamboat Company came back from bankruptcy in 2002 under new ownership. The line's three classic paddle wheelers returned to the rivers: *Delta Queen, American Queen,* and *Mississippi Queen.*

ResidenSea launched its *World* in 2002. The ultraluxury 43,000-ton ship is operated like a condominium, with most of her 110 furnished residences and 88 guest suites owned by travelers. A small number of suites are available for booking for short cruises. The ship will travel continuously around the world.

ABOUT THIS BOOK

The main purpose of this book is to help you choose the right ship, the right itinerary, the right cabin, and even the right dining options. I'll also tell you how to find ways to be alone among a few thousand other passengers and how to pick and choose your activities to make the cruise ship meet your expectations, not the other way around.

My staff and I have collected information on the best cruises at any price, along with details of how to get the most for your money, no matter how much you spend, as well as advice on how to travel in economic style from coast to coast.

In the 2004 edition we cover every major cruise line marketing cruises to Americans and Canadians in U.S., Canadian, Caribbean, Mexican, and South Pacific waters. We also cover seasonal cruises in the Mediterranean, the Baltic, elsewhere in Europe, and transatlantic repositioning trips.

We offer a selection of money-saving coupons from travel providers. There is no connection between the information in this book and the coupons we publish, except that *everything* between the covers is intended to save you money.

Pardon us for saying so, but we think the cost-effectiveness of this book will speak for itself. With its assistance, you should easily be able to save many times its price while enjoying your cruise.

CHAPTER ONE

How to Choose a Cruise

THE FIRST DECISION is the easy one: Do you want to check into a fine hotel and sit back and relax as it floats from one fascinating place to another, all the while plying you with gourmet food and great entertainment?

Now comes the slightly harder part—the *Econoguide* **top-ten questions for cruisegoers:**

■ Would you prefer a gigantic floating city with a population of a few thousand strangers and dozens of dining and entertainment options? Or would you instead choose a well-equipped but small, intimate vessel that is more like a semi-private yacht?

■ Do you want to laze your way through the blue Caribbean, be thrilled by the Inside Passage of Alaska, venture way out to sea on a transatlantic or transpacific crossing, explore the remains of the ancient civilizations of Central America, cruise the Mississippi on a paddle wheeler or a river barge, or join a growing number of travelers who use a cruise ship as their hotel between ports in the Mediterranean, Baltic Sea, Irish Sea, and the English Channel?

■ Is the itinerary the most important factor in your decision, or do you want to choose a ship and ride her wherever she travels?

■ Are you the sort of person who looks forward to a cruise that goes for a long haul with full days at sea? Or would you prefer a new port every morning: Go to sleep in Aruba and awake in Curaçao; lights out in Boston, daybreak in Nova Scotia; good night Saint Martin, good morning San Juan?

■ Does the stateroom of your dreams include a sitting room, bedroom, private balcony with hot tub, and a butler? Or do you just need a place to store your stuff and lay your head when you're not out at the pool, in the dining room or the casino, or at the barbecue, the theater, or the midnight buffet?

■ Are you a blue jeans and T-shirt kind of person, or are you looking for a place to break out the tuxedo or cocktail gown?

■ Do you want familiar food and hometown customs, or would you like to sail on a ship with a bit of a foreign flavor: British, Dutch, German, Greek, or Italian-style cruising?

- Do you enjoy being assigned a dining time and the company of six strangers for the duration of your cruise, or do you prefer a table for two in the corner, whenever you choose to use it?
- Are you looking for particular sports and health club facilities, such as a golf simulator (or a miniature golf course), a luxurious spa, an indoor swimming pool, or (really!) an ice-skating rink and a rock climbing wall out at sea? Or are you more interested in the thickness of the cushions in the lounge?
- For some people this is the killer question: How much are you willing to pay? Are you looking for a bargain price for good value, or is money no object to your pursuit of pleasure?

There are no right or wrong answers to any of these questions. The wide range of choices available to cruisegoers is a good thing. The purpose of this book is to help you find the perfect cruise for you. Before you sign on the bottom line for a seaborne vacation, make yourself an expert on the world of cruising.

In this book we'll explore ships from massive megaships that would have dwarfed the *Titanic* to luxurious superyachts and intimate adventure boats. We'll look at the latest and greatest, and we'll examine a few floating antiques, stylish reminders of the days of the great ocean liners.

THE LIST PRICE AND THE REAL PRICE

Cruise and new car brochures have a lot in common: gorgeous pictures of the hardware, photo spreads of handsome models having a great time in exotic places, and a price list that could stop a heart.

But for both cars and cruises, only a few unfortunate and generally uninformed people actually pay the sticker price. Let me put it another way: Those relative few who pay list price subsidize the rest of us who search out the best bargains.

In many instances, there's the list price and there's the real price. There are many ways to save. In fact, with some cruise lines, you may find it hard to pay the list price; there are sales to be found almost all the time. If you choose cruises and the time of year carefully, discounts of 50 percent or more off the brochure rate are quite ordinary.

Start out with a determination not to pay the prices you see quoted. Contact a cruise specialist or a travel agent who has some expertise in cruises, or check with the cruise line directly for special rates. Consult the Internet to research cruise lines, and use what you learn to obtain the very best prices—whether you book directly or through a travel agent.

Be direct and to the point: Ask the agent or reservationist to save you money off the published list price. This accomplishes two goals: First, it announces right at the start that you're aware the list price is often a starting point in a sales negotiation. It also puts the agent on notice that you expect a close eye on the bottom line.

DO YOU NEED TO USE A TRAVEL AGENT?

You do not *need* to work with a travel agent to book *most* cruises. You may, though, *want* to consult an expert for advice about ships, itineraries, and special deals.

You've got most of the basic information about cruises and cruise ships right here in this book, and every cruise line offers extensive information about its offerings in brochures, telephone help lines, and Internet Web sites. Although some cruise lines insist that you book your trip through a travel agent, most will also work directly with travelers by telephone or over the Internet.

Here's my advice: Spend a week or so collecting information from this book, Web sites, and other sources, and then contact cruise lines directly to find out about availability and special promotions.

Among cruise lines that take direct bookings over the Internet or by telephone are Royal Caribbean, Celebrity Cruises, Carnival Cruise Line, Holland America, Costa Cruises, Norwegian Cruise Line, and others. Most allow you to "reserve" a cruise for a few days without putting down a deposit; this is a good way to compare the best rate you can find for yourself with one that is arranged by a travel agent.

Then look for a knowledgeable travel agent; ask friends and acquaintances for recommendations. Be specific in your criteria: the type of cruise ship, itinerary, and cabin you're looking for.

Compare the suggestions of the travel agent with the results of your own research. If the agent can save you money or time or get you an upgrade, go ahead and lay down your credit card.

If the agent's prices are significantly higher than ones you can get on your own, or if he or she seems to be pushing a different cruise line or itinerary than the one you've identified, ask yourself—and the travel agent—if there is some ulterior motive here. The fact is that some travel agents receive additional commissions or special rebates from particular cruise lines; a handful of travel agents specialize in just one or two cruise lines for that reason.

If you're not convinced the agent is looking out for your interests first, or if you discover that you know more about the business than the supposed "expert," move on to another agent or do it yourself.

TRICKS TO GETTING THE BEST RATE

Here are some of the best ways to pay less than the list price:
- Book early.
- Book late.
- Cruise in the off-season.
- Choose a repositioning cruise.
- Cruise a new itinerary.

- Extend a cruise with back-to-back trips.
- Take advantage of special offers for frequent cruisers.
- Take advantage of special discounts.
- Buy from a cruise consolidator or major cruise travel agency able to negotiate special deals for its customers.
- Buy directly from a cruise line, grabbing last-minute deals or Internet-only specials.
- Be flexible on the ship's itinerary or date of departure.
- Upgrade your cabin onboard.
  Or, if you insist, here's how to end up paying top dollar for a cruise:
- Choose a hot new ship in its inaugural season.
- Insist on sailing during a holiday period.
- Be rigid in your sailing date or itinerary.
- Insist on a particular class of cabin.
- Require a particular bed configuration, especially for a cabin for more than two persons.

■ BOOK EARLY

Many cruise lines offer discounts of as much as 50 percent off bookings made six months to a year in advance. If you sign up for such a deal, be sure you understand your rights in case of an unexpected need to cancel; you might also want to include trip cancellation insurance in your purchase.

If you are planning a major celebration—a wedding or anniversary, for example—or hope to travel on a special occasion such as New Year's Eve or a solar eclipse, you might have no choice but to commit to a cruise six months to a year in advance.

■ BOOK LATE

If you are flexible on departure date and itinerary, you can really clean up with a last-minute deal. An unsold cabin is a loss that can never be recouped. Cruise lines just hate to sail with an unused cabin, and they'll carve deeply into list prices to fill those empty berths.

The downside is that in some cases, cruise lines will upgrade their customers who paid full- or near-full rates. This leaves last-minute cruisers the least attractive cabins, albeit at a deeply discounted rate.

In general, the first cabins to sell out on a cruise ship are those at each end of the spectrum: the lowest-priced staterooms and the most spectacular (and relatively scarce) suites.

Register with a cruise agency or, in some cases, directly with a cruise line, and indicate your willingness to take whatever is available on a particular date or itinerary, then be ready to make a last-minute dash to the port.

It is hard to predict when a cruise line will offer these deals. Sometimes the unsold cabins are on the most desirable cruises: Christmas and New Year's in the Caribbean, or the heart of summer in Alaska or the Mediterranean. At other times, the best deals are available on repositioning cruises and trips at the "shoulders" leading up to or out of peak season.

Disadvantages to last-minute booking: You may have to pay top dollar for last-minute air travel to the port unless it is within reasonable driving distance. Be sure to figure in airfare costs to see if the bottom line for a spur-of-the-moment cruise still makes sense. Also, the last-minute cabins are almost always the least desirable staterooms.

■ CRUISE IN THE OFF-SEASON

As with most everything you buy, you can expect a better price when there are more sellers than buyers.

In many cases, you'll find cruising in the off-season just as attractive as in the heart of the season; happily, you'll have less company and pay less for the privilege. You could, though, run into problems caused by the weather, such as late-season hurricanes or unusually rough seas. Do the research and know your preferences before you book off-season—or any other time of the year, for that matter.

Here are a few *off-season* times for cruising:

■ **Caribbean and Mexican Riviera.** After Labor Day to pre-Christmas, early January, and April through Memorial Day.

■ **Panama Canal.** January and February; repositioning cruises in spring and fall.

■ **Alaska.** Beginning and end of the season: May and September.

■ **Europe.** Beginning and end of the season: May and September.

■ **Bermuda.** Beginning and end of the season: May and September.

There are usually a few dead periods too, even in what might otherwise be considered prime season. In most markets, for example, the period between Thanksgiving and Christmas is relatively quiet, as is the period immediately after New Year's Day.

PRIME TRAVEL SEASONS

	Jan	Feb	Mar	Apr	May	Jun	Jul	Aug	Sep	Oct	Nov	Dec
Alaska						★★	★★★★	★★★★	★★★			
Bahamas	★★★★	★★★★	★★★★	★★★★	★★★★	★★★★	★★★☆	★★★☆	★★★☆	★★★	★★★	★★★★
Bermuda					★★★★	★★★★	★★★★	★★★★	★★★★	★★★★		
Caribbean	★★★★	★★★★	★★★★	★★★★	★★★★	★★★★	★★★☆	★★★☆	★★★☆	★★★☆	★★★☆	★★★★
Western U.S.	★★★★	★★★★	★★★★								★★★★	★★★★
Hawaii	★★★★	★★★★	★★★★	★★★	★★★	★★★	★★★★	★★★★	★★★★	★★★	★★★	★★★★
Mexico, Central America	★★★★	★★★★	★★★★	★★★	★★★	★★★	★★★	★★★	★★★☆	★★★☆	★★★☆	★★★★
New England									★★★	★★★★	★★★	
Canada							★★★	★★★★	★★★★	★★★		
Eastern U.S.					★★★★	★★★★	★★★★	★★★★	★★★★	★★★		
Europe						★★★★	★★★★	★★★★	★★★★			
Transatlantic reposition				★★★					★★★			
World cruise	★★★★	★★★★	★★★★	★★★★								★★★★

★★ Low   ★★★ Good   ★★★★ Prime   ★★★☆ Prime, but hurricane season

■ CHOOSE A REPOSITIONING CRUISE

There is nothing scarier to a cruise line bean counter than a $350 million ship with nowhere to go and no incoming payments to apply to the mortgage. The Caribbean is pretty much a year-round destination, but most other areas of the world are more seasonal in their draw.

One example of a seasonal schedule puts a ship in Alaska for the summer, then down the West Coast to the Panama Canal in the fall and through to the Caribbean for the winter. The process is reversed in late spring. The ship might also make a wide detour to Hawaii on its way south to the canal.

These repositioning cruises are sometimes less popular than regular itineraries for a particular ship or cruise line. They may call at unusual ports or spend several days out to sea instead of in port, but to some travelers, these are the very things that make repositioning cruises so attractive. You can expect significant discounts as well as cabin upgrades on many repositioning itineraries.

(In chapter 11 you can read a cruise diary of a weeklong repositioning cruise from Harwich, England, to Boston, Massachusetts, on Holland America Line's *Maasdam*.)

■ CRUISE A NEW ITINERARY

A careful shopper may be able to find a bargain fare on a cruise ship pioneering a new port or a new itinerary. In some cases, the cruise line might be testing the appeal of a new schedule, or the line may be just beginning to build its business in a new area. Sometimes the first few sailings from a new port are fully booked by those who seek out new and different ports, then there is a period of lower bookings while the cruise line markets its new offering.

Once again, try to take advantage of any situation in which there may be more cabins than passengers.

■ EXTEND A CRUISE WITH BACK-TO-BACK TRIPS

Many cruise lines will offer significant discounts to travelers who book more than one trip in a row. For example, many ships offer alternating east and west Caribbean itineraries and will reward passengers who book a cabin for both legs.

You could also receive a discount for booking multiple legs of a round-the-world cruise or other long-term cruises.

■ TAKE ADVANTAGE OF SPECIAL OFFERS FOR FREQUENT CRUISERS

Many cruise lines make special offers to members of their own clubs of former passengers. Companies might maintain a more formal "club" of passengers with newsletters and get-togethers, or they may merely send offers to former clients.

Typical offers range from discounts to upgrades. Some companies offer special discounts if you make a booking for another cruise while onboard ship.

■ TAKE ADVANTAGE OF SPECIAL DISCOUNTS

Keep your eyes open for special deals offered directly by the cruise line as well as those offered in conjunction with associations, credit card companies, and other groups.

For example, some cruise lines offer special rates to AARP or AAA members. I have often received discount coupons for cruise vacations with my monthly credit card bills.

Be on the lookout—and don't be afraid to ask—for special programs that offer reduced rates for third and fourth passengers in a room, for single passengers willing to be matched in a double cabin, and other such deals.

Some cruise lines also offer a "guaranteed outside cabin" deal, priced at or below the lowest specific outside cabin class. In other words, you won't be choosing a particular deck or type of room but are willing to accept whatever outside stateroom is available. You just might be lucky enough to get a better accommodation than you would receive by specifying a particular class.

■ BUY FROM A CRUISE CONSOLIDATOR OR MAJOR CRUISE TRAVEL AGENCY

Consolidators purchase large blocks of cabins on particular sailings at deep discounts and resell them to consumers. You'll sometimes find great deals here, but be sure to compare the agent's price with one you could obtain on your own. And don't let yourself be talked into a ship or cruise line that is not what you originally decided on. Look for consolidators at Internet Web sites.

■ BUY DIRECTLY FROM A CRUISE LINE

Some cruise lines are cautiously exploring selling trips directly to the consumer at a discount. I say cautiously because they do so at the risk of alienating their primary source of sales: travel agents. Look for the best price you can find online, and then ask a travel agent to beat it.

■ BE FLEXIBLE ON THE SHIP'S ITINERARY OR DATE OF DEPARTURE

If you can adjust your travel plans to take advantage of the best available offerings, you are sure to save money.

Let's say you are able to tell a travel agent or cruise line that you are interested in cruising sometime in February or March, are willing to consider a wide range of ports of embarkation and itineraries, and are willing to travel on any of a wide range of available ships.

In a way, you are putting your business out for sale to the lowest bidder. Of course, you do need to look closely at any offers, and your agent should be able to give you a full and honest answer about why a particular cruise is being discounted.

Matching Services for Singles

▶ **Connecting: Solo Travel Network.** www.cstn.org; (800) 557–1757. A fee-based listing service that helps singles find each other, the network also posts information on cruises and other travel packages, making special discount offers to single travelers.

▶ **Travel Companion Exchange.** www.travel companions.com; (631) 454–0880. This fee-based matching service requires participants to fill out a detailed information and preferences form.

▶ **Vacation Partners.** www.vacationpartners.com; (800) 810–8075. Vacation Partners is a fee-based matching service for cruises and other travel.

▶ **Travel Chums.** www.travelchums.com. A free bulletin board service, Travel Chums helps match single travelers, but performs no verification of the identity of members.

■ UPGRADE YOUR CABIN ONBOARD

Another strategy is to search for upgrades to cabins once you're onboard the ship. Visit the reception or purser's desk after the ship sets sail and ask about any available cabins. Nearly all cruise lines offer reduced rates on premium staterooms when there is no longer any chance of selling that cabin to a last-minute arrival. This scheme will not work, of course, if the ship is fully booked.

SINGLE CRUISERS

Like it or not, cruise lines base their fares on double occupancy, building in the costs of meals, entertainment, and other services. For that reason, single travelers face "premiums" or "supplements" of as much as 200 percent if they choose to reserve a cabin for themselves.

Some cruise lines are a bit more reasonable, charging only 110 to 150 percent of ordinary rates, and several lines offer special deals from time to time, selling double-occupancy cabins to singles at regular fare.

Here are some money-saving options:

■ Ask if the cruise line has a singles-matching program. The company will pair you with another single traveler of the same sex, and you will each pay the standard double-occupancy rate. In many cases, if the cruise line is unable to pair you with another single you will end up with a cabin to yourself at half the double rate. Some cruise lines offer to fill up a triple or quad cabin with singles, reducing the cost markedly for all travelers.

■ Look for a cruise line that offers cabins specifically designed for singles. Not all that many of these staterooms are available, and they are generally found on older ships. Single cabins are often the least impressive inside staterooms, but they do save travelers a bit of money. (Among the vessels with single cabins is the still-impressive *Queen Elizabeth 2.*)

■ If the cruise line is going to charge you as though you had a second person in your cabin and you don't want to travel with a stranger, why not invite a friend or relative to join you? For the cost of an airline ticket to the port, you'll have comfortable company.

You can also cautiously explore several services that promise to help match up singles to share rooms; my recommendation would be to arrange to meet with a potential roommate for a weekend trip before booking a cruise. Some single travelers use services to match up with a traveling companion for a cruise but still book separate single rooms for the trip.

COMPARING THE COST OF A CRUISE WITH ANOTHER VACATION

Cruises sound expensive, and, indeed, the most luxurious suites onboard a modern ship can cost hundreds of dollars per person per night. But the cost for a cabin in the middle range compares well with other types of vacations when you look at the entire picture.

Think of the cruise equation as:

Cruise Ticket = Transportation + Room + Meals + Entertainment + Sports Activities

Of course, the more cruise amenities you use, the better the deal. If you're planning to stay in your room and skip the sumptuous meals, the midnight buffet, and the nightly theatrical shows, perhaps you should stay in a room at a motel on the shore.

The following example is based on a middle-of-the-market, seven-day cruise in a midrange cabin on a premium carrier such as Holland America or Norwegian Cruise Line, compared with a week's stay at a good-quality resort in Florida or the Caribbean.

	On a Cruise	On a Land Vacation for Two
Cruise fare for two	$2,500	$0
Hotel room	Included	$875 (7 nights)
Transportation	Included	$400 (7 days car rental)
Entertainment	Included	$500 (7 nights)
Sports activities	Included	$280 (7 days)
Breakfast	Included	$200 (with gratuity)
Lunch	Included	$300 (with gratuity)
Dinner	Included	$600 (with gratuity)
Snacks	Included	$200 (with gratuity)
Drinks	$150	$150
Other gratuities	$210	$50
TOTAL	**$2,860**	**$3,555**

Not included in either package are airline transportation and airport transfers. Note that some cruise packages include air transportation.

CRUISERS' FREQUENTLY ASKED QUESTIONS

Won't I get seasick? Modern cruise ships are very comfortable in most seas; most include high-tech stabilizers that act like underwater wings to even out much of the side-to-side roll that upsets some travelers.

You can also pick your cruise itinerary to try to avoid rough seas. For example, Caribbean waters are generally calm except for short periods of time during hurricane season. Trips on the Inside Passage from Vancouver or Seattle to Alaska are usually smooth and offer many opportunities to get off the ship and onto land.

If you are prone to motion sickness, I would avoid trips with full days at sea, and especially transatlantic and transpacific crossings, during which you might not set foot on land for as much as a week at a time.

If you are concerned about sway, you can consider the location of your stateroom. The least rocky rooms are on lower decks, toward the center of the ship; on most ships these are also less expensive cabins.

Medication such as Dramamine tablets or doctor-prescribed long-term scopolamine patches work well for those particularly prone to problems; be sure to check with your physician if you have any special medical conditions. Other remedies that work for some travelers include acupressure bracelets or herbal treatments such as ginger.

In these troubled times, is it safe to go out on a cruise? Alas, it may be that no place in today's world is completely free of the threat of terrorism. That said, cruise lines have done a lot to improve security in recent years. Luggage and freight are routinely inspected, passengers are checked at embarkation and at each port, and crew members are closely screened.

In American waters and nearby, cruise lines work closely with the U.S. Coast Guard and local port authorities to guard ships in port.

Because many travelers are more concerned about flying from their home to the port, most cruise lines have increased their "homeland" itineraries, sailing from the United States and Canada. Passengers can drive to departure cities on the East or West Coast or the Gulf of Mexico, or fly in on domestic airlines.

Operations in foreign waters, especially in the Middle East and Asia, have been curtailed in recent years. Many cruise lines have also reduced the number of ships sailing in the Mediterranean and Baltics.

The smart traveler does not throw caution to the wind on any vacation. Pay attention to the world situation; be on the lookout for suspicious persons or activities—you should do nothing less at home.

I heard about epidemics at sea. Will I get sick on a cruise? There is nothing particular about a cruise ship that causes epidemics, except that there are a lot of people in a relatively small enclosed space. Of course the same thing can be said about shoreside theaters, schools and universities, day care centers, and hospitals, as well as airports, planes, buses, and trains.

The best protection from disease at sea is common sense. Wash your hands frequently, especially before eating, and keep away from anyone who's visibly ill.

Maiden Voyages

Do you dream of being first to sleep in a new cabin, first to belly up to the buffet, and first to a new port? There'll be grand speeches, free-flowing champagne, and a sky filled with fireworks . . . kind of like the *Titanic*, presumably without the icebergs.

With a dozen or so major new cruise ships being launched each year, your chances of getting on a maiden voyage are better than ever. You'll find information about many of the upcoming launches in this book.

Many cruise lines will accept reservations for maiden voyages as much as a year ahead of scheduled dates; in some cases, first choice is offered to preferred customers.

The bad news, though, is that as ships become larger and more complex, the chances of delays in announced maiden voyage dates are also better than ever. If a cruise ship is not available for her scheduled maiden voyage, you might be offered a trip on another ship or a high-priority reservation on the actual first sailing. Some lines offer discounts or upgrades to soothe customers made unhappy by delays.

By the way, "maiden" voyages are not always the true first trip for a new ship. Modern cruise ships are generally built at yards in Europe or Scandinavia and go through several "shakedown" cruises near the yards before making a transoceanic crossing; some cruise lines schedule several weeks or months of trips before the formal start of service. Contact the cruise line to see if space is available on these pre–maiden voyages.

Will I go crazy being confined in a small place for a week? First of all, modern cruise ships hardly qualify as small places. The largest cruise ships afloat, classified in this book as a *Megaship, Colossus,* or *Gargantuan,* are more like midsize towns, with many restaurants and clubs, movie theaters, show rooms, gyms, jogging tracks, shops, and much more. A complete circuit of each deck on a Gargantuan ship is nearly a half mile in length. In my experience, any ship with at least 20,000 tons of capacity is big enough to allow a few changes of scene.

You can also choose an itinerary with lots of port calls; many ships in Europe and the Caribbean sail by night and are in port every day.

Help! I want my privacy; I don't want to share my dinner with six strangers. Choose a cruise that offers free choice for dining, a growing trend. Let your travel agent or the cruise line know of your preference for a private table at the time of booking. If you're unable to confirm a table to your liking, head directly for the maître d' when you board the ship; on most crews, the dining room managers are available for changes to table assignments or seatings on the day of embarkation.

On most ships you will find that the early seating is more fully booked; you should have an easier time selecting a table if you're willing to eat later.

On ships with open seating, let the maître d' know of your preference early in

Cruise Demographics

The passenger mix will vary across cruise lines and itineraries, but here's an example of one cruise on Holland America Line's *Veendam* in the Caribbean: Forty-two percent of passengers were age fifty-four and younger, and 58 percent were fifty-five and older. About 56 percent of the guests were female.

the cruise, and keep your elbows out to protect your privacy. Find the best time to show up; on many ships you can have your pick of tables early or late in the evening.

I hate the feeling that every waiter and cabin attendant looks at me as a walking gratuity. Is there another way? You're hardly alone; many lines have moved away from the awkward passing-of-the-envelope ceremony on the last night of the cruise. You might want to look for a cruise that includes tips in your fare or automatically adds them to your account. This system is becoming increasingly popular as cruises move away from assigned seatings for passengers.

Cruising is too expensive, isn't it? For many people, it is difficult to look past the bottom line on a cruise contract. There's one large figure, and it has to be paid for with a check or credit card. But as I've shown already, if you break it down and consider the cost of transportation, food, entertainment, and lodging, most cruise vacations turn out to be comparable with other types of travel.

You can also find ways to dramatically reduce the cost of a cruise. Look for trips at the start and end of a season, the so-called "shoulder seasons" when prices are often slashed. Some cruise lines commonly offer two-for-one deals to fill their ships.

Consider a repositioning cruise, when a ship is sent from one part of the world to another to prepare for the coming season. Sign up for notification of last-minute special offers.

Cruising is just for old folks. Won't I be the only one under seventy? Not anymore, if this ever was true. The biggest area of growth for many lines is among first-time cruisers and younger travelers. That's why they've added discos, rock climbing walls, skating rinks, and more.

All cruise lines welcome adult travelers of all ages, although a handful do not encourage or accept young children. Spend the time to learn a bit about the cruise line's policies and atmosphere.

The "party" lines, including Carnival and Royal Caribbean, may have a slightly younger crowd. The premium lines, including Norwegian Cruise Line, Celebrity, and Holland America Line, attract a slightly older audience, as do superluxury lines such as Crystal, Silversea, and Seabourn.

Cruising is just for young folks. Aren't I too old for this sort of thing? Not at all. A cruise ship is a wonderful way to travel for many people who want to take it easy. You'll check in once and unpack your bags for an extended period of time. Modern ships have ramps and elevators, making it easy to get about. Cruise lines are quite capable of dealing with guests in wheelchairs, with oxygen tanks, and with other special needs.

All major cruise lines have a medical clinic and doctor on board, and most lines will work with you and your doctor to accommodate special medical needs. It's also possible to arrange for special dietary requirements. You can find out from the shore excursions staff about port trips that meet your needs.

I don't want to learn how to carve ice. What will I do all day? Not interested in napkin folding either? Many cruise lines have moved beyond some of the silly old standbys to offer much more substantial courses. I've sat through fascinating lectures on anthropology and geology on a cruise in Alaska, heard a maritime historian tell the inside story of the *Titanic* on a transatlantic cruise that passed very close to the spot where the ship went down, and sailed through the Caribbean on a jazz cruise with some of the best musicians in the world. And of course, some of us enjoy seven days of pampered indolence.

I don't want to take a bus tour in each port. How can an independent traveler enjoy a port call? There is no requirement that you take a guided bus tour when you arrive in port. Spend the time before you leave home to investigate renting a car, hiring a vehicle and driver, or traveling by local train on your own. Be sure to allow a comfortable cushion of at least an hour at the end of the day to make sure you don't miss the boat; the main advantage of taking a cruise line–endorsed shore excursion is a guarantee that the ship will wait for passengers on the tour.

Hiring a car and driver, especially for a group of four people, is almost always less expensive than traveling on a chartered bus. You can impress the rest of the ship when they clamber down the gangplank to their bus and see a driver holding a card bearing your name.

Do the research in advance of your trip. Know more about the ports than the shore excursion staff does. Make phone calls to tourist bureaus; hire guides by phone or over the Internet.

How long a cruise should I take? First-time cruisers might want to take a three- or four-day voyage, although the best values are usually for seven-day or longer trips. More important to some is the nature of the itinerary. Are there days at sea? Some inexperienced cruisers may find that prospect a bit anxiety-inducing, while some veterans seek out relaxing days beyond sight of land. Does the ship spend every day in a port? You'll see less of the ship and more of the shore, which may or may not be your goal, but cruisers with a fear of seasickness will be able to regain their footings every morning.

CHAPTER TWO

HOW BIG IS BIG?

HOW BIG IS BIG ENOUGH? Everyone has his or her own answer. Some people yearn for a floating city with theaters, nightclubs, ice rinks, rock climbing walls, shopping malls, and a different restaurant for each night of the cruise. Others prefer a small but safe and comfortable raft in the vastness of the open ocean, their entertainment coming from the ever-changing sea.

Today's biggest ships are rated as 100,000 or more tons in size, a Brobdingnagian stature that was considered unrealistic a few years ago.

Royal Caribbean's *Voyager of the Seas,* a Gargantuan 142,000 tons, nearly overshadowed the skyscrapers of Miami when she arrived at her home port in late 1999. She has since been joined by sister ships *Explorer of the Seas, Adventurer of the Seas, Navigator of the Seas,* and *Mariner of the Seas.*

But wait: In early 2004 Cunard Line will introduce the *Queen Mary 2,* a massive vessel of more than 150,000 tons, 1,132 feet in length, and with a beam of 135 feet.

Each of these modest little boats is three times the size of the *Titanic* and more than double the magnitude of one of the Megaships that were the harbingers of the cruising boom of the 1990s.

Many cruise lines have chosen to keep their ships within the "Panamax" specifications, the maximum width and length for a ship to be able to pass through the Panama Canal between the Atlantic and Pacific Oceans. The locks of the canal are 110 feet wide and 1,000 feet long; any ship wider or longer than that must go the long way around the tip of South America if she is to be repositioned from one ocean to another. The new *Queen*

Royal Caribbean's *Voyager of the Seas* and her sisters are the largest cruise ships now in service. *Courtesy of Royal Caribbean International*

Mary 2, the Royal Caribbean Voyager-class ships, and a few other whoppers are bigger than the locks at Panama.

And how big is too big? Some dreamers—and a few planners—envision a future floating resort that will be a palatial waterworld.

The concept of economy of scale pushes cruise ships to either end of the spectrum—to small, ultraluxury (and ultra-high-priced) vessels or to Gargantuan ships that have cabins for more than 2,000 guests. On the small luxury ships, cruise lines can charge very high rates per passenger; on huge ships the costs of the construction of the ship, fuel, show rooms, and other fixed expenses are spread over a large number of guests.

AN ECONOGUIDE TO SMALL, MEDIUM, LARGE, AND GARGANTUAN

Size does matter—in facilities, atmosphere, and the overall experience of a cruise. There are those who prefer citizenship in a city at sea and others who would rather be in a floating supper club.

I divide cruise ships into classes based on gross registered tons, a measure of capacity I'll define in a moment. Here are the *Econoguide* size classes:

Gargantuan	130,000 or more tons
Colossus	100,000 to 130,000 tons
Megaship	70,000 to 100,000 tons
Large	40,000 to 70,000 tons
Medium	10,000 to 40,000 tons
Small	Less than 10,000 tons

So, how big is big enough? If you have a large cabin, a comfortably uncrowded dining room, and more deck chairs than people, you might consider a Medium 20,000-ton ship big enough. If you're one of 3,000 guests on a 100,000-ton Colossus and find yourself standing in line for a half hour to get to the buffet table, you may decide that the ship is way too small.

(Cunard's Gargantuan *Queen Mary 2* will carry a relatively small passenger load and offer an exceptionally large amount of public space, which should leave a lot of room to roam.)

Any ship 70,000 tons or larger will have multiple restaurants, large clubs, and other indoor and outdoor facilities.

So let's look at two important measures of size: gross registered tons and passenger-space ratio. We'll also define another way to think about quality of service: the passenger-to-crew ratio.

◼ GROSS REGISTERED TONS

First of all, it is important to understand that *tonnage* is not a measure of the weight of the ship. A ship of 100,000 tons does not weigh 200 million pounds.

Royal Olympia Cruises' *Olympia Voyager,* a 25,000-ton Medium-size ship for 836 passengers, tied up at Progreso, Mexico, alongside *Carnival Pride,* an 84,000-ton Megaship with cabins for 2,112 guests. *Photo by Dan Michalski*

In nautical terms, a ton is actually derived from a French measure known as *tonneaux,* which referred to a particular size of wine cask.

The concept of gross registered tons (GRT) was developed as a means of taxing vessels based on their cargo-carrying capacity. GRT is a measurement of the total permanently enclosed spaces of the ship, excluding certain essential areas such as the bridge and galleys. In modern terms, one GRT is equal to 100 cubic feet of enclosed, revenue-generating space.

Here is another way to think of GRT: A typical four-door compact car occupies roughly 300 cubic feet, or three tons. A basic kitchen refrigerator is between 40 and 50 cubic feet in size, equivalent to four-tenths to one-half GRT. So a 100,000-ton Megaship has revenue-generating space equivalent to about 33,333 compact cars or 250,000 kitchen refrigerators.

Some ships—freighters and smaller vessels among them—are measured in net tonnage, which is the gross tonnage minus certain additional spaces, such as crew and officer quarters and a calculated portion of the engine space.

■ PASSENGER-SPACE RATIO

Another way to look at the size of a ship is to compare the gross tonnage with the number of passengers onboard. The passenger-space ratio, which you'll find listed in charts later in this book, divides gross tonnage by a ship's standard double-occupancy capacity. The higher the space ratio, the less likely you'll find a stranger in a bath towel in your personal space by the pool or be assigned a seat at a dinner table for twelve. In this book, the range of space ratios for cruise ships runs from about 19 to 57, with most ships in the mid-30s range.

Passenger-space ratios are very rough measures. Some ship designers make staterooms large at the expense of public spaces; other ships have sprawling casinos and magnificent open atriums but offer broom-closet cabins. As we'll discuss later, some guests are willing to accept a small sleeping room because they don't intend to spend much time behind its closed door.

The space ratio does not work very well when applied to small adventure ships and sailing vessels that have different designs, including small bridges, galleys, engine rooms, and multipurpose public rooms. This class of ship also typically makes use of open deck space for viewing and dining.

IS BIGGER BETTER?

If you're looking for a Broadway theater at sea, a waterborne ice-skating rink, or a choice of five restaurants for dinner, sometimes bigger is better. A bigger ship may also offer larger cabins with more amenities. However, sometimes smaller is better—if you're looking for more personalized service, easier embarkation and disembarkation, and calls at less often visited ports.

Following is a plus-and-minus comparison of large and small cruise ships.

◼ LARGE SHIPS

Plus

+ Large ships are generally more stable in rough seas, although roll may be more pronounced in certain conditions because of top-heavy construction.

+ More activities are offered: theaters, show rooms, casinos, ice-skating, and so on.

+ Passengers can take advantage of multiple dining choices.

+ Many newer large ships have more verandas, larger windows, and more cabin choices.

+ Shore excursion programs are larger and more diverse.

Minus

− Deeper draft may limit ports or require passengers to transfer to small boats (called tenders) to go ashore.

− A small city's worth of people can be accommodated in the show rooms.

− Large dining rooms may result in more institutional-style food and service.

− Large passenger capacity may result in long lines for embarkation, immigration clearance, and disembarkation.

− Thousands of guests will descend upon small ports at once, lessening the quality of your visit.

■ SMALL SHIPS

Plus

+ Shallower draft may allow visits to smaller ports and require less frequent use of tenders.

+ Public rooms are relatively intimate.

+ More personalized service is available from cabin and restaurant staff.

+ Less structured, sometimes open seating is available in the dining room.

+ Small ships may have water-level water sports platforms or internal docks.

+ There is less of an impact on ports of call from smaller passenger loads.

+ A smaller number of passengers allows for easier embarkation at the start of a cruise and disembarkation at the end.

Minus

− Smaller ships are generally less stable in rough seas.

− There are fewer choices for entertainment.

− Fewer verandas and categories of cabins are available.

− Few or no choices are offered for dining.

IS A NEW SHIP BETTER THAN AN OLD CLASSIC?

The only thing you can say for certain about a new ship versus an old one is that a modern ship is, well, newer. Some spectacular new vessels include amenities well beyond the dreams of the most luxurious queens of the sea. But some new ships also have sections akin to a shopping mall food court. Some older vessels are tired relics counting the days until the scrap yard. But other veteran ships are handsome classics, offering a sense of elegance and class not duplicated by new construction. Two fine examples are the *Norway* and the *QE2*.

A typical life for a new cruise ship in the hands of a major cruise line is approximately ten to fifteen years, after which the ships are pushed along to a succession of secondary cruise companies. That doesn't mean there is anything wrong with these older ships or with the cruise companies. It just means the ships might not match a line's current marketing plan.

There are some areas of concern: A handful of very old ships may not fully meet the current safety regulations, operating under temporary or permanent exemptions. For example, these include old riverboats, antique Tall Ships, and a few older cruise ships that are due for retrofitting with sprinklers and other safety systems. Older ships are also not likely to be very accommodating to persons in wheelchairs and to others who may require an elevator.

New ships include state-of-the-art propulsion, air-conditioning, television, telephone, theater, and other facilities. They also are constructed using the latest safety regulations and equipment. Cabins usually have internal hallway entrances, permitting portholes, windows, or verandas along the sea.

Many new ships have shallower drafts, which allow visits to smaller ports and less frequent use of tenders; bow and stern thrusters allow maneuvering in narrow ports. On the minus side, a shallower draft may mean less comfortable cruising in rough weather.

CHAPTER THREE

WHERE IN THE WORLD DO YOU WANT TO GO?

WHERE IN THE WORLD do you want to go? Well, let me refine that a bit: Where in the world's oceans and major rivers do you want to go?

The waters around the United States are the world's most popular for cruising. In this book we cover any ship that touches an American port or sails nearby. Under that definition we include New England, Canada, the East and West Coasts, the Caribbean, Bermuda, the Bahamas, the Mexican Riviera, Hawaii, and Alaska. And we add coverage of voyages in Europe offered by the same major cruise lines.

In the wake of the terrorist attacks of 2001, most major cruise lines repositioned their ships to avoid trouble spots and to allow Americans to drive to many ports. That trend continues, with an increasing number of sailings from U.S. and nearby ports.

Many cruise lines have sharply reduced or completely canceled sailings in Europe, the Middle East, and Asia due to security or health concerns. You can, though, still find a good selection of cruises in the Mediterranean, the British Isles, the Baltic, and Scandinavia on many lines.

There has been a significant increase in departures from such domestic ports as Florida (Tampa, Port Canaveral, Fort Lauderdale, and Miami), New York, Boston, Philadelphia, Baltimore, Galveston, Houston, Los Angeles, and Seattle. Cruise industry officials point out that these domestic ports are within a half-day's drive of 40 percent of the households in North America.

Itineraries from East Coast ports include the Caribbean, the Bahamas, Bermuda, and Canada. From Gulf of Mexico and Florida ports, there are more cruises to the Western Caribbean, South America, and the Panama Canal than ever before. From West Coast ports ships head north to Alaska, west to Hawaii, and south to Mexico, South America, and the Panama Canal.

Travelers willing to fly to familiar nearby ports will also find increased service from Puerto Rico, Antigua, Aruba, and Honolulu.

I'll discuss many of the most popular cruising destinations a bit later in the chapter. First, though, let's explore the political and economic reasons behind most cruise itineraries.

OCEANS AWAY: INTERNATIONAL AFFAIRS

Cruising is one of the most international of businesses, and its operations are very much shaped by politics, economics, and protectionism.

I first wrote these words onboard a cruise liner built in Spain, registered in Panama, and leased from a Scandinavian holding company by Norwegian Cruise Line, a Norwegian corporation that had its headquarters in Miami. We were sailing through the American Hawaiian Islands with a 2,400-mile round-trip detour to stop at an undeveloped beach on Fanning Island in the South Pacific Republic of Kiribati.

Let's deconstruct that global stew.

Today's modern cruise ships are mostly built at a handful of giant shipyards in Italy, France, Germany, and Scandinavia. There is hardly any American shipbuilding industry left.

The ownership of cruise ships follows the financing; a new Gargantuan ship can cost upward of $400 million. The largest cruise lines—Carnival and Royal Caribbean among them—are huge multinational companies. Some of the smaller cruise companies, like Crystal and MSC Italian, are related to major freight shipping lines in Europe, Scandinavia, and Japan.

A ship's registry is for the most part a legal fiction. The great ships of old represented their nation's political and economic strengths, were proud to bear their country's flags, and, most important, abided by their home nation's laws, regulations, and customs. The Cunard Line's historic ships *Queen Mary* and *Queen Elizabeth,* for example, flew the Union Jack of Great Britain. From the stern of the *France* fluttered the Tricolor. Great American vessels such as the *United States* hoisted Old Glory. Each acted as a floating extension of its homeland.

Today, though, a new cruise ship is most likely to fly the flag of countries such as Panama, Liberia, or the Bahamas. They do so because the accountants and lawyers have determined that the cruise line can save money on construction costs, taxes, and operating expenses by doing so. In addition, if a ship is registered in the United States, labor and immigration laws require that crew members be American citizens or legal aliens.

Many of the vessels flying these exotic flags have never touched the waters of ports in those nations. These are "flags of convenience."

■ PROJECT AMERICA

In 2003 there was not a single major cruise ship flying the American flag. In recent years there had been two U.S.-flagged ships: the elderly *Independence* of American Hawaii Cruises and the reflagged *Patriot,* the former *Nieuw Amsterdam* of Holland America Lines. Both of these ships were laid up with the bankruptcy of the reborn United States Line.

A few smaller ships fly the American standard: The historic *Delta Queen* and her modern cousin the *Mississippi Queen* sail the rivers of the heartland. There are also a number of small American cruise ships on the East Coast and several boats in Alaskan waters.

Norwegian Cruise Line, one of the few major lines not part of either Carnival or Royal Caribbean, made a bold move in early 2003 with its "Project America" plans. NCL had previously purchased the uncompleted hull of a new cruise ship under construction in Mississippi but abandoned in the bankruptcy of American Classic Voyages. That hull and the components for a second ship were taken to Germany for completion.

Then NCL announced the purchase of the S.S. *United States,* one of the most venerable ships from the glory days of transatlantic sea travel. NCL said it would convert the ship—first launched in 1952—into a state-of-the-art, modern cruise ship and add her to NCL's planned U.S.-flagged fleet.

Considered by some to be the greatest superliner ever built in the United States, the *United States* was engineered to be faster, safer, and more technologically advanced than anything else afloat when she was christened. At 990 feet, 6 inches, the ship is the longest passenger vessel ever built in the United States. Her Atlantic crossing record on her eastbound maiden voyage—three days, ten hours, and forty minutes at an average speed of 35.59 knots—has never been matched, and she remains the holder of the fabled Blue Riband.

The refurbishment of the hull and superstructure will be done at U.S. shipyards, with the outfitting completed overseas. NCL is no stranger to such conversions, having converted the fabled North Atlantic liner the S.S. *France* into cruising's first Caribbean Megaship, S.S. *Norway.*

NCL also announced the purchase of another classic American-built ship, the S.S. *Independence,* which had been sailing in Hawaii before the failure of American Classic Voyages.

All these ships will operate under a U.S. flag, which will allow them to sail between American ports without having to visit a foreign country. NCL has not disclosed specific plans for introduction of the ships or their itineraries.

■ THE JONES ACT

Why does a ship sailing from New York on a cruise to New England have to make a port call in Canada? Why does a ship from Honolulu have to steam thousands of miles to Vancouver, Canada, or Ensenada, Mexico, or a tiny dot of a Pacific island nation before returning? Why can't you cruise up or down the California coast? Why do most Alaska cruises originate in Canada or make a stop in that country as they go to or come from the forty-ninth state?

The answer comes from a nearly two-century-old set of laws intended to protect U.S.-flagged vessels from unfair foreign competition.

The Jones Act requires that cargo moving between U.S. ports be carried in a vessel that was built and maintained in the United States and is at least 75 percent owned by American citizens or corporations. The Jones Act actually refers to Section 27 of the Merchant Marine Act of 1920; prior legislation to accomplish essentially the same thing has been in effect since 1817.

The act has actually done very little to preserve the U.S. shipping industry, of which there is not much left. The same applies for the American cruise industry, where the bill has had the unintended effect of boosting the economy of some otherwise obscure foreign ports whose main advantage is that they are within a reasonable cruising distance of a U.S. port. (Witness the Republic of Kiribati I mentioned earlier.)

Nearly fifty countries around the world have laws similar to the Jones Act. The United States is especially tough in its ban against flying an American flag on a foreign-built vessel; Canada permits importing ships but requires payment of a tariff equal to 25 percent of the vessel's value, which all but makes foreign vessels economically infeasible.

While the Jones Act applies to cargo, the Passenger Vessel Act of 1886 declares that "no foreign vessel shall transport passengers between ports or places in the United States." Cruise companies face a substantial fine for violating the law.

Railroads, airlines, bus lines, and trucking companies in the United States must follow similar rules of ownership and operation.

■ STRANGE ITINERARIES

Until and unless changes are made to the Jones Act, cruise vacationers have options like these:

■ Take a cruise from a U.S. port in Florida or a Gulf of Mexico port (including New Orleans and Galveston) that makes a visit to a Caribbean nation or Mexico.
■ Leave from a Canadian port on the East or West Coast and sail to an American destination such as Boston, New York, or Alaska, or the reverse.
■ Follow an unusual itinerary on a repositioning cruise, such as a trip from Vancouver to Hawaii, Hawaii to Mexico, or Florida through the Panama Canal to California.

As more and more ships are launched, and more and more ports are opened to welcome their business, cruise lines are on the lookout for new places to visit. A number of new destinations have been developed in the Mexican Riviera, and some U.S. ports have made major improvements to their facilities as a point of embarkation.

Here's the reason behind my visit to Kiribati: For the past few years, Norwegian Cruise Line has operated cruises among the Hawaiian Islands in the spring and fall in between winter assignments in the Caribbean and summers in Alaska. To sail from Hawaii and meet the requirements of the Jones Act, the vessels sail a 1,200-mile side trip to an island in the Republic of Kiribati near the equator.

■ THE BATTLE FOR REPEAL

In recent years several attempts have been made to repeal or modify the Jones Act, led in one way or another by cruise lines or their American representatives and supporters. Opposition to change has come from what remains of the U.S. shipping industry and from American unions. It is unclear whether the U.S. Congress will change the law.

One bill would have removed most restrictions, allowing foreign-flagged ships to cruise between U.S. ports. A more modest version would create waivers to permit ships that are repositioned from the Caribbean to Alaska and the Mediterranean to make multiple U.S. port stops along the West and East Coasts and grant a limited number of thirty-day permits for foreign-flagged ships to sail between U.S. ports. It would also permit U.S. companies to reflag foreign ships.

According to its supporters, the removal of the Jones Act could virtually destroy the U.S. domestic shipping industry and its 124,000 jobs. According to an industry association, owners and builders of U.S.-flagged vessels pay approximately $300 million annually in federal taxes and $55 million annually in state taxes. The foreign-ship cruise industry operating out of U.S. ports earns hundreds of millions of dollars a year from American consumers, yet pays no taxes on that income.

American employees pay some $1.1 billion in federal income taxes and $272 million in state taxes; again, foreign workers on foreign-flagged ships do not pay taxes. Foreign operators are also exempt from minimum wage laws, the provisions of the National Labor Relations Act, the Occupational Safety and Health Act, and some safety regulations applied to U.S. ships and industries.

It is important to note, though, that foreign-owned cruise lines do contribute to employment of port personnel, purchasing supplies from domestic sources and supporting American travel agencies, airlines, hotels, and other elements of vacation travel.

PORTS OF EMBARKATION AND PORTS OF CALL

Three-quarters of the earth is covered by the oceans, forming the highway to thousands of wondrous ports on the continents and islands of the world. The busiest ports for cruise ships are in the Caribbean, the Mediterranean and northern Europe, and Alaska. In this section I'll discuss some of the most interesting places where cruise ships call.

■ THE CARIBBEAN

The Caribbean basin is the most popular cruising area in the world, and for good reason. There are dozens of attractive and interesting small island nations, lovely beaches, and easygoing and friendly cultures that have their roots in Africa and Europe.

The Caribbean islands are made up of the Greater Antilles and the Lesser Antilles. The first group is closest to the United States and includes the large islands of Cuba, Jamaica, Hispaniola (which includes Haiti and the Dominican Republic), the U.S. territory of Puerto Rico, and the Cayman Islands.

The Lesser Antilles occupy the southern portion of the Caribbean, comprising the Virgin, Windward, and Leeward Islands. Included here are the U.S. Virgin Islands of Saint John, Saint Thomas, and Saint Croix, as well as Dutch/French Saint Martin, Saint Eustatius, Tortola, Virgin Gorda, Anguilla, Saint-Barthélemy, Saba, Saint Kitts, Nevis, Montserrat, Antigua, Guadeloupe, Dominica, Martinique, Saint Lucia, Saint Vincent, Barbados, the Grenadines, Grenada, and Trinidad and Tobago. Just off the coast of Venezuela are the ABCs: Aruba, Bonaire, and Curaçao.

(By the way, the generally preferred pronunciation is *kar-ih-BEE-en,* as opposed to *kah-RIB-ee-en.* The name is derived from Caribs, the indigenous people of the area who were mostly killed by imperial explorers or died as the result of diseases brought to the islands by outsiders.)

Cruises to the Caribbean leave from Florida ports that include Tampa, Miami, and Port Canaveral and from Gulf of Mexico ports, including Galveston, Houston, and New Orleans. Other major ports of embarkation located in the islands themselves are San Juan, Puerto Rico; Santo Domingo, Dominican Republic; and Montego Bay, Jamaica.

Caribbean cruising is usually a series of short island hops. A typical schedule has a ship arriving in port (or offshore for transfer by ship's tender) in the early morning and departing in the evening. This is enough time to get a brief taste of the islands: a shopping expedition, a visit to a beach or historical site, or a jaunt to an island casino, but not much else. And there may be relatively little pure cruising—days when the ship is out to sea.

June through November is hurricane season; August is generally the most active month. That does not mean there are constant storms. In some seasons hurricanes miss the area; even when they do arrive, the storms can hit one port and miss another, and ships can alter course.

You can count on cruise operators to exercise due caution with their expensive ships and litigious passengers. They reserve the right to reroute ships, cancel port calls, and, in rare circumstances, cancel an entire trip. It's all spelled out in the fine print in cruise brochures and contracts, along with policies on refunds and credits that result from cruise changes.

Another feature of some Caribbean cruises is a visit to a private island, an extension of the sealed world of the ship. Just as the cruise ship is a city unto its own, a private island is a way to spend some time ashore without the hassles of tourist traps, or other tourists for that matter (other than the few thousand or so close friends traveling with you). To some, that's a real appeal; to others, it's an unreal way to travel.

Among the private islands:

- Disney Cruise Line's Castaway Cay in the Bahamas near Nassau.
- Costa Cruise Line's Catalina Island off the coast of the Dominican Republic.
- Royal Caribbean's Coco Cay in the Bahamas.
- Royal Caribbean and Celebrity's Labadee off Haiti.
- Norwegian Cruise Line's Great Stirrup Cay.
- Holland America Line's Half Moon Cay.
- Princess Cruises' Princess Cay in the Bahamas.

In most cases the cruise ships will anchor offshore and guests will have to transfer to the island by tender, which can result in delays and a shorter visit. (And in rough seas, the tenders might not run or could be uncomfortable for some guests.) Disney Cruise Line, which sails year-round to the Bahamas and the Caribbean, is the only line to construct a pier to tie up its ships at its private island.

If you are booked for a visit to a private island, be sure to inquire about what is included in your cruise package. Some of the private islands are clearly profit centers for the cruise lines, with extra charges levied for water sports and other services.

Selected Caribbean Ports of Call

- **Anguilla.** A relatively quiet British dependency, first settled in 1650, it was named by Columbus, who thought the wandering coastline looked like an eel.
- **Antigua.** Largest of the British Leeward Islands, it was headquarters to Admiral Horatio Nelson's fleet in the colonial era. The island is home to at least 365 beaches, one for each day of the year if you're on a very long shore leave. The main port town is Saint John's. Another port, for smaller vessels, is at English Harbor in Falmouth, where Admiral Nelson set up the base for the British Navy in 1785. Many of the naval facilities have been restored to their Georgian splendor at Nelson's Dockyard.
- **Aruba.** A mostly independent piece of the Netherlands, the "A" of the "ABC" Islands of Aruba, Bonaire, and Curaçao. The desertlike island of cactus, jungles, and shopping lies just off the coast of Venezuela. The cruise port is at Oranjestad.
- **Bahamas.** The capital city of the Bahamas and one of the busiest cruise ports anywhere is Nassau on New Providence Island. Cruise ships pull up to Prince George Wharf at the foot of town, a short walk to the shops and the famed straw market where native handicrafts and souvenirs are sold.
- **Barbados.** The port at Bridgetown is still a bit of Britain, with its own Trafalgar Square complete with a statue of Lord Nelson; out of town, the island is a sea of green sugarcane that stretches to the white granulated beaches. Bridgetown is a lively commercial center that has a distinctly British flavor; out in the countryside are forests of flowers, caverns, and beaches. The island is the

The dock in Nassau is regularly a billion-dollar parking lot; from left to right are *Norwegian Wind, Carnival Ecstasy,* and *CostaAtlantica. Photo by Corey Sandler*

farthest east of any of the Caribbean islands, sitting on the line between the Atlantic and the Caribbean, approximately 100 miles east of the Lesser Antilles.

■ **Curaçao.** A mixture of Dutch, Spanish, English, and native cultures in the Netherlands Antilles, Curaçao is 35 miles off the coast of Venezuela. The famed Queen Emma Floating Bridge will move to the side to permit your cruise ship to enter the harbor at Willemstad. Beaches are more rock and coral than sand, and there is a busy refining industry. Willemstad was established by Dutch settlers in the 1630s, about the same time as other Dutch settlers arrived on Manhattan Island. Curaçao has maintained much of its original color, including red-tiled gable roofs.

■ **Dominica.** One of the most naturally diverse and relatively unspoiled islands of the Caribbean, Dominica is an independent nation; it is not related to the Dominican Republic, which lies on the island of Hispaniola. The interior is mostly an inaccessible rain forest; something like 365 rivers cascade down three mountain ranges. A few ecotours enter the rain forest by boat. The island, whose name is pronounced *dom-in-EEK-ah,* is also home to one of the last surviving groups of Caribs and a thriving set of folklore and superstitions that have their roots in Africa. The main port is at Portsmouth; some ships also call at Roseau in the southwest and at Prince Rupert Bay.

■ **Grand Cayman.** A former hideout for pirates, today George Town is legal home to offshore tax shelters and trendy shops. The island's beaches and coral reefs are among the best in the Caribbean. The conservative culture there has banned cruise ship visits on Sunday and has taken unfriendly positions against what it broadly defines as "undesirable" elements.

■ **Grenada.** The Spice Island of the Caribbean, Grenada is known for its nutmeg, cinnamon, and cocoa in particular. Formerly a British colony, it had a rocky beginning as an independent nation in the late 1970s and early 1980s, including a questionable U.S. intervention and "rescue" of some medical students. More recently, the island has concentrated on tourism and agriculture. The famed Grand Anse beach is about ten minutes away by bus or taxi from the cruise dock in Saint George's Harbour. Plans are under way for the construction of a new deepwater cruise ship port on the western side of the capital city of Saint George's, including a visitor reception area, duty-free shops, restaurants, and a bus terminal.

■ **Guadeloupe.** Two French islands in one: Basse-Terre has volcanic peaks and a mountainous coast; Grande-Terre has beaches and shopping. The port is at Pointe-à-Pitre. The two islands are separated by the River Salée. Basse-Terre is dominated by La Soufrière, an active volcano; hot water cascades down its sides in several streams. Cruise ships pull into a bay near Pointe-à-Pitre, billed as the "Paris of the Antilles." Guadeloupe is a region of France, along with Martinique, Saint Bart's, and half of Saint Martin.

■ **Îles des Saintes.** This very French set of islands off Guadeloupe was originally settled by Breton fishermen. More recent arrivals include some of the jet set of Europe who have built fancy vacation homes.

■ **Jamaica.** The famed resort port of Montego Bay is on the north shore of Jamaica, home to modern high-rise hotels and all the tourist amenities that go with them. The showplace beach is Doctor's Cave, which stretches for nearly

5 miles. Cruise ships also land on the north shore of this large independent island at Ocho Rios. The rivers of Ocho Rios include the one that tumbles down famed Dunn's River Falls, a 600-foot-high waterfall that has a well-worn set of natural steps, allowing visitors to climb its wet face. The bustling capital of Kingston lies on the other side of the Blue Mountains that run down the spine of Jamaica. Kingston, with nearly a million residents, is the largest English-speaking city south of Miami.

■ **Jost Van Dyke.** A tiny island northwest of Tortola, renowned as the "party island" of the British Virgin Islands, it has a port for small vessels at Great Harbour. There are fewer than 200 permanent residents, a dozen restaurants and bars, and a stunning white sand beach at White Bay.

■ **Martinique.** Very French—still a region of France—and very pretty, Martinique is abloom with orchids, hibiscus, and other tropical flowers. The island is also blooming with expensive shops in Fort-de-France, and it offers a European-tinged nightlife.

■ **Puerto Rico.** The capital port city of San Juan is home to ancient forts and cobblestone streets in Old San Juan, as well as some of the liveliest modern nightspots, casinos, and restaurants in the Caribbean. San Juan is also the most active cruise port in the basin. The island itself, a semiautonomous territory of the United States, is 110 miles long and 35 miles wide and home to nearly four million residents.

■ **Saint-Barthélemy.** Just eight square miles, this is considered one of the most attractive of the islands. The town of Gustavia, still tinged with Swedish and French designs, is a world-class shopping district. By the way, everyone calls the place Saint Bart's.

■ **Saint Croix** is one of the largest and more developed of the U.S. Virgin Islands. Christiansted, its capital and principal port, offers superb golf courses, beaches, and shopping. Another cruise port is located at Frederiksted on the west side of the island, near the popular West End beaches and the island's rain forest. Parts of the island have experienced high crime rates, and Carnival canceled its calls there in 2002.

■ **Saint Eustatius (Statia).** This Dutch island was historically the merchant center of the Caribbean, at least until the U.S. Revolutionary War, when a British fleet destroyed many of the island's structures because of minor support of the upstart Americans by the local governor. The port is at Oranjestad. The waters surrounding it are cluttered with shipwrecks, coral reefs, and rare fish. Hikers can climb to the rim of an extinct volcano and look into the cone. By the way, anyone with a clue calls it "Statia," pronounced *STAY-sha.*

■ **Saint John.** About 3 miles east of Saint Thomas, this island in the U.S. Virgin Islands is an unusual

U.S. Virgin Islands

The islands of Saint Thomas, Saint Croix, and Saint John have been under Spanish, French, English, and Dutch control. Saint Croix was at the heart of the slave trade, a way station from Africa to the West Indies, America, and South America. All three islands were sold by the Dutch to the U.S. government in 1917 during World War I, amid American fears of the Germans establishing a U-boat base in the area.

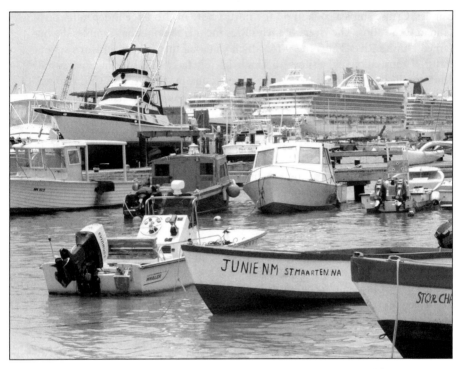

A billion or so dollars in cruise ships join more humble fishing vessels in Phillipsburg Harbor on the island of St. Martin. *Photo by Corey Sandler*

mix of luxury resorts and a wondrous protected natural park preserve that occupies two-thirds of the island. The main port anchorage for smaller vessels is at Cruz Bay.

■ **Saint Kitts.** This island was the first English settlement in the Leeward Islands. Most ships visit Basseterre. Today Saint Kitts has moved from a sleepy sugarcane economy to an increasingly upscale tourist industry, including quite a few restored plantation houses. Across the sound is the sister island of Nevis, a near-perfect volcano cone that still belches sulphur. Together the two islands are now an independent nation.

■ **Saint Lucia.** The lush port on the northwest coast of the island is at Castries, not far from the twin peaks of Les Pitons at Soufrière Bay and La Soufrière herself, sometimes referred to as the "drive-in volcano." Saint Lucia, an independent member of the British Commonwealth, had a small coal mining industry until early in the twentieth century; a sugarcane economy continued until later in the century, supplanted by bananas, and, relatively recently, by crops of tourists.

■ **Saint Martin/Sint Maarten.** On the French side of this binational island, Marigot has a pretty harbor, an old fort, and an attractive shopping district. The beaches on the French side are all lovely, and many of the sunbathers seem to have misplaced their suits. Philipsburg is the cosmopolitan port at the capital of the Dutch half of this split-personality island. The Dutch area is more built up, with large hotels and resorts, a few casinos, and a shopping district. The best beaches are at Mullet Bay and Cupecoy and across the unpatrolled border on the French half.

- **Saint Thomas.** The port city of Charlotte Amalie (*a-MAHL-ya*) is the capital of the U.S. Virgin Islands, but its roots as a Dutch port are very much evident in the architecture. One of the busiest cruise ports in the world, it is home to a staggering assortment of duty-free shops and other commercial ventures aimed at visitors who have dollars to spend. Outside of town is the famed Magen's Bay beach, a white swath of sand that follows the outline of a horseshoe bay.
- **Tortola.** The largest and most populated of the British Virgin Islands, Tortola is home to the major airport of the area. The port is at Road Town. The best beaches lie on the north side of the island, more or less easily reached on a day trip by car on some rather primitive roads.
- **Venezuela.** The coastal port of La Guaira offers access to the inland capital city of Caracas.
- **Vieques.** A lovely, lightly developed island, Vieques is part of Puerto Rico, just off the east coast of the main island. The island's bays are home to microscopic bioluminescent organisms that put on a light show in the wake of your boat. The U.S. Navy ran a controversial bombing range for many years at one end of the island. Most of this land was transferred in 2001 to Puerto Rico and the U.S. Department of the Interior. More than 3,800 acres will be wildlife refuge; the Navy retains 100 acres.
- **Virgin Gorda.** Supposedly named by Columbus because the island's rolling hills somehow reminded him of an overly ample young woman (the name translates to "fat virgin"), the island is best known for its interesting beach and rock formation at The Baths, where gigantic boulders form grottoes, caves, and pools. Its man-made jewels include the opulent Little Dix Bay, Biras Creek, and Bitter End Yacht Club resorts. The principal port is at Spanish Town. Roads are very limited; the best way around is by boat.

◼ BERMUDA

Britain's oldest colony, dating back to the early seventeenth century, Bermuda is still very much a bit of Old England, from afternoon tea to cricket matches to a good-natured formality in business and social matters. The island was first settled in 1609 by the survivors of the shipwrecked *Sea Venture,* British colonists who had been heading for Jamestown, Virginia.

Bermuda, about 600 miles east of Cape Hatteras, North Carolina, actually includes some 150 islands, with the six main islands connected by bridges and causeways. The preferred method of transportation is moped or bicycle.

The climate is temperate, not as hot as the islands of the Caribbean, which lie much farther south. The season runs from May through September. The best bargains are often available at the beginning and end of the season, before Memorial Day and after Labor Day.

The port of King's Wharf is at the tip of Bermuda's West End, home to the Royal Naval Dockyard and the Bermuda Arts Centre and Crafts Market. Saint George is another port on Bermuda, known for its narrow cobblestone streets and the restored 300-year-old King's Square on the waterfront. Although discovered by Spanish explorer Juan de Bermúdez in 1515, Bermuda was first occupied by Sir George Somers and other British colonists who were shipwrecked there in 1609, an event noted by William Shakespeare in *The Tempest.* The island was a haven for pirates and privateers and later used as a base for Confederate blockade runners during the U.S. Civil War.

■ CUBA

Politics aside, one of the most appealing cruise destinations is the island nation of Cuba. It has beautiful beaches, a lively culture, and ports just 90 miles off the coast of Florida.

Cuba is, of course, off-limits to ships sailing from U.S. ports and to most U.S. passport holders. It is legal for journalists and educators with a particular reason to visit Cuba; consult the U.S. Department of State for details. But the political climate could change rapidly.

A number of cruise ships visit Havana from ports in the Dominican Republic, Mexico, or Jamaica without touching American ports. In 2002 European lines making port calls at Cuba included Festival (the *Mistral*); Fred Olsen Cruise Line (the *Black Watch*), and Sun Cruises (*Sundream*).

All the major cruise lines have plans to bring their ships to Cuba as soon as they are permitted.

■ ALASKA

The hottest waters for cruising in recent years have been in the Inside Passage to Alaska, with nearly a half million passengers visiting coastal towns each year.

The *Regal Princess* under way in Alaska's Inside Passage. *Courtesy of Princess Cruises*

Alaska has some magnificent appeals: the spectacular frozen rivers of Glacier Bay and other inlets; the fascinating native, Russian, and American cultures of trading and fishing towns such as Ketchikan and Sitka; and the Gold Rush history of Skagway. Just as appealing: a pod of whales shadowing your ship in a narrow passage between thickly forested slopes, and frolicking families of seals on bobbing ice floes.

Alaska is still one of the last great frontiers of the world, and it's certainly among the most remote places in North America. There are almost no roads between towns in the state; residents are served by a fleet of small floatplanes and ferries.

For the cruise passenger, one of the major appeals of an Alaskan visit is that your ship will be within sight of land in protected waters for most of the cruise. The Inside Passage is sandwiched between the mainland and a series of large and small islands. You can expect generally calm waters in the sheltered arms of the Pacific, with only an occasional jaunt into the open ocean to visit ports such as Sitka.

Many of the cruise ships depart from Vancouver in Canada's British Columbia; Vancouver is one of the most attractive ports I know, combining a thriving cosmopolitan city with mountains and the ocean. It's worth a few days as a stopover at the start or end of a cruise. Another beautiful Canadian port is Victoria on Vancouver Island. You can also sail to Alaska from Seattle, and some repositioning cruises depart from elsewhere on the West Coast or from Hawaii.

Most of the cruises visit the southernmost reaches of Alaska, from Ketchikan to Juneau and Glacier Bay. The more adventurous ships venture farther north through the open waters of the Gulf of Alaska and Prince William Sound to Seward.

Many larger ships must anchor offshore because they are unable to enter shallow or narrow harbors.

Holland America Line and Princess Cruises are major players in Alaska, and both have extensive facilities on shore, including hotels and tours. In fact, Holland America is one of the state's largest private employers.

It's not quite accurate to say that the Alaskan towns visited by cruise ships are untouched. You'll find more than your share of T-shirt and gift shops, tacky tourist bars, and unimpressive bus tours. The appeal of Alaska instead lies off the beaten path in the pristine bays and fjords of places such as Glacier Bay, Tracy Arm, and the sprawling Misty Fjords National Park.

Don't go for the weather. It can be cold and rainy any day of the year, although you could be blessed with a spectacular, warm day when you least expect it.

Selected Ports of Call in Alaska

■ **College Fjord.** In Prince William Sound, College Fjord is home to twenty-six glaciers, each named for an Ivy League college by the Harriman Expedition in 1899; the trip was financed by the schools.

■ **Haines.** Gateway to a rich Gold Rush history, thousands of bald eagles, and the Tlingit and Chilkat Indian cultures, the tiny town at the dock is not geared to tourists.

- **Juneau.** This is the nation's only state capital with a glacier in its backyard; the Mendenhall Glacier is just outside town, reachable by public bus, taxi, or guided tour. Juneau is also home to the Alaska State Museum and other cultural attractions.
- **Ketchikan.** Ketchikan lays claim to the largest collection of totem poles in the world, at Totem Bight and elsewhere around town. It's also the gateway to floatplane and boat expeditions into the spectacular Misty Fjord National Park, which spreads over more than two million acres and includes sheer granite cliffs that rise thousands of feet out of the water. The area has countless lakes and ponds and sprawling forests that are home to bears, deer, mountain goats, and other wildlife.
- **Prince William Sound.** A large saltwater bay northwest of Juneau, the sound is some 15,000 square miles in size and as much as 2,850 feet deep. It contains more glaciers than any other single area in Alaska.
- **Seward.** This tiny fishing village is the gateway to some of America's natural jewels: Chugach National Forest, Kenai Fjords National Park and Wildlife Refuge, and the Alaska Maritime National Wildlife Refuge.
- **Sitka.** The keeper of Alaska's Russian heritage, Sitka's attractions include an onion-domed cathedral, a restored fort site, and a cultural center. The harbor looks out on a dramatic volcano.
- **Skagway.** The northernmost point in the Inside Passage, this was the jumping-off point for many Gold Rushers of the 1890s. Its history is saluted by many shops and restaurants. It is also the terminal for the White Pass & Yukon Railroad, which retraces some of the routes taken by the Gold Rushers.
- **Tracy Arm.** Tracy Arm is a fjord that wends its way to the face of two dramatic glaciers, North and South Sawyer.
- **Valdez.** Laying claim to the title of the "Switzerland of Alaska," with its perch beneath the snowcapped peaks along Prince William Sound, Valdez is the southern terminus of the 800-mile trans-Alaska oil pipeline.
- **Yakutat Bay.** The bay is home to Hubbard Glacier, which let loose in 1986 to advance more than a hundred feet in a single day, blocking off Russell Fjord. At more than 6 miles in width and nearly 500 feet in height, Hubbard is the largest valley glacier in North America.

Selected Ports of Call in Western Canada

- **Vancouver, British Columbia.** One of the most cosmopolitan cities in Canada, Vancouver shares British, Asian, native, and many other cultures. It's home to the spectacular Capilano footbridge that sways over a deep gorge; sprawling Stanley Park with its world-class aquarium; several significant museums of science, anthropology, and art; and a thriving commercial district and Chinatown.
- **Victoria, British Columbia.** A very English outpost on the far western edge of Canada on Vancouver Island, Victoria is the capital of the province of British Columbia and home to the famed Royal British Columbia Museum and the Empress Hotel. Just outside town are the world-famous Butchart Gardens.

■ HAWAII

Hawaii's weather is fine year-round. Norwegian Cruise Line circles the islands, making a long detour to the Republic of Kiribati. Other major cruise lines visit Hawaii mostly as part of repositioning schedules. A typical schedule has ships coming to Hawaii in the fall as they move south from Alaska en route to the Panama Canal and the Caribbean Sea. The schedule is reversed in the spring.

The complication comes from the provisions of the Jones Act, which requires foreign-flagged cruise lines to visit at least one other country after embarkation from a U.S. port. Itineraries sometimes begin in Vancouver or Mexico for repositioning trips. A few lines, including Norwegian Cruise Line, have extended their Hawaiian seasons with long detours to obscure island nations such as the Republic of Kiribati.

American Hawaii Cruise Line and its sister company, United States Line, which operated the American-flagged *Independence* and *Patriot* in the Hawaiian Islands, went bankrupt at the end of 2001.

Selected Ports of Call in Hawaii

■ **Hilo, Hawaii.** Hilo is a commercial center on the east coast of the Big Island of Hawaii. The island is nearly twice the size of all the other Hawaiian Islands combined, and it is still growing as lava slowly but steadily flows into the sea from several active volcanoes. A visit to Volcanoes National Park by vehicle, or overhead by helicopter or plane, is a tourist highlight.

■ **Honolulu, Oahu.** The best-known city of Hawaii is located on the island of Oahu. Near the port is the famed beach at Waikiki, as well as the U.S. naval base at Pearl Harbor. The waterfront Aloha Tower has greeted ships since 1926.

■ **Kona, Hawaii.** The second port on the Big Island, on the west side, is a quiet backwater. Expeditions leave to tourist destinations and several nearby golf courses and resorts.

■ **Lahaina, Maui.** Lahaina has some touches of an old New England fishing port, a remembrance of its days as an important Pacific port for the whaling ships of Nantucket and eastern America. The whaling ships are gone, but the whales still swim by in winter. The island is also home to some of the best beaches in the Hawaiian chain. Another port on the island is Kahului, 24 miles from Lahaina.

■ **Nawiliwili, Kauai.** The very lush and mountainous island of Kauai includes the colorful Waimea Canyon, a small-scale geological feature somewhat grandly billed as the "Grand Canyon of the Pacific," as well as some spectacular waterfalls that are like a scene from Shangri-la.

■ EAST COAST

New York and Boston were once among the great transatlantic ports; today they are busy in season with cruise ships to Atlantic Canada, Bermuda, and the occasional crossing of the pond to Europe.

A typical cruise heads north from New York along the coast, sometimes through the Cape Cod Canal, to Boston and on to Nova Scotia and sometimes Montreal. Some ships leave from Boston and head north to Canada.

So many cruise ships, so few American ports. That's one of the problems faced in 2002 by cruise lines as they expanded their fleets and reworked some of their schedules to emphasize "homeland" cruising from ports within driving distance of much of the country.

One of the beneficiaries of new itineraries was the port of Galveston, Texas. This is hardly a new port; in fact, Galveston is one of the busiest cargo ports in the United States. In the early part of the twentieth century, Galveston was the second busiest port in the country for European immigrants, after New York's Ellis Island. In the time since, though, calls by cruise ships had been infrequent.

In 2002 the historic Pier 25 became home to three major cruise ships with plans for at least 145 embarkations; by mid-2002 one or another ship was unloading and loading passengers four days a week. Carnival Cruise Lines' *Celebration* and *Jubilee* sailed four- and five-day trips to Playa del Carmen/Cozumel and Calica/Cancun, Mexico. Royal Caribbean International's *Rhapsody of the Seas* was scheduled for seven-day trips to Playa del Carmen and Cozumel, Mexico; Georgetown, Cayman Islands; and Key West, Florida.

(The Port of Houston, a container port about 30 miles north on the Houston Ship Channel, gained seasonal service from Royal Olympic Cruises' *Olympia Voyager.*)

Although the sailings from Texas are mostly aimed at the regional market, Galveston has a lot to offer travelers. It's a place with a great deal of history and an attractive downtown arts and shopping district frozen in time from the early part of the twentieth century.

When the first Europeans landed on Galveston Island in 1528, it was already home to Akokisa and Karankawa Indians. Galveston was named for Bernardo de Galvez, a Spanish colonial governor and general who dispatched surveyors to chart the Gulf of Mexico from the Texas coast to New Orleans in 1786.

Pirate Jean Laffite arrived on the island in 1817, making it his base of operations and naming it Campeche. The little village contained huts for the pirates, a large slave market, boardinghouses for visiting buyers, a shipyard, saloons, pool halls, gambling houses, and Laffite's own house, the "Maison Rouge." Laffite remained neutral during Texas's fight to gain independence from Spain and Mexico, but he was forced to leave the island in 1821 after his pirates attacked an American ship. It is believed that he had buried treasure on the island, but it has never been found.

The town prospered as a trading port until September 8, 1900, when the deadliest natural disaster in United States history hit Galveston Island. A storm with winds exceeding 120 miles per hour and the subsequent tidal surge devastated the island and killed more than 6,000 people.

At the time of the 1900 storm, Galveston had a population of 37,000. It was the fourth largest city in Texas, following Houston, Dallas, and San

Antonio, and was the most sophisticated city in the state. The storm completely destroyed one-third of the city, more than 3,600 buildings.

To prevent such a natural disaster from devastating the island again, the city built a seawall 7 miles long and 17 feet high and began a tremendous project to raise the level of the island. Galveston's seawall now extends more than 10 miles and covers one-third of Galveston's Gulf side. The story of the flood, *The Great Storm*, is a multimedia show presented at Pier 21. For information call (409) 763–8808.

Today Galveston boasts four districts on the National Register of Historic Places: the Strand National Historic Landmark District, East End National Historic Landmark District, Silk Stocking District, and Central Business District. In all, there are about 1,500 Galveston structures on the National Register of Historic Places.

One of Galveston's most popular attractions is Moody Gardens, which includes the ten-story Rainforest Pyramid, housing thousands of exotic plants, birds, butterflies, and fish in a tropical environment complete with waterfalls, cliffs, caverns, wetlands, and forests. The Aquarium Pyramid showcases the waters of the North Pacific, Edge of the Antarctic, Tropical Pacific, the Great Barrier Reef, and the Caribbean. The Discovery Pyramid hosts traveling exhibits. For information, call (800) 582–4673 or visit www.moodygardens.com.

Pier 21's Texas Seaport Museum highlights the workings of the nineteenth-century port; visitors can search a computer database with information about more than 133,000 immigrants and their countries of origin, dates of arrival, and planned destinations. Docked alongside is the Tall Ship *Elissa*, launched in Scotland in 1877 and later used in commerce in and around Galveston. For information on the museum and ship, call (409) 763–1877 or visit www.galvestonhistory.org.

The historic sailing bark *Elissa* frames Carnival's *Celebration* in Galveston.
Photo by Corey Sandler

Guests arriving ahead of their cruise ship departure can take advantage of a special offer made by a group of historic bed-and-breakfasts on the island, including free long-term parking after an overnight stay.

For more information on Galveston, call the Galveston Island Convention and Visitors Bureau at (409) 763–4311 or (888) 425–4753, or visit www.galvestoncvb.com.

The season for cruises runs from May to October, with the best bargains available before Memorial Day. Weather in New England and Atlantic Canada can be very capricious, especially in the spring and fall. There can be some spectacular October days and ferocious nor'easter storms.

Selected Ports in New England, Atlantic Coast, and Eastern Canada

■ **Baltimore.** The port of Baltimore, founded in 1706 on the banks of the Patapsco River, is just minutes from Interstate 95, the main north-south highway of the East Coast.

■ **Boston.** A modern metropolis, Boston also has a great colonial and Revolutionary War history. The port lies directly across the water from Logan Airport and just a few miles by taxi from South Station for Amtrak and bus connections.

■ **Halifax, Nova Scotia.** Halifax is a historic fishing town of maritime Canada. Many victims of the sinking of the *Titanic* were buried in Fairview Cemetery, where rows of headstones form the shape of a ship's hull. Nearby is picturesque Peggy's Cove, a tourist magnet that has engulfed a little fishing village.

■ **Martha's Vineyard, Massachusetts.** The tony resort island off the coast of Cape Cod, Massachusetts, is home to artists, musicians, and fine Atlantic Ocean beaches.

■ **Montreal, Quebec.** The largest French-speaking city outside France, Montreal is one of the most cosmopolitan cities anywhere.

■ **Nantucket, Massachusetts.** A onetime whaling island 30 miles south of Cape Cod, Nantucket is now primarily a tourist community of galleries, shops, museums, and beaches—and home to the author of this book. The narrow and shallow harbor does not permit large ships to enter; they set anchor well outside the harbor and send guests ashore by tender.

■ **New York.** The Big Apple was once one of the most important ports for transatlantic ocean liners. Today the port is home to seasonal service to Bermuda and to maritime Canada, as well as transatlantic crossings. Sailing into or out of New York is one of the most dramatic transits anywhere in the world.

■ **Norfolk, Virginia.** A newly renovated pier, capable of handling Megaships, adjoins Nauticus, the National Maritime Center, home to the USS *Wisconsin*. In the heart of the Mid-Atlantic coastal region, Norfolk was founded in 1862.

■ **Quebec City, Quebec.** Cruise ships dock on the river below the famed Château Frontenac Hotel.

■ **Saint-Pierre and Miquelon.** This pair of tiny fishing outposts of France lies just south of Newfoundland, Canada.

▮ FLORIDA AND THE GULF OF MEXICO

From Florida to Texas, the Atlantic and Gulf of Mexico ports are the busiest cruise ports in the United States. Ships travel deep into the Caribbean and west to Central America, South America, and through the Panama Canal to the Pacific Ocean.

Selected Ports in Florida and the Gulf of Mexico

- **Fort Lauderdale.** The third busiest domestic cruise port, Port Everglades has eleven terminals that are used by more than fifty ships each year, with more than 2,000 departures annually. Fort Lauderdale Airport is a few miles away; the larger Miami International Airport is 25 miles to the south.
- **Galveston.** The historic port of Galveston was the second busiest port of immigration, after New York's Ellis Island, in the early part of the twentieth century. Today's terminal is a block away from the historic Strand shopping and entertainment district. Air service is through Houston, about ninety minutes away.
- **Houston.** The Port of Houston is part of the 25-mile-long Houston Ship Channel that leads to the Gulf of Mexico at Galveston. The port is the busiest in the United States in terms of foreign commerce. Cruise ships tie up at Barbour's Cut Terminal near La Porte, less than an hour from Houston.
- **Miami.** The port sits at the feet of the shorefront skyscrapers of Miami, along the causeway to Miami Beach; it's one of the most attractive cruise terminal locations anywhere. In 2003 nearly twenty-four cruise ships had their home port at Miami; one out of every three North American cruise passengers sailed from there.
- **New Orleans.** More than 125 ships make calls or depart from the Julia Street terminal at the foot of downtown on the Mississippi River. The *Delta Queen* docks nearby at Robin Street Wharf.
- **Port Canaveral.** The protected harbor is about an hour east of Orlando, within sight of the launch pads of the Kennedy Space Center at Cape Canaveral. Disney built its own impressive terminal for the three weekly departures of its ships; other lines have their own structures.
- **Tampa.** The busy port of Tampa is about twenty minutes from the international airport there. The thriving downtown, including the Cuban-flavored Ybor City, is nearby.

▇ MEXICAN RIVIERA AND CENTRAL AMERICA

The sunny ports of upper Mexico are becoming more popular each year, with ships making calls at port cities on the Pacific side, including Ensenada near the U.S. border with California and farther south at Cabo San Lucas at the tip of Baja California. Pacific mainland ports include Mazatlán, Puerto Vallarta, and Acapulco. On the Caribbean side are Calica, Cancun, and Cozumel.

Some cruise ships heading through the Panama Canal make port calls in Caldera, Costa Rica, and points off the eastern coast of Panama, including San Andrés Island, a northern outpost of Colombia.

The Mexican Riviera has generally fine weather year-round, with high season in the winter.

Selected Ports in the Mexican Riviera

- **Acapulco.** The most famous and most developed port in the Mexican Riviera, Acapulco has grown from a sleepy fishing village to a world-class resort during the past few decades. Among the best-known sights of the area are the cliff divers of La Quebrada, who plunge more than 100 feet into the waters below.

■ **Cabo San Lucas.** Cabo San Lucas lies at the extreme southern tip of Baja California, between the Pacific Ocean and the Sea of Cortez. The bay once sheltered treasure ships from the Orient—and pirate ships waiting to prey on them. The pounding surf has carved some spectacular sea arches and rock formations.

■ **Calica.** A recently developed port on Mexico's Quintana Roo coast on the Yucatan Peninsula on the Caribbean Sea, Calica provides access to the Mayan ruins at Tulum and the lagoons of Xel-Há.

■ **Cozumel.** Just off the coast of the Yucatan Peninsula in Mexico, Cozumel is near the Mayan ruins at Chichén Itzá and San Gervasio. Palancar Reef, discovered by Jacques Cousteau about thirty years ago, is the second largest known reef in the world.

■ **Huatulco.** On Mexico's Oaxaca coast, set against the dramatic backdrop of the Sierra Madres, the area's resorts lie along Tangolunda Bay.

■ **Manzanillo.** This small but very stylish port of call was built around the Las Hadas resort and its dreamscape of a beach.

■ **Mazatlán.** This is Mexico's largest Pacific port.

■ **Playa del Carmen.** The gateway port to the resort center of Cancun, which is almost entirely made up of fancy tourist hotels and pricey shops, Playa del Carmen, referred to as Playa by residents, has the nicer beach and is a bit less developed. You can also catch a ferry (about an hour) from Playa to Cozumel.

■ **Progreso.** The port city for Mérida, the capital of Yucatán, Progreso is the gateway to numerous Mayan ruins, including Chichén Itzá and Uxmal.

■ **Puerto Vallarta.** A small fishing village on the Bay of Banderas, it has embraced visitors and has become a world-class resort.

Selected Ports in Central America

■ **Belize.** The principal port and city of Belize, formerly British Honduras, is Belize City. North of the port is Altun-Ha, a significant Mayan ruin accidentally discovered in 1957 by a road construction crew.

■ **Colombia.** At the top of South America on the Caribbean Sea, the port of Cartagena was one of the principal ports from which the riches of the New World were sent back to the Old in the days of colonial control. The walled city on Colombia's northern coast was built centuries ago to protect against pirate raids. Today the port is famed as a shopping mecca, especially for emeralds. San Andrés Island is a small piece of land off the eastern coast of Panama that is home to a Colombian naval base and not much else. The island is a reminder that Panama was once part of Colombia, before a U.S.-backed revolution, which helped pave the way to American development of the Panama Canal.

■ **Costa Rica.** On the Pacific coast of Central America, the commercial port of Puerto Caldera is the gateway to a tropical paradise, home to exotic birds, butterflies, and tourists enjoying its white- and black-sand beaches. The port lies below San José, Costa Rica's capital.

■ **Honduras.** The port city of Puerto Cortes is an industrial center for San Pedro Sula, the commercial center of Honduras. Many visitors head for the Mayan ruins at Copán. Honduras was severely damaged by Hurricane Mitch.

■ **Panama.** Cruise ships rarely make calls at Cristobal or Balboa, the ports at either end of the Panama Canal, although some ships send shore excursions to plantations on Gatun Lake in the middle. More popular ports for ships are the San Blas Islands, a group of 360 lush, low-lying isles off the east coast. They are little changed from the way they were when Columbus visited more than 500 years ago and are home to the Cuna Indians.

■ PANAMA CANAL

The Panama Canal was built to speed transit of ships from the East Coast of the United States to the West Coast, allowing vessels to avoid the lengthy and sometimes dangerous 8,000-mile passage around Cape Horn at the bottom of South America. The canal still serves that purpose, but its extraordinary man-made and natural wonders are today a tourist draw of their own.

From the Caribbean to the Pacific, ships are lifted 85 feet in three steps at Gatun Locks to Gatun Lake. They cross Gatun Lake to Gaillard Cut, where the canal passes the Continental Divide. From there ships are lowered 31 feet to Miraflores Lake and then proceed through two more locks at Miraflores Lock before entering the Pacific Ocean. The 50-mile transit takes approximately nine hours.

Until recent years, cruise ships passed through the canal only on repositioning itineraries, usually on journeys from Alaska or Hawaii to the Caribbean and returning. Now you'll find some cruise ships that pass back and forth from the Pacific to the Caribbean for much of the year. Other ships make a partial transit, entering from the Caribbean side and going as far as Gatun Lake midway across; there they turn around and exit.

The United States completed the turnover of the canal to Panama at the end of 1999. Most experts expect little or no change in its operations, although the possibility of political instability worries some.

■ EUROPE AND THE MEDITERRANEAN

Europe is one of the fastest-growing cruise markets and will continue to expand as a number of cruise companies position their ships there for the summer.

Many of the finest cities of Europe are ocean harbors, including Amsterdam, Barcelona, Copenhagen, Genoa, Helsinki, Lisbon, Monte Carlo, Nice, Oslo, Saint Petersburg, Stockholm, and Venice. London is up the Thames River from the sea.

Selected Ports in Europe and the Mediterranean

■ **Crete.** The fabled birthplace of Zeus and home of the ancient Minoans is Iráklion; you can visit the 4,000-year-old Knossos Palace.

■ **Croatia.** The ancient city of Dubrovnik, repaired from war damage, is one of the world's treasures.

■ **Germany.** The port for the bustling city of Berlin is Rostock.

■ **Greece.** The cruise port for Athens is Piraeus. Newcomers visit the Acropolis; veteran travelers head for the wineries, nightclubs, and shops. Among many Greek islands visited by cruise ships is Corfu in the Adriatic.

■ **France.** The queen of the French Riviera is Cannes, home to some of the most ostentatious displays of wealth in Europe. Ships dock a few miles away from La Croisette, the seafront promenade. Le Havre has served as the port for Paris since the sixteenth century. Marseille is the gateway to Provence, about an hour from the ancient hilltop town of Aix-en-Provence. Corsica, birthplace of Napoleon, is a French island with an Italian temperament. The principal port is Ajaccio. Located south of Marseilles, Corsica offers spectacular mountains and seashore and a culture just a bit different from elsewhere in the Mediterranean.

■ **Italy.** The ancient port of Civitavecchia is about an hour's bus, taxi, or train ride from Rome, the Eternal City that is home to the Vatican, the Colosseum, and hundreds of thousands of awestruck tourists. Livorno, also known as Leghorn, is the port for Florence, about an hour away. Among the treasures of Florence are Michelangelo's *David,* the Pitti Palace, and Santa Croce, the burial place of Galileo and Machiavelli. Also near Livorno is Pisa. Bella Napoli, the port city of Naples, is worth a visit of its own; Mount Vesuvius and the Isle of Capri are nearby. Cruise ships can also pull into a port complex just outside the heart of Venice. A vaporetto or water bus takes visitors to Saint Mark's Square, the Doge's Palace, the Bridge of Sighs, and the canals, which are every bit as thrilling as you've imagined. Messina is one of the most handsome cities in Sicily, within sight and visit of Mount Etna and the ancient Greek theater at Taormina.

■ **Malta.** The capital city and principal port of the ancient island nation of Malta is Valletta. The vibrant city has churches, mosques, museums, and stores. Worth a visit by public bus, taxi, or tour is the nearby old city of Mdina, a spectacular living museum.

■ **Netherlands.** Amsterdam is a lively center of culture in Western Europe.

■ **Russia.** Saint Petersburg is home to the fabulous Hermitage art museum.

■ **Spain.** Cruise ships bound for Barcelona dock a few minutes away from Las Ramblas, the famed downtown promenade. You can hop on the subway for a visit to Gaudi's quirky Sagrada Familia. Alicante is a jewel of the Spanish Riviera, with a Carthaginian fortress above the harbor dating from about 3 B.C.

■ The **Balearic Islands** of Majorca, Minorca, and Ibiza lie south of Spain, of which they are part. Palma de Mallorca on Majorca is the most cosmopolitan city of the Balearics, home to a medieval cathedral that took more than 400 years to complete. Downtown shopping is among the best in the Mediterranean.

■ **Turkey.** The famed Blue Mosque of Istanbul holds the culture, the Grand Bazaar holds the pursestrings. Some cruise lines canceled calls here in 2002 and 2003 because of security concerns.

■ REPOSITIONING CRUISES

The cruise companies have to move their ships from place to place to accommodate changing itineraries; the trips between ports of embarkation are known as "repositioning" cruises. Many cruise veterans seek out these trips because they often offer unusual ports of call, extra days at sea, and generally lower prices.

Many cruise ships follow a seasonal schedule, matching the changing interests of travelers. Here are a few typical cycles:

■ **Alaska/Caribbean.** Ships may spend the summer in Alaska, then move south through Hawaii or the Mexican Riviera in the fall, passing through the Panama Canal before winter, and finishing out the season in the Caribbean. In spring the migration is reversed.

■ **New England/Bermuda/Caribbean.** Some ships finish up their winters in the Caribbean and head north to New York or Boston for cruises to Bermuda in the spring. They then cruise New England and Atlantic Canada in summer and early fall.

■ **Caribbean/Europe.** After finishing Caribbean winter runs, some cruise ships then sail across the Atlantic to the Mediterranean for the summer. A typical itinerary runs from Florida or the Caribbean to Italy or Spain, or in the other direction.

CHAPTER FOUR

HOW TO BUY A CRUISE

THE MAJORITY OF CRUISE BOOKINGS are made through travel agents, although some cruise lines sell a portion of their available space directly.

In theory, it shouldn't matter to you as a buyer. Most travel agents do not charge customers a fee for cruise bookings. Instead they make their income from commissions received from the cruise lines and most other elements of a travel package they put together, including airlines, hotels, and car rental agencies.

Sometimes the best prices can be found by buying directly from a cruise line, especially when it comes to last-minute bookings. On the other hand, cruise lines recognize that the major portion of their sales still come from travel agencies, and they don't want to damage that relationship. A travel agent who sells a large volume of cruises often receives special offers at deeper discounts than are available elsewhere.

Airlines have been cutting back or eliminating commissions to travel agents, and some agencies have instituted a charge to book airline tickets. Because agents continue to receive significant payments from cruise lines, though, I don't think a fee to the consumer is appropriate. In any case, be sure to compare the bottom line—the cost, convenience, and special features—put forth by a travel agent with a booking you can put together yourself.

Most larger travel agencies are members of or associated with a national association, such as ASTA (American Society of Travel Agents), the CLIA (Cruise Line Industry Association), or NACOA (National Association of Cruise-Oriented Agencies). If you see one of these logos on the door of an agency, on a brochure, or on a Web site, you have some assurance the agency meets some level of industry standard. Among other things, the company may have posted a bond to protect deposits and advance payments made by clients; you may be able to enlist the association in any dispute you have with the agency.

Some industry groups offer training for members, awarding "master" and other titles to agents with particular expertise on cruises or other specialties. However, no matter what the string of letters after a travel agency's or agent's name, you should closely judge the quality of service you receive from any travel agency. Be willing to take your business elsewhere if you do not feel you are receiving proper treatment and the best available deal.

My recommendation is that you begin with research of your own, starting with this book, before you speak with a travel agent. Understand the industry, learn about the cruise lines and their ships, and find out about destinations. Check prices in newspaper and magazine ads, then make a phone call to the cruise line or check its Web page on the Internet, or both. Some cruise lines have begun accepting direct bookings from their Web sites, and it is reasonable to expect special deals, especially on unsold cabins close to the sailing date.

HOW TO CHOOSE A TRAVEL AGENT

Good travel agents remember whom they work for: you. There is, though, a built-in conflict of interest here because the agent is in most cases paid by someone other than you. Agents receive a commission from the sellers of the products they recommend. The more they sell (or the higher the price), the more they earn.

I recommend that you start planning for any trip by calling the cruise lines and airlines, and even a few hotels if you'll need to stay over at a port. Find the best package you can put together for yourself; then call a travel agency and ask them to do better.

If your agent contributes knowledge or experience, comes up with money-saving alternatives to your own package, or offers some other kind of convenience, then go ahead and book through the agency. If, as I often find, you know a lot more about your destination and are willing to spend a lot more time to save money than will the agent, you can do some or all of the booking yourself.

You'll have to judge whether an agent is looking out for your best interests by determining the best cruise line, vessel, and itinerary for you, or whether the promise of a higher commission is clouding your agent's judgment.

My best advice: Interview a travel agent carefully, and don't be afraid to ask questions about commissions and special promotions the agent receives from the cruise lines. If the agent refuses to discuss the matter or does so in a rude manner, take your business elsewhere. Remember that this is a business transaction, and it is your money and your vacation that are at stake.

Bids and Rebates

If you are booking an expensive cruise, don't be afraid to devote a little time and effort to saving some money:

▶ **Put your business out to bid.** There is nothing that says you cannot call two or three agencies and ask for a price on a particular cruise. Some agencies might have better pricing than others or could be receiving a bonus from the cruise line, and they may be willing to share some of that money with you to get your business.

▶ **Ask for a rebate from your agent.** If you're booking a $10,000 two-week luxury cruise, the agency stands to earn as much as $1,500 in commission for perhaps an hour's work. Ask for a reduction in price, a free cabin or hotel upgrade, first-class airline tickets, or something else back from the travel agency. It's not an unreasonable thing to do, and it's common practice in dealings between agencies and business clients.

Inside Info

The ordinary commission payment from cruise lines to travel agents is 10 to 15 percent, with some companies paying bonuses above that level for promotions. Most airlines have reduced their commissions significantly or have completely ended payments to agencies.

If you go to a travel agency with one cruise line in mind and are steered toward a different line, make sure the switch makes sense to you. Ask yourself: *Who gets a better deal because of the switch, me or the travel agent?*

■ UNBUNDLING THE PACKAGE

You might want to consider "unbundling" a vacation by giving your cruise business to a travel agency or consolidator, your airline reservations directly to the air carrier or a consolidator of tickets, and so on. Your goal, of course, is to compare the bottom line of a mixed purchase with the all-inclusive package put together by a travel agent.

In some cases, a cruise line may have negotiated special prices for airline tickets from many major gateway airports. Some cruise packages include airfare from these cities. Either way, you should compare the airfare price you could obtain by directly booking a flight to the cost in the package. Find out from the cruise line the credit you would receive if you were to make your own arrangements.

All this said, keep in mind that if you provide your own transportation to the ship, the cruise line is not likely to be very accommodating if your flight is late or canceled. If you purchase a package that includes airfare, the cruise line usually will take responsibility for getting you and your baggage to the ship, from the moment your journey begins. You'll read more about embarkation in Chapter 10.

INTERNET AND DISCOUNT TRAVEL AGENTS

Some large agencies offer travelers rebates on part of their commissions. Some of these companies cater only to frequent fliers who will bring in a lot of business; other rebate agencies offer only limited services to clients.

You can find discount travel agencies through many major credit card companies (Citibank and American Express among them) or through associations and clubs. Some warehouse shopping clubs have rebate or discount travel agencies. If you establish a regular relationship with your local travel agency and bring in enough business to make the agent glad to see you walk through the door, don't be afraid to ask for a discount equal to a few percentage points.

One other important new tool for travelers is the Internet. Here you'll find computerized travel agencies that offer airline, hotel, car, cruise, and package reservations. You won't receive personalized assistance, but you will be able to make as many price checks and itinerary routings as you'd like without apology. Several of the services feature special deals, including companion fares and rebates you won't find elsewhere.

Some of the best Internet agencies include:

- **Microsoft Expedia,** www.expedia.com.
- **Orbitz.com,** www.orbitz.com.
- **Travelocity,** www.travelocity.com.
- **Trip.com,** www.trip.com.

You can link directly to Travelocity from the *Econoguide* Web site: www.econo guide.com.

You can also book directly with a number of major airlines, sometimes taking advantage of special Internet prices or bonus frequent flyer mileage. Among the airlines that offer on-line booking are:

- **American Airlines,** www.aa.com.
- **Continental Airlines,** www.continental.com.
- **Delta Airlines,** www.delta.com.
- **Jet Blue,** www.jetblue.com.
- **Northwest Airlines,** www.nwa.com.
- **Southwest Airlines,** www.southwest.com.
- **United Airlines,** www.united.com.
- **US Airways,** www.usairways.com.

Don't be afraid to do your business over the phone or on the Internet. You should expect the same sort of personalized attention and service over the phone. In many instances I have received better service than I would have received had I walked into a travel agency.

You can also check Internet portals such as AOL or links from major newspaper or magazine Web sites.

UNDERSTANDING CANCELLATION POLICIES

One of the problems with booking a cruise is that you are paying in advance for a product not yet delivered. If you take advantage of some discount programs, you could be laying out thousands of dollars as much as a year before your cruise date.

In theory, that's OK. You're reaping the benefits of a discount for advance payment or securing a reservation for a commodity that's in very limited supply. There is a value that can be assigned to either situation, and if it makes sense to you, making an advance deposit and payment is acceptable behavior.

But what happens if your vacation schedule changes? What if there is an illness in your family? What if the cruise line changes the itinerary or substitutes a different ship? And, alas, what if the threat—or reality—of terrorism changes your dream into a nightmare?

I'll start with the last question first: In light of recent terrorist activities and the war in Iraq, most cruise lines and airlines have relaxed their cancellation policies. Most companies will permit travelers to cancel or postpone their trips on short notice because of military action; the value of any prepayment can usually be applied to a future trip without penalty or for a small charge. Keep in close contact with the cruise line if you have travel plans during such periods.

Other than terrorism and acts of war, if you are unable to show up at the appointed time, cruise lines generally claim the right to keep some or all of your

A Sample Cancellation Policy

Here's an example of a basic, inflexible policy from a major cruise line:

All cancellations and requests for refunds must be submitted in writing to the cruise company. All documents (deposit receipt or tickets) must be returned before the refund can be processed.

The cruise company will assess cancellation charges as follows:

- *76 or more days prior to sailing: Full refund*
- *75–46 days prior to sailing: Loss of deposit of $100 per person*
- *45–15 days prior to sailing: 50 percent of cruise/package price per person*
- *14–3 days prior to sailing: 75 percent of cruise/package price per person*
- *Less than 3 days prior to sailing: No refund, 100 percent cancellation charge per person*

These charges are just for the cruise portion of the trip and do not include cancellation or change fees that may be applied by air carriers, hotels, shore excursion suppliers, and others.

To add insult to injury, some cruise lines will add an "administrative fee" for changes to bookings after cruise documents have been issued.

deposit or advance payment. Some lines are more accommodating than others. The careful buyer spends the time to closely read the small print at the back of the cruise brochure.

On the other hand, if the cruise line makes a substantial change—such as changing the port of departure, changing the dates, or substituting a different ship—you don't have to accept the new deal; you can ask for all of your money back.

Enlist the assistance of your travel agency, the cruise line, and experienced travelers. But remember this: Put no trust in anything you are told verbally. The only thing that really matters is the written contract. If the cruise line or a travel agent tells you something different from what you see in the brochure or on the booking papers, ask that it be put in writing, signed, and made part of the contract.

TRIP CANCELLATION INSURANCE

So what is there to do about the not insignificant risk to your wallet from cancellations?

You might want to consider buying trip cancellation insurance. These policies pay the penalties assessed for any cancellation or interruption due to unforeseen, nonpreexisting medical conditions of travelers, their immediate family members, or traveling companions. Cancellation insurance will also often add coverage for illness or injury while on the cruise, including emergency evacuation, as well as damage, loss, delay, or theft of baggage.

As with other forms of insurance, the higher the potential payout, or the more likely it is that the insurance company will have to pay it, the higher the premium. Spend the time to read the insurance offering carefully. Pay special attention to the medical sections that cover preexisting conditions, generally excluded from coverage.

Unforeseen circumstances might include a traffic accident while en route to the port of departure, jury duty or subpoena, quarantine, a hijacking, or a home rendered uninhabitable by natural disaster. In all of these cases, you'll have to provide legal proof.

If your trip is interrupted midway because of illness, the refund will most likely be for the unused, nonrefundable portion of your cruise payment, plus the cost of returning home. For example, if you must leave the ship eight days into a ten-day trip, the insurance policy might pay only 20 percent of the cruise cost.

Take care not to purchase more coverage than you need. If you have a $5,000 prepayment on a cruise but the cruise line's cancellation policy says you will lose 50 percent of your advance payment in the case of a late cancellation, you need $2,500 in coverage, not $5,000. Be sure to include in your calculations all the elements of the package, such as airfare, noncancelable hotel reservations, and other bills explicitly covered by the insurance policy.

ACCIDENT AND SICKNESS INSURANCE

The idea of falling ill or suffering an injury while hundreds or thousands of miles away from home and your family doctor can be a terrifying thought. Although nearly all cruise ships have a medical doctor and small infirmary aboard ship, in the event of serious illness or injury, you'll almost certainly have to be taken to a hospital onshore or even airlifted home.

On one cruise I took, the captain told me that on the previous sailing the ship had to reverse course and sail several hours out of the way to meet up with a Coast Guard helicopter for an at-sea transfer of an ill passenger. On another cruise, an elderly passenger suffered a serious cardiac problem and was treated in the ship's hospital overnight until he could be transferred to a shoreside facility the next morning.

On a transatlantic repositioning cruise from Europe to New York on Silversea's *Silver Shadow*, a passenger with chest pains was left in a hospital in the remote Faroe Islands in the North Atlantic between Scotland and Iceland. He remained there for a week before being released to fly home.

As we'll discuss in greater detail in Chapter 7, most standard medical insurance policies do not cover expenses incurred onboard a cruise ship or in foreign countries. Consult your own insurance agent or your company's personnel office to see how far your personal medical insurance policy will reach. Does the policy cover vacation trips but exclude business travel? Are all international locations excluded? Can you purchase a "rider" or extension to your personal policy to cover travel?

Travel Insurance Providers

Here is a listing of some of the companies that sell travel insurance directly to travelers or through travel agents. If you purchase insurance, be sure not to buy more than you need; check with your own insurance agent to determine the coverage provided by your own medical policy. If you plan to make more than one trip in a year, it is usually less expensive to purchase a policy that covers the entire year rather than individual policies for each trip.

▶ **CSA Travel Protection.** www.csatravelprotection. com; (800) 873–9855

▶ **Global Travel Insurance.** www.globaltravelinsurance. com; (800) 232–9415

▶ **Travelex.** www.travelex insurance.com

▶ **Travel Guard.** www.travelguard.com; (800) 826–4919

▶ **Travel Insurance Services.** www.travelinsure. com; (800) 937–1387, (925) 932–1387

If you are not covered under your own policy, you can choose to buy coverage that is part of the trip cancellation insurance packages sold by cruise companies; many include some level of accident and sickness coverage.

The only reason to purchase an accident and sickness policy is to fill in any gaps in the coverage you already have. If you don't have health insurance of any kind, a travel policy is certainly valuable, but you might want to consider whether you should spend the money on a year-round policy instead of taking a vacation in the first place.

Also be aware that nearly every kind of health insurance has an exclusionary period for preexisting conditions. If you are sick before you set out on a trip, you might find that the policy will not pay for treating the problem.

CRUISE LINE BANKRUPTCIES

Every year or so, the cruise industry adds—and loses —a few lines. Competition is very fierce among cruise lines, and some, especially those in the second tier of companies, operate on very tight margins. It doesn't take much to push some smaller cruise lines into treacherous waters.

If you purchase your cruise through a travel agency, the agent should be able to inform you about the financial viability of a line. In some cases, a cruise line will bolster its image by promising to place all advance payments in an escrow account that cannot be tapped until after completion of a voyage.

All ships embarking from American ports must post a performance bond administered by the Federal Maritime Commission that is intended to cover refunds to passengers if the line is unable to provide promised transportation. If you are departing from a foreign port, you might not be covered for financial failure.

You can also protect yourself by purchasing a traveler's insurance policy that specifically provides coverage for trip cancellation for any reason, including financial problems by the cruise line. If the insurance company refuses to cover a specific cruise company, that's a pretty good indication of potential problems.

Note that the cancellation coverage sold directly by cruise lines might not offer protection against financial difficulties; insurance companies don't want to encourage cruise lines to be fiscally irresponsible.

You should also pay for your cruise with a major credit card if possible. If the line fails to provide a promised trip, the credit card company may be able to assist you.

HOW TO PAY FOR YOUR CRUISE VACATION

In general, the best way to pay the fare for your cruise vacation is with a major credit card. This also applies to all the other elements involved, including airfare to the port and any necessary hotel and car rental expenses.

I am not endorsing paying high credit card interest rates. Rather, my advice is to pay for vacations from savings: Charge the expenses to your credit card, and pay the bill when it arrives. This allows you to take advantage of a credit card's built-in protection against fraud and other problems.

Here are some reasons to use your credit card:

■ You can enlist the bank or card issuer in any dispute with the seller. Although you have authorized a charge to be put on your account, you hold on to your money for the moment. If the seller does not deliver the goods, or if whatever you bought is not what you contracted for, you can withhold payment and enlist the assistance of the company that issued the credit card.

■ You'll have the federal Fair Credit Billing Act on your side, which allows you to refuse to pay for a purchase and any finance charges while you make good-faith efforts to resolve a dispute. Your credit card company can put pressure on the merchant on your behalf, too.

Be sure to follow the rules for disputing a credit card charge; they're generally listed on the back of your monthly statement. You can also discuss these rules with the customer service department of the credit card company.

■ It's fun to go "native" when you travel in a foreign land, paying for your meals and souvenirs with euros in Europe, pounds in England, and pesos in Mexico. But you could end up losing 10 to 20 percent or more of your purchasing power by cashing in your dollars at a money-changing counter at the airport or a hotel, where you may have to pay a service charge and almost certainly will receive less than the best rate. You'll get a better exchange rate at a major bank and an even squarer deal by using your credit card.

When you are traveling abroad and are paying local currency, your credit card company will convert the bill to dollars at the bank rate, almost always lower than the rate charged by local merchants or money-changing outlets. (Call the customer service department for each of your credit cards and find out how they calculate foreign transactions, then use the card that has the lowest markup fee.)

■ Use your credit card's automobile insurance coverage when you rent a car. Many credit cards, especially "gold" and "platinum" cards, offer special automobile insurance coverage for rentals made using the card. Be sure to read the fine print from the credit card company, and don't hesitate to call customer service for clarification before you use the card to rent a car. The insurance coverage usually has exceptions that exclude luxury cars, and payment can be withheld if it is deemed that an accident was due to negligence by the driver. Finally, some credit card companies do not extend coverage to international rentals.

▪ You can obtain free airline accident insurance on tickets purchased with your credit card. Special insurance coverage for airline flights, purchased from an airport kiosk or directly from an insurance company, is generally not a good deal; you're better off buying and maintaining a good life insurance policy. But if your credit card company offers free coverage for tickets purchased with its card, take advantage of the offer.

▪ You want an interest-free loan from your credit card company from the time you make your purchase until the due date on your statement. Here's one of the best uses of a credit card, but it's only for the financially well disciplined: Make as many purchases as you can on your credit card—and then be sure to pay off the entire bill when it is due. The finest art here involves making major purchases just after the closing day of one billing period, which can give you thirty days until the next statement and up to thirty more days until the bill must be paid.

▪ PAYING FOR A VACATION ON THE INSTALLMENT PLAN

Do you really want to be paying for your vacation memories for years after you're back home? That's what you'll be doing if you put your cruise on an installment plan, credit card, or other loan arrangement. What's even worse is taking out a home equity loan or a second mortgage for a vacation. In this case, you could be putting the roof over your head at risk.

All that said, if you do use a loan or credit card, be sure to pay close attention to the APR (annual percentage rate) for the interest charged. Don't be shy about changing credit cards to get a lower rate or asking your current card issuer to reduce the APR to match another offer you have received.

One plan I cautiously endorse is a pay-in-advance installment plan—sort of a layaway plan for a cruise. Here you put away money before you travel. The sponsor of the plan should pay you interest on your money or offer some other enticement to you, such as a discount or upgrade. Be sure to understand your rights to receive a full or partial refund if you must cancel your plans before you travel.

CHAPTER FIVE

YOUR HOME ON THE WATER

HERE'S MY IDEA of the perfect ship's cabin (and hotel room): a comfortable, clean, and quiet home away from home with a fabulous and regularly changing view out the window or off the private balcony.

What's your idea of the perfect cabin? As you thumb through cruise line brochures you'll see glorious color photos of spectacular suites and glimpses of the better-looking portions of the smaller outside cabins. If there is a picture of one of the lowest-priced inside cabins at all, it is usually with a wide-angle view that rarely hints at just how minimal the accommodation is.

My wife and I like to watch the sunrise and sunset in privacy and to retire to our cabin on a sunny afternoon to read and write. My children love the guilty pleasure of room service between lunch and late-seating dinner.

But some travelers use their rooms only as a place to sleep and hang their clothes. If you spend all your waking time outside on the pool deck, you might not want to spend money on a veranda or panoramic window; if you don't expect to make it down to your room until way after dark, you might be perfectly happy with a windowless inside stateroom.

Think, too, about the nature of the cruise itself. If you're on a Caribbean island-hopper, the ship will travel by night and tie up or set anchor in a new port each morning. On this sort of cruise, you might be willing to accept a lesser cabin than you would prefer on an itinerary with several days between ports.

Once you're out of your room, there's no class distinction on most modern ships: All guests eat in the same restaurants, swim in the same pools, traverse the same promenades and lobbies, and participate in the same onboard and shore excursions. (The exception: On some very luxurious cruise ships, a few suites have their own pool or deck area and a concierge area.)

CHOOSING A CABIN

Are you the sort of person who wants to spend time lounging around your luxurious cabin, or would you rather spend time (and the money you've saved) in luxurious public spaces and onshore shopping expeditions?

This is not to say you should seek out (or accept) substandard accommodations, but there have been many times when I've checked into a first-class hotel room at midnight and left at six o'clock the next morning for a business appointment. The sitting room was unsat in, the luxurious bathrobe unlounged in, and the spectacular view unviewed.

The same goes for cabins on a ship. Ask yourself how important it is to have a window. Are you willing to accept an obstructed view or an inside cabin with no view at all? You can save big bucks if you choose to spend most of your time up on deck or in one of the public rooms of the ship.

One step deeper into the budget section are especially small inside cabins, or staterooms in a particularly unappealing location such as the very bottom of the ship or next door to the disco or the laundry room. If you can put up with living in the low-rent district, you can expect to pay a lower rent.

Going in the other direction, there is little to match the luxury of a private veranda at sea, especially when there are spectacular sights to see—in Europe, in Alaska, entering a big city port, and sometimes merely watching the sunset over an empty sea.

Study the cabin diagrams and ship layouts carefully before booking passage, and have all your questions answered before you commit to a cruise. Although it is sometimes possible to upgrade to a better class of cabin once onboard the ship, you cannot rely on that on all cruises, especially those taken during peak seasons when ships may be completely booked.

Cabin size can vary from a tiny closet to a penthouselike suite. In recent years the trend has been toward smaller cabins on modern ships, for no other reason than to maximize income for the owners. But that trend has reversed lately with the largest Megaships.

Suites offer superior accommodations; some of the most expensive come equipped with concierge or butler service, and a few may have access to a private swimming pool or lounge.

■ A ROOM WITH A VIEW

A balcony or veranda is a lovely extra, especially on a warm-water cruise. It's a great place to salute the sunset or the sunrise or to conduct a romantic interlude. Be aware, though, that not all balconies are that private; there could be a view from above, or there might not be full partitions on the sides. And the open veranda may be a concern to families with young children.

A handful of ships include forward-facing balconies at the bow. This affords a great view, but in most conditions, you'll also have something like a 20-knot wind in your face when the ship is moving.

Some newer vessels, including *Carnival Pride* and sister ships, have decks full of balconies on the stern. You'll have a great view of where you've been, with less breeze than at the bow unless you've got a following wind. (The downside: the absence of the traditional multideck lido restaurant and bar at the ship's stern.)

Study the ship's diagrams and check with the cruise line or a trusted travel agent to learn if your chosen cabin has an obstructed or partial view. What does

Cabin Locations to Avoid

Here are locations on the ship to avoid:

▶ **Near the disco** or near the gathering place for a public area, such as the theater or dining room.

▶ **Below the jogging track** or the exercise room.

▶ **Staterooms near the ship's machinery.** All things being equal, the quietest rooms are amidships (the middle of the vessel), away from the propeller at the stern and the anchor and winch mechanisms at the bow and stern. The midship area may also be less susceptible to roll and pitch.

▶ **Obstructed views.** Read the plan carefully to understand whether an available room has a veranda, a full window, or a large or small porthole. (Inside cabins, of course, have no windows or portholes.) Then check to see if the view out the window is obstructed by a lifeboat. Note that some "outside" cabins may lie across from an open promenade instead of being directly over the water. It's still a view, but you might have less privacy than you'd like.

that mean? On many ships, the lifeboats and other necessary equipment are mounted on the side of the ship or on an exterior deck. Try to get as much information as you can from the cruise line: A small winch in a corner of your view is very different from the broad side of a lifeboat completely filling your window.

Is there a promenade deck outside your cabin window or porthole? If so, you can't count on much privacy when the curtain is open.

By the way, on most ships the windows or portholes can't be opened. The exceptions: suites on upper decks and cabins that have verandas.

■ MAKING YOUR BED

Many cabins are equipped with twin beds, even on the "Love Boats." It may be possible to have the beds moved together to create a double bed, albeit one with a small gap between the mattresses.

In some especially small cabins, the beds are arranged in an L-shape. Some older boats use upper and lower berths with twin mattresses on each level. A few cabins have pulldown beds that fold up against the wall when they are not being used.

If you have any particular requirements or desires, study the ship diagrams before you book a cabin; you may also want to call the cruise line and discuss specific staterooms.

By the way, don't move furniture in your cabin. Ask the stateroom attendant whether beds can be rearranged, and allow the ship's staff to make changes and add appropriate bed linens.

WHERE ON THE SHIP?

The better and higher priced cabins are generally on the upper decks because these afford better views and larger windows or even verandas. As you move lower in the ship, the windows or portholes become smaller, and the chance you will feel vibrations or hear engine or machinery noise increases. (But lower decks experience less side-to-side roll than upper levels.) On some older vessels, elevators do not go all the way to the lower levels, requiring the use of stairs for the final approach.

Cabins at the front of the ship may have an angular outer wall because of the shape of the bow. More important, these cabins can be noisier during the time the ship is departing or arriving in a port because of the location of the anchor chain or docking ropes. Cabins at the stern, especially those on low decks, may be more susceptible to engine noises and heat.

An outside cabin offers views, light, and sometimes air. Watch out for obstructed views, usually lifeboats or docking winches on the outside decks.

The middle of the ship is usually less likely to carry engine noise and vibration. Cabins amidships (the middle of the ship in nautical terms) are affected less by the up-and-down pitching of the ship.

Avoid rooms that are located near nightclubs, lobbies, elevators, and other locations likely to have late-night noise.

■ INSIDE AND OUT

The most important distinction between cabins is that of "inside" and "outside" locations.

An outside cabin, as the name suggests, includes at least one wall that is part of the exterior of the ship, usually one of the sides but sometimes overlooking the bow or stern. You can expect at least one porthole or window; on new ships many outside cabins include a veranda with a glass door.

Posh Digs

According to some maritime historians, the preference for location on the ship is the source of the term "posh." British travelers heading out on grand expeditions on P&O ships to India and Asia would specify "port outbound, starboard home" to seek shelter from the sun.

An inside cabin is one that has no windows or portholes; on many ships these are also the smallest accommodations onboard. Some passengers will find them unbearably claustrophobic, while others will see them as a comfortable den to sleep in when they are not moving about the ship's public places.

There's one other class of inside cabins on some of the newest and grandest of ships: those with an inside balcony and a view of the ship's interior atrium. The first major ships with this sort of accommodation were Royal Caribbean's Voyager-class vessels, which offer a set of "Atrium Staterooms." (This strikes me as wholly unappealing, like a veranda in a shopping mall. Then again, it might match some travelers' concept of nirvana.)

The deck plan for the *CostaVictoria,* a modern 76,000-ton Megaship that has 964 cabins and nine decks. *Courtesy of Costa Cruises*

■ LEFT OR RIGHT?

You might also want to pay attention to whether your room is on the port (left) or starboard (right) side of the vessel. Only one side of the ship will be facing the sunrise or sunset or will receive direct sunlight during the course of the day. Just as on land, the southern exposure receives more sun than east, west, and, especially, northern exposures. If your vessel is heading west, the port side faces south; heading east, the starboard side will receive more sun.

Some travelers also pay attention to the orientation of their beds in relation to the ship. If the berths are parallel with the sides of the vessel, your head and feet will rise and fall with the pitch of the ship; if the berths lie across the beam, your head and feet will rise and fall with the ship's roll.

Which is better? Beats me. I sleep like a bobbing log either way.

■ YOUR FLOOR, PLEASE?

The "floors" of the ship, known as decks in marine parlance, run down the length of the ship and are stacked from the keel to the topmost sundeck.

The lowest level decks are used for the ship's mechanical rooms, including the engines, fuel tanks, saltwater desalination machinery and freshwater storage, and some of the refrigerators, freezers, and larders for the galley. The lowest decks are below the water level and there are no windows. It's a dark, sometimes noisy underworld.

On a ship of any significant size, the next few decks are given over to the galley or food preparation areas as well as cabins for most of the crew. On many ships, the lower decks may also house a movie theater or show room, where the absence of windows is not a problem.

The restaurant deck or a combined stateroom and restaurant level is typically three or four passenger decks up the ship or about six decks from the keel. On many modern ships, the dining room is at the stern, allowing a wall of windows.

The main deck is the central deck of the ship, usually the home of the purser's office and the reception desk. On many ships, this is the level where you will board the ship at the port of embarkation.

One level is often denoted as the boat deck, because that is the location of the boarding areas for most or all the lifeboats. Most modern ships hang their lifeboats way up high to avoid blocking the views from staterooms. The lifeboats would be lowered to a boarding platform if needed.

The promenade deck offers an open or enclosed walkway down one or both sides of the ship. An open walkway is pleasant for strolls or power walks in good weather, although high winds or rain can make the promenade disagreeable. On older vessels the promenade deck was often up high, between the main and boat decks; on more modern ships the promenade deck may be the same as the boat deck. On some ships the promenade has been shortened at the bow or stern or both by placement of luxury suites; walkers will have to reverse course for longer walks.

CHAPTER SIX

EXPENSES ONBOARD THE SHIP

YOUR CRUISE FARE is an all-in-one ticket for transportation, meals, a hotel room, and entertainment. Does that mean you can leave your wallet behind? No way.

There are many, many ways to spend money aboard ship and in ports of call. There are bars, health spas, art auctions, gift shops, and much more. There are shore excursions, bingo games, and casinos.

The truth is, most cruise lines realize a great deal of their profit from shipboard activities. You can run from their entreaties, but I'm afraid you can't completely hide.

ALCOHOLIC DRINKS AND SODA

On most cruise ships, you'll have to pay for drinks from the bar as well as wine at the table or drinks in your room. You can expect to find waiters hovering over you any time you sit down by the pool, in one of the lounges, and at your dining table. You may also find waiters standing by with a tray of welcome-aboard concoctions as your ship prepares to depart the terminal.

On all but the topmost ranks of cruise ships, the drinks are on you. It's perfectly fine to just say no. You don't have to order a drink to visit any part of the ship, including lounges and show rooms.

The waiters quickly learn to distinguish their best customers from those who don't indulge. By the end of a weeklong cruise you may have to wave very insistently to nab a farewell drink if waiters are not used to taking your order.

As with most other expenses onboard ship, if you do order a drink, you'll likely be asked to sign a receipt or hand over your onboard credit card, and the charge will appear on your final bill for the trip.

Drink prices onboard ship are usually comparably priced with what you'll find in an upscale bar on land, approximately $3.00 to $5.00 for most selections. Many cruise lines feature a drink of the day at a reduced price; you'll often find the specialty listed in the daily onboard newsletter.

Watch out for bottles of water, soda, or wine on the dresser in your room or in a minibar in some cabins. Find out from your cabin attendant whether there is a charge for opening one of the bottles (there usually is).

Here are some ways to save: First of all, juice, iced tea, and ice water are free, usually available in cafes and lounges onboard.

Most ships have rules against guests bringing their own alcohol aboard. Just between you and me: I have been known to pack my bags with a few bottles of wine from home or from a shoreside liquor store, keeping the bottle discreetly out of sight in a drawer or a closet. I can't imagine that a room steward is going to risk a gratuity by turning me in to the purser.

You may also choose to purchase some wine in ports of call; on one cruise I took in the Mediterranean, we engaged in a floating wine tasting, sampling local offerings from Croatia, Greece, Italy, Corsica, and Spain. (Some cruise lines will insist on collecting any liquor purchased ashore to store it for you until the end of the cruise; there's no good reason for this except to protect their onboard liquor sales.)

Speaking for myself, I can accept the exclusion of alcohol from freebies—I don't want to subsidize someone else's binges—but I do think that paying for soda is a bit of an imposition, especially when I travel with my kids. They are, alas, used to traveling by airplane, where the soda flows free and freely. On a weeklong cruise, it's easy to run up a bill of $50 per kid for a few $2.50 Cokes a day. (A few lines, including Disney, Holland America, and others, offer all-you-can-drink soda cards at a discount for kids.)

If you want to be really tight—and I'm willing to include myself in that category when appropriate—bring a few six-packs of soda in your luggage or buy them from a store in port and keep them cool with a free bucket of ice or the refrigerator found in some cabins.

ALTERNATIVE RESTAURANTS

Eating is at the heart of the daily routine on most cruise ships. Your basic vessel includes a dining room, a lido or poolside buffet, and a pizza and ice-cream counter. They're all included in your cruise fare, and the food is usually good and always plentiful.

As ships grew in size and passengers increased in number, cruise lines began to add more options for dining. Today, nearly all Megaships and larger ships offer main restaurants as well as "alternative" dining places: Italian, Asian, seafood, and other specialties. Then there are the "gourmet" restaurants (which makes me wonder whether cruise lines are admitting that their standard dining rooms are subgourmet).

Although some lines offer the alternative restaurants as just another option in the basic package, an increasing number of cruise lines levy an extra charge for the special service and food. Fees range from as little as $5.00 to as much as $25.00 per person.

Is that a good deal? Perhaps. The alternative restaurants deliver an unusually high level of service, even by cruise ship standards. You can expect tableside preparation of salads, entrees, and desserts. The dining "experience" is more leisurely, and in most cases you can expect a small table matched to the size of your party.

You can also expect a bit more persistent sales pitch from wine stewards and cocktail waitresses for added-cost beverages during the meal, and you should take into account the fact that you have already paid for your meal in the main dining room, whether you eat there or not.

SHORE EXCURSIONS

Within hours of departure at the start of a cruise, you can expect to hear the persistent drumbeats of the shore excursion staff. You'll be invited to a meeting where you will hear about the wondrous excitement of a guided tour to Mayan ruins or the Alaskan bush or a Hawaiian volcano. The shore excursion host or hostess might tell you, in a hushed, conspiratorial tone, about the fabulous bargains available at a particular shop in an upcoming port. The deals get even better, you're told, if you flash your cabin key or wear a cruise line sticker.

In a phrase: Caveat emptor . . . let the buyer beware. Although the shore excursions offered by most cruise ships may well be worthy of your time, they are almost always marked up in price from a tour you might arrange for yourself. The stores touted by the staff are often advertised for a reason: They might pay the cruise line to be included in the excursion spiel or in some way make the ship or the cruise director's staff happy for delivering a boatload of tourists.

One advantage of booking a tour through the shore excursion desk is that the cruise line will then know where a group of its passengers is for the day, and will generally promise to hold the ship if an excursion is delayed.

Here are some important questions to ask before you purchase a shore excursion onboard a ship:

■ What kind of transportation will be provided? How large is the vehicle? Is it air-conditioned? Is there a rest room onboard?

■ Will an accredited guide accompany the group?

■ How long is the drive? Are there any intermediate stops for comfort, shopping, or sight-seeing?

■ Will you have free time in cities or tourist destinations to explore on your own?

■ Will you return in the same vehicle? Will it remain locked and attended while you are away, allowing you to leave personal possessions at your seat?

■ Are there any extra charges for admission to attractions? If a meal is offered, are drinks included?

■ How much walking or climbing is involved? Is the trip appropropriate for your physical condition?

■ What time is the group due back at the ship?

Be aware that in many ports, excursion operators have booths on shore offering tours. These might be the same companies and tours sold by the cruise

Too Good to Be True

In some ports you'll see booths touting "free" or deeply discounted tours with deals that seem too good to be true. In many cases, that's exactly what they are. These are come-ons for time-share vacation offers, and the price for the free helicopter tour or luau or submarine trip is that you'll have to sit through several hours of a high-pressure sales presentation.

First, a real estate or time-share presentation is not a very good use of your precious shore time; you might not have enough time for both the sales pitch and the "free" excursion anyway. Second, in my opinion, time-shares are not a good investment nor a rational way to plan future vacations.

Just say no.

line, or they could be similar trips offered by independent operators. If you haven't made arrangements in advance, be one of the first passengers off your ship when it docks and look for the booths; ask for a discount.

You can also hire a taxi or van and ask the driver to take you to the same places that the cruise line's bus will visit.

My recommendation for shore expeditions: Research the ports of call before you set out on your cruise. Buy a good travel book specific to your destinations and learn about the best sights to see and the recommended shops as laid out by a writer who has no vested interest in anyone but you. Make a few phone calls to the visitor bureaus for the ports before you travel, and ask about places to go on your own. The Internet is a wonderful source of information; many visitor bureaus maintain Web pages with links to individual tour operators.

Some cruise lines will send you a brochure of shore excursions a few weeks before you leave for your trip, to whet your appetite for their offerings. I use that brochure as the basis for my own research.

One word of warning: In some cases, a major cruise line may have locked up a particular excursion for its passengers, booking the only floatplane, for example, or arranging for the best seats at a particular show or event. Before you pay top dollar in the face of that sort of argument, make a phone call and see what you can arrange. In my experience, there's almost always something you can do for yourself.

I consulted some Web pages and made a few phone calls before I embarked on an Alaskan cruise; I found that I could save $50 per person on a seaplane tour of the bush by booking it myself instead of paying the price asked by the shore excursion desk onboard the cruise.

In the Caribbean, I regularly rent a car from a dockside agency and drive to the same beaches others take taxis or buses to reach. Some of the best islands for drives include Saint Martin and Saint Thomas.

In Europe, many ports are served by high-speed rail links to major cities, making it easy to make your own tour and save money.

Here are further savings opportunities:

■ A submarine voyage to the floor of the harbor in several Hawaiian ports is $20 to $30 cheaper when you buy a ticket onshore instead of from the shipboard excursion desk.

▪ You should be able to negotiate a better price for a private guided tour by taxi, Jeep, or limousine by contacting ahead of time tourist agencies in the ports you will visit. Split the fare with someone else you meet onboard the ship to save even more.

▪ Floatplanes for visits to the Alaskan bush, an experience I recommend very highly, can be reserved ahead of time by calling tour operators directly or by calling tourism agencies in the ports. The same goes for helicopter trips to the volcanoes of Hawaii.

▪ If you are planning to make a shopping expedition to a specific store and are reasonably certain you will be making a purchase there, why not call ahead to the store and make an appointment to come in? You can hope for more personalized attention, and the shop may even arrange to pick you up at the dock.

▪ You can often catch a water taxi to a Caribbean beach at a much lower price than you'd pay to take a party boat.

▪ When it comes to bus tours to tourist attractions and natural wonders, I figure that if the bus can drive there, so can I. It is almost always much more satisfying to rent a car in port and drive wherever you want, whenever, and with whomever; sometimes it's even considerably less expensive. You can set your own itinerary and stop at any shop or attraction. Best of all, at least in my view, you're not a sardine on a bus.

▪ RENTING A CAR

Start out by calling major car rental agencies. You'll generally find rental companies at airports of most any size and in many important towns and cities. Bear in mind that the port where your ship docks or drops anchor could be some distance away from an airport. Call directly to a rental counter to arrange for shuttle service. If the car company wants to charge for a pickup and delivery, try another agency.

You should be able to save $20 or more per day on a car rental in port if you make a few phone calls to rental agencies ahead of time instead of relying on the excursion desk to make arrangements for you.

Car rental rates in obscure locations may be slightly higher than you would find at home, and gasoline prices are almost certainly more expensive on distant islands and ports. But I have yet to see a case in which renting a car is not less expensive or comparable in price to a prepackaged tour for two to four travelers.

Check with your insurance agent about your liability and collision coverage, and make sure you make the agent aware of your itinerary if it includes a stop in a foreign country. Some insurance companies will not extend coverage for rental of four-wheel-drive off-road vehicles. In any case, you probably should not use your vacation as the place to learn to drive off-road.

Be aware, too, that on islands with a British heritage, including a number of ports in the Caribbean, cars travel on the left side of the road. For some drivers, the changeover to the "wrong" side of the road is a simple adjustment; for others, it is an exercise in terror.

◼ A WORD OF WARNING

When you go it alone onshore, you assume the responsibility for getting back to your ship before it leaves port at the end of the day. If you drive too far away from port, if your car suffers a flat tire, if your fishing expedition makes a wrong turn, or if you simply make a mistake in your planning, you could end up with the extra expense of catching up with your ship at its next stop.

If you're driving, discuss local road conditions and travel times with the rental company, and carry a good map. Ask about how breakdowns are handled, and bring with you the phone number for the local office, not the toll-free number for reservations. Plan your trip to give yourself at least an hour's cushion at the end of the day.

If you're taking a tour, make sure the operator knows when you need to be back onboard the ship. Again, leave yourself an extra cushion of time.

Finally, any time you leave the ship, be sure to carry with you the ship's identification number and the name and telephone number of the cruise line's local agent in the port; it is usually listed on the day's newsletter. In case you run into trouble or miss the departure of the ship, the local agent should be able to help you communicate with the line and help you catch up with the ship in a later port—at your expense.

TELEPHONE SERVICE

One of the reasons to travel by cruise ship is to cut the cord to the "real world." But, alas, there is always the tug to stay in touch with the family and the office. In today's world of cellular and digital communication, it is relatively easy to make phone calls as you travel. You will, however, have to pay a premium rate to use the ship's long-distance services.

Until fairly recently, communications from a ship were exclusively by radio. The ship's radio officer could patch a cabin telephone or a phone on the bridge into a radio signal to shore, where it could be tied into a land-based telephone system. You may still find radio-based telephone service on some older vessels; typical radio charges range from $10 to $15 per minute.

The latest in shipboard telecommunications, however, is the satellite phone. On most ships, passengers can place calls from their cabins directly to a phone located anywhere on the planet. Typical charges range from about $6.00 to $10.00 per minute; billing sometimes starts as soon as the call is initiated, and a session of two minutes and one second is billed at three minutes.

Either telephone system will work quite well in the most popular cruising areas, including the Caribbean, but there are still places that even satellites don't cover.

On one cruise I found myself at Fanning Island, which lies just above the equator, nearly 2,000 miles west of South America and a thousand miles south of Hawaii. The standard satellite links for the ship, including telephone and television, were useless in the vast emptiness of that part of the South Pacific. I was able, though, to visit the radio officer on the bridge and place a call that bounced off a satellite somewhere over Japan and then back to my home in Massachusetts; I've got the bill to prove it.

■ BETTER WAYS TO KEEP IN TOUCH

Before you travel, think about your telephone and Internet needs and strategies. In this modern age, you will rarely be out of reach of an electronic connection, but some arrangements are much better than others.

The most expensive way to call is to use the phones onboard the ship. Make your phone calls as short as possible. Prearrange with family or the office to set a particular time for your call—you don't want to be put on hold at $10 per minute—and keep the calls businesslike. You can always discuss the weather when you return.

You'll do much better by calling from shore. Use a telephone credit card with a reasonable per-minute charge. If you are going to be calling to or from a foreign country, check with your long-distance credit card provider before you set out on your cruise and inquire about the most economical way to place the call.

The lowest calling card rates are found in countries that have deregulated their phone companies. Rates from Europe are generally about 30 to 50 cents per minute plus a service charge of about $1.00 for the first minute. At the other end of the spectrum are Mexico and Central America and parts of the Caribbean, where you can expect to be charged about $3.00 to $4.00 per minute plus a service charge of about $4.00.

Apply for several telephone calling cards before you leave. AT&T will usually work in ports both familiar and strange, but the company's prices are generally the highest. Slightly better deals are available from Sprint and other carriers. Before you leave for your voyage, check with the issuers of each of your cards to obtain the latest local access phone numbers.

Another way to keep in touch is to purchase phone cards in port; visit the shops that cater to members of the crew. Ask your dining room waiter or stateroom attendant where he or she goes to call home. In Mexico, for example, phone cards cost about 100 pesos for 12 minutes, a bit less than $1.00 per minute for calls to the United States. In Europe, phone cards cost about 30 to 50 cents per minute.

■ CELL PHONES

One way to keep in touch is to use a cell phone, but don't expect to receive a signal when your ship is way offshore or in an obscure port. Be sure you understand your cell phone company's policy on roaming out of your home area.

You should be able to use a U.S.-based cell phone in major ports in Alaska and Hawaii; some companies have local connections in American territories in the Caribbean, including Saint Thomas and Puerto Rico, and a few companies extend their coverage into major cities in Canada.

Most domestic cell phones will not work in Europe, Asia, South America, and elsewhere, but a new class of "world phones" can extend your digital phone to roam in many other countries; check with your cellular company. My "triband" phone works throughout most of Europe and Asia, at a rate of about $1.00 to $2.00 per minute; it does not work in Mexico and Central America, and coverage in the Caribbean is spotty.

Another solution is to rent a cell phone with a foreign account, either before you travel or on arrival. Expect to pay a few dollars per day for rental of the phone plus about $1.00 to $3.00 per minute for calls. I took one such cell phone with me on a cruise around the Mediterranean. The phone, from Roadpost (formerly RentExpress), came equipped with a telephone number in England; it worked in that country as well as in most of my ports of call in Italy, Greece, France, Spain, and even in parts of Croatia.

One nice feature of some world phones is the ability to receive text messages sent over the Internet. Messages cost less than a dollar to send or receive, a reasonable way to keep in touch between voice calls. For information call (888) 290–1616 or visit www.roadpost.com.

INTERNET CAFES

Communicating by e-mail offers many advantages, including cost (if you're careful) and a way to get around time zone differences. The beauty of using the Internet is that messages can be sent on an asynchronous basis, meaning that both parties do not need to be on-line at the same time.

I'd suggest that you set up an account with one of several free-mail Web sites. You don't even need to have a regular Internet account to use one; you can sign up on a free terminal at a library or school or borrow a friend's system. Among mail Web sites are www.hotmail.com and www.juno.com. You should also be able to set up a Hotmail account that can retrieve messages from your regular e-mail provider.

Some computer users make arrangements for an AOL Instant Messenger account and try to coordinate being on-line at the same time as friends or family members; be sure to take into account time zone differences. AIM permits near-instantaneous messaging among users.

Many cruise lines now have Internet cafes onboard their ships, allowing guests to sign on to mail Web sites or Internet providers, including America Online. The cafes at sea typically charge 75¢ cents to $1.00 per minute, which is rather pricey, and connection speeds can be slow in some parts of the world. Expect to spend at least five minutes on-line to retrieve messages and dash off a reply.

Some cafes offer unlimited service for a onetime fee, usually about $100 for a week's pass.

A better deal is to visit an Internet cafe on land. You'll find one in nearly every port; check in the terminal for advertisements, or ask a crew member for advice. Typical rates are about 10 cents per minute; I've found charges as low as a few pennies per minute in Europe. Check to see if the cafe is part of a chain with locations in other stops on your itinerary. If so, it probably makes sense to purchase a block of time that can be used at several ports.

SHIP'S PHOTOGRAPHER

On some cruise lines the ship's photographers will be on you like flies on jam, happy to document your every moment for posterity. They'll be there as you come onboard for the first time, they'll be there at the captain's welcome-aboard dinner, and they'll be there at most every onboard activity.

If you'd like to come home from your trip with pictures to prove you've really been on a cruise, or to show yourself stuffed into a tuxedo and cummerbund or a cocktail dress at the captain's dinner, the photographers will be happy to oblige.

On some of the most spectacular of the modern ships, you'll even find a state-of-the-art "blue screen" studio, where a bit of electronic magic can place you against most any backdrop. Didn't quite make it to the lip of the volcano? Who's to know? Even stranger: How about a picture of you in front of an Alaskan glacier, taken onboard your Caribbean cruise?

Photographs are not cheap; on most ships a 5 × 7 picture costs $5.00 to $10.00. Multiple copies of the same picture should be priced at a lower rate; ask for a discount if one is not offered. Formal studio portraits cost more.

You are under no obligation to make a purchase. If you don't like the picture, don't buy it. There is nothing wrong with waving off the photographers if you're not interested in posing; tell them to save their film or digits for someone else. As with waiters in the bars, by a few days into the cruise, the ship's photographers will have a pretty good idea of which passengers are going to be their customers and which ones don't want to be spotted.

On many cruises you can also sit for a formal family portrait in a studio setting; in this instance there may be an obligation to make a purchase. Be sure you understand the terms before saying cheese.

One deal you might want to consider: On the most modern of ships you can arrange to have your own film developed, printed, and delivered to you within a day or so. Compare the prices with what you would pay onshore and add in the convenience and amazement factor: You can show off your pictures on the plane ride home.

GIFT SHOPS

On most modern ships, a small shopping arcade offers a reasonable selection of gifts and necessities. Many of the items are duty-free; that makes a difference on certain items such as some liquor, jewelry, and perfume. You'll also find cruise clothing, pharmaceuticals, cosmetics, cameras, binoculars, and all manner of souvenirs. The shops seem to be constantly offering some sort of a "once in a lifetime" sale.

My opinion, since you asked, is that you should consider these shops as emergency resources, kind of a floating 7-Eleven for things you need in a hurry and can't wait to purchase in the next port of call. The only exception: On most ships the prices for liquor are about the same or a bit less than you'll find onshore; it's a lot more convenient to buy on the ship. Note that the selection is usually limited to major brands. If you're looking for unusual local wines or liquors, you're still going to have to shop onshore.

The shops may be of value if you are unexpectedly invited to sit at the captain's table and your most formal outfit is a T-shirt that proclaims, I'M WITH STUPID. Many shops sell or rent formal wear, albeit at premium prices.

Another reason to visit the ship's gift shop is if you absolutely must own a T-shirt or a jacket emblazoned with the name of the ship or cruise line.

Remember that on most ships, you can obtain free aspirin or Tylenol, Band-Aids, shampoo, and other sundries from your cabin attendant or from the purser's office. You should also be able to obtain seasickness pills and Tylenol from the office of the ship's doctor.

ART AUCTIONS AND GALLERIES

We all know the official slogan of the amateur art collector: "I don't know much about art, but I know what I like."

That's all very well and good, but do you also know how much the art you like is worth? On many cruise lines, especially those in the mid- to upper price range, you'll find an onboard art gallery or auction.

On one cruise I took, an earnest young man was passing himself off as an expert in "fine art" and conducting several auctions of paintings and sculptures that he declared at various times to be priced at either "80 percent off retail" or "80 percent of retail." There's a huge difference between those two discounts; even more scary is the fact that I have absolutely no idea what the true "retail" price for a piece of art should be.

The auctions he conducted were also not pure exercises in capitalism. The seller had a reserve price—a minimum price—for each piece, and although the bidding might start low, the painting or sculpture was not going anywhere until someone offered at least that minimum amount.

So is an onboard art auction a fraud? I couldn't tell you because, as I said, I have no idea of the true value of the items. My advice: If you know the value of art, go forth and drink the free champagne and hunt for a bargain. If you don't know the value of art, but you find something you really like, decide for yourself what the item is worth to you and see if you can buy it for that price. Don't, however, try to make an "investment" in art unless you do know the value of the items for sale.

Oh, and be sure you understand any shipping costs, duties, and other charges that might be assessed on your purchase before you make a bid.

HEALTH SPA AND BEAUTY SALON

If the rockabye motion of the ocean, lying by the pool, and the overall cruise experience are not quite relaxing enough—or if you feel the urge to beautify yourself or undertake a new course of exercise—most ships offer an onboard health spa that is fully prepared to coddle you in luxury. The spa is also ready to give your credit card a serious workout.

Disney Magic and *Golden Princess* tied up in St. Maarten. *Photo by Corey Sandler*

Basic facilities include everything from beauty parlors and barbers to manicures, massage rooms, saunas, and steam rooms. But on many ships, that's just the starting point. On a typical voyage you might find such offerings as a full body massage with aromatic oils and therapeutic heat for about $90, a reflexology consultation and analysis for about $70, and something called an Ionithermie superdetoxification treatment for about $120.

(That last is described as a regime in which lotions rich in kelp, ivy, and seaweed are placed on the body and covered with a blue clay, then excited with electrodes. The treatment is supposed to reduce cellulite and remove toxins in the body that contribute to cellulite and reduce energy. Or so they say.)

SPORTS AFLOAT

Swimming in the pool, working out in the gym, playing basketball on the sundeck or shuffleboard alongside the pool, hiking around the promenade deck, and repeated trips to and from the buffet line are all included in your fare. You'll also find some additional sports facilities that are offered at an extra cost. These include:

- **Golf.** The offerings here include driving ranges and golf simulators that allow you to step up to the tee with a real club and drive a ball into a screen that carries the image of a famous fairway. On some cruises you'll also find a PGA-certified instructor who can help you with your game. Some of the golf programs are tied into shore excursions to courses in ports of call.

■ **Specialty sports.** The biggest of the new ships include some unusual sports options, including rock climbing on an artifical wall attached to one of the ship's funnels or ice-skating on a small rink. You can expect to be charged for the right to tell your friends and family, "You won't believe what I did on my cruise."

■ **Water sports.** In warm waters you may be able to rent snorkeling or scuba diving equipment or sailboats or arrange for waterskiing and other activities in port. (You'll need to be certified to use scuba devices; some cruises can arrange for the training onboard the ship.)

■ **Skeet shooting.** This holdover from the glory days of the transatlantic liner is available on a few ships. The modernized version uses biodegradeable targets and quieter guns.

Some of the smaller luxury ships make their advanced sports part of the basic package. For example, the Radisson *Diamond* includes a marina at the stern used to launch watercraft available to all guests in certain ports.

BABY-SITTING AND KIDS' ACTIVITIES

Many cruise lines offer free activities for children. Among the best programs are those offered by Disney Cruise Line. Other companies that promote kiddie-friendliness include Holland America, Carnival, Royal Caribbean, and Princess.

You'll likely have to pay for private baby-sitting in your room or for special group baby-sitting activities. You'll also have to pay for video arcades. Some companies, including Disney Cruise Line, make it very easy to run up a bill. Kids (if you give the cruise line permission) have their own credit cards they can use to purchase arcade time, as well as soda and gifts from the stores.

GRATUITIES

Like it or not, nearly all the service staff onboard most cruise ships receive very little in the way of salary, sometimes the equivalent of only a few dollars a day. They make their incomes from gratuities offered by guests.

There is no requirement that you give a tip, but the fact is, tipping is considered part of today's cruise environment. Most cruise lines will helpfully provide passengers with a "suggested" schedule of tips. On most ships the amount ranges from $7.50 to $12.00 per person per day.

Here's a typical breakdown:

Cabin attendant	$3.50 per person per day
Waiter	$3.50 per person per day
Busboy	$1.50 per person per day

The cruise line may also recommend that you tip the headwaiter and/or maître d' another $1.50 per person per day. Those tips are truly voluntary. If the managers of the restaurant have performed some especially notable service for you, go ahead and remember them with a gratuity. If not, take solace in the fact that the managers are paid a reasonable salary, while the cabin attendants and waiters are not. (Want some scary math? Multiply 2,000 passengers times $1.50 per day for the headwaiter and maître d' and ask yourself if you're in the wrong business.)

Drinks from the bar and many other special services, such as the health spa and special-order room service deliveries, will typically have a 15 percent service charge added to the bill.

As I have noted earlier, on many ships you can charge the gratuities to your shipboard account and hand your servers a card indicating that. You can also give cash.

The traditional time to extend gratuities is at the final dinner before disembarkation, known among the staff as "the last supper." You can expect all the service staff to be especially attentive to your needs that evening.

If you do expect to give a tip, some veterans recommend giving your room steward and dining room staff $20 or more at the start of the cruise; you can expect just a bit more attention and special service if they envision you as a big tipper. It'll be up to you whether to stay with the standard amount of gratuity when you make a second gift at the end of the trip.

A handful of cruise lines charge their passengers enough of a premium to allow a "no tipping permitted" or a "no tipping required" policy. The lines that completely prohibit tipping include Seabourn and Silversea. Among lines that say tipping is not required are Cunard, Holland America Line, Radisson, and Windstar.

Note that it is also customary to extend a small gratuity to the escort on a shore excursion.

PORT CHARGES

Many cruise lines advertise their rates without including port charges and fees levied by the various places the ship departs from and visits. These can easily add $150 or more to each ticket on a seven-day cruise, and much more on a longer voyage. Be sure you know whether these fees are included in the price of your cruise.

FLOATING CRAPS GAMES AND SLOT MACHINES

If you want to gamble, many cruise ship companies are perfectly happy to take your money. Onboard casinos range from a few slot machines in a bar to glitzy miniatures of Las Vegas.

You won't find casinos on many smaller ships and adventure cruises and the Disney Cruise Line decided to forgo gambling on its family-oriented vessels.

In most cases, the casinos do not operate when the ship is in port.

Let's get a few things straight right away: First of all, the fancy casino onboard your ship, just like those of Las Vegas, Reno, Lake Tahoe, Laughlin, southeastern Connecticut, Atlantic City, and everywhere in between, was not built as

The casino onboard *Celebrity Millennium. Photo by Corey Sandler*

entertainment but as a place of business. That business is the extraction of cash from your wallet or purse.

Second, the success of that business is based on the fact that nearly every visitor can be counted on to lose money at gambling tables and slot machines. Some will lose more than others, and a few will even come away with an occasional small or large or huge win; but always remember that the pockets of the casino operators are lined with the money left behind by the losers.

Third, if you are a serious gambler, shipboard casinos may not be the best place to invest your capital. Passengers on a ship are a captive audience, and slot and video poker machines might not be as liberal in their payouts as their land-based equivalents.

I'm not going to offer lessons on gambling here. If you're going to bet serious money, I'd suggest you buy a book or two about gambling. I will, though, offer my **Three *Econoguide* Rules of Gambling**.

- **Rule Number One for Gamblers:** Don't bet more than you can afford to lose.
- **Corollary to Rule Number One:** Don't bring with you to the table (or with you onboard the ship) more money than you can afford to lose.
- **Second Corollary to Rule Number One:** Don't beg, borrow, or steal more money than you can afford to lose. The casinos will make it very easy for you to tap into credit cards or savings accounts, and they may even offer unsecured loans. Whatever the source, it will still be a debt, and it probably will include an unpleasant interest rate.

■ SLOT MACHINES

At one time, the conventional wisdom may have been that table games, from roulette to 21 to baccarat, were where the real action was at a casino. Slot machines were looked down upon as the province of the low roller.

The average bet in a casino is still considerably higher at the tables, but don't believe for a moment that casinos look down on slot machines. At most casinos, slots deliver about half the revenue. That percentage is even higher on most cruise ships.

Here's the rap on slots: They are dumb, require no skill, and provide no human interaction. They are pure exercises in luck, and, like other casino bets, they ask the player to put aside the knowledge that the casino is almost sure to win over time. They aren't called "one-armed bandits" for nothing.

The odds against winning are based on the number of reels (rolling sets of symbols), the number of symbols on each reel, and the computer settings made by the casino operator. A "liberal" machine is one that returns about 98 percent of the money put into it. What that means is that over an extended period of time, the machine pays out about $98 for every $100 bet. In practice, this could mean that unlucky players might lose nearly everything they bet, while a lucky bettor could walk away with a nice payoff. The highest-payoff five-reel machines may work out to a chance of something like 1 in 3.2 million pulls for the jackpot.

Most slot machines pay better jackpots to bettors who play the maximum number of coins on a pull. If you are willing to bet about $1.00 per pull, you generally would be better off at a quarter machine putting in five coins at a time ($1.25 per pull) than putting in a single dollar token at a dollar machine.

■ VIDEO POKER

Video poker machines are very popular, offering the chance for a bit of reward to players who have a bit of skill. There are dozens of different formats, but most of them come down to versions of stud poker. The machine will deal you five cards; you can choose to hold any or all of them or draw up to five new cards. After the second round of cards, the hand is evaluated and winning hands are paid off.

Most machines pay off only on a pair of jacks or better. In addition, the relative payoffs are much higher for the best hands. Therefore, professional video poker players generally recommend throwing away any low hands and always making a play for the high-payoff hands. For example, in standard poker you would almost never draw to an inside straight (seeking to fill out a straight with a gap in the middle, as in 9-10-Q-K), but in video poker it might be worth a chance.

■ THE ROULETTE WHEEL

Round and round she goes; where she stops, nobody knows. Some historians track the roulette wheel back to the ancient Chinese or Tibetans of 1,000 years ago. Famous French scientist and mathematician Blaise Pascal is credited with adapting the wheel to a casino game in 1655.

Of the four major table games (roulette, craps, blackjack, and baccarat), roulette offers the poorest odds to the player. It is, though, one of the simplest of games to play. In the standard game as played in Nevada and onboard most ships, the wheel is divided into alternating red and black compartments that are numbered from 1 to 36; in addition, one compartment is numbered 0 and another 00. A player can bet on any of the 38 numbers directly and is paid off at 35:1. (Here is the house advantage presented about as clearly as possible: There is a 1 in 38 chance of a particular number coming up, and the winning payoff is 35:1.)

The 0 and 00 are excluded from the payoffs on red/black, odd/even, columns, or rows. In other words, the casino wins all bets on color, odd/even, or groups of numbers if 0 or 00 comes up.

The American game with the 0 and 00 numbers added to the layout gives the house a 5.26 percent advantage on most bets; the worst gamble for the player is the five-number bet, which gives the house an advantage of more than 7 percent.

■ BLACKJACK (21)

Blackjack, also known as 21, is one of the more popular casino games and, on one level, one of the easiest to play. All you have to do is request cards from the dealer, one at a time, until you get as close to a card value of 21 as you can. If you get closer to 21 than the dealer, you win; if you go over 21 or if the dealer is closer to that magic number, you lose. If you and the dealer tie, your bet is returned to you.

Betting is relatively simple too. You are always betting against the dealer that your card value will be better than the dealer's. But although blackjack is easy to play, it is not easy to win. It is, however, one of the few games at the casino that can be consistently beaten, or at least fought to a draw, by a well-educated and careful player.

A player who understands the basic strategy and bets conservatively can expect to win about 1 percent of total action over the course of time, which doesn't sound like much, but it can quickly mount up to serious money. Players who can count cards and adjust the levels of betting and strategies based on the current condition of the deck can expect to win much more.

The line between winning and losing is always slim, and the casino always stands to benefit from a player's mistake.

Watch the players at the table or ask the dealer about the protocol for indicating whether you want to hit or stand. Some casinos are more picky than others about hand signs used at the table. In most casinos, you indicate you want another card by scratching your current cards toward you on the felt or by waving at the dealer with a "come to me" gesture. (Looser dealers will permit you to nod your head "yes" or perform some other positive signal.) To indicate that you want to stand, you can slip your cards, face down, under your bet or give some sort of a "wave off" signal. The reason casinos are sometimes picky about the signals used is they don't want a bettor to ask for his money back on a losing bet because of any ambiguity about betting intentions.

Other casino protocol: Handle the cards with one hand only; don't take the cards off the table, and don't touch your bet once cards have been dealt. If you are busted, turn over all your cards and watch the dealer take away your bet.

CRAPS: A FLURRY OF ACTION

Craps is one of the more exciting games at the casino, one in which the players and even various casino employees are encouraged to yell, shout, and otherwise encourage the little cubes of plastic to come up properly.

The thrower (called the shooter) makes a money bet, covered by one or more opponents. The shooter throws the two dice against the far wall of the craps table. (This is an important rule of the casino; the boxman or pit boss may halt the game if they don't feel you are throwing the dice with enough force to ensure an honest tumble.) If the first throw totals 7 or 11, the player wins; but if 2, 3, or 12 is thrown, the player loses. In any of these cases, betting and throwing are repeated.

If the throw totals 4, 5, 6, 8, 9, or 10, that number becomes the player's point, and throwing is continued until the same point is made again or a 7 is thrown. If the point is made, the player wins, but if a 7 is thrown, the player loses both the bet and the right to throw again.

Even more complex is the betting protocol for craps. If you're going to be risking your capital at the craps table, pick up a specialized book on gaming or ask the casino management for a lesson.

THE BINGO PARLOR

Your grandma might not refer to bingo as gambling, but that's what it is, and on many ships this is where you'll find the big action.

Every ship has its own prices and special promotions, but in general, bingo is bingo. You'll find traditional games, the goal of which is to fill in a straight or diagonal line, as well as "coverall" versions, in which the winner must fill in all the numbers to win.

There are basic prizes of $25 to $100 per game, and there are jackpot and progressive rounds, with the prize rising after each unsuccessful game until one player takes home a large payment.

And then there are lotteries intended to keep you coming back for more bingo games. A number of cruise lines, including Holland America and Norwegian Cruise Line, routinely award a grand prize of a free cruise to the winner of a lottery or a special high-priced round of bingo.

Bingo cards typically cost between $5.00 and $10.00 per game. Less expensive cards and twofer promotions are offered on most cruises, too, although the prize payout for lower-priced cards is usually concomitantly lower.

Don't look to finance your kids' college education or even your next cruise vacation on the basis of your bingo winnings. The careful player performs a rough calculation of the odds of winning based on the number of players, and then looks at the price to play and the possible prize. If you go to all of that trouble, you'll probably decide the game is a pretty poor bet. Instead, if you think of an hour of bingo as fun, pay the price as entertainment.

A CASHLESS SOCIETY

On most cruise ships, cash is either not expected or not accepted. Instead, you'll be asked to establish a credit account with the purser's office when you board. From that point on, you'll be able to sign for all expenses onboard the ship. If you do not have a credit card or choose not to use one, you will likely be asked to make a cash deposit to open an account.

Some ships issue a magnetically encoded charge card for use aboard. Others give you a printed card with your name and cabin number on it, while on some cruises all you need to do is announce your stateroom number. On the most modern of ships, your cabin key is also your personal credit card as well as your embarkation and disembarkation pass.

On many ships you can also charge gratuities to your charge account. You should receive a receipt for the tips and a card to give to your room attendant, waiter, and busboy to inform them you have paid for a tip that should be credited to their accounts.

Some ships provide a preliminary accounting of your bill a few days before the end of the trip; take the time then to check over the statement and bring any errors to the attention of the purser's office. You'll receive a final itemized bill early on the morning of disembarkation. If the bill is correct, you're usually set to leave; on some ships you'll have to visit the purser's office to check out.

If there are errors on the bill, head for the purser early. It is not unheard of for someone else's charges to be applied to your account, or for accidental double billing. Stand your ground and politely demand that the purser show you the signed receipts for all charges posted to your account.

On most ships, the one place where the onboard charge card is not valid is at the casino. Here they expect visitors to use (and lose) cash or traveler's checks. You can, though, arrange for a separate line of credit with the casino manager. Some shipboard casinos also have credit card cash-advance ATMs, a convenience I find fiscally appalling.

CHAPTER SEVEN

SAFETY AT SEA

BEFORE THE TERRORIST ATTACKS in 2001, the most common fear among cruisegoers was an errant iceberg: Precious few travelers could resist making nervous jokes about the famous marine disaster when they put on their life vests for lifeboat drills. And some nervous cruisers kept a lookout for icebergs in waters, like the Caribbean, almost warm enough to make tea.

Today the travel industry has been forced to be on the lookout for threats from terrorists as well. A cruise ship on the open sea is a rather remote target, although experts do express concern about threats from within, either from passengers or from crew members with ill intent. More worrisome is the huge target presented by a cruise ship in a harbor or tied up at a dock.

In our changed world, cruise lines have stepped up their inspection of checked and hand-carried luggage. You can also expect to have your passport or other identification closely examined at embarkation. The cruise lines promise more close screening of the crew as well.

In ports, the U.S. Coast Guard and foreign equivalents are keeping a close eye on ships in the harbor. It's definitely in the government's interest to do so; a cruise ship with 2,000 guests brings with it hundreds of thousands or even millions of dollars in spending.

Cruise lines also realize that an incident on one of their ships could deeply injure the industry. The cruise lines' immediate reaction to the attacks was to reposition most of their fleets from Europe and Asia, sailing from American ports and nearby ports in the Caribbean and Canada for the winter of 2002. In 2003 most lines offered reduced service in distant waters, moving more ships to the Caribbean, the Northeast, and the Gulf of Mexico.

No one I know is able to predict world events very well. We may have peace, or we may have to endure a long period during which whole sections of the world—the Middle East, Asia, and parts of the Mediterranean among them—present real or perceived threats to cruisegoers. I intend to keep traveling, but with a new attention to security in the ports I choose to visit.

In the aftermath of the terrorist attacks, cruise lines went to "Level 3" security in cooperation with the U.S. Coast Guard. Here's part of what that means:

- Advanced screening of passengers and crew based on passport and visa information before departure; commercial vessels must give ninety-six hours advance notice before entering a U.S. port.
- Screening of passenger baggage and carry-ons as well as supplies and cargo loaded on ships at various ports. Cruise lines are expected to check in guests with photo ID or ship's identification. Some lines have added metal detectors at entry points.
- Cruise lines have beefed up their onboard security staff with former military personnel or police officers; Princess Cruises has employed Gurkhas, former members of the specialized Nepalese brigade of the British Army.
- There is greatly tightened access to sensitive areas of the ship, including the bridge and engine room. Many cruise lines have ended tours of the bridge.
- In U.S. ports, the Coast Guard maintains a security zone around cruise ships in the harbor and escorts them into open water.

Safety at sea is not a joking matter. In a real disaster, passengers and crew can find themselves with nowhere to go but into the water, hundreds or even thousands of miles away from the security of dry land and shelter.

In the past few years, there were about a dozen significant accidents involving cruise ships: One liner sank off Malaysia, a classic eighty-three-year-old Tall Ship was blown from her moorage and lost at sea in a hurricane in the Caribbean, another lost power in the Gulf of Mexico as a tropical storm bore down on her. Three small vessels ran aground in Alaska, one Megaship on her maiden voyage washed up on the rocks in the Saint Lawrence River, and another large cruise ship had a middle-of-the-night collision with a freighter in the English Channel. That sounds scary, but consider this: In all of these accidents, not a single person was killed, and only a handful of injuries were sustained.

Today the biggest fear doesn't have to do with striking an iceberg in the North Atlantic. Radar, satellite navigation systems, and improved construction have pretty much solved that problem. Instead, the real threats to travelers are fire at sea, contagious diseases, or contaminated food.

In May 2003, the classic steamship *Norway* suffered a boiler explosion as the vessel was preparing to disembark passengers in Miami at the conclusion of a cruise. Seven crew members were killed and more than a dozen others injured; no passengers were hurt.

MODERN SAFETY: AFTER THE *TITANIC*

For the record: The "unsinkable" RMS *Titanic* struck a glancing blow against a large iceberg some 400 miles from Newfoundland in the cold North Atlantic on April 14, 1912, at 11:40 P.M. The ship sank two hours and forty minutes later.

Although the ship went down quickly, that would still seem to be more than enough time to evacuate the 2,200 passengers and crew. However, the designers of the *Titanic* trusted too much in the promises of technology; the supposedly unsinkable ship did not have enough lifeboats to carry all aboard, and the lifeboats were not designed well enough to overcome the severe list of the sinking ship. Only about 700 people survived.

SOLAS: THE LEGACY OF THE TITANIC

From the *Titanic* disaster came one positive development: the convening in 1914 of the first international convention for the Safety of Life at Sea, which became known by its comforting acronym, SOLAS. This agreement among shipping nations has been updated and expanded numerous times since.

Today most of the world's nearly 140 seagoing nations are parties to the agreement. The countries that subscribe promise to apply the regulations of SOLAS to any ships that fly their flag. (Panama, the Bahamas, and Liberia, common "flags of convenience" for cruise lines, are signatories.)

In North American waters, the cruise industry cooperates with the U.S. Coast Guard, which inspects all foreign-flagged vessels operating from American ports and issues certification that is required before U.S. passengers can embark. Coast Guard certification also includes quarterly lifeboat and firefighting inspections.

The original SOLAS convention set rules that ships have enough lifeboat seats for every person aboard and mandated a lifeboat drill on each voyage. Ships were required to staff their radio rooms at all times.

The SOLAS regulations have been improved over the years. Modern ships now must have partially or totally enclosed lifeboats as well as other equipment, such as self-righting rafts.

In recent years, much attention has been shifted to fire safety at sea. Nearly all older vessels are now under orders to be refitted to add fire sprinklers and automatic controls of fire doors.

SAVE OUR SHIP!

With the advent of satellite navigation, improved radar and radio systems, and computers, the chances of collisions between ships or accidents involving obstacles in the water have become more and more remote. This is especially true for modern cruise ships. The owners of your basic $300 million Megaship that has a few thousand vacationers aboard have what lawyers would call a huge liability exposure; most cruise lines are extremely conservative in their operations. That doesn't mean, though, that accidents don't happen.

Royal Caribbean's *Monarch of the Seas* struck a rock off the coast of Saint Martin just after midnight on December 15, 1998; three of her eighteen watertight compartments began taking on water. The captain was able to steer the ship back to port, where it was intentionally beached on a bed of sand. Meanwhile, all 2,557 passengers were called from their cabins and sent to their muster stations. By 4:15 A.M., all had been evacuated from the ship in tender boats, without injury.

In May 1999, the 30,000-ton *Sun Vista* suffered a fire in its engine room; all 1,104 passengers and crew were forced to take to lifeboats off the coast of Malaysia in the middle of the night, where they watched the ship go down.

In September of the same year, a fire on board Carnival's *Tropicale* disabled its engines, leaving it to drift in the Gulf of Mexico as Tropical Storm Harvey approached. The ship, with 1,700 passengers and crew aboard, drifted for nearly a day in rough seas before the crew was able to restart one of the engines and move slowly out of the way of the storm, eventually heading back to port in Tampa. Passengers complained of lack of air-conditioning, faulty toilets, and other issues of comfort, but there were no injuries.

In summer 1999, three small ships had problems in Alaska's Inside Passage. The *Spirit of '98* struck a shoal in Tracy Arm, a narrow fjord that leads to a pair of glaciers, about 40 miles southeast of Juneau. All ninety-three passengers were transferred by raft to another ship. Earlier, the *Wilderness Adventurer* ran aground in Glacier Bay National Park, and a sister ship, the *Wilderness Explorer,* ran aground in an inlet 70 miles west of Juneau.

In August and September 1999, Norwegian Cruise Line suffered a pair of costly mishaps. First, the *Norwegian Dream* inexplicably collided with a large freighter in the English Channel; passengers were able to stay onboard as the ship continued to port in England, but the ship was disabled for more than a month for repairs. And then the line's brand-new *Norwegian Sky,* on its first official cruise after arriving from the shipyard in Europe, ran aground in the upper Saint Lawrence River at the mouth of the Saguenay River in Quebec. Ferries, whale-watching vessels, and private boats were mobilized to help evacuate passengers, but the ship eventually floated free and was brought into Quebec City for repairs to its hull, rudder, and one of its propellers. NCL was forced to cancel the next six weeks of sailings for the much anticipated ship.

HURRICANES AND BAD WEATHER

Cruises are rarely canceled because of storms, but the weather can result in a choppy ride, a rerouting that may include cancellation of a port visit, or substitution of a destination out of the way of the storm. In some extreme cases the ship may be unable to return to its planned port of disembarkation, and passengers may have to travel by bus or other conveyance to their intended destination.

All that said, it would take one heck of a storm to threaten a large cruise ship. But cruise companies don't want to risk their customers' falling or have a ship full of vacationers too green to come out of their cabins. Modern weather equipment, including satellite receivers aboard ship, permit captains to outrun a hurricane or steer around massive storms.

In late October 1998, disaster struck the venerable *Fantome,* flagship of the Windjammer fleet, a 282-foot-long, four-masted schooner built in 1927.

As Hurricane Mitch approached Central America, the *Fantome* was ordered to stop at Belize City to drop off its passengers so that they could be flown back to Miami. The ship then headed out to sea with its crew of thirty-one to avoid the storm, but the hurricane kept changing its path and eventually overtook the

Fire!

In 1996, five crew members of the *Universe Explorer* were killed in a laundry room fire as the ship sailed near Admiralty Island, west of Juneau, Alaska. Seventy-three passengers were hospitalized, mostly for smoke inhalation.

The ship, built in 1958, had passed its quarterly Coast Guard fire inspection the week before, but it was operating under an exemption from fire regulations that required refitting to install a fire sprinkler system. The sprinklers and other safety equipment have subsequently been installed.

As this book went to press, some dozen older ships had been given until the year 2005 to fully comply with fire safety regulations.

In the summer of 1998, the decades-younger *Ecstasy* of Carnival Cruise Lines caught fire just off the port of Miami. That blaze, blamed by the cruise company on sparks from welding that was going on even while the ship was at sea, caused significant damage to some of the work areas on the ship. But there were no fatalities; some passengers were treated for smoke inhalation. The ship returned to port, and the cruise was canceled.

Disney Cruise Line's modern *Disney Magic* suffered a minor fire in its funnel in March 2002; guests were roused from bed in the middle of the night, but the fire was extinguished by the crew with little damage, and the cruise continued.

ship. The *Fantome*'s last radio message said it was experiencing 100-knot winds and the ship was rolling 40 degrees. After more than a week, the search for the ship and its crew was abandoned.

In late November 1999, the cruise world lost another classic when the eighty-three-year-old *Sir Francis Drake* apparently broke free of her mooring in a hurricane and was swept out to sea and lost. Hurricane Lenny, one of the most severe storms of the twentieth century, parked off the Caribbean island of Saint Martin for several days.

The 165-foot-long ship had been built in Germany in 1917 and in recent years had sailed throughout the British Virgin Islands. She was in port at Marigot for repairs on her auxiliary engine. As the storm approached, all passengers and crew were disembarked to shore. The ship was secured with fifteen lines and both anchors at a huge commercial-ship mooring buoy in Marigot Harbor. When visibility returned after three days, the *Drake* and another Tall Ship were gone. An intensive search with private aircraft and ships, aided by U.S. Coast Guard satellite data, was unsuccessful. No trace was found of either vessel, except for a floating life raft, later identified as being from the *Sir Francis Drake*.

(See the cruise diaries in Chapter 11 for stories of cruises that were forced to make changes because of nearby hurricanes.)

DOCTORS ONBOARD

Cruise ships carrying more than fifty passengers will have a doctor onboard; some smaller luxury ships, especially those that venture to remote corners of the world, also carry a doctor. Most ships also have an infirmary or hospital and nursing staff. Few on-ship facilities are suitable for surgery, though.

That said, there is no guarantee that a ship's doctor will be well qualified or that the ship's hospital is well equipped for such critical emergencies as heart attacks. The goals of most medical facilities are to treat any minor illnesses or injuries and stabilize seriously injured patients until they can be transferred to a full-service hospital. If you have any particular medical concerns, be sure to discuss your travel plans with your own physician and with the cruise line.

Medical services aboard most ships are not free; passengers must pay consultation fees (typically about $50) plus charges for medication and tests. Most private health plans and Medicare do not cover the costs of medical care at sea and in foreign ports; consult your insurance agent or corporate benefits department. You might want to consider purchasing supplemental health and emergency evacuation insurance; this coverage may be included as part of a cancellation policy offered by many cruise lines or available separately from the cruise line or through your own insurance agent.

In recent years, some cruise lines have upgraded their medical facilities as ships have grown into small floating cities. As an example, most modern ships have an infirmary equipped with much of the equipment used in hospital emergency rooms, including an X-ray machine, defibrillator, electrocardiogram machine, and an intensive care unit.

Princess is among the major lines offering a telemedicine program that links the ship's medical staff with the emergency department physicians and specialists at a major American hospital onshore. This "virtual ER" allows X rays, electrocardiograms, and other monitoring signals to be transmitted from the ship to the hospital by satellite.

Just for the record: Most cruise ships have a small refrigerated morgue below decks. I've inspected a few . . . from the outside.

TRAVELERS WITH MEDICAL CONDITIONS

Most cruise lines will not book passage to a woman in the third trimester of pregnancy. Beyond that, most companies require that passengers notify them at the time of booking of any physical or mental illness or disability for which special services or the use of a wheelchair may be necessary.

Cruise lines reserve the right to refuse passage or terminate a vacation if the ship's doctor determines travel may pose a risk to the passenger or others.

■ A PRECRUISE MEDICAL CHECKLIST

There are few of us who don't have a health or diet concern of some sort. Consider the fact that soon after you embark on a cruise you will find yourself hundreds or even thousands of miles away from the nearest full-service pharmacy and potentially in the hands of a doctor and clinic that have no record of your medical history.

Here are some ways to protect yourself; these suggestions are adapted from Holland America's excellent precruise brochure.

■ Gather a supply of all prescription drugs and medications sufficient to cover your trip from home to the port of embarkation, the entire cruise, your return home, plus a few extra days in case of delay. Most major cruise ships have a supply of common medications onboard, but they might not have your precise prescription.

■ Place all medications in a carry-on bag that is not checked on your airplane flight and not given to the stevedores at the cruise port. In other words, carry your medications with you from home to your stateroom.

■ Carry a written list of all medications with the brand names and generic equivalents and the dosage you take. Put the list in a separate place from the carry-on bag with the medications.

■ Bring with you the names and phone numbers of your doctors at home.

■ If you have a medical condition, consult with your doctor about your cruise plans, including flights from home to the port of embarkation. If you have a significant medical condition, bring a copy of your medical records. If you have a heart condition, bring a copy of your most recent EKG.

■ Make sure you or your travel agent conveys all special needs to the cruise company before you travel. Inform the company about the need for a wheelchair, oxygen, or other equipment.

■ Consider the purchase of travel insurance to cover cancellations due to medical conditions. If you have a medical condition that is of concern, look for a policy (more expensive, but more valuable) that does not exclude preexisting conditions from coverage.

■ Consider purchase of supplemental insurance to cover medical expenses at shipboard infirmaries or in foreign ports. This sort of coverage may be included with trip cancellation policies. Again, pay attention to exclusions of preexisting conditions.

■ If you require a special meal, such as low-sodium, low-cholesterol, low-fat, or other arrangements, be sure to inform the cruise line several weeks in advance of your trip.

■ TRAVELERS WHO HAVE DISABILITIES

Although most cruise lines can be counted on to be accommodating to persons with disabilities, the fact of the matter is that not all ships are appropriate for persons in wheelchairs or those who have significant medical problems.

To begin with, many older ships were designed before consideration was given to persons with special needs. It's possible that only a handful of rooms and few, if any, public rest rooms are accessible to guests in wheelchairs. Antique ships, such as Tall Ships and windjammers, do not have elevators and so present difficulties for persons with disabilities.

If you do book passage on a ship that claims wheelchair accessibility, be aware that not all areas of the vessel may be served by elevators. You may also find that some ports of call are not equipped to handle all visitors. In some ports the cruise ship might not tie up at a dock, instead transferring guests to shore by tender boats, which might not be easily navigated by all guests. This is an area where you may be able to ask your travel agent to do some detailed research for you.

SEASICKNESS

Could there be anything worse than spending thousands of dollars, traveling thousands of miles to a port, setting sail on a fabulous cruise ship, and then finding yourself so seasick you cannot leave your bed?

That scary thought keeps many travelers away from cruises and causes more than a bit of concern among those who do go down to the sea in ships.

The good news is that modern ships are pretty stable, and there are a number of things you can do, from common sense to common medication, that can help you ignore the rolling and pitching of a cruise ship. (Rolling is the side-to-side motion caused by seas that move across the beam of the ship; pitching is the up-and-down movement of the ship as the bow rides waves coming at the ship or a following sea that attacks from the stern.)

Modern ships use one or more forms of stabilizers to reduce roll. These devices are like underwater wings that work against the motion of the ship in rough water. The size and length of larger ships goes a long way toward reducing pitch, and sailing ships are relatively less likely to roll because they are held to an angle of heel by the pressure of the wind on the sails.

Here are some things you can do to reduce your chances of seasickness:

■ Give some thought to the waters your ship will travel. The Caribbean and the Inside Passage of Alaska are usually calmer than the waters of the Pacific and the North Atlantic. The Gulf of Mexico can vary weekly, from dead calm to moderately or severely rough. The Mediterranean is usually calm in summer.

■ Choose the time of year you cruise. June through late fall is hurricane season along the East Coast and sometimes the Gulf of Mexico. That doesn't mean the seas are always stormy at that time of the year, but, on average, one or two hurricanes a year disrupt the cruise calendar.

■ Pay attention to the cruise itinerary. Some ships spend one or more days out to sea without making a port call. Most cruisegoers relish the calming effects of nothing but ocean, but if you do suffer from occasional seasickness, you might want to seek out an itinerary that allows you to set foot on land every eight or twelve hours.

- Select a more stable cabin. Most cruisegoers find that a cabin amidships (in the middle of the ship) and on a lower deck will roll and pitch less than a cabin that is up high and at the stern or bow.
- Reduce your alcohol intake. Alcohol can make you dizzy and disoriented and upset your stomach. Need I say more?
- Consider taking a seasickness medication such as Dramamine or Bonine before the ship gets under way. In my experience, both work quite well, although they may make you drowsy. (Be sure to consult with your physician if you have any other medical conditions that might complicate use of such medication.) Many cruise ships have stocks of seasickness pills available for guests; check with the purser's office or the medical office. Some travelers find relief with the use of accupressure wristbands and other devices.

EPIDEMICS ONBOARD

Cruise ships are a near-perfect environment for the transmission and spread of disease. You have passengers gathering from all over the world, then mingling in enclosed dining rooms, theaters, and show rooms. Add to the equation the large central kitchens and the tons of food that must be stored onboard the ship and prepared for the almost continuous round of meals, snacks, and buffets. Finally, consider the fact that passengers are visiting remote ports where the sanitation may not be as advanced as onboard ship or at home.

In 2002 and early 2003, several hundred cruise vacationers suffered from a series of nasty viruses at sea. Television crews met cruise ships as they docked, interviewing passengers about their ordeal.

The primary culprit: the Norwalk virus or something just like it. As a cause of illness, the Norwalk virus—your basic stomach bug—is second only to the common cold. According to the Centers for Disease Control and Prevention (CDC) in Atlanta, each year more than twenty-three million persons in the United States are infected by that virus—and only a few thousand are on cruise ships. That compares with 1.4 million illnesses caused by salmonella, 79,000 cases from *E. coli* contamination, and 2,500 instances of listeriosis.

The problems reported in 2002 and 2003 affected about 1,200 cruise guests and crew, including a few hundred each on Carnival's *Fascination,* Holland America Line's *Amsterdam* and *Ryndam,* Disney Cruise Line's *Disney Magic,* Princess's *Ocean Princess,* and several other ships. The CDC typically requires a cruise line to immediately file a report when more than 3 percent of passengers are ill.

In early 2003 every major cruise line stepped up its surveillance for passengers who might be carrying SARS (Severe Acute Repiratory Syndrome). Guests were asked if they had experienced any symptoms of the disease or had traveled to areas in Asia where the disease was reported.

The key to stopping epidemics onboard a cruise ship is to step up the already-continual cleaning process and to break the cycle of transmission. Cruise ships pay special attention to sanitizing handrails and doorknobs touched by guests and to request regular handwashing by all onboard (it's required for employees after rest room use). If an epidemic does occur, the ultimate solution is to take a ship out of service for a week or two to prevent passing the disease to and from the crew and passengers.

During the removal from service of the *Amsterdam,* virtually everything on the ship was cleaned—from TV remotes to ice buckets and Gideon bibles—and pillows and bedding were replaced.

Most cruise ships visiting American ports do a good job of maintaining proper hygiene under the watchful eye of the CDC. Every vessel that has thirteen or more passengers is subject to inspections at least twice a year by the CDC. The resulting scores are published every two weeks in the *Summary of Sanitation Inspections of International Cruise Ships,* known in the industry as the Green Sheet.

A ship must receive a score of 86 percent or higher to be acceptable; ships that fail are subject to reinspections and could eventually be prevented from sailing from a U.S. port if problems are not fixed. The CDC also distributes the list of inspections to travel agents and the press.

You can view a list of recent cruise ships inspections on the Internet at www2. cdc.gov/nceh/vsp/vspmain.asp. You can also contact the CDC by phone at (888) 232–6789 and request a copy of the most recent Green Sheet, although I was warned that the agency is understaffed and may not be able to respond quickly over the phone.

And you should use good judgment. Don't eat foods onboard you wouldn't have at home. Make sure hamburgers and seafood are fully cooked, for example. And take special care with anything you eat or drink in foreign ports.

In many parts of the world, it's a good idea to avoid drinking the local water and any products prepared with unsterilized water. That means limiting yourself to commercially bottled water or bottles filled with the water prepared on your cruise ship, sodas, and beer and avoiding unpeeled and uncooked fruits and vegetables. (This is not to say that water in other countries is necessarily "bad," but it may contain organisms that your body is not prepared to deal with without a few weeks of acclimation.)

CRIME ABOARD SHIP

In recent years, several newspapers and television shows have made a big deal about a supposed "crime wave" aboard cruise ships. Here are the facts: Cruise ships are a relatively safe environment, less dangerous than most small towns. But like a small town, they are not without an occasional problem.

Onboard, there are two sources of threat to your possessions and personal safety: the crew and the passengers. A third danger lies in some ports of call.

The fact is that cruise ships draw their crews from all over the world, often from areas of relative poverty. The crew is often out to sea for six months or longer, without return visits to their homes. Add to all this the fact that some travelers, including single women, may be overly relaxed on their sea vacations.

Most cruise lines are very specific in their instructions to crew members regarding prohibitions on fraternization with passengers outside their official duties in the dining room, bar, or elsewhere. But that does not mean you should totally abandon any concern for safety: Lock your door when you are in your cabin, keep valuables in the safe (or at home), and take the same sort of care with strangers you meet on ship that you would with someone you met in a bar in your town.

Finally, there is this: When you are in international waters in a vessel that (like nearly all cruise ships) flies a foreign flag, you are outside the reach of U.S. laws and enforcement agencies. Theoretically, the laws of the nation of registry apply while on the seas. How much do you know about the legal code of Liberia, Panama, or the Bahamas? For most intents and purposes, a cruise ship is like an independent floating nation.

If a crime or incident does occur while you are at sea, be sure to document every detail for the ship's officers, as well as for yourself. Then do the same when the ship reaches its next port of call, and again with the U.S. Coast Guard if the ship touches an American port.

Most cruise lines do not permit visitors onboard ship without prearrangements through the purser or other officer. Hand-carried luggage is X-rayed, and passengers go through a metal detector prior to boarding.

The most modern of ships include a passenger cruise card ID with a magnetic strip. The card is used as an identity instrument to disembark or reboard the ship at port calls (allowing the purser to know if all of the guests have returned at the end of the visit), as a shipboard charge card, and as an electronic key to the stateroom.

SHORE EXCURSIONS

When you leave the ship, you are out of the cruise line's protective cocoon of security and safety. In a foreign country, you could find that American definitions of safety—shaped by lawyers, lawsuits, and legislation—do not apply.

Rental cars might not have seat belts, and they often are closer to "rent-a-wreck" condition than the near-new condition we expect at home. Buses can be overcrowded and rickety. (In some countries, including parts of Central America, you'll discover where all the old American school buses and city buses go after they have been "retired" from our streets and highways.)

Part of the charm of many attractions in strange places may also bring some serious safety hazards. I've climbed trails hacked into the sides of mountain canyons with nothing between me and the edge but the tread on my sneakers. I've crossed bridges in the jungle that Indiana Jones would have turned away from; I fell through the planking of a pontoon bridge on a lake in Honduras, coming within millimeters of snapping my leg on the support below. And my wife and I have strolled through areas of some ports where even the police demand escorts.

Does this mean you shouldn't leave the ship? Of course not, but you do need to be on guard for your own safety. Here are some suggestions:

■ A cruise ship's excursion desk should vouch for the quality of any bus or car provided for an excursion. If you're on your own, take a look at the tires and general condition of a taxi before you enter for a long trip. If you don't feel comfortable with the safety of the transport, reconsider your trip.

■ Carefully follow any safety instructions given by tour providers. Wear life preservers if asked. Don't undertake an activity you know to be beyond your physical abilities.

■ Never carry nonessential valuables. Leave your jewelry in the safe in your cabin, and bring only enough spending money for minor purchases. Credit cards are accepted almost everywhere and, in any case, are generally the best way to pay for items in a foreign currency.

■ If you are accosted, give over what little you have with you without a fight. Objects are not worth endangering your life for.

■ Carry the name and phone number of the ship's agent with you. If you are stranded or injured, the agent should be able to help you make contact with the ship.

■ In subtropical and tropical climates, bring with you a high-SPF sunscreen—and use it regularly. Drink plenty of liquids and wear a hat. Consult with your family doctor for advice on innoculations and preventive medications recommended for the destinations you will visit.

■ If you're in a country where you are concerned about the water or food, bring your own. You can purchase bottled water onboard ships, or fill your own bottle from the water in your cabin. It is generally considered safe to drink bottled beer or soda; avoid ice cubes and fruits and vegetables washed in local water.

CHAPTER EIGHT

DINING ON THE HIGH SEAS

SOMETIMES IT SEEMS as though the logic of many cruise vacationers is this: I paid $250 a night for this cruise, and by God, I'm going to eat $250 worth of food every day.

It doesn't help your waistline one bit when you realize that most cruise lines go out of their way to encourage you to eat. In fact, there's a bit of a war of the restaurants and buffets among most of the major cruise lines: Call it the Floating Battle of the Bulge.

The staff is going to be pushing food at you at most every turn, and in most cases the food ranges from good to excellent. When you sit down to dinner, your waiter is going to encourage you to sample anything and everything on the menu: Look twice at the dessert offerings, and he is likely to bring you both the cheesecake *and* the double dark chocolate dream cake.

I am particularly partial to salad, and I enjoy freshly grated pepper on most everything; my wife's secret indulgences are a piece of blue cheese as an inter-mezzo before the main course and a cup of cappuccino at the end of the meal. And my daughter fell in love with kalamata olives on a Greek cruise ship. We can judge the quality of the service we receive onboard a ship by how long it takes before our waiter and assistant learn to automatically stand by with extra salads, pepper, cheese, a bowl of olives, and coffee at the appropriate times in the meal.

EAT UNTIL YOU DROP

There's a lot of eating onboard a cruise ship. In fact, on some ships you could just about go from meal to snack to meal, from dawn until after midnight. And then you could probably order room service to get you past the munchies at 3:00 A.M.

Here's a typical meal lineup, in this case from the SS *Norway*, the classic, older flagship of the NCL fleet:

6:00–8:30 A.M.	Eye-opener, Great Outdoor Restaurant
7:30–10:00 A.M.	Breakfast service, Windward and Leeward dining rooms
8:30–11:00 A.M.	Late breakfast, Great Outdoor Restaurant
Noon	Lunch (first seating), Windward and Leeward dining rooms
12:30–3:00 P.M.	Lunch buffet and barbecue, Great Outdoor Restaurant
1:30 P.M.	Lunch (second seating), Windward and Leeward dining rooms
4:00–6:00 P.M.	Coffee and snacks, Great Outdoor Restaurant
6:00 P.M.	Dinner (main seating), Windward and Leeward dining rooms
6:00–11:00 P.M.	Le Bistro Supper Club (by reservation), Pool Deck aft
8:30 P.M.	Dinner (late seating), Windward and Leeward dining rooms
Midnight–1:00 A.M.	Mini midnight buffet, Casino
Midnight–1:00 A.M.	Chocoholic midnight buffet, Windward and Leeward dining rooms

But wait: If you're in one of the suites, your cabin attendant will deliver a small tray of hors d'oeuvres in late afternoon to stave off sudden pangs of hunger. And, oh yes, there is also twenty-four-hour room service if you have a sudden need for a turkey sandwich between dining room seatings.

To me, that late-night buffet, sometimes known as the midnight buffet, is the ultimate in wretched excess—and an occasional wicked delight. Typical offer-

The Grand Restaurant on Celebrity's *Century. Photo courtesy of Celebrity Cruises*

ings range from crab legs to steamship round of beef to gourmet pizza. On all Norwegian Cruise Line ships, one night of each cruise is given over to the aptly named Chocoholic Buffet, an absolutely sybaritic exercise in late-night gluttony. Oh, yes, we gave in to our baser instincts too.

Royal Olympia Cruises' *Olympia Voyager* offers a different mix, including a British tradition of "elevenses," a light midmorning breakfast.

6:00–7:00 A.M.	Early Risers, Horizon Garden Lounge
6:00–9:30 A.M.	Breakfast buffet, Horizon Garden Lounge
6:30–9:00 A.M.	Breakfast buffet and a la carte menu, open seating, Selene Dining Room
10:00–11:00 A.M.	Elevenses, Horizon Garden Lounge
11:00 A.M.–2:00 P.M.	Pizza, Avra Cafe Pool Bar
Noon–2:00 P.M.	Light lunch barbecue, Avra Cafe Pool Bar
Noon–2:00 P.M.	Lunch buffet, Horizon Garden Lounge
12:30–2:00 P.M.	Lunch, open seating, Selene Dining Room
4:00–4:45 P.M.	Afternoon tea and cookies, Alexander the Great Lounge
5:15–6:00 P.M.	Wine tasting, Selene Dining Room
5:30–6:30 P.M.	Happy hour and hors d'oeuvres, Anemos Sky Bar
6:00–7:00 P.M.	Ouzo party with Greek appetizers, Avra Cafe Pool Bar
6:30 P.M.	Dinner, first seating, Selene Dining Room
8:30 P.M.	Dinner, late seating, Selene Dining Room
11:30 P.M.–12:15 A.M.	Late-night snacks, Horizon Garden Lounge

Room service is available twenty-four hours a day, in case you find yourself in dire need of food between scheduled feedings.

DINNER SEATINGS

For some travelers, the most exciting news in recent years is the arrival of "freestyle" or open seating at restaurants. Today you can choose when, where, and with whom you dine on many ships. Cruise lines have added alternative restaurants and more staffs to accommodate freedom of choice.

Still, on most ships, the dining rooms have two seatings: a main or first seating and a second or late seating. On many ships, breakfast is open to all from about 7:00 to 9:00 A.M.; lunch may have a first seating at noon and a second seating at 1:30 P.M., or it may be open seating. Dinner is usually served at 6:00 or 6:30 P.M. and again at about 8:00 or 8:15 P.M.

For most Americans, an 8:00 P.M. dining time is a bit later than we're used to. You'll waddle out of the dining room close to ten o'clock, perhaps to catch a show, and then be well situated for the midnight buffet. Still, it can be gotten used to.

If you are flying from the East to the West Coast, however, factor in the time change. When we flew from Massachusetts to Honolulu to pick up a cruise there,

Room Service

Most cruise ships offer room service food without extra charge. On some lines, you can order from that day's restaurant menu; other ships offer a more limited menu for meals taken in the cabin.

You can also pay for drinks and wine from the bar and order canapés—a bucket of shrimp, for example—if you have an appetite for something special.

we lost six hours. Our internal clocks were set at 2:00 A.M. for the 8:00 P.M. seating for the first few days of the cruise; we quickly changed to the 6:00 P.M. main seating, which was ever so slightly better. The same would apply for Europeans flying to Florida or the Caribbean to pick up a cruise. Coming from the West Coast to Florida, the late seating will be more comfortable, at least for the start of the trip.

Know thyself. If you're the sort of person who expects to enjoy every possible moment in port, taking shore excursions or going native, choose the late seating for dinner. You don't want to cut short your time ashore to rush back for a 6:00 P.M. assignment. On the other hand, if you value your time on the ship above all else, you'll probably want to eat early and then enjoy the shows and other activities aboard. This is another reason many travelers prefer cruises without assigned times for meals. You can adjust your onboard schedule to your plans for each day at sea or in port.

If you have a strong preference for a particular seating, make your wishes known early and often; enlist your travel agent if necessary. In some cases, you may find that your preference is not available; some cruisers don't accept no for an answer and take up the issue with the maître d' on arrival. Remember: Most cruise crew members depend on tips for much of their income, and a subtle reminder of this may grease the way to the dining time or table you want.

On many ships, you can expect to find yourself assigned to a table with others. A typical dining room has tables for four, six, eight, and occasionally even more. You should also be able to find a two-seat hideaway, although the "deuces" are often tucked away in corners. My wife and I are quiet and private by nature, and we always push for a table for two; one way or another, we always get one.

You can expect that the occupants of your cabin will be seated together; you may have to work to bring together friends or family members in other cabins.

Can you change your table assignment once you are onboard? Perhaps. A lot depends on how full the vessel is and the reasonableness of your request. If you cannot stand your tablemates, take the subject up quietly and in private with the maître d' or the cruise director.

For many cruisers, the freestyle or open dining is a welcome change. Depending on the size of the ship and the number of dining rooms, you might be free to show up whenever and wherever you want, or you may need to make a reservation for a table. You could still end up at a large table with whoever arrives at the same time you do, or the cruise line may be flexible enough—like a shoreside restaurant—to rearrange tables to suit the sizes of the parties. Cruisers who look forward to making friends onboard can still do so, gathering their own tables.

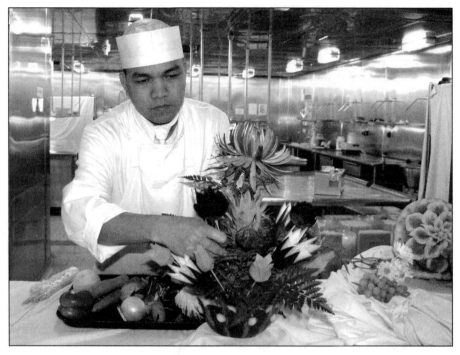

A cook carves a decorative vegetable display in the galley of Holland America's *Veendam*.
Photo by Corey Sandler

The downside, for some, of freestyle dining is that you won't have the same servers and tableside staff throughout the cruise. (For that reason, most cruise lines that have gone away from assigned seating have also instituted an automatic gratuity program that pools tips and distributes them among the dining room staff.)

CRUISE CUISINE

Start with this: Imagine the challenge of every day preparing 2,000 sit-down breakfasts, 2,000 lunches, and 2,000 dinners, plus buffets for breakfast, brunch, lunch, afternoon, and midnight. Then prepare to carry nearly all your food supplies with you, reprovisioning once every seven to ten days.

And, oh yes: Your cramped kitchen is in a pitching, rolling ship. You cannot use an open flame because of safety concerns, and your staff is a mini United Nations.

Then there are the passengers, many of whom look at their all-inclusive cruise fare as a license to make demands of waiters and the chef—demands they would never attempt at home or at a restaurant where they were paying a la carte.

All that said, it is nevertheless true that most cruise cuisine is pretty good.

In general, the budget end of the cruise market delivers decent institutional-quality food. The top-of-the-line ships offer quality approaching that of a first-class restaurant on land. The ultraluxury ships add caviar, champagne, and an extra level of personal attention.

The most luxurious ships will sometimes offer to prepare any special request the galley can possibly accommodate. Don't assume they'll be able to rustle up some fresh venison in the middle of a transatlantic crossing, but if you give the chef enough advance notice, he may be able to find some at an upcoming port of call.

Most cruise lines offer vegetarian and low-calorie alternatives on every menu. If you require a special diet beyond that, such as kosher, low-sodium, or gluten-free, be sure to advise the cruise line several weeks before sailing. In some cases, the special meals will be prepared and frozen off the ship and then warmed as needed.

A SENSIBLE DINING STRATEGY

Face it: You're going to go off your diet on a cruise vacation; that's one of the appeals of cruising. But you don't have to overdo it. Here are a few tips:

■ **Choose your meals.** You don't really need to visit every food offering every day. Pick the ones that most appeal to you.

■ **Eat in moderation.** Take smaller portions or avoid cleaning every morsel off your plate. You might be able to get your waiter to deliver half portions.

■ **Consider the "spa" dishes**—low-calorie or heart-healthy offerings found on most menus. Eat an extra portion of salad, with a fat-free dressing, instead of a cream-based chowder.

■ **Increase your level of exercise,** especially on days at sea when you won't be walking onshore. Use the health spa or take a half dozen laps around the promenade deck. It's romantic, fun, and helps work off the calories.

■ **Don't be afraid to skip a meal.** Missing an occasional breakfast or lunch won't kill you.

CHAPTER NINE

GET ME TO THE PORT ON TIME

FOR MOST OF US, before we get onboard our cruise ship, we have to travel to the port, which could involve a lengthy flight or a long drive. Among your first decisions as a savvy consumer is whether to book your own transportation from home to the port or to take advantage of travel packages offered by the cruise companies.

In some cases, the cruise line may be able to offer you a discounted airline ticket because of arrangements with major carriers. You might, though, find you can do better by yourself. In any case, making your own arrangements offers you the greatest flexibility with your schedule, including the ability to stay over en route or before or after your cruise.

Following the terrorist attacks of 2001, many cruise lines chose to reposition many of their ships to sail from U.S. ports and to emphasize that travelers could drive to a port from much of the country.

THE ADVANTAGES OF BOOKING A PACKAGE

One advantage of booking your travel package through the cruise company is that the line may take responsibility for you from your home airport to the ship. Many cruise lines dispatch employees to arrival airports to help with transfers to the ship. If your flight is delayed, canceled, or diverted, they'll know about the situation and may help you get to the ship.

Be sure you understand the commitment of the cruise line to tracking its incoming passengers. In some instances, the cruise line might hold the departure of the ship by a few hours to accommodate late arrivals. In other situations, the line will make arrangements to fly passengers to the next port call.

During a "sickout" by one airline's pilots in 1999, several major cruise lines chartered planes and made other special arrangements to get their guests to the waiting ships.

The cruise line should also take responsibility for matching you up with misdirected luggage. On an Alaskan cruise I took, a group of passengers made it to the ship while their baggage took a vacation somewhere else. The cruise line delivered the guests to their cabins, offered a basic kit of personal supplies, and arranged to have their bags catch up with them two days later at the first port call.

A few weeks later, I was cruising in the South Pacific and met a couple whose clothing was a week behind them. They had to do without their luggage for six days out of a ten-day voyage because the ship was heading out to sea for a stop at a remote island that had no airport. The cruise line chose to offer them a few sets of T-shirts and shorts from the gift shop, outfits that did not work very well on formal nights in the dining room.

Note that I say the cruise line "may" be able to help. Be sure to check with the company and discuss their policies before you book tickets. Then make certain everything you are told verbally is also presented in writing in the cruise line's brochures, contracts, or other confirmations you receive.

WHY YOU MIGHT MAKE YOUR OWN ARRANGEMENTS

If, on the other hand, you make your own arrangements to get to the port, you could end up waving at the stern of your cruise ship as it leaves the pier. The cost of overnight accommodations and transportation to the ship's next port of call will probably be your responsibility.

That said, making your own arrangements is usually less expensive than the flights and transfers offered by the cruise line. I'd suggest that you do the research yourself before you accept the cruise company's travel arrangements. For domestic departures you may well be able to obtain a lower price or make a better set of connections. If your ship is departing from an unusual location, the cruise company might be able to offer better prices, sometimes using a charter airline.

Here are a few tips to lessen the chances of missing your ship:
- Consider traveling to the port the night before your departure.
- Notify the cruise line of the flight arrangements you have made. The line might have other passengers on the same plane and may be making special arrangements for them.
- If you encounter problems with the airline, be sure to inform them you are flying to catch a cruise departure. They may be able to rebook you on another flight or another airline if necessary.

If you do end up missing the ship, immediately call the cruise line's port representative. Most companies have an office at ports of embarkation; if not, call the phone number listed in your cruise confirmation papers.

If you arrive at the port but your bags are off on a trip of their own, you should be able to engage the assistance of the cruise line in notifying the airline of your ship's schedule and providing the names and phone numbers of the ship's agents in upcoming ports. Be sure to keep copies of the missing baggage form you file with the airline, and record the names of any airline personnel you speak with and the details of conversations you have with them.

If you've planned ahead properly, you should have your passports, cruise tickets, medications, and a change of clothing in your carry-on bag.

ARRIVING EARLY

There is one other situation in which you might have to make your own arrangements: if you choose to fly to the port the day before your cruise (my preference) or stay afterward in the final port.

Why do I prefer to fly to the port a day ahead of departure? First of all, I don't want the stress of worrying about missing a departure because of a delay while flying to the port. This is especially true in the wintertime, when bad weather can wreak havoc on airports and schedules everywhere in the country.

Second, I prefer to spend a day of rest in a port city before getting onboard the ship. Many cruise travelers pass too quickly through some of the most interesting cities in the world, rushing from the airport directly to the ship and missing exciting places such as Vancouver, Miami, Boston, New Orleans, and other points of departure.

This also allows me a day or so to become acclimated to time zone changes in distant ports before I get on the ship. On the day of the cruise, I take a quick taxi to the port instead of suffering through a day of high-stress airline travel. In that way, while the passengers who have been traveling all day to get to the port head for bed, I'm immediately ready to enjoy the cruise.

GETTING FROM THE AIRPORT TO THE SHIP

Your cruise company is likely to offer a service to transport guests from the airport to the ship. This could be included in your cruise if you have booked airfare through the cruise line, or you might be able to purchase the transfer service separately.

I can see the advantages of having a prearranged service with a direct connection to the cruise company, but I also know that in general, transfer service is overpriced and can be less convenient than arrangements you make on your own.

Do a little research and compare the cruise line's transportation with the cost and convenience of a taxi, a rental car, or a limousine service from the airport to the pier.

Just how overpriced are transfers? On one trip in the Hawaiian Islands, the cruise line charged $20 per person for a bus trip from the pier to the Honolulu airport, a distance of just a few miles. Guests had to wait while their bags were collected and loaded onto a huge bus and then wait again at the airport while the bus was unloaded and bags distributed. Meanwhile, my wife and I got off the ship a half hour later and grabbed a taxi. The fare was $17 for the two of us, including a tip, and we got to the airline counter ahead of the bus-borne horde.

The same applied in Vancouver on the return from a voyage north to Alaska. The cruise company's bus was not only overpriced, but it would have delivered us to the airport four hours before we needed to be there. Instead, we arranged for a rental car that was delivered right to the dock; we spent the morning at a museum, had lunch in Chinatown, and drove to the airport on our own schedule.

Among ports that are very close to major airports are Boston and Fort Lauderdale. North American ports that are distant from airports include Houston (about seventy-five minutes) and Galveston (about ninety minutes). Port Canaveral is about an hour from Orlando and just a bit farther from Daytona Beach. Long Beach is about a half hour from Los Angeles International Airport.

If you're concerned about making a tight connection, contact a taxi company or a limousine service before you embark, and arrange for a pickup at the dock when your ship returns.

AIRLINE TRAVEL

Why is there a section about airline travel in a book about cruising? Simply because the vast majority of cruise passengers begin their vacations by boarding an airplane and flying to a port in Florida, San Juan, Vancouver, New Orleans, or other major locations.

Let's start with a real-life scenario: It's May 2003, and I'm flying south from Providence to Fort Lauderdale to pick up a cruise from the bustling port there. My ticket, a special deep-discount Web fare, cost a mere $207 round-trip. The businessman across the aisle will suffer through the same plastic baggie of fried something-or-other, watch the same crummy movie, and arrive in Florida at the same millisecond I do. The only difference: He waited until the last minute and ended up paying $589 for his ticket. And in first class, someone who (in my humble opinion) has more money than sense has paid an astounding $892 for a slightly wider, slightly plusher seat and a relatively better meal. (I'd rather spend just some of that money on a better place to sleep and a meal at a restaurant where half the meal doesn't end up in your lap.)

All of those prices are real, as I write these words. Now consider a few more positive examples.

Somewhere else on this same plane is a couple who were bumped off a previous flight because of overbooking. They are happily discussing where to use the two free round-trip tickets they received in compensation.

And up front in first class, where you arrive at your destination a millisecond earlier, a family of four is traveling on free tickets earned through Mom's frequent flier plan.

Me, I'm perfectly happy with that cut-rate ticket. I use some of the money I saved to buy a bag lunch to eat on the plane, and I'm daydreaming about where to use the frequent flier miles I'm earning on the airfare, hotel, and car rental.

■ ALICE IN AIRLINELAND

In today's strange world of air travel, there is a lot of room for the dollarwise and clever traveler to wiggle. You can pay an inflated full price, you can take advantage of the lowest fares, or you can play the ultimate game and parlay tickets into free travel.

There are three golden rules when it comes to saving hundreds of dollars on travel: Be flexible, be flexible, and be flexible. Here's how to translate that flexibility into extra dollars in your pocket:

■ Be flexible about when you choose to travel. Go during the off-season or low season when airfares, hotel rooms, cruises, and attractions are offered at substantial discounts. Try to avoid school vacations, Spring Break, and the prime summer travel months of July and August, unless you enjoy a lot of company.

■ Be flexible about the day of the week you travel. In many cases you can save hundreds of dollars by bumping your departure date one or two days in either direction. Ask your travel agent or airline ticket agent for current fare rules and restrictions. If this puts you into port a day or two ahead of the departure of the ship, use the time to become acclimated to a new time zone and to explore.

The lightest air travel generally occurs midweek, Saturday afternoon, and Sunday morning. The busiest times are Sunday evening, Monday morning, and Friday afternoon and evening.

You may find the lowest possible fare if your stay includes a Saturday overnight; this class of ticket is sold as an excursion fare. Airlines use this as a way to exclude business travelers from the cheapest fares, assuming that businesspeople will want to be home by Friday night. Many air carriers have given up on this sort of fare structure in recent years, but you may still run into situations where a weekend stay will significantly reduce the ticket price.

■ Be flexible about your hours of departure. There is generally lower demand, and therefore lower prices, for flights that leave in the middle of the day or very late at night. The highest rates are usually assigned to breakfast time (7:00–11:00 A.M.) and cocktail hour (4:00–7:00 P.M.) departures.

■ Be flexible on the route you will take, and be willing to put up with a change of plane or a stopover. Once again, you are using the law of supply and demand to your advantage. For example, a nonstop flight from Boston to Tampa for a family of four may cost hundreds more than a flight from Boston that includes a change of planes in Atlanta (a Delta hub) before proceeding to Florida.

Consider flying on one of the newer, deep-discount airlines, but don't let economy cloud your judgment. Some carriers are simply better run than others. Read the newspapers, check with a trusted travel agent, and use common sense. As far as I'm concerned, the best thing about the cheapo airlines is the pressure they put on the established carriers to lower prices or even to match fares on certain flights. Look for the cheapest fare you can find and then call your favorite big airline and see if it will sell you a ticket at the same price; it just might work.

■ Don't overlook the possibility of flying out of a different airport. For example, metropolitan New Yorkers can find domestic flights from LaGuardia, Newark, White Plains, and a developing discount mecca at Islip. Suburbanites of Boston might want to consider flights from Providence as possibly cheaper alternatives to Logan Airport. Chicago has O'Hare and Midway. From Southern California there are major airports at Los Angeles, Orange County, Burbank, and San Diego.

■ Plan way ahead of time and purchase the most deeply discounted advance tickets, which usually are noncancelable. Most carriers limit the number of

Airline Speak

In airline terminology, a "direct" flight does not mean a "nonstop" flight. Nonstop means the plane goes from Point A to Point B without stopping anywhere else. A direct flight may go from Point A to Point B, but it might include a stopover at Point C or at more than one airport along the way. A connecting flight means you must get off the plane at an airport en route and change to another plane. And to add one more level of confusion, some airlines have "direct" flights that involve a change of plane along the way: The flight number stays the same, but passengers have to get off at an intermediate stop, dragging all their carry-on luggage to another gate and aircraft. Go figure.

discount tickets on any particular flight. Although there may be plenty of seats left on the day you want to travel, they might be offered at higher rates.

■ Understand the difference between nonrefundable and noncancelable. Most airlines interpret *nonrefundable* to mean that they can keep all your money if you cancel a reservation or fail to show up for a flight. You can, though, apply the value of the ticket (minus a fee of as much as $150) to the purchase of another ticket. A *noncancelable* fare means that you have bought a specific seat on a specific flight, and if your plans change or you are forced to cancel your trip, you lose the value of the tickets. (Think of missing a concert performance; you can't use your ticket another day.) Of course, if the airline cancels your flight or makes a schedule or routing change you find does not meet your needs, you are entitled to a refund of your fare.

■ If you're feeling adventurous, you can take a big chance and wait for the last possible moment, keeping in contact with charter tour operators and accepting a bargain price on a leftover seat and hotel reservation. You may also find that some airlines will reduce the prices on leftover seats within a few weeks of your departure date; don't be afraid to check with the airline regularly or ask your travel agent to do it for you. In fact, some travel agencies have automated computer programs that keep a constant electronic eye on available seats and fares.

■ Take advantage of special discount programs such as senior citizens' clubs, military discounts, or offerings from other organizations to which you belong. If you are in the broadly defined "senior" category, you might not even have to belong to a group such as AARP; simply ask the airline ticket agent if there is a discount available. You might have to prove your age or show a membership card when you pick up your ticket or boarding pass.

■ Consider doing business with discounters, known in the industry as consolidators or, less flatteringly, as bucket shops. These companies buy airlines' slow-to-sell tickets in volume and resell them to consumers at rock-bottom prices. Look for their ads in the classified listings of many Sunday newspaper travel sections. Be sure to study and understand the restrictions; if they fit your needs and wants, this is a good way to fly.

■ Shop on-line through one of the Internet travel sites or the Web sites of individual airlines. You can expect to receive the lowest possible airfares—usually a few percent below the best prices offered if you call the airline directly—but little assistance in choosing among the offerings. Be sure to pay close attention to details such as the number of connections required between origin and destination. Note too that tickets sold in this way may have severe restrictions on changes and cancellations.

I list some of the best Internet agencies and airline Web sites in Chapter 4.

■ Consider, very carefully, buying tickets from an on-line travel auction site such as www.priceline.com or www.hotwire.com. These sites promise to match your travel plans with available seats on major airlines at deep-discount prices, but you will not be able to choose departure or arrival times or a particular airline. The way to use these sites is to do your research beforehand on one of the regular Web sites to find the best price you can; compare that with the "blind" offerings from the auction sites. Although the auction sites can often deliver the best prices, the tickets come with some detractions: You cannot time your arrival to meet cruise ships and may have to build in an extra hotel stay at each end of the trip; it may be impossible to make changes or obtain a refund if your plans change; and you might not be permitted to stand by for another flight with your limited ticket. Read the fine print carefully: Prices might not include taxes and fees, and the sites could tack on a service charge. Be sure to compare the true bottom line with the price quoted on other Web sites or from a travel agent.

■ STANDING UP FOR STANDING BY

Until our world was turned upside-down by terrorists in 2001, one of the little-known secrets of air travel on most airlines and for most types of tickets was the fact that travelers with valid tickets were allowed to stand by for flights other than the ones for which they have reservations; if there were empty seats on the flight, standby ticket holders were permitted to board at no additional charge.

Today, though, be sure to check airlines' current policies. Some companies will allow holders of full-fare tickets to stand by for other flights without charge. Others apply a reticketing charge, and some airlines have banned the practice completely.

If I have a changeable ticket, here's my strategy: If I can't get the exact flight I want, I make the closest acceptable reservation available after that flight, then I show up early at the airport and head for the check-in counter for the flight I really want to take. Unless I am traveling during an impossibly overbooked holiday period or arrive on a bad-weather day when flights have been canceled, my chances of successfully standing by for a flight are usually pretty good.

One trick is to call the airline the day before the flight and check on the availability of seats for the flight you want to try for. Some reservation clerks are very forthcoming with information; many times I have been told something like, "There are seventy seats open on that flight."

Be careful with standby maneuvers if your itinerary requires a change of plane en route; you'll need to check the availability of seats on all legs of your journey.

The fly in the ointment in today's strict security environment is this: Airlines are required to match bags to passengers before a flight takes off. It is difficult, if not impossible, to stand by for a flight other than the one you hold a ticket for if you have checked a bag. Your chances are much better if you limit yourself to carry-on bags. Security screeners might not let you into the concourse for flights more than two hours before scheduled departure. Consult with the ticket agents at check-in counters *outside* the security barriers for advice.

A final note: Be especially careful about standing by for the very last flight of the day. If you are unable to get on that flight, you're stuck for the night.

■ YOUR RIGHTS AS A CONSUMER

The era of airline deregulation has been a mixed blessing for the industry and for the consumer. After an era of wild competition based mostly on price, we now are left with fewer but larger airlines and a dizzying array of confusing rules.

The U.S. Department of Transportation and its Federal Aviation Administration (FAA) still regulate safety issues. Almost everything else is between you and the airline. Policies on fares, cancellations, reconfirmation, check-in requirements, and compensation for lost or damaged baggage or for delays all vary by airline. Your rights are limited and defined by the terms of the contract you make with an airline when you buy your ticket. The contract might be included with the ticket you purchase, or the airlines may "incorporate terms by reference" to a separate document that you will have to request to see.

Whether you are buying your ticket through a travel agent or dealing directly with the airline, here are some important questions to ask:

■ Is the price guaranteed, or can it change from the time the reservation is made until you actually purchase the ticket?

■ Can the price change between the time you buy the ticket and the date of departure?

■ Is there a penalty for canceling the ticket?

■ Can the reservation be changed without penalty or for a reasonable fee? Be sure you understand the sort of service you are buying.

■ Is this a nonstop flight, a direct flight (your plane will make one or more stops en route to its destination), or a flight that requires you to change planes one or more times?

■ What seat has been issued? Do you really want the center seat in a three-seat row, between two strangers?

You might also want to ask your travel agent:

■ Is there anything I should know about the financial health of this airline?

■ Are you aware of any threats of work stoppages or legal actions that could ruin my trip?

■ OVERBOOKING

Overbooking is a polite industry term for the legal business practice of selling more than an airline can deliver. It all stems from the rudeness of many travelers who neglect to cancel flight reservations that will not be used. Airlines study the patterns on various flights and city pairs and apply a formula that allows them to sell more tickets than there are seats on the plane in the expectation that a certain percentage of ticket holders will not show up.

But what happens if all passengers holding a reservation do show up? Obviously, the result will be more passengers than seats, and some will have to be left behind. The involuntary bump list will begin with passengers who check in late. Airlines must ask for volunteers before bumping any passengers who have followed the rules on check-in.

Now, assuming that no one is willing to give up a seat just for the fun of it, the airline will offer some sort of compensation, either a free ticket or cash, or sometimes both. It is up to the passenger and the airline to negotiate a deal.

Some air travelers, including this author, look forward to an overbooked flight when their schedules are flexible. My most profitable score: $4,000 in vouchers on a set of four $450 international tickets. The airline was desperate to clear a large block of seats, and it didn't matter to us if we arrived home a few hours late. We received the equivalent of three tickets for the price of one, and you can bet that we'll hope to earn some more free travel on future tickets purchased with those vouchers.

The U.S. Department of Transportation's consumer protection regulations set some minimum levels of compensation for passengers who are bumped from a flight due to overbooking. If you are bumped involuntarily, the airline must provide a ticket on its next available flight. Unfortunately, there is no guarantee that there will be a seat on that plane or that it will arrive at your destination at a convenient time. If you are traveling to the port on the day your ship is scheduled to depart, you probably don't want to even consider the possibility of being bumped. Let the airline staff know you are flying to a cruise, and stand your ground if you feel your vacation is threatened.

If the airline can get you on another flight that will get you to your destination within one hour of the original arrival time, no compensation need be paid. If you are scheduled to get to your destination more than one hour but less than two hours late, you're entitled to receive an amount equal to the one-way fare of the oversold flight, up to $200. If the delay is more than two hours, the bumpee will receive an amount equal to twice the one-way fare of the original flight, up to $400.

It is not considered bumping if a flight is canceled because of weather, equipment problems, or lack of a flight crew. You are also not eligible for compensation if the airline substitutes a smaller aircraft for operational or safety reasons, or if the flight involves an aircraft with sixty seats or less.

How to Get Bumped

Why in the world would you want to be bumped? Well, perhaps you'd like to look at missing your plane not as an annoyance but as an opportunity to earn a little money for your time. Is a two-hour delay worth $100 an hour to you? For the inconvenience of waiting a few hours on the way home, a family of four might receive a voucher for $800; that could pay for a week's hotel plus a heck of a meal at the airport.

If you're not in a rush to get to your destination or to get back home, you might want to volunteer to be bumped. We wouldn't recommend doing this on the busiest travel days of the year or if you are booked on the last flight of the day, unless you are also looking forward to a free night in an airport motel.

■ THE NEW WORLD OF AIRPORT SECURITY

Travel has become all the more complicated and less convenient in the wake of the terrorist attacks of 2001. The bottom line for well-meaning business and pleasure travelers is this: You'll need to add an hour or more to the check-in process, and your options to stand by for a different flight or make other changes to your itinerary are severely limited.

Here are some things you can do to lessen the pain:

■ Consult with the airline or your travel agent about current policies regarding check-in times.

■ Consider your departure time. Lines for check-in and security clearance are longest during peak travel times: early morning and late afternoon.

■ An alternate airport might have shorter lines. Some major hubs are, by necessity, more efficient at processing huge crowds, but smaller airports with fewer crowds can be easier to navigate.

■ Try to avoid carrying unnecessary metallic items on your person. Choose a belt with a small buckle rather than the one with the three-pound championship steer-wrestling medallion. Put your cell phone, keys, coins, and wristwatch in a plastic bag and place it in your carry-on bag as you approach the magnetometer; this will speed your passage and reduce the chances of losing items.

■ Travel in a pair of simple sneakers instead of heavy boots or high heels; you are less likely to have to remove your shoes.

■ Be cooperative, remember that the screening is intended to keep you safe, and hope that the guards do their job well.

SHOULD YOU DRIVE?

Everyone's conception of the perfect vacation is different, but for me, I draw a distinction between getting there and being there. I want the getting there part to be as quick and simple as possible and the being there part to be as long as I can manage and afford. Therefore, I fly to just about any destination that is more than a few hundred miles from my home. The cost of driving, hotels, meals en route, and general physical and mental wear and tear rarely equals a deeply discounted excursion fare.

If you do drive to the port, you can save a few dollars by using the services of AAA or another major automobile club. Before you head out, spend a bit of time and money to make certain your vehicle is in traveling shape: A tune-up and fully inflated, fully inspected tires will certainly save gas, money, and headaches. If you are taking your own car to the port, be sure to inquire ahead of time about parking facilities. Find out the charges, and determine what level of security is provided. You might want to look into leaving your car at a secured garage away from the port.

■ RENTING A CAR

Your travel agent can be of assistance in finding the best rates on rental cars; make a few phone calls on your own, too. Sometimes you'll find significant variations in prices from one agency to another. Be sure to check Web sites as well; sites such as www.expedia.com and www.travelocity.com allow you to compare rates from several rental agencies for the dates and locations you specify.

You might also find lower rental rates at the Web sites of the rental car companies themselves. Join the agencies' priority clubs, which usually are free, to receive special offers.

In 2003, prices for rental cars were on the climb, although they still represent a relative bargain. Think of the deal as borrowing $15,000 for a $35 fee to put things in perspective.

Car rental companies will try, with varying levels of pressure, to convince you to purchase special insurance coverage. They'll tell you it's "only" $7.00 or $9.00 per day. What a deal! That works out to about $2,500 or $3,330 per year for a set of rental wheels. Of course the coverage is intended primarily to protect the rental company, not you.

Before you travel, check with your insurance agent to determine how well your personal automobile policy will cover a rental car and its contents. I strongly recommend using a credit card that offers rental car insurance; such insurance usually will reimburse you for the deductible and other out-of-pocket expenses under your personal auto insurance policy. The extra auto insurance by itself is usually worth an upgrade to a gold card or other extra-service credit card. The only sticky area comes for those visitors who have a driver's license but no car, and therefore no insurance. Again, consult your credit card company and your insurance agent to see what kind of coverage you have or what kind you need.

Pay attention, too, when the rental agent explains the gas policy. Under the most common plan, you must return the car with a full tank; if the agency must refill the tank, you will usually be billed a very high per-gallon rate and sometimes a service charge as well.

Under an optional plan, the rental agency sells you a full tank when you first drive away and takes no note of how much gas remains when you return the car. Unless you somehow manage to return the car with the engine running on fumes, you are in effect making a gift to the agency with every gallon you bring back.

I prefer the first option, which requires making it a point to refill the tank on the way to the airport on getaway day.

Although it is theoretically possible to rent a car without a credit card, you will find it to be an inconvenient process. If the rental agency can't hold your credit card account hostage, it will most often require a large cash deposit, perhaps as much as several thousand dollars, before it will give you the keys.

CHAPTER TEN

BEFORE YOU SET SAIL

WHAT KIND OF WEATHER can you expect at your destination and your ports of call? If you're sailing from Vancouver to Alaska, you can expect a wide range of conditions, from warm and sunny to cold and drizzly. If you head to the mountains on a shore excursion, you could find a bit of winter in July on a glacier. In eastern Canada, it can be damp and cool in spring and fall; the inland port of Montreal can be surprisingly cold in spring and immoderately hot in summer and fall.

In Hawaii, the Caribbean, and Mexico, temperatures are generally moderate to hot all the time; of more import is the difference between the dry and wet seasons. In Central America and Mexico, it's hot all the time, with a rainy season that begins in early May and continues through October and November, when hurricanes sometimes arrive in the Gulf of Mexico. European coastal ports can reach extremes of cold and heat.

Wherever you go, pack some light sweaters or jackets to wear on deck in the evening when temperatures drop. Your ship will be moving, too, usually adding a 15- to 20-mile-per-hour breeze to whatever wind there is at sea.

The Internet offers a great way to check average weather and specific forecasts around the world. Among the sites you should visit are:

- www.accuweather.com
- www.cnn.com/weather
- www.intellicast.com/Travel
- www.mytravelweather.com
- www.travelforecast.com
- www.usatoday.com/weather
- www.weather.com

FASHION TIPS

Find out from the cruise line about the dress suggestions for dinner; details are usually included in the packet of information that arrives with your cruise tickets. Most ships have one or more "formal" nights. Many add optional theme nights: Western, the '50s, Island, Mexican, Greek, and so on.

Like it or not, the definition of "formal" has loosened up greatly on most ships. Only a few lines require men to wear tuxedos; a conservative suit or a blue blazer and gray slacks will not raise any eyebrows. On nearly every cruise I've taken, at least one man has chosen to arrive at the formal dinner in a kilt. Women have a range of options, from cocktail gowns to pantsuits. Put another way, on most ships "formal" means the night when you don't wear a T-shirt and jeans.

What happens if you show up at dinner on a formal night inappropriately dressed? On some ships, the maître d' may discreetly suggest that you return to your cabin and seek new attire. On other ships, he might suggest that you visit an alternative casual dining room that night. Or he might look away, preferring to keep his relations with you—and his potential gratuity—undamaged. You might have to endure some sideways glances from cruisers in fancy duds though.

On some ships you can arrange to rent a tuxedo and other formal wear; check before you depart to see if such services are available.

Ask if the ship has an onboard Laundromat or a reasonably priced laundry or dry cleaning service. On a longer cruise this can allow you to pack less clothing.

Find out about health club and sports facilities onboard the ship, and think about whether you will be visiting any beaches onshore. Pack a bathing suit, sandals, sun hat, sneakers, and any other appropriate articles, including sunblock. The cruise line will provide beach towels and might offer other amenities such as bathrobes and slippers for some or all of its passengers, sometimes discriminating on the basis of your class of cabin.

One other thing: Think twice and even three times about whether you want to bring any valuable jewelry with you. You'll have to worry about its security while getting to the ship, onboard the ship, in port, and getting home.

Another worthwhile fashion accessory: a pair of neat rubber-sole shoes for strolls on the promenade deck or other outside parts of the ship. Plastic or leather soles might be too slippery for comfort.

PAPERWORK AND PASSPORTS

Almost every cruise visits a foreign port. That's part of the romance of it all, as well as a legal requirement for any vessel that does not fly a U.S. flag.

Many tourist ports in the Caribbean and Canada do not require visitors to have a passport to enter and will accept a birth certificate or a driver's license. The same generally applies for U.S. citizens returning to this country from those destinations. Immigration laws and regulations can change, however, and you might find some immigration inspectors are more picky than others. In today's heightened security atmosphere, you should be prepared for a more stringent examination at border points.

I strongly recommend that you bring a passport. If you don't have one, it's not a huge bother to obtain one. Your travel agent, U.S. post office, or county clerk can usually help you with the paperwork. The standard process can take a few months, but for an extra fee, there are ways to speed it up considerably.

The cruise line will also likely send you some embarkation papers to fill out and bring with you to the port. One form is used for immigration purposes; inspectors at foreign ports and in the United States on your return will likely work from a list provided by the cruise company.

On most cruise lines, U.S. immigration officials board the ship on the last morning of the trip; all guests are required to come before them with their passports and immigration forms before any passengers are permitted off the ship. Customs officials either board the ship or wait to meet guests as they pick up their bags in the terminal.

Some cruise lines will send passengers a personal questionnaire to be used in producing a shipboard newsletter or a registry that will allow people to locate guests with similar interests or backgrounds or those from particular locations. You do not have to participate or fill out this sort of form. The forms ask for your date of birth and sometimes for your wedding anniversary. Don't be surprised if this information is conveyed to the serving staff in the dining room.

The cruise line will likely send you a set of luggage tags. If you have purchased an airport transfer service from the cruise line, these will be used to identify your bags when you arrive at the airport. If you make your own way to the ship, these luggage tags will be used by cabin attendants who deliver bags to staterooms. Fill out the tags, including your cabin number, which you should find on your cruise contract.

MEDICAL NEEDS AND PERSONAL SUPPLIES

If you are taking any medications or have any significant medical conditions, speak with your doctor before heading out on your trip. Consider bringing a copy of your current medical records in case you need to visit the shipboard clinic or an onshore facility. If you have a heart condition, for example, your doctor might want you to bring a copy of a recent electrocardiogram.

If you are on medication or have a medical condition, ask your doctor whether you can safely take one of several commonly used seasickness preventives or remedies. (Most are considered quite safe and effective, but the question is worth asking.)

Be sure to pack a full supply of required medicines; bring along a few additional days' worth to deal with possible delays on your return. You might want to ask your doctor for a backup set of prescriptions in case you need to replace bottles during your trip. Pack your medication in a carry-on bag that does not get checked at the airport or at the dock.

Although most cruise ships can supply you with seasickness pills, aspirin, and most personal toiletries, you're better off bringing your own supply. Again, pack these in your carry-on bags.

I also recommend bringing a sunscreen that has an SPF rating of at least 30, especially on Caribbean, Mexican, Central American, and Hawaiian voyages but also for Alaska and other destinations. It is quite easy to ruin your vacation with a bad sunburn, and overexposure to the sun's rays is a long-term health risk.

In some areas, including Central America and Mexico, it can be worthwhile to take a prescription antimalarial drug; most require that you begin the course of medication a week before arrival in the region and continue for several weeks after your return. Seek the guidance of your physician.

Finally, consult with your insurance agent or personnel office about the limits of your health insurance. Most policies don't cover emergency medical treatment onboard a ship, and many exclude coverage for treatment in foreign countries. Policies also might not pay for expensive emergency medical evacuation from a ship or from a foreign port.

You can, however, purchase special medical insurance for your trip. Policies are offered by most cruise lines and some travel agencies or insurance agencies. Be aware that most policies exclude coverage for pre-existing conditions. Be sure you understand all the terms of a policy before you buy one.

Centers for Disease Control

The Centers for Disease Control and Prevention maintains an excellent Web site with advisories for travelers: www.cdc.gov/ travel. You can also call a toll-free hot line at (877) 394–8747 or request information by fax at (888) 232–3299.

CAMERAS

Most travelers document their vacations on film, but not everyone is happy with the results.

If you're strictly an amateur, consider buying an autofocus, autoexposure, pocket camera with a zoom lens. These cameras do just about everything but take the picture for you, and the quality is generally quite good. Expect a decent model to cost approximately $100 to $200.

A standard lens for 35mm film is about 50mm, a typical wide-angle lens is 35mm, and a moderate telephoto focal length is 100mm. Therefore, a zoom lens that runs from 35mm to 100mm covers most situations; even better is a zoom that is slightly wider and longer, say 28mm to 135mm.

When you buy film, pay attention to the speed, also called ASA or ISO rating. The higher the number, the "faster" the film. A fast film allows you to shoot in lower-light conditions, at a higher shutter speed to stop the action, or at a smaller lens aperture, which generally gives you a sharper image with a better depth of field. Professional photographers will tell you that faster film doesn't deliver perfect color or that your photos may be more grainy in appearance when larger prints are made. That is true, but you are taking vacation snapshots, not studio portraits. And today's "fast" films have nearly as fine a grain and as much color saturation as the slower films of just a few years ago.

I recommend using film that has a rating of at least 400, which allows picture-taking at the midnight buffet as well as on deck and in port. If you know you're going to be shooting mostly low-light images in museums and onboard, look for film with an 800 rating.

It's a good idea to buy your film at a reputable dealer before you leave for your trip. You'll pay less than at a tourist port, and you can expect that the film is fresh and has been stored properly.

A word of caution: Film can be damaged by exposure to heat. Don't leave your film out in the sun. You'll also get the best results if you have your film processed sooner rather than later. Try to avoid leaving a roll of film in your camera for months just because there are a few unexposed frames.

In theory, airport X-ray machines will not harm film in carry-on bags. However, faster film, such as ASA 800 stock, is more susceptible than slower film, and there can be a cumulative effect from passing through six or eight machines over the course of a trip. In today's security-conscious airports, you might have no choice but to pass your film through the screening machines. Don't put film—exposed or unexposed—in checked luggage. The X-ray equipment used for checked luggage is much stronger and can "fog" or damage film in just one pass.

You can do without film entirely by using a digital camera that records images in magnetic memory. You can transfer the data from the camera to your personal computer and send the images to a laboratory for prints, or stay electronic and transmit the pictures to friends and family by e-mail. A basic point-and-shoot digital camera, acceptable for e-mail and small prints, starts at about $200. More sophisticated digital cameras are capable of storing higher-resolution images that can be enlarged to wall-size frames. The key to look for is the "pixel" (picture element) rating for the camera. A camera that records 640 kilobyte images is appropriate for Web and e-mail use. In order to make large prints, look for a camera that records at least two megabytes.

It's also a good idea to pack one or more sets of replacement batteries for your camera; even better are rechargeable batteries. You don't want to discover that you've run out of juice just at the moment a humpback whale breaches alongside your ship.

If you are traveling with a video camera, be sure to bring the battery charger with you. Most modern cruise ships offer standard 110-volt electrical outlets in the cabins. You might need a voltage adapter on some older ships and certain European cruise ships that supply 220 volts. And if (like me) you travel with a suitcase full of electronic and electrical devices—a digital camera, a personal computer, a cell phone, a shaver, and a CD player—you might want to also carry a multiple-outlet plug with you. Most cruise ships offer only one or two outlets. Even better is a multiple-outlet device with a surge protector.

ARRIVING AT THE PIER

Most ships have a window of several hours for arriving passengers to check in and get onboard. Cruise ships generally depart in the early evening, and may be open for check-in as early as 1:00 P.M. You'll probably find that lunch will be served to arriving passengers, sometimes in the dining room but more often as a casual buffet.

When you arrive at the pier, you might find a curbside check-in for your bags.

Be sure to determine that the persons reaching for your bags are legitimate employees of the cruise line or stevedores from the port; look for an ID badge or card. Cruise line staff might have a list of arriving passengers. Be sure, too, that they are checking in your ship and not another one at the same port.

At some ports, you might have to drag your bags into the terminal for check-in. Again, be sure that you deposit your bags with the right cruise line. Your luggage tags should have your name and cabin number clearly marked on them. Double-check to see that the tags have not come off en route to the pier.

Hold on to your overnight bag with a change of clothes, medications, cameras, jewelry, and other valuables. Be sure you also hold on to your cruise documents, including your passport.

On nearly every ship, your bags will be delivered to your cabin. Sometimes they will arrive before you get to your cabin, but they might not make it to your stateroom until after the ship has sailed from the port. (On most ships, the first night's dinner has a casual dress code.)

It is not necessary to tip a cabin attendant who brings your bags to your room onboard the ship; protocol calls for a tip to be delivered at the end of the voyage. If your bags are taken at the curb by a stevedore or employee of the port, a tip may be in order; check with the cruise line in advance or ask a representative of the cruise company at the dock whether the service is included in your fare.

BOARDING THE SHIP

When you get onboard, you will likely be escorted to your room by a cabin attendant. (The fancier cruise lines make this into a bit of an event, outfitting the attendants in starched jackets and white gloves.) Check out your room. Be sure the attendant shows you how to operate the heating and cooling system. Find out if there is a safe in the room. If you're lucky enough to have a veranda, learn how to open and close the door. Locate the life vests. If you want extra pillows or blankets, ask for them. If the cabin has two single beds that can be brought together to serve as a queen-size bed, ask the attendant to rearrange them.

Of course, if you find that the cabin is not what you thought you had purchased—it has a porthole instead of a window, there are upper-and-lower berths instead of a double bed, it's an inside broom closet rather than the Owner's Suite—now is the time to make a beeline to the reception desk or purser's office onboard the ship. It may be possible to switch to another cabin if the ship is not full.

If no mistake has been made, you may still be able to upgrade your cabin if better accommodations are available. On many ships, this is one way to obtain an upgraded room at a decreased price: The purser or onboard hotel manager might offer deep discounts on any available upgraded cabins once it is absolutely impossible to sell them to someone not already onboard the ship.

Your first few hours on the ship may also be the time to visit the dining room to meet with the maître d' to attempt to change your dining room assignment if it is not to your liking.

IMMIGRATION AND CUSTOMS INFORMATION

There are two official steps in the process of entering a foreign country and returning to your home nation: immigration and customs.

Put simply, *immigration* is the process of clearing you into a country, and *customs* is the process of allowing your possessions the same privilege.

In this section, I'll concentrate on customs and immigration processes for American citizens leaving and returning to the United States. Similar requirements apply to citizens of other countries; ask the cruise line or your travel agent any specific questions about your situation.

▇ IMMIGRATION

The Immigration and Naturalization Service (INS), part of the Department of Justice, is responsible for the movement of people in and out of the United States.

The cruise line will ask to see your passport or identification papers before you embark on the ship. This allows the company to certify to foreign destinations that all passengers are legally able to enter; in most cases you will not have to produce your passport to actually enter the country at the port. The next time you will have to produce your passport is likely to be upon your return to the United States. Under tightened security controls, cruise lines may supply information to the INS and the U.S. Coast Guard ahead of time to speed up the processing of passengers when they return to the United States.

Depending on the itinerary and the cruise line's policy, your passport may be held by the purser's office and returned at the end of the trip when immigration officials are onboard to clear the reentry of passengers. Be sure you understand the official policy before you leave your passport in someone else's hands.

For information on obtaining a passport or other immigration questions, contact the nearest passport agency in person or by mail or phone. You may also be able to obtain assistance from some U.S. post offices and some town or city clerks of court. Your travel agency should also be able to direct you to the nearest and most convenient office.

You can write for information by addressing a letter to the passport agency at the nearest of the following zip codes: Boston 02222-0123; Chicago 60604-1564; Honolulu 96850; Houston 77002-4874; Los Angeles 90024-3614; Miami 33130-1680; New Orleans 70113-1931; New York 10111-0031; Philadelphia 19106-1684; San Francisco 94105-2773; Seattle 98174-1091; Stamford, Connecticut 06901-2767; Washington, D.C. 20524-0002.

Be aware that if a single parent is traveling with a minor child, the cruise line or immigration authorities may refuse boarding or entry without a legally binding letter from both parents, even if they are divorced, granting permission for the minor to leave the country. Consult an attorney and the cruise line for advice if you fall into this category.

■ CUSTOMS

On the customs side, administered by the U.S. Customs Service, there are two principal concerns: security and duties.

Obviously, it is not a smart idea to go through an inspection point with illegal drugs or weapons. Also prohibited are foreign lottery tickets, obscene articles and publications, seditious and treasonable materials, and hazardous articles such as fireworks, dangerous toys, and toxic or poisonous substances.

In most ports, visitors are on the honor system; customs agents do not inspect every incoming bag. Some travelers may be honored with a random search of their person and possessions. Many ports are adding X-ray machines and devices that screen for explosives.

It's a good idea to carry prescription drugs in a pharmacist's bottle or with a copy of the prescription from your doctor. In a pinch, your hometown pharmacy should be able to give you a letter certifying that the pills you carry have been ordered by an accredited physician. Be especially careful to obtain this sort of proof if you are carrying any painkillers or sedatives.

Duties are a special form of taxes levied on certain types or amounts of imported goods. As this book goes to press, each returning U.S. resident is permitted to bring home up to $800 in goods without having to pay duty. Included in that $800 exemption is up to one hundred cigars and two hundred cigarettes; residents over age twenty-one can also bring back one liter (33.8 ounces) of alcohol duty-free. The next $1,000 worth of items is taxed at a flat duty rate of 10 percent.

Note that certain items, including Cuban cigars and other products, are generally not allowed into the United States, even though they are readily available in nearby countries. Although you can purchase Cuban cigars in Canada, Jamaica, Mexico, and elsewhere, you cannot bring them back to the United States; the only exception is if you are returning from Cuba itself, and that requires a special license that is generally limited to American journalists and academics. In 1998, restrictions on travel to Cuba were relaxed slightly, and U.S. residents who are allowed to visit are now permitted to bring back up to $100 in Cuban goods purchased in Cuba.

Other acquisitions may qualify for duty-free treatment under other exemptions, such as the generalized system of preferences, which awards duty-free treatment to many goods from developing countries. Fine art (not handicrafts) and antiques older than one hundred years are commonly acquired items that also do not require the payment of duty. There are all sorts of interesting side trips in the regulations. For example, although fine art is exempted from duty, you may be liable for tax on the picture frame that surrounds it.

If your cruise includes a visit to one of the U.S. Virgin Islands, the personal exemption is $1,200, although no more than $800 worth of items within that $1,200 exemption can come from foreign nations outside the U.S. Virgin Islands ($600 for Caribbean Basin countries).

The "Duty-Free" Confusion

In most seaports and airports, the streets and corridors are chock-a-block with "duty-free" stores. You'll also find some duty-free items available onboard cruise ships. If you didn't know better, you could reasonably assume this meant that items for sale there are free from duty when travelers return home. That's not the case.

Articles sold in duty-free shops are free of duty and taxes for the country in which the shop is located, and items sold there are intended for export. When you arrive in the United States, these items are subject to duty after you exceed your personal exemption.

If you are returning directly from any of the following countries, your customs exemption is $600: Antigua and Barbuda, Aruba, Bahamas, Barbados, Belize, British Virgin Islands, Costa Rica, Dominica, Dominican Republic, El Salvador, Grenada, Guatemala, Guyana, Honduras, Jamaica, Montserrat, Netherlands Antilles, Nicaragua, Panama, Saint Kitts and Nevis, Saint Lucia, Saint Vincent and the Grenadines, and Trinidad and Tobago. If you make an intermediate stop at another country, say, Venezuela, the $800 exemption applies, although only $600 may come from the noted Caribbean countries.

Finally, to qualify for an exemption, you must be returning from a stay abroad of at least forty-eight hours and you cannot use more than one exemption within a thirty-day period. If you have been out of the country more than once in a thirty-day period, or if your trip out of the United States lasted less than forty-eight hours, you will be limited to bringing back $200 free of duty and tax.

Be sure to check with the cruise line or the U.S. Immigration and Customs Service for the latest regulations. The Customs Service lists some valuable information on their Web site at www.customs.ustreas.gov/xp/cgov/travel/vacation.

Regulations for returning Canadian citizens are similar, with an exemption of up to $750 (Canadian) for travelers who have been out of the country for at least seven days, including up to forty ounces of alcohol, two hundred cigarettes, and fifty cigars. Canada Customs and Revenue Agency maintains a Web site at www.ccra-adrc.gc.ca/menu-e.html.

■ REGISTERING FOREIGN-MADE VALUABLES

If you cross through customs with an expensive Japanese camera on your shoulder, an Italian scarf on your neck, and a fancy watch or piece of jewelry on your arm, the inspector can assume that all these items were purchased abroad and not in your neighborhood mall.

To establish that you brought these items from your home, bring proof of purchase, an insurance policy, or jeweler's appraisal. You can also register the serial numbers or other marks with customs before you leave home.

Customs pays particular attention to expensive cameras (including special lenses and video equipment), binoculars, radios, foreign-made watches, and other similar items. To register items, take them to the customs office and obtain a validated Certificate of Registration (CF 4457) form; bring the form with you on your travels.

■ PROHIBITED FOOD PRODUCTS

In general, you can bring home packaged foods in sealed cans, bottles, and boxes. Baked goods and cured cheeses are also permitted.

Most fruits and vegetables are either prohibited from entering the country or require an import permit. Every fruit or vegetable must be declared to the customs officer and must be presented for inspection, no matter how free of pests it appears to be. Note that Hawaii and California also have very strict prohibitions against the import of fruits and vegetables; the regulations are in place to protect against the introduction of pests and diseases that could be damaging to the native crops. Plants, cuttings, seeds, unprocessed plant products, and certain endangered species either require an import permit or are prohibited from entering the United States.

Unpasteurized cheeses, meat, poultry, and processed food products including ham, frankfurters, sausage, and pâté are either prohibited or restricted, depending on the animal diseases prevalent in the country of origin. Canned meat is permitted if the inspector can determine it is commercially canned and can be kept without refrigeration.

■ TRANSPORTATION OF CURRENCY

You may take on your trip as much currency or monetary equivalents as you wish. However, if you take out or bring into the United States more than $10,000 in cash, you are required to file a report with the U.S. Customs Service.

LIFEBOAT DRILLS

One of the first scheduled events on a cruise is the lifeboat drill, often conducted in port before departure. It's something that could save your life in the extremely unlikely event of an emergency at sea, and it's a requirement of vessels operating throughout most of the world.

When you arrive in your cabin, you should find one life vest for each person who will sleep there; ask the cabin attendant for assistance if you cannot locate the vests or if the number is incorrect. On many ships, the vests themselves are marked with a letter or number code for an "assembly station." You'll also find information about your assigned assembly station on a placard near the door of your cabin.

Listen for the instructions that will be announced over the ship's public address system; you'll likely be asked to return to your cabin, pick up your life vest, and proceed to the assembly station. When you arrive, a member of the crew will check your name off the list of passengers assigned to that lifeboat; in theory, a

A lifeboat drill aboard Royal Caribbean's *Rhapsody of the Seas* while in port in Vancouver.
Photo by Corey Sandler

crew member will come looking for you if you don't show up.

Finally, you'll be instructed on how to put on the vest properly, shown the location of the emergency whistle and beacon on each vest, and given an explanation of how the lifeboats are lowered into position for boarding.

Pay attention to any instructions about fire safety. As I've already noted, although fires are very rare, they are much more of a threat on a modern ship than is a collision with an iceberg.

CHAPTER ELEVEN

CRUISE DIARIES

EVERY CRUISE HAS A STORY: an amazing sight, a particular luxury, an exciting encounter. Here are cruise diaries from a few of my favorite recent trips in Central America, the Caribbean, north to Alaska, and across the pond from Europe to America. It's a tough job, but someone has to do it.

SILVER SHADOW: THE LUXE BOAT

I have always wanted my own luxurious yacht, staffed with an attentive crew, stocked with the finest food and drink, and sailing to the most exotic locations. Until the day comes when I have several hundred million dollars to spare, the next best thing may be a cruise aboard one of the four vessels in the Silversea fleet.

Nothing about a Silversea cruise is cheap: not the luxurious appointments in the suites, not the food and wine and other drinks (all included), and certainly not the level of service delivered to the passengers. And though the fare for a cruise on this line is not cheap, either, when it comes to value for your money, Silversea is a great deal.

If I had that luxury yacht of my own, I'd be able to sail on my own schedule. Silversea comes pretty close with their unique Personalized Voyages program that permits guests to put together their own trip, getting on and off the ship from a selection of ports.

And though the daily rate for a cruise on Silversea is higher than the charges on a lesser line, there are still occasional sales and discounts available through the cruise line and travel agents. Whatever you pay, though, it is gratifying to see where your money goes.

■ VALUE FOR MONEY

Your Silversea cruise dollars pay for quality, service, and space. There's not a spot on the ship that is crowded. You cannot walk from the luncheon buffet to your seat without a waiter taking your plate. And at dinner, the staff quickly gets to know your every want . . . and delivers it without an outstretched palm.

Silversea's *Silver Shadow* tied up in St. John's, Newfoundland. *Photo by Corey Sandler*

And then there are the dozens of little luxuries, like wine and drinks without additional charge and free laundry service for certain classes of suites (more about that later.)

On many lines you get the feeling that everything is designed from the bottom line up. From the moment you step onboard, you'll be accosted by staff selling tropical drinks with paper umbrellas; at dinner you get the feeling that your wait staff is calculating the gratuity they expect you to pay at the end of the cruise. In the restaurant the beef is good but you've had better, the lobster tail is recently defrosted, and the chocolate in the cake looks great but tastes quite ordinary.

Not so on Silversea. When it comes time to make a decision between good and excellent, ordinary and extraordinary, budget or expensive, this cruise line always seems to choose excellence.

But enough about money. Allow me to rhapsodize about our cruise.

■ ACROSS THE NORTH ATLANTIC IN STYLE

We tried out Personalized Voyages by joining up with *Silver Shadow* in Reykjavik, Iceland, midway on her September fourteen-day transatlantic repositioning cruise from Europe to New York. As it turned out, the rest of the passengers had boarded at the official start of the voyage in Dublin. The ship made a call at the wild Faroe Islands in the North Atlantic northwest of Scotland, halfway between Iceland and Norway, before sailing to Reykjavik.

From Iceland, *Silver Shadow* crossed the remote waters off Greenland and dropped down toward northern Canada, calling at St. John's, Newfoundland, after three pampered days at sea. We ducked into the protected harbor there just ahead of an oncoming storm, and high winds and seas kept us there for two extra days, forcing cancellation of port calls scheduled at the French island protectorate of St. Pierre and Miquelon, and Sydney, Nova Scotia. We did make our

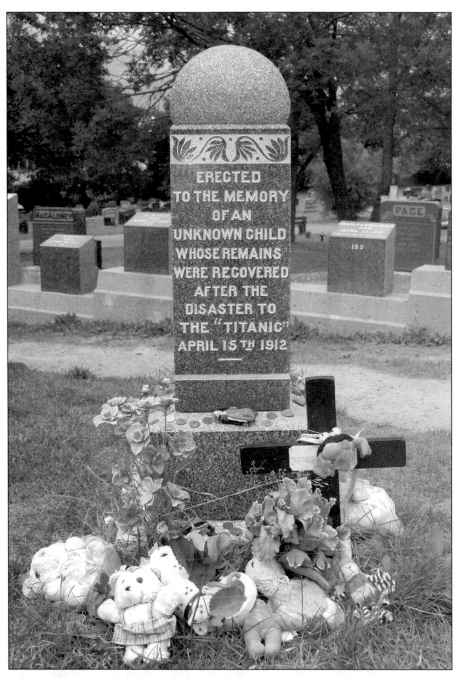

The marker for an unknown young victim of the S.S. *Titanic* in Halifax, Nova Scotia. *Photo by Corey Sandler*

scheduled port call at Halifax, making a pilgrimage to the quiet cemetery that holds many of the recovered victims of the *Titanic* disaster.

Disappointed as we were by missing two ports, we hunkered down in our suite, calling up room service for a few extra bottles of champagne, ordered some new music for the suite's CD stereo system, and otherwise made do. Three days later, we cruised into New York harbor at sunrise and enjoyed another occasional Silversea luxury: a full day to explore New York without having to check out of our five-star hotel parked on the West Side of Manhattan. (With advance reservations, passengers could also invite guests to come onboard the ship for dinner.)

■ OUR MODEST PIED-À-MER

The basic accommodation on *Silver Shadow* and her sister ship *Silver Whisper* is the Vista Suite. A mere 287 square feet in size (about 50 percent larger than the lowest category cabin on most other ships), the room includes a panoramic window, a refrigerator and cocktail cabinet, walk-in closet, sitting area and writing desk, and a marble bathroom with bathtub and separate shower. The most common suite is the Veranda Suite, at 345 square feet, which adds a teak veranda.

Our accommodations were in a Silver Suite, an especially elegant and spacious home at sea. Spread across 701 square feet was a bedroom, a dining room, a living room, a double-size veranda, a walk-in closet, two televisions with VCRs, a CD player, a whirlpool bathtub, and many other lovely little touches. There are thirteen such Silver Suites on Deck 7 of the two sister ships, and they are very popular.

(There are even more spectacular digs: the Owner's, Royal, and Grand Suites—as big as 1,435 square feet, larger than many landlocked apartments.)

Accommodations on the slightly smaller *Silver Cloud* and *Silver Wind* sisters are similar, although a bit downsized.

Everything is up a notch or two—or three—from most other cruise lines. The furniture is more like an upscale home than a budget motel. The beds are appointed with luxurious Frette bed linens from Italy, and the marble bathrooms are stocked with Bulgari amenities.

■ SETTING A GOURMET TABLE

Philipponat champagne flows like water throughout the ship and in the suites; guests can also order complimentary wine, beer, and spirits from an extensive selection for delivery to their rooms or at any of the bars, lounges, and restaurants.

The Restaurant is large and bright, more like a traditional dining room on a cruise ship. Meals are served on an open seating, and the quality of food is like that of a gourmet restaurant on shore.

The Terrace is a small, lovely hideaway up top, presenting a preset menu that's mostly Italian with an occasional French evening. Many of the dishes are finished tableside, with personal visits to every table by the chef.

The wine steward quickly learned that I prefer an interesting beer at dinner, and with each visit he tried to surprise me with something special. *Silver Shadow* had sailed in the Baltic earlier in the summer, and for one meal he produced a few bottles of an unusual Russian beer that had been squirreled away in the galley.

Here's a sample offering served in the middle of the North Atlantic between Greenland and Newfoundland:

- An appetizer medley of stuffed baby squash with wild mushrooms, fresh mozzarella and cherry tomato salad, seared fresh tuna with vegetables, and marinated fried chicken bits with Marsala wine.
- Linguine with lobster, scallops, and tomato sauce, or fresh pasta rolls with ricotta and spinach stuffing with creamy pesto sauce.
- Roast veal rack with sautéed onions and polenta.
- Mint-infused strawberries with lemon-ricotta ice cream.

All this is served with wedges from a gigantic wheel of Parmigiano Reggiano cheese, a bread basket of grissini and focaccia, and accompanied by a changing selection of wines, champagne, or other libations.

A few decks below, guests at The Restaurant could choose from a full menu. On that same night, the menu offered:

- Appetizers including carpaccio with crispy Parmesan; Gorgonzola tart with pesto and tomato; or seared scallop, tiger prawn, and lobster skewer.
- Venetian fish soup, or cream of chicken soup with pistachio nuts.
- Tricolor salad of endive, radicchio, and arugula with mimosa garnish and oregano vinaigrette.
- Limoncello lemon liqueur sorbet.
- Entrees including grilled swordfish fillet with tomato and roast pepper compote; pink roasted veal rack in crispy sour cream dough with foie gras macaroni; spiced roast filet of beef tenderloin with sweet red onions and garlic sauce; and Crespelle alla Fiorentina pancakes filled with creamy spinach and baked in tomato sauce.

Many Silversea guests avail themselves of yet another unique luxury from time to time: ordering from the menu and having it served course by course in the privacy of your suite. Room service will also bring up your choices of wine. That is, without a doubt, the way I would enjoy dinner on my private yacht.

Once each cruise, The Restaurant opens the doors at the back of the dining room for an unusual luncheon buffet: a fabulous spread of dishes on steam tables, countertops, and machinery in the sparkling galley. Of course, on Silversea there are also liveried waiters standing by to carry your treasures to the table and music by the ship's classical trio.

Le Champagne, an intimate wine room, offers the complimentary house wines as well as special vintages. And for those who absolutely must spend more money onboard, the room can be reserved for a private dinner party for as many as twelve guests, with selections from an ultrapremium menu and a sommelier at your beck and call.

Nearby, The Humidor dispenses premium cigars and cognacs in a universe of wood paneling, leather-upholstered chairs, and a high-tech ventilation system that keeps blue clouds away from the rest of the ship.

SOPHISTICATED ENTERTAINMENT

This is not, in oh so many ways, a Carnival fun ship; you're not going to find rock-climbing walls, art auctions, and ice-carving demonstrations.

The Show Lounge presents a program of basic cruise line entertainment, augmented from time to time by special appearances. In coming years, Silversea plans to add more guest performers and special appearances. On our cruise renowned mezzo-soprano Cecilia Bartoli was crossing the Atlantic in style on her way to an American concert tour; she offered a performance as the *Silver Shadow* departed the Faroe Islands. Bartoli is scheduled to sail on four cruises in 2004.

Silversea also regularly offers sophisticated enrichment lectures. We heard a series of presentations from a flight engineer of the supersonic *Concorde* and a set of fascinating lectures on Islam by a distinguished professor of religion.

THE BOTTOM LINE

Now back to money. The typical Vista Suite fare—taking advantage of advanced booking and payment fares—can be as low as about $350 per person per night; a Silver Suite would go for about $1,500. Specially priced Silver Sailings itineraries, including repositioning cruises, offer discounts of as much as 50 percent off the list price when you take advantage of early booking and advance payment programs.

All Silversea fares include complimentary champagne, wine, beer, and spirits from an extensive list at restaurants and lounges and for room service. Gratuities are not accepted from guests.

You can save as much as 20 percent off fares with early booking incentives, plus an additional 5 percent with advance payment. Guests who have sailed previously on Silversea can save an additional 5 to 15 percent on Venetian Society sailings, for a total discount of as much as 40 percent off list price.

The deepest discount fares are offered on repositioning cruises, including transatlantic and transpacific itineraries.

The fare for Personalized Voyages varies by the ship's location and time of year, and only about 20 percent of suites are available for the program. Trips must be for at least five consecutive nights. Fares range from about $495 to $995 per night for a Vista or Veranda Suite and higher for larger suites.

GETTING THE PRIORITIES RIGHT

We were sailing just south of Greenland on the way to Newfoundland. The winds were howling and the seas moderately rough, a harbinger of the storm we were going to meet in St. John's in a few days. However, the modern *Silver Shadow* handled the seas well, her stabilizers smoothing out most of the side-to-side rolls.

It was dinner time, and we were ensconced at our usual private table at The Terrace on Deck 7. We had just finished our appetizer of *Conchiglie ai Gamberoni* (shell-shaped pasta with prawns) and expecting the serving of *Costata di Manzo alla Griglia con Salsa al Barolo* (grilled prime rib with Italian vegetable compote). The table was set with a *panettiere* of grissini and focaccia breads, a tub of *bresaola* butter, and elegant crystal stemware for *Vernaccia di San Gimignano* and *Dolcetto DOC,* the white and red wines of the evening.

Suddenly, the ship heeled all the way over to starboard in a slow roll. Plates and glasses and wine bottles flew off the tables. From the back of the room, we heard a cacophony of crashes as hundreds of additional plates and glasses fell to the floor in the galley. Waiters, sommeliers, and deck crew appeared from every direction to help a few guests who had undergone a slow-motion fall.

The ship returned to its steady upright position. The captain later told us that the ship's computer-controlled stabilizer had suffered a once-in-a-lifetime hiccup.

The room was quiet as we all surveyed the thousands of dollars in broken glass and dishes, the overturned wine coolers, and the crumbled grissini. We then heard a weak little voice from a table by the window: "Excuse me? More wine please."

All was back to luxurious normalcy on the *Silver Shadow.*

And finally, about the laundry service: Sometimes it's the little things that count. Each morning we filled a linen bag with clothing to be washed or pressed. When we returned to our suite in the afternoon, we would find a beautifully wrapped package of clean clothing on our bed: crisp white tissue paper sealed with a hand-tied bow.

The packages were almost too pretty to open—we took one package of socks home in our luggage, and it was weeks before we could bring ourselves to untie the bow and end our last direct connection to a fabulous cruise on our Silversea yacht.

DISNEY MAGIC: **THE KIDS ARE ALL RIGHT**

Dear Mom and Dad:

While you were sleeping, I was hanging out under the stars in the Caribbean, dancing with my new friends and visiting the late-night all-dessert buffet extravaganza. We partied in the atrium, went to teens-only shows, and strolled around the promenade in the dark. One night we watched a cool lightning storm way out to sea.

When you were upstairs at that fancy adults-only restaurant, nibbling eggs Benedict and sipping champagne for Sunday brunch, we were ordering pizza, fabulous french fries, and ice cream from the restaurants around the pool deck: all the basic food groups for the healthy teenager.

We were doing the hokey-pokey while you were watching Roxie Hart and Velma Kelly put on their moves in the movie *Chicago,* part of the nightly double feature of first-run movies in the gorgeous Buena Vista Theatre. Then we all went to see *Holes,* which debuted on the ship the same week it opened on land.

I don't know about you, but this was pretty close to my perfect vacation: Mom and Dad took care of all the details. They got me down to Florida and on the ship, and then we had our own separate holidays. You were up early to sit out on the veranda or go to a cooking lesson. I was out all night, coming back to the cabin about 2:00 A.M. and sleeping late in the morning. We met to attend the stage shows and go to dinner every night, and then you headed off to bed while the teens took over the ship.

They call this *Disney Magic* a cruise ship, but I think of it more as a floating city that traveled to some great places and a fantastic beach. We partied hearty every day, and I felt safe everywhere I went. And I didn't have to pack up and un-pack every day.

I really enjoyed the three days at sea and the shopping and sight-seeing in St. Martin and St. Thomas, and then there was Castaway Cay, where I soared like a bird. More about that later.

This was my sixth cruise; it's pretty nice having a dad who travels for a living. I've liked all the ships I've been on, but Disney is definitely the best when it comes to things for kids of all ages.

◼ NO ADULTS ALLOWED

Our headquarters was Common Grounds, a club where no parent is allowed. About fifty kids, age thirteen to seventeen, hung out there. It was our home base from noon to 2:00 A.M., with couches, a huge television set with a library of tapes and video games, Internet terminals, board games, and a coffee and soft drink bar.

We had three crazy Canadian counselors, and on the first night we were told the rules: no swearing, no fighting, and no forgetting that there were coun-selors—and video cameras—watching us in the club and nearly 1,000 members

Disney Magic at dock in Key West. *Photo by Corey Sandler*

of the crew in one place or another on the ship. No problem: We had way too much fun to get into trouble.

Those Canadians were obsessed with the movie *Coyote Ugly*; they danced on top of the bar when they showed the movie one night.

I mentioned that there were about fifty older teens; there had to be three or four hundred younger kids on board. Many of them spent a lot of time at the Oceaneer Club, for kids from three to twelve years old; the little babies were parked at Flounder's Reef Nursery while their moms and dads chilled. And there was a lot going on at Mickey's Kids' Pool, with the big water slide, or at Goofy's Family Pool. Several nights they pulled the cover over Goofy's and made the whole middle of the ship into a dance floor facing the stage; we had a great sail-away party the night we left St. Martin.

After the young kids went to bed most nights, we took over the Studio Sea club for midnight dances and karaoke sessions. Other times we made our own animation cels; I brought "Stitch" home in my suitcase.

One day at sea we played "Gotcha." Everyone was given a secret assignment to track down another kid somewhere on the ship and kill them off in the game: You got points for stabbing with a paper spoon, delivering the kiss of death on their hand, giving a water torture on the pool deck, or poisoning them by slipping a piece of paper marked POISON under their drink without being noticed. You never knew who had your name—until they got you. Let me tell you, this is a big ship with ten decks, four restaurants, three pools, a whole bunch of elevators, and lots of stairs. I put up a good fight.

One of the best things about this cruise is the way they treat kids; we felt like full citizens in this city. Of course I also really liked the way our Filipino servers Andrew and Rowena fussed over us at dinner. Disney does this cool thing: They have three restaurants, and our servers travel with us to a different one each night.

They did a great job of figuring out what I liked to eat, and they had my soda and steak sauce and my favorite green tea at the table before I even thought to order. Andrew had a new puzzle for me to solve each night. Rowena, who was so sweet, insisted on calling my dad "Sir Corey."

On the last night of the cruise, Andrew gave me a stainless-steel plate cover to bang during the servers' parade; maybe it was because he heard me running around on the deck with a cow bell given to me by one of those crazy Canadians.

Back in the room, our stewardess Lijljana made a different animal out of towels each night. Dad found out that she was a former journalist with a degree in political science who was earning some money before heading back to Croatia, where she hoped to work as a diplomat. That was cool, too.

■ BROADWAY AT SEA

I loved the shows, even if they kept bringing out Mickey and Minnie at the end of each performance. I mean, please, I'm almost eighteen years old. (I prefer Pluto and Belle.)

They did this comedy and magic show called "Morty the Magnificent" about a pretty bad magician. His girlfriend, Daphne, made a wish on her birthday candles, and the Sorceror's Apprentice (Mickey) made Morty magnificent. The magic tricks were cool, and the singing and dancing was really good.

Dad, you told me the little inside joke about the name Morty; it's short for Mortimer, Walt Disney's intended name for his cartoon mouse before his wife convinced him to go with Mickey. It had nothing to do with the show, but, as always, you see things differently than most other people do.

The best magic trick was when Morty sawed the stage manager in half. He said he needed a single woman for the trick because she had to remain unattached. Anyhow, after sawing, the stage manager's legs danced away all by themselves.

There were two other shows. "Hercules—A Muse-ical" was really funny, full of wisecracks and references to pop songs and singers. Hades, lord of the underworld, and his goofy imps sang a few lines of "It's a Small Underworld After All." The big production number was "Zero to Hero."

"Disney Dreams" is like a review of all the Disney favorites, with Peter Pan helping a wishful little girl, Anne-Marie, to find her own magic. We meet Cinderella, Belle, the Beast, Ariel, the Lion King, and all the usual suspects . . . and Mickey.

The Walt Disney Theatre is just fabulous. There are three stage elevators, a fly loft for sets, indoor fireworks, fog machines, laser lights, video screens, and a starfield in the ceiling. And how many theaters on a ship have flying rigs so that Peter Pan can help a little girl soar out the window?

"Who wants to be a Mouseketeer?" was a game show named after guess-what, with prizes from $20 to $400 in shipboard credit and a top prize of a free seven-day cruise. Contestants are randomly selected from the audience, and I had it all worked out. I was going to go up there with dad; I could answer all the questions about *Lion King* and *The Little Mermaid* and dad could answer questions about Mortimer Mouse and all those other little details he knows about ships, theme parks, and other stuff.

They also had this really funny ventriloquist onboard; he had this hilarious routine where he took a five-year-old kid from the audience and made him into his dummy. And this juggler guy did some amazing tricks on stage. Both of them also appeared later in the smaller Off-beat and Rockin' Bar D clubs for some close-up tricks.

And then there was Castaway Cay, on the last full day of the cruise. I remember how you told me that when Disney was planning its cruise ships, the designers thought about how kids would imagine a fabulous ocean liner. That's why they gave it a pointy prow, a black hull, and two big funnels—even though only one of them is real.

I think they did the same thing when they worked on their private island: It's just the way I would want it. The beach is beautiful, there's a big barbecue, and there's snorkeling and floating and a fort with ropes to swing on. Inland, there are bike paths and hiking trails. The little kids have their own beach.

I know you both visited the adults-only beach at the other end of the island. I know that sounds pretty risqué, but this is a Disney place, right? It's a nice, quiet beach with no kids, its own restaurant, and private cabanas for massages.

I hung out with my friends at the teen beach, until the afternoon, when I met up with Dad at Marge's Barges at the end of the breakwater that protects the beach. We climbed into a speedboat and headed out into the open ocean beyond the *Disney Magic* at her dock. A guy strapped me into a harness, attached me to a parachute, and gunned the engine.

For the next ten minutes or so, I parasailed high above Castaway Cay, making a turn around the stern of the cruise ship. We had a nice wind, and once I was about 200 feet in the air, the speedboat stopped and I just hung there—a human kite.

I soared higher than Wendy ever did with Peter Pan; it was my Disney Dream. Dad, you did pretty well, too—for an old man.

I know I'm headed off to college in the fall, and I expect I'll find a few things to do there for the next four years. But if you need me to go with you on a cruise as a reporter, I'm there.

—Tessa

OLYMPIA VOYAGER: RACING BACK IN TIME

"Fasten your seat belts," said Captain Antonios Kritikos, master of the *Olympia Voyager*. "We're going to let the horses run."

The horses—the diesel equivalent of 55,000 of them—combine with an unusual hull design to make Royal Olympia Cruise Line's *Olympia Voyager* and her sister ship *Olympia Explorer* the fastest cruise ships currently in service. About an hour after we had cleared the harbor at Belize City, Belize, en route to Progreso, Mexico, the horses were let loose and the 25,000-ton ship steadily accelerated until she reached 30.5 knots, a bit more than 35 miles per hour.

Twin plumes of water streamed off the stern of the ship; we were moving fast enough to tow a fleet of water-skiers. Cruising, of course, is not about speed; today's travelers are looking for comfort and style, and the *Olympia Voyager* delivers both. But the extra speed, about 7 to 10 knots faster than most other passenger vessels, allows the *Olympia* twins to travel to farther destinations or to spend a few extra hours in port.

(For the record, a few of the older transatlantic liners were able to steam at 32 and even 35 knots, albeit with huge consumption of coal or oil. With their retirement or reconfiguration as cruise ships, as was the case with the *QE2* and the *Norway,* the typical cruising speed for modern ships was reduced to about 20 knots.)

Royal Olympia Cruises is a Greek company, with majority ownership by Louis Cruise Lines, a tourism company in Cyprus. It can trace its history back to Epirotiki, founded in the mid-nineteenth century as a cargo line. In 1954 Epirotiki began cruise ship operations in the Aegean Sea under the Epirotiki and Sun Line brands. Today the company is the largest cruise operator in the eastern Mediterranean. Over the years it has offered cruises in the Caribbean and the Gulf of Mexico aimed at Americans.

We sailed on the *Olympia Voyager* on a weeklong "Mayaribbean" cruise from

Houston to Playa del Carmen, Mexico; Puerto Cortes, Honduras; Belize City, Belize; and Progreso, Mexico. The company plans sailed from Fort Lauderdale or Los Angeles to Central America in 2004.

Olympia Voyager is a Medium ship, about one-third the size of a typical Megaship, with cabins for 836 passengers. Don't expect to find a rock climbing wall, an ice-skating rink, alternative restaurants, and a Broadway-style show room. Here's what else you won't find: several thousand strangers crowding the deck or descending en masse on a tiny exotic port.

The two Olympia-class ships are more like superyachts than Megaships. Think of them as five-star hotels that deliver pampered guests from one spectacular destination to another—at a good clip. In port, guests desert the ship in droves, heading for shore excursions that keep them on land for as long as twelve hours.

Many cruisegoers were disappointed at the financial scuttling of Renaissance Cruise Lines in late 2001; that company operated a fleet of ships of a similar size in Europe, Asia, and the South Pacific. Royal Olympia Cruises goes a long way toward offering the same sort of product. The ship's cabins are smaller and the food is good but not great, but *Olympia Voyager* and *Olympia Explorer* are clearly ships for travelers who have destinations in mind and want to sail there in a fine hotel, not in a neon piece of Las Vegas at sea.

The angular, yachtlike lines of the ship are noticeably different from the rounded, porpoiselike design of many larger modern ships. Cabins are attractive and functional, albeit on the small side; the basic oceanview stateroom comprises just 140 square feet. (Most modern ships offer cabins starting at about 180 to 200 square feet.) On the *Olympia Voyager* only the twelve Deluxe Sky Suites offer balconies; the *Olympia Explorer* has twelve additional balconies in the Deluxe Suite category.

The two ships were built in Hamburg, Germany, at the Blohm and Voss yards, one of the oldest in the country, dating back to 1877. The company built the famed *Vaterland* transatlantic liner and, in 1939, one of Germany's most famous combat vessels, the *Bismarck*.

The *Vaterland* was launched in 1913 as Hamburg Amerika Line's answer to the Cunard and White Star liners, including the *Titanic*. At 54,282 tons, when she took to service in 1914 she was the largest ship in the world. The ship was at dock in New Jersey when World War I began; it was seized by the United States and converted into a troop carrier. After the

Royal Olympia Cruises' speedy *Olympia Voyager* at rest in Progreso, Mexico. *Photo by Corey Sandler* war she sailed as the *Leviathan* for United States Lines. The battleship *Bismarck*, one of the most feared vessels of World War II, sank in the Atlantic after a battle with the British battle cruiser *Hood* and the battleship *Prince of Wales.*

The military history of the Blohm and Voss shipyard came into play with the design of the *Olympia Voyager.* The ship is built on a "fast monohull" derived from the design of modern frigates. The hull includes a knifelike bow and a submarine-like displacement for the main body of the hull. From about midships to near the stern, water is channeled through open tunnels to a pair of large propellers near the centerline. The result is an undisturbed flow of water to the propellers and greater efficiency. In sea trials, the ship achieved a top speed of 31.5 knots. On our trip north from Belize, we came within a knot of the maximum, with the aid of a slight current.

Olympia Voyager delivers a slightly jumpy or "stiff" ride, with relatively little roll but a lot of sharp little movements and vibration at certain speeds. Some of the buzzing was smoothed out a bit with the *Olympia Explorer,* which joined the fleet in mid-2002, nearly a year behind schedule.

The interior design is modern but understated. A small casino is out of the flow of traffic, allowing guests to come inside to gamble or happily ignore its presence. The two main stairwells are adorned with a pair of Greek odes to the joys of travel.

We found the mostly Greek officers and dining room crew and the mostly Eastern European cabin attendants to be among the friendliest and most accommodating we have sailed with. The waiters picked up on my daughter's newfound love of kalamata olives and delivered a bowlful anywhere she sat down for dinner; each night our Ukrainian cabin attendant, not much older than she, earnestly wished her "a sweet dream."

The attractive and uncrowded Selene (Greek goddess of the moon) dining room offered international fare and Greek specialties. The Horizon Garden Lounge presented buffets throughout the day, with indoor seating as well as tables on three of the four outdoor lido decks at the stern. The service was exemplary, although the food itself was merely good, not great. The ship did not include an Internet cafe, although we were told one was due to be added soon.

The small Alexander the Great lounge is home to lectures by, among others, visiting professors discussing Mayan culture and chefs from shoreside restaurants delivering cooking demonstrations, as well as nightly entertainment. The singers and dancers on our cruise were an unusual mix of nationalities, including Latvians, Moldavians, Romanians, and Russians. (Sammi, our talented cruise director, told us there was not a single common language among them; she communicated in pidgin Italian with one singer who started a chain of instructions from one to another, like an international game of "telephone.")

Someone somewhere decided that it would be appropriate to present several shows that saluted Texas and the United States, and so we were entertained by Eastern European farm girls in cowboy hats and tasseled hot pants phonetically singing "Cotton-Eyed Joe" and "Yellow Rose of Texas." It was a show that would have made Mel Brooks proud.

Many guests preferred more native presentations, including Greek singing and dancing and solo performances on pan pipes and a cembalo. One evening, a small group of Greek waiters and cabin attendants performed a set of native dances.

One area in which Royal Olympia Cruises excels is its shore excursion offerings. Passengers are offered a wide range of trips in each port, including visits to Mayan sites, snorkeling and scuba diving, golf, and shopping. In Playa del Carmen, trips visited the dramatic ruins of Tulum, an ancient maritime city of the Mayans that sits on a cliff overlooking the Caribbean Sea. Another trip went to the Coba ruins, a lesser known and not fully excavated Mayan site that's home to more than 3,500 sacred structures set among four lakes. A shopping expedition went to Cancun; passengers could also travel on their own by ferry to Cozumel. We chose to shop in the silver markets of Playa; after lunch on the ship we returned to enjoy the white sand beach just steps away from the heart of town.

From the industrial dock at Puerto Cortes, Honduras, we drove by van through the city of San Pedro Sula toward the capital of Tegucigalpa. Our goal was Lago de Yojoa, the largest natural lake in Honduras, at the base of interior mountains about 60 miles from the port. The lake, at an elevation of 2,063 feet, is home to nearly 400 species of birds and teems with largemouth bass and tilapia. Lording over the lake is Cerro Santa Barbara, the second highest peak in Honduras, at 8,000 feet above sea level.

A thousand years before the birth of Christ, the shores of the lake were inhabited by natives believed to be of the Lenca culture. Some of their descendants still live in western Honduras; although their language has disappeared, many of their pre-Columbian customs and beliefs survive. Los Naranjos is under exploration along the shore of the lake; it appears that several thousand persons once lived in a community there.

The lake is drained to the north by the Río Blanco, which powers a hydroelectric plant at Cañaveral and also spills into the Río Lindo, which leads to the 140-foot-high Pullhapanzak Falls. We descended 138 rough-hewn steps to a series of pools at the base of the falls, where some visitors dived from cliffs into the deep water. The sight was spectacular enough, but the once-in-a-lifetime view came after my daughter and I hired a local boy to guide us along a steep and narrow path on walls of the canyon that led to a cave behind the waterfall. There we looked up at the curl of water breaking over the top of the falls and felt the hurricane-like rush of wind and water.

Serious explorers could instead have taken a twelve-hour expedition to the Copán ruins, about three and a half hours by bus from Puerto Cortes to the other side of the coastal mountain range, at an elevation of 2,000 feet. Copán is considered the most artistically embellished Mayan site; its central acropolis includes pyramids, a ball court, temples, and decorative stelae. Some archaeologists believe that the sculptures of the Maya ruins of Copán were done by the Lencas, who lived in peace under the influence of the Maya during the height of Copán's importance, from about the fifth through the eighth century.

Tourists climb El Castillo at the Mayan city of Chichén Itzá in Mexico. *Photo by Corey Sandler*

The most unusual shore excursion and one of the most popular offerings of the ship was found in Belize. We took a van from Belize City along the Western Highway toward San Ignacio and into the jungle to the Jaguar Paw Resort, a trip of about ninety minutes. The small ecoresort, named after a renowned Mayan leader, spreads across 200 acres. It includes the mouths of three large caves that extend more than 7 miles, carrying the slow-moving Caves Branch River. We hiked into the jungle to the upper mouth of one cave and then took to individual truck inner tubes. Wearing miner's headlamps, we slowly drifted through more than a mile of the cave. It was like a "lazy river" ride at a water park, except that the cave was pitch dark and very real. A colony of bats bemusedly observed the floaters-by from above.

The cruise port of Progreso, Mexico, about twenty minutes from the historic city of Merida, is a new destination for ships in the Gulf of Mexico. Merida, established in 1542, was modeled after its namesake in Spain. Some of its earliest buildings and roads were constructed from debris from the Mayan city of T'ho, which was destroyed by Spanish conquistador Francisco de Montejo.

From Progreso, it is about ninety minutes by road to the fabled Mayan city of Chichén Itzá. (It is also possible to take a longer trip from Cancun or Playa del Carmen.) Our guide, Juan, came from a Mayan background and spoke with pride of the accomplishments and culture of his forebears. "The Yucatan is not the land of the mariachi and tequila," he told us. "Don't look for Pedro in a blanket under a tree. This is the land of the Maya." Satellite surveys have disclosed the presence of some 2,000 Mayan sites in Mexico; only about 450 have been explored and, of those, only a small number excavated.

Chichén Itzá was founded about A.D. 432, spreading over six square miles. At its heart is the Pyramid of Kukulcan, also known as El Castillo. We joined visitors hiking 180 feet up the 91 steep steps on one side of the pyramid (four sides times 91 steps plus the platform at the top equal 365 days, a calendar year). At the top was a fabulous view of the surrounding structures and the flat jungle; between the abandonment of the city about 1194 and its rediscovery in the mid-nineteenth century, the jungle had grown up around the buildings to obscure them. We descended—carefully and without benefit of guardrail or safety net—to the base. (Two of the four faces of the pyramid have been restored; preservationists have called on the Mexican government to end the practice of allowing visitors to climb the architectural treasure, and that ban may take effect in coming years.)

Nearby is the impressive ball court, the largest such athletic site found in Mexico. Archaeologists believe the Mayans played a game that was something of a cross between soccer and basketball, with royalty and commoners observing from the stone stadiums alongside and at each end. There is some confusion about some of the carvings found at the site, which seem to indicate that the *winners* of the game were killed in ritual sacrifice; some experts point out the obvious disincentive against victory this would present to athletes.

Docked alongside us in Progreso was one of the newest and most tricked-out cruise ships in service, *Carnival Pride,* an 84,000-ton Megaship with a two-story dining room, a huge theater, a dance club, several alternative restaurants, hundreds of balconies, and 2,112 passengers. She was able to stay just the morning, while our ship was tied up at the pier for more than twelve hours.

Captain Kritikos, who has been at sea for more than thirty-seven years, commands a bridge on the *Olympia Voyager* that is equipped with all the latest electronic devices, including a joystick maneuvering control. He prefers the tried-and-true ship's wheel, he said. He sniffed in the direction of the *Carnival Pride.* "These are not cruise ships," he said. "These are boxes."

The *Olympia Voyager,* Kritikos continued, "is for real travelers."

CARRYING CULTURE TO SEA: *VEENDAM* IN THE CARIBBEAN

Every modern cruise ship is globalization in action, a mini United Nations of guests, crew, cuisine, and culture. But few cruise lines are as conscious of their history and cultures as is Holland America Line.

We sailed on the *Veendam* from Fort Lauderdale on a basic weeklong eastern Caribbean cruise: Saint Thomas, San Juan, and Nassau. But we were surrounded by an often elegant, sometimes wondrously confusing, and always fascinating global stew of cultures on an exceptionally handsome ship. (*Veendam* is one of four nearly identical sisters in the fleet, along with *Maasdam, Ryndam,* and *Statendam.*)

We were aboard an Italian-built ship, registered in the Netherlands by the Holland America Line division of the American company Carnival Corporation. The ship's captain and principal officers were British, while the dining room staff and cabin attendants were mostly Indonesian. We were sailing in the Caribbean, which is itself a mix of native, American, British, Dutch, French, and Spanish cultures, and we were carrying with us a floating art museum with pieces from as far away as Egypt and China.

Holland America Line (HAL) helped bring the huddled masses to the New World, carrying nearly a million European emigrants in the late nineteenth and early twentieth centuries. The company was founded in 1873 as the Netherlands-America Steamship Company.

HAL celebrates some of its own history in the forward staircase with a set of paintings of the four company ships that have carried the *Veendam* name. The first was built as the *Baltic* for White Star Line. It entered service in 1871, was purchased by Holland America Line in 1888, and served until 1898. The 426-foot-long vessel, just 3,707 tons in capacity, carried 166 passengers in first class and 1,000 more in third class or steerage. The painting shows *Veendam* in New York's Upper Bay, off today's Liberty Island, at the start of a voyage to Rotterdam in summer 1891.

The second *Veendam* sailed from 1922 to 1953. *Veendam III* joined the fleet in 1972 and served until 1984; the ship was the reflagged liner *Argentina*, launched in 1958, which was the last major passenger liner built in the United States. *Argentina*'s sister ship *Brasil* sailed until 2002 as the *Universe Explorer*.

On today's modern *Veendam*, the entire ship is a floating art gallery, with hundreds of items small and large on walls and in display cases. Many of the pieces celebrate the connection of Holland to its former colonies and trading partners around the world.

Indonesian carvings, paintings, and fabrics adorn the walls of the piano bar. Within the Explorers Lounge on the upper promenade is a collection of feather masks and headdresses from the Tapirape, Kayabi, and Txukaramac tribes of Brazil. Nearby is an elegant mantel clock from mid-nineteenth-century France

Holland America's *Veendam* tied up at the dock in Nassau. *Photo by Corey Sandler*

and a set of pewter plates from late-eighteenth-century England.

In a showcase outside the handsome library are some ancient artifacts from Mexico and Central America. Among the oldest items on the ship is a statue of a sower, holding a planting stick and a seedbag, from the Jama-Coaque culture of Ecuador and dated from 500 B.C. Nearby is an earthenware dog from the Colima culture of western Mexico, about 100 B.C.; the dog, which has a hollow space within to hold corn wine, was meant as a companion for the dead in the afterlife.

Near the puzzle room is an interesting mix of Chinese and Dutch porcelain and delft items. A Chinese dinner service and serving bowls dating from the seventeenth and eighteenth centuries sits alongside earthenware and delft pottery from Holland of about the same time. Some of the Chinese items were commissioned by Dutch traders and imported into Europe.

A corner of the Half-Moon Room holds a display of *ushabiti,* small mummy-like statues from about 1085 to 935 B.C. The 3,000-year-old icons were supposed to perform farm work in the afterworld for the deceased.

The attractive two-level Rubens Lounge was used for nightly entertainment, including a magician, an "edgy" juggler, and an above-average corps of singers and dancers. Special events included a "Rockin' Rolldies Show" that engaged some of the guests in some very funny (intentional and otherwise) send-ups of golden oldies; the highlight was a rendition of Bobby Darin's "Splish Splash," featuring a septuagenarian man in a towel and snorkel mask and a dancing chorus of good-natured women who had made more than a few extra trips through the buffet line in their lives.

But for many of us, the entertainment highlight was the Indonesian Crew Show, presented by a group of waiters from the dining room as we sailed toward San Juan, Puerto Rico. Dressed in spectacular native costumes, they performed a version of the classical Balinese *Kecak Ramayana* dance that tells the sad story of King Dasaratha and the unhappy succession of his less favored son to the throne. The finale of the show was a presentation by the Angklung West Java Bamboo Orchestra.

Captain James Russell-Dunford, master of the vessel on our cruise, was born in southern England and went to sea as a cadet on cargo ships at age eighteen. In 1978 he joined Cunard as a second officer and worked his way through the ranks to become the youngest chief officer on the transatlantic liner *QE2*. In 1982 he was aboard ship when the liner was taken over by the Ministry of Defence to transport troops during the Falklands War between Great Britain and Argentina. When not aboard ship, the captain, who joined HAL in 1998, lives in a small fishing village in Cornwall, England. On our cruise he was joined by his wife, Lynne, who served as social hostess for special events.

Holland America offers most of the amenities of the Megaships, although it does so with a nicely cultured restraint. You can play bingo or go to the casino or bid on art at an auction, but the ship's loudspeakers don't assault your senses with announcements.

The small movie theater is in regular use; we stocked up on fresh popcorn from the stand outside, augmented by cappuccino, espresso, and dessert—the sort of free snack bar every landside cinema ought to offer. The ice-cream bar and pizzeria on the lido deck were open most of the day as well.

We made good use of the attractive Internet cafe onboard the ship; on our cruise, the operator was offering a package deal of unlimited service for seven days for $99, which is a relatively good deal for those of us who need to or want to remain in near-constant touch with the office, friends, family, and the rest of the world. I joined a group of Canadians in listening to the Olympic gold medal hockey game over the

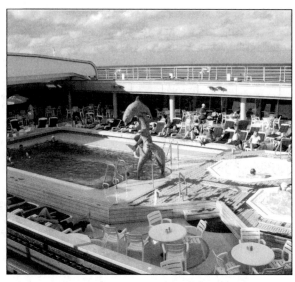

Holland America ships, such as the *Veendam,* have a rolling roof over the swimming pool that allows for year-round and all-weather use. *Photo by Corey Sandler*

Internet as we sailed near the Bahamas, yet another wondrous dish of global stew.

Another interesting package deal on our sailing was unlimited laundry service for $45 per cabin, or unlimited clothes pressing for $30.

As on any other cruise ship, much of the focus of the day revolves around three—or four or five—meals. We were not disappointed; the quality and presentation of food were excellent, several notches above the middle of the road. Each night's menu included an unusually expansive choice, typically offering five appetizers, several soups, and five entrees. Some sample entrees: sesame potato-crusted coho fillet; seared tuna steak with charmoula vinaigrette; grilled venison rack chop; pan-seared five-spiced duck breast; and sautéed garlic prawns. One dinner featured Dutch specialties, including *Zeevruchten Zeeland* (bay shrimp, scallops, mussels, and mushrooms in lobster sauce), and *Hutspot met klapstuk* (boiled brisket of beef over mashed potatoes).

There was also a separate vegetarian menu chosen by one of our tablemates; it included some dishes that deserved a spot on the menu alongside the thick steaks, fresh fish, and other specialties.

After I made a special request that our waiter visit the crew's galley below deck, my meals were accompanied by a bowl of Indonesian *sambal,* a fiery-hot chili sauce.

The exceptional pastry chef prepared a changing rotation of desserts and baked goods. Two of our tablemates, friends of the executive chef, reached an anniversary on our cruise: They were feted with a huge marzipan dessert that celebrated a few notable personal events.

In between stage shows, meals, dessert, and more dessert, we sailed happily through the Caribbean—although our visit to Holland America's private beach resort, Half Moon Cay, was canceled because of high winds and waves. We strolled the streets of San Juan and visited El Morro Castle. In Saint Thomas we rented a car and circled the mountainous island on our own, stopping for a swim at famed Magens Bay. We've explored Nassau enough times to know by heart its limited charm, but our daughter enjoyed bargaining for trinkets at the Straw Market.

On this cruise, the excitement and entertainment came from the ship and not the destinations. Happily, the *Veendam* held up her part of the bargain as a comfortable and cultured place to hang our sandals.

CELEBRITY *MILLENNIUM*: HIGH-TECH ON THE HIGH SEAS

Celebrity Cruises' *Millennium,* a technologically advanced beauty, was the first passenger ship to be powered by gas turbine engines. She also is equipped with state-of-the-art propulsion pods, advanced Internet connections aboard, Pay-Per-View movies in the cabins, and a show stage with a control panel that would be at home on the space shuttle.

All of this would mean nothing were it not for the fact that *Millennium* is a stunner inside and out. The 965-foot-long, 105-foot-wide, 91,000-ton cruise ship is the first of at least four vessels in Celebrity's Millennium class. *Infinity* joined the fleet in 2001; *Summit* and *Constellation* were added in 2002.

The dark blue hull of the ship is topped with a white superstructure and a large blue funnel about two-thirds of the way to the ship's stern. Two smaller funnels, one near the stern and another near the bow, are for decoration only. The main funnel carries the large *X* of Celebrity's fleet, with a horizontal bar like the scarf of Hermes, messenger of the gods. (The *X* is a Greek chi, as in Chandris, founders of the line.)

Millennium boasts the first glass-enclosed panoramic elevators on a cruise ship; the lifts near the midships atrium offer unusual views of the sea as they traverse the decks. Eighty percent of the 975 staterooms have ocean views, and there are 578 cabins with private verandas. An interactive television network aboard the ship allows passengers to order room service, shore excursions, and Pay-Per-View movies.

The ship features a pair of handsome two-story libraries. "Words" offers one level of English-language books and a second in other languages. "Notes" is a music library offering 1,500 selections of music accessible from listening stations.

Online@CelebrityCruises, one of the first Internet cafes designed with the ship, has eighteen LCD screen stations and an ocean view. The Emporium, the largest retail shopping area on any current ships, includes name-brand shops such as DKNY, Versace, H. Stern, La Perla, Swarovski, and Fossil.

On our cruise we were entertained in the Celebrity Theater by high-energy

The high-tech Celebrity *Millennium* in the harbor at Saint Thomas. *Photo by Corey Sandler*

stage shows, including *Spectacle of Broadway* with singer and actor Joel Grey as video host, and an interactive game show, *Dream Ticket,* in which members of the audience entered their answers by remote control from their seats to win the right to come up on stage and compete for prizes.

AquaSpa is among the largest and most luxurious floating spas. You'll find your basic thermal suite with a tropical shower, laconium grotto steam room, and fog shower. If that's not exotic enough, you can lose yourself in the ancient oriental ceremony of rasul, which demands the application of purifying muds followed by an herbal steam bath. There's also a thalassotherapy pool under a glass dome in a garden setting.

One of Celebrity's claims to fame is the quality of dining, and *Millennium* does not disappoint its many frequent eaters. Renowned chef Michel Roux oversees the fleet's dining rooms and specialty restaurants.

The Metropolitan Restaurant is lit from above by a blue faux skylight. At the back of the room a full-window wall looks out at the sea to the stern of the ship; by night, projectors can paint maritime scenes on a curtain at the stern. The upper level of the two-story dining room is a horseshoe-shaped balcony that overlooks the main floor. Galleys for the restaurant are one deck below; hidden escalators are used by servers.

The culinary star of the ship is the Olympic Restaurant, an elegant and oh-so-fancy eatery that includes some of the design elements and actual paneling from the famed SS *Olympic,* sister ship of the *Titanic.*

Cova Cafe Milano, an outpost of the famed cafe near the La Scala Opera

House in Milan, offers coffees and pastries from an a la carte menu. Michael's Club, an English Georgian-style cigar lounge, is another premium room.

At the forward end of the Sunrise Deck is Cosmos, an observation lounge with a glass wall that replicates the sweeping view from the navigational bridge below. By night Cosmos becomes a cocktail lounge and later a disco. At the top of one of the stairwells on this deck is the Conservatory, a small greenhouse at sea that's filled with arranged plants, trees, and flowers.

We sailed from Fort Lauderdale to San Juan, Saint Thomas, Nassau, and Catalina Island, which is a private beach resort off the coast of the Dominican Republic. In winter, *Millennium* sails eastern Caribbean itineraries like ours, alternating with western Caribbean journeys to Key West, Calica and Cozumel in Mexico, and George Town, Grand Cayman.

■ THE GEE-WHIZ FACTOR

At her christening in Southampton, England, *Millennium*'s name was preceded by a new prefix, GTS, for gas turbine ship. Nearly every other modern cruise ship uses diesel engines as the source of power, carrying the label MS for motor ship. The diesels spin generators that produce electrical power for motors to turn the propellers. A few older ships directly drive the propeller shafts from diesel engines, and a handful of venerable antiques use steam turbines, classified as SS (steamship) vessels.

The state-of-the-art *Millennium* ship produces much less pollution from the combustion of its engines and its associated lubrication system. Gas turbines are adaptations of jet engines. Although they may be slightly less efficient than equivalent diesel engines, they produce only a small fraction of the noxious emissions of a diesel, and they are also much simpler to maintain. Diesels use oil for lubrication, and the material breaks down into sludge and waste over time.

The gas turbines do without the need for bulky and environmentally hazardous oil storage and oil separation systems. And because the turbines are much smaller than diesels and do not require oil storage tanks, the space devoted to mechanical systems is reduced. What that means to a cruise line is more space for staterooms or public rooms.

The smaller gas turbines produce power by rotation rather than up-and-down reciprocation, which means they produce less vibration. Diesel engines emit low-

An engine room video display monitors the starboard engine pod on the Celebrity *Millennium*. *Photo by Corey Sandler* frequency noise that is difficult to muffle, while the jet engine/gas turbines produce noise in a much higher frequency range that is easier for engineers to quiet.

The two turbines spin generators rated at fifty megawatts; an additional nine megawatts are produced by a low-pressure steam turbine spun by the exhaust gases from the turbines. *Millennium* uses a pair of General Electric LM2500+ gas turbine engines, manufactured in Cincinnati. They were sent by freighter to the Chantiers de l'Atlantique shipyard in Saint-Nazaire, France, to be installed in the hull under construction; this marked the first time in more than forty years that engines for a new cruise ship have been built in the United States.

When the shipyard completed *Millennium* in 2000, it was the largest vessel ever built there, surpassing the legendary *Normandie,* which launched in 1935 and weighed in at 82,799 tons.

The next design improvement for *Millennium* addressed the propulsion mechanism. The standard design for ships built in the past few decades placed large electric motors in chambers toward the back end of the ship; they spun propellers attached to shafts at the stern. Also at the stern were one or two huge movable rudders that could change the angle of the bow as it moved through the water. Rudders have been used on ships for thousands of years; among their drawbacks are mechanical complexity and the fact that ships have greatly reduced steering when they are moving at low speed.

Millennium is among the first cruise ships to use propulsion pods, which are like huge outboard motors. Forward-facing propellers, 19 feet in diameter, are mounted in units that can swivel in any direction. The ship's generators feed power to the electric motors in the pods by cable; the motors are directly connected to the propellers.

In ordinary operation the propulsion pods pull the ship through the water like airplane propellers; to turn, the angle of the pods is changed. Because the pods can swivel and produce thrust in any direction, the massive ship has no need for rudders and can quickly change from forward to reverse without the need for the propellers to come to a complete stop and change direction. And because the pods can generate thrust to either side, there is no need for separate stern thrusters like those used on nearly every major ship. (*Millennium* still has electric bow thrusters to swing the front of the ship in port and in emergency situations.)

I visited the engine control room of the *Millennium* as we sailed between Saint Thomas and the Bahamas. The video display panel used by the engineers to control the machinery showed that one pod was facing straight ahead while the other was angled slightly; the ship's computer had directed the unusual configuration to deal with a crosscurrent.

All of this high-tech equipment practically guaranteed some teething pain for the new class of ships. *Millennium* had to be pulled from service twice in her first six months, once to slightly modify the shape of the hull underwater to deal with an unexpected vibration detected during her initial cruises in Europe, and once in February 2001 to repair a problem with one of the electric motors within the propulsion pod. Neither problem was a threat to the safety of the passengers.

■ THE OLYMPIC RESTAURANT

This most modern of cruise ships reaches back almost a century for some of its design. In 1909 the famed White Star Lines announced construction of three 45,000-ton ocean liners. The first was *Olympic,* huge for its time (about half the tonnage of today's *Millennium*). The ship was capable of carrying more than 2,400 passengers in three classes, including more than a thousand in cramped third class. The second ship in the series was the ill-fated *Titanic.*

One reason the huge ships of the time had relatively small public spaces and cabins was the need for huge mechanical spaces. *Olympic,* as originally built, had immense coal-fired boilers served by hundreds of stokers with shovels. She was later converted to oil burners.

Nevertheless, *Olympic* included the first indoor swimming pool at sea and a squash court, both located deep within the hull. The jewel of the ship was an alternative restaurant, an a la carte dining room for first-class passengers. The restaurant was paneled with elaborate hand-carved wood that was accented with gilded moldings and ornaments.

After *Titanic* sank in 1912, *Olympic* was withdrawn from service and renovated to improve its safety, with features including additional lifeboats and improvements to the ship's watertight compartments. The alternative dining room was expanded at that time as well.

The fabled *Olympic* came to the end of the line during the Depression, when she was cut up for scrap, but not before some of her finest appointments were set aside. In 1935 the paneling from the restaurant was sold at a pierside auction to a family who used the wood to decorate their own home in England. Celebrity purchased the paneling at a second auction in 1998.

Just as with the high-tech machinery on *Millennium,* the design of the Olympic Restaurant is merely a stage setting. The room seats just 134 guests, with a serving staff of ten chefs, ten servers, five sommeliers, and five maître d's. Reservations are necessary, and guests are charged a stiff $25 per person fee for gratuities.

The emphasis of the restaurant is placed on tableside finishing, with servers showing off their skills on appetizers, entrees, and desserts, including an elaborate Caesar salad, steak Diane, flambéed shrimp scampi, and crepes Suzette. Other attractively presented dishes included monkfish with sauce Nantua, saltimbocca alla Romana, and rack of lamb en croute.

On sister ship *Infinity,* the specialty restaurant is patterned after the decor of the famed liner *United States; Summit* salutes the French liner *Normandie.*

NORWEGIAN SKY: ON THE ROUTE OF THE GOLD RUSHERS

Here's the way to prepare for a cruise aboard the *Norwegian Sky* from Seattle into the Inside Passage of Alaska: Before you embark, make a stop at the Klondike Gold Rush Historic Park in downtown Seattle. Spend the time to absorb a bit of history about the years 1897 and 1898, when a hundred thousand prospectors set out on an almost impossibly difficult and unpleasant trek in search of gold.

The gold rushers were headed north, mostly to the new tent-and-shack towns of Skagway and Dyea in Alaska. From there they faced a 600-mile passage to the goldfields near Dawson in Canada's Yukon.

Alaska and the Yukon were almost completely wilderness made worse by severe winter weather and extremely difficult mountain passes. And then there was the "one ton" rule, enforced by Canada's Northwest Mounted Police: Every prospector had to carry with him a full year's provisions, which amounted to about a ton in weight.

At Dyea, the trail led to the shorter but extremely steep Chilkoot Trail, where prospectors had to carry their ton of supplies up the "Golden Stairs" carved in the ice; they had to make as many as thirty-five round-trips to the summit with their supplies. The longer, less steep White Pass Trail left from Skagway and allowed packhorses. Both trails led about 40 miles into the interior; from there the gold rushers had to build their own rafts and boats for a 550-mile trip on lakes and rivers.

Consider this: Of about 100,000 who sailed out of ports in the Pacific Northwest, only about 30,000 actually reached the goldfields in the Yukon. Of those, only about half actually did some prospecting, and only 4,000 or so found some gold. A few hundred became rich, and just a handful managed to hold on to their wealth and bring it back to the United States.

Now you've got a bit of perspective before you are shown to your luxurious stateroom, where you'll effortlessly float your way into Alaska.

The *Norwegian Sky* at anchor in Juneau, Alaska, her masts reaching the low-lying fog.
Photo by Corey Sandler

■ ONBOARD THE *SKY*

We thought about the Chilkoot Trail and the White Pass as we sat on our private veranda, eating a room service breakfast and watching the green hills and the sky blue glaciers as we cruised north.

The *Norwegian Sky* is a very comfortable ship, operated by one of the more accommodating mass market cruise lines. I've sailed with Norwegian Cruise Lines (NCL) in Hawaii and the South Pacific, the Caribbean, and from Seattle to Alaska, and I have hardly a complaint about the ships, cabins, food, or staff. NCL delivers a uniformly good product; some other cruise lines might have flashier ships or fancier dining rooms or more spectacular cabins, but few put it all together like NCL does.

Norwegian Sky joined the fleet in summer 1999. In 1997 NCL acquired the unfinished hull of what was to be the *CostaOlympia* before a German shipyard went bankrupt; the hull was towed to another shipyard and recast as the *Norwegian Sky,* allowing completion within a speedy twenty months.

After her first full season in the Caribbean, she moved to Seattle's new cruise terminal for summer cruises to Alaska. In fall she reverses the schedule, heading down the coast of California to the Panama Canal and back to Florida and the islands.

Most of the cabins are on Decks 8, 9, and 10, well above the lifeboats on Deck 7; a bit more than 200 other cabins are spread among the lower decks. About a quarter of the ship's 1,000 staterooms have a private teak-floored balcony, and four owners' suites also have private outdoor hot tubs. Up top are three pools, including one with a waterfall. The focus of the interior is a pair of glass-domed atria. Aft, there's Neptune's Court, with a grand stair tower; midships is The Atrium, eight decks high with four panoramic lifts.

The main knock on the *Norwegian Sky* is the fact that the attractive staterooms are a bit on the small side; a sister ship, the *Norwegian Sun,* delivers slightly larger accommodations.

■ CRUISING THE INSIDE PASSAGE

Our cruise departed Seattle's new cruise terminal on a glorious late-summer Sunday. The first day was spent "at sea"—more properly, cruising the Inside Passage to the east of Canada's Vancouver Island and up toward the panhandle of lower Alaska.

Alaska has a longer coastline than the combined lower forty-eight states. Unlike cruises in the Caribbean and Europe, we could see land on one or both sides of the ship at all times. In some places, the channel between the islands and the mainland was only a few hundred feet wide; the 853-foot-long, 106-foot-wide *Norwegian Sky* eased its way through like a recumbent skyscraper with a propeller.

Except for a handful of small towns and cities, you won't see many signs of civilization. You'll see many more whales, eagles, and the occasional bear or mountain goat than you will humans. The huge state of Alaska (615,230 square miles) has the lowest population density of any state, just 1.1 residents per square mile. The cruise industry, however, has been a steadily growing influence in the state. Juneau, the state capital and a regular port of call, received about 718,633 cruise-borne visitors in 2002, a number about equal to the state's entire population.

On Tuesday we made a slow passage up Tracy Arm to the face of Sawyer Glacier, which is among the most spectacular sights on the planet, especially when you arrive in luxury on a cruise ship. (Some of the *Norwegian Sky*'s cruises visit Glacier Bay instead; cruise ships are allotted only a limited number of slots to enter the narrow and environmentally fragile glacial bays.)

The steep-walled watery canyon is approximately 50 miles south of Juneau, branching eastward off Stephens Passage. The *Norwegian Sky* steamed slowly through the fog at the entrance to the deep fjord, then followed the twists and turns of the canyon for nearly two hours, steering around some large ice floes along the way. Finally the ship came to the end of the passageway and we were face to face with an electric-blue wall of ice.

The color of a glacier is almost always a surprise to visitors. The ice at the face has been compressed, and most of the air has been pressed out. What remains is highly crystallized; as light strikes the surface, all colors of the spectrum are absorbed except blue, which is reflected back.

The next day we arrived in Skagway, the principal objective of the gold rushers. There we changed modes of transportation for a few hours, traveling back in time on the incredible White Pass & Yukon Railroad (WP&YR).

The White Pass route was discovered in the early 1890s—before the Gold Rush—by a survey team mapping the 141st meridian, the boundary between the United States and Canada. The extremely difficult Chilkoot Pass had already been found, but it was much too rugged for pack animals or vehicles. The longer White Pass route was a series of steep climbs and perilous switchbacks that finally leveled out at Lake Bennett near the headwaters of the Yukon. (The pass, by the way, was named not for the glaciers and snow, but instead for the Canadian Minister of the Interior at the time, Sir Thomas White.)

When the Gold Rush began in 1897, tens of thousands of prospectors came to the panhandle to cross over to the Yukon. Those who arrived in Dyea hand-carried their ton of supplies up the icy steps at the face of the Chilkoot Pass; eventually a primitive cable tramway was used to carry supplies to the top of the pass. At Skagway many gold rushers attempted to climb the White Pass using pack animals—horses, mules, and dogs. Thousands of the animals died along the way, and many of their skeletons can still be seen at Dead Horse Gulch partway along the trail.

In 1897 a former construction engineer on the Northern Pacific Railroad attempted to construct an improved toll road up the canyon. George Brackett's road eventually extended 12 miles before he ran out of money. The next year, though, a group of British financiers and a Canadian railway contractor met in the bar of a Skagway hotel, and by May 1898 work was under way on a narrow-gauge railroad.

Work on the northernmost railroad in the Western Hemisphere was extremely difficult. The first stage of the track was a climb from sea level in Skagway to 2,865 feet at the summit, with grades as steep as 3.9 percent. Workers had to hang from

A White Pass & Yukon Railroad train climbs White Pass along the route of the gold rushers. *Photo by Corey Sandler*

ropes to blast and hack their way through granite walls. At mile 16, Tunnel Mountain, crews had to cut through the side of a 1,000-foot-high cliff.

Heavy snow and temperatures as low as 60 degrees below zero hampered the work. Many workers were killed or injured; others quit with each new rumor of a gold strike. On February 20, 1899, in the dead of winter, crews reached the summit of White Pass; by July 6 they reached Lake Bennett. At the same time, another crew worked south from Whitehorse in the Yukon. The two crews met, and the road was completed on July 29, 1900, at Carcross.

Alas, the completion of the railroad came at nearly the exact moment the Gold Rush went bust. Instead of carrying prospectors over the White Pass from Skagway, the railroad found business carrying copper, silver, and lead ore from large corporate mines in the Yukon. The WP&YR expanded to include stern-wheeler freighters that carried ore south to processing plants. During World War II the railroad helped supply the U.S. Army as it built the Alaska Highway as part of the defense of the West Coast. Steam engines were still in use until 1954.

In 1982 market prices for metals plummeted, and the major mines in the Yukon shut down. The WP&YR was forced to close. But in 1988 the historic railroad benefited from a new gold rush: tourism by cruise ship. Today the tracks of the railroad extend down onto the piers where the *Norwegian Sky* and other ships tie up for the day.

The three-hour trip from Skagway up to the summit is quite simply one of the most extraordinary journeys in the world. Diesel engines pull vintage passenger cars up the grade to the international border at the Canadian Yukon and then return. The views at every turn are spectacular, and guides explain the history of each mile.

Every cruise ship that visits Skagway sells shore excursions that include the WP&YR. You can also book your own tickets directly from the railroad; be sure to take a trip that returns you to the pier in time to reboard your ship. For information call (800) 343–7373 or visit www.whitepassrailroad.com.

From Skagway we progressed to Juneau. One of the highlights here is the small but rich Alaska State Museum. Among its treasures are the remains of a prehistoric mammoth found at Tolovana; the tusks are 11 feet long with a diameter of 7 inches at the base. You'll also find exhibits on the Tlingit and Athabascan Indians. One of the most poignant exhibits is a pom-pom dipped in oil that was used in the cleanup of the spill from the *Exxon Valdez* in March 1989.

The museum dates from 1900, when it was originally in Sitka, the capital of Alaska at the time. Some of the exhibits about Alaska include the returned showcases from the Louisiana Purchase Centennial Exposition in Saint Louis in 1904 and the 1905 Lewis and Clark Centennial Exposition in Portland.

After a day cruising back south, we arrived in Vancouver, British Columbia, one of the prettiest and most vibrant big cities in the world. Vancouver is heavily influenced by its trade with the Pacific Rim, which is evident in its lively Chinatown and international shopping district.

■ FREESTYLING

Our trip was among the first after NCL began converting its ships to what it calls "freestyle" cruising. The new regime is most notable for what is missing: No longer are guests given a particular time to eat breakfast, lunch, or dinner: You won't be assigned to share your dining with six strangers, and you can leave your formal gowns and tuxedos at home.

The concept is to treat the dining rooms as though they are restaurants. You can show up any time during operating hours and request any available table. Of course, just as on shore, if you choose to arrive at, say, 7:00 P.M. for dinner, you might not get the romantic table for two by the window, or you might have to wait a while for it to open.

We found that we could grab that private "deuce" easily if we showed up early in the evening, which suited us just fine. We could also choose to eat in one of three alternative restaurants instead of the main dining room; the *Norwegian Sky* has since added a fourth specialty restaurant.

One of the interesting things about the arrival of freestyle is the effect it has on the ebb and flow of the ship. There is no longer a crush of bodies heading for dinner at 6:30 and 8:30 P.M., and no longer are there dead times on the ship when half the passengers are chowing and the other half are at the stage show. Lounges and public rooms are in use almost all the time. On the *Norwegian Sky*, the new regime required the addition of about 150 dining room and lounge crew to clear tables and prepare food throughout the day instead of just for two shifts.

The shipboard dress code was also altered at both ends of the scale; the new style is called "resort casual" and means that just about anything except shorts and T-shirts is acceptable. One night of our seven-night cruise was designated as a formal night in the main restaurant, requiring gowns or cocktail dresses for the women and tuxedos or suits for the men; if that didn't agree with your personal dress code, you could dine at one of the alternative eateries.

One other element of freestyle that we liked: the end of the awkward final-night ritual of the passing of the gratuity envelopes to waiters, busboys, and maître d's. Instead, suggested gratuities are billed to onboard accounts and automatically distributed to staff. Guests can choose to adjust the amount at the purser's desk or make additional personal gifts.

■ SHIPBOARD LIFE

The crew on an NCL ship is almost without exception pleasant and helpful, a notch above many other cruise lines. Food is very good to excellent in the two main dining rooms, the Four Seasons and the Seven Seas.

On the Sports Deck is Le Bistro, the most formal of the alternative restaurants; the menu features French Mediterranean fare. Ciao Chow on the pool deck is a casual Italian and Chinese eatery (ciao, chow—get it?) where you can mix and match pizza and pot stickers. The Garden Cafe, also on the pool deck, is used for breakfast and lunch buffets and as a casual alternative dinner spot with buffet and chef stations.

In early 2001 NCL converted the Horizon Restaurant, formerly a side room between the two main dining rooms, into Trattoria, an upscale Italian specialty restaurant. Menu items include mushroom ravioli in roast onion broth, herbs and root vegetables, and zabaglione with fresh fruits. As with Le Bistro and Ciao Chow, reservations are necessary, and there is a $10 per person service charge.

We especially enjoyed the international specialties offered at lunch in Ciao Chow (udon soup, sushi, Indian fare, and outstanding pizza) and at the bar in the observation lounge before dinner (Indonesian and Asian hors d'oeuvres).

SEA CLOUD: A CLASSIC AT SEA

I've always wanted my own sailing yacht. Until my ship comes in, I'll make do with the memories of a week of luxury aboard the *Sea Cloud* in the Caribbean.

The largest private sailing yacht ever built, *Sea Cloud* now carries passengers and crew on cruises around the world. On our round-trip from Antigua, we sailed in the company of thirty-seven guests (a full load is sixty-nine guests) and sixty crew.

The seventy-year-old ship is exquisite above and below decks; it is a place of marble and teak and gold-plated fixtures. Some of the original staterooms are beyond compare on land or sea, and several of the original owners' cabins include fireplaces. The service is impeccable, and the food is superb. Oh, and the prices. . . .

The *Sea Cloud* at anchor off the little-visited Caribbean island of Carriacou. *Photo by Corey Sandler*

Rates for a week onboard *Sea Cloud* can be as much as $17,000 for a cabin for two. How can they justify a fare equal to a year's college tuition? In a word, overhead.

You can rent a huge suite on a luxury cruise liner, but you won't be sleeping on a classic vessel with a storied history, almost certainly the last of her kind. You won't be able to watch the exquisite ballet of twenty able-bodied seamen (and a few women) climbing the twenty-story masts to let loose the sails by hand. You won't sail into port and find guests onshore and aboard cruise ships lining up to take pictures of your vessel.

If you're lucky (and you can pay the price), you might have the key to Cabin 1, a seagoing palace complete with a fireplace and bathroom of Carrara marble, mahogany furniture, Louis Philippe chairs, and an antique French bed. But even the lesser cabins are rather grand, outfitted with marble and fine furniture.

The restaurant, created from the ship's original salon, is like a fine private club. And the food: If there were any complaints on our voyage, I didn't hear them. In any case, if you don't like the menu posted each afternoon, all you need do is leave word with the chef, and he'll fix almost anything you can request. Beer and fine wine are included. Lunch is often served beneath a canopy on the fantail.

There's no television, no movie theater, no stage show, no casino, and no pool. There are also no kids, no ship's photographer intruding on your privacy, no art auctions, and no rah-rah cruise staff. Guests sail along in a semiprivate fraternity of privilege.

We were treated to a slide show of Tall Ships from the personal collection of the captain, a lecture about the history of the ship from the accommodating but most discreet cruise director, and a private performance by a twenty-piece steel band while we enjoyed a nighttime barbecue off Grenada. But our primary entertainment was the ship herself, a most elegant way to travel.

■ A CLASSIC SHIP

Sea Cloud stretches a bit more than a football field (360 feet) from stern to the end of the bowsprit, a little less than half the length of a typical cruise ship. About half the length of the ship is accessible to guests; the rest is given over to crew work areas. There are twelve of the original cabins on the main deck and fourteen more on the promenade deck. When the ship was refurbished for use as a passenger ship, eight simpler but still elegant cabins were added to the upper captain's deck.

Sea Cloud is classified as a bark or barkentine, and its sails are mostly near-square or rectangular. In the right conditions, the crew can hoist, by hand and winch, thirty sails from her four masts, about 32,000 square feet of canvas. The crew has to unravel a maze of ropes and operate a shipyard's worth of pulleys; guests can sit and watch, following along on a rigging chart.

At the very front of the ship is the bowsprit, extending nearly horizontally out over the water; here the captain can order an inner, outer, and flying jib. The first vertical mast is the foremast; the uppermost of five large sails here is the fore royal, followed by the fore topgallant. The main mast is the tallest of the uprights and holds six large sails, from the skysail (the origin of the term skyscraper) to the main royal and down to the mainsail. The third mast is the mizzenmast, which holds aloft four nearly rectangular sails plus the triangular mizzen course or crossjack. Near the stern is the spanker topmast, with two sails that together form a triangle. By night the sails are lit from below, like a ghostly galleon.

Even with all her masts and canvas, *Sea Cloud* cannot sail very close into the wind like a modern sailboat; the wind has to be behind the sails or no more than 90 degrees across the direction of forward motion. When the wind does not cooperate, the ship's four diesel engines can move her through the water at a respectable 12 knots.

The ship is very stable in most conditions, and under

Cabin 1, an original stateroom on the *Sea Cloud*. *Photo by Corey Sandler* sail the ship does not roll much because of the pressure of the sails against the ship. The sails do keep the ship at a near-constant heel of a few degrees; sometimes you might wonder if your downwind leg will become shorter over time. Sleeping under sail is also a bit unusual; rolling over against the direction of the heel can take a bit of extra effort.

Sea Cloud was built in 1931 for cereal food heiress Marjorie Merriweather Post by her husband, Wall Street broker Edward F. Hutton. Post, famous for her parties and social events, turned the ship into a gathering place for royalty, heads of state, and society hobnobbers. The ship was built during the Depression; the Post cereal empire was privately owned and not much affected by the stock market crash. *Sea Cloud* was constructed, at a cost of just over $1 million, by the Krupp shipyard in Germany, later to become the builder of much of the Nazi fleet. From the deck down, the steel-hulled *Sea Cloud* is designed almost as though she were a submarine, with ten hermetically sealed watertight compartments.

Marjorie Post and E. F. Hutton lived aboard for nearly four years, sailing in the Caribbean and Europe. When they divorced in 1935, Marjorie took the ship as part of the settlement, renaming her *Hussar V.* In the prewar years, the ship served as a floating diplomatic residence in the Soviet Union; during that time Marjorie Post bought millions of dollars worth of Russian art, including Fabergé eggs. Many of the eggs are now on display at the Hillwood Museum in Washington, one of her homes.

During World War II, the ship was leased to the U.S. Coast Guard for a nominal $1.00 per year. Her rigging was stripped down and she was equipped with guns, cannons, and depth charge launchers. Sailing as the *IX-99*, her primary assignment was as a weather observation ship (during the D-Day invasion in June 1944, she was stationed off the coast of Normandy to broadcast weather reports). She was, though, involved in several submarine spottings.

After the war the ship came into the hands of Dominican dictator Rafael Trujillo and was renamed *Angelita*. Son Rafael Trujillo Jr. took the ship to Los Angeles as a party boat while he was in school from 1954 to 1958; his crew of fifty-three included a nine-piece mambo band. During that time the original Krupp engines were replaced with motors from Dominican Republic gunboats.

In 1961 Trujillo Sr. was assassinated; his son took over for four months, just enough time to gather much of the national treasure and load it, along with the body of his father, aboard *Angelita* and attempt to flee to Cannes in France. The ship was seized and much of the treasure returned. Trujillo Jr. went into exile, a wealthy socialite. He died in 1969 from injuries suffered in an automobile accident.

The ship was taken to Panama, where she lay at anchor for eight years, rotting and filling with water while owners sought a new buyer. In 1975 Hugh Hefner was said to have offered the asking price of $5 million to buy the ship for use as a floating Playboy club, but the offer was refused. Two years later, Ross Perot reportedly tried to buy the ship and give it to the U.S. Navy while he retained tax advantages and visitation rights, but the Navy decided it didn't need the ship.

The dining room belowdecks of the *Sea Cloud*. *Photo by Corey Sandler*

In 1978 a group of German businessmen and shipowners decided to resurrect *Sea Cloud*. They managed to bring the ship across the Atlantic to Germany, sailing her up the Elbe River; in 1979 she arrived in Kiel, where she had originally been built. Her steel hull was still in good condition, as were the original owners' cabins; much of the remainder of the ship had to be rebuilt. The original cabins have the same floor plan and are furnished with antiques, but not all are from the original ship. (Cabin 2 boasts a pair of Chippendale chairs valued at $15,000 each.)

In 1980 *Sea Cloud* returned to the seas but wasn't a success until she was used for an episode of the German equivalent of *The Love Boat* in 1988. The ship is often chartered for private groups or resold by various travel agencies and charter companies. At the busiest times of the year, you can expect to be asked to pay full rate. At other times, though, you could see discounts and special offers that reduce the fare by as much as 50 percent. Because of all of the wood paneling and furnishings aboard, *Sea Cloud* might have only a few more years at sea before she's no longer able to operate under exemptions from Safety of Life at Sea (SOLAS) regulations.

In 2001 the fleet doubled with the addition of *Sea Cloud II*, built in the style of her famous cousin. The new ship is slightly larger and includes some more modern features and amenities. She will follow a similar schedule, sailing in the Caribbean in winter and the Mediterranean in summer.

▇ SAILING IN STYLE

In port in Antigua, we were tied up alongside the superluxury cruise ship *Crystal Harmony*. Many of the 900 passengers onboard lined the rails as she left port at sunset; most were admiring the *Sea Cloud* instead of the bright orange sun descending into the Caribbean Sea.

Captain Richard Shannon, one of several masters of the vessel, was in charge; Shannon is among the world's most experienced Tall Ship skippers and is a former captain of the Coast Guard sailing vessel *Eagle.* On the *Sea Cloud* he commanded a United Nations of a crew: Swiss, Russian, and Ukrainian officers and mostly German and Filipino deckhands and stewards.

The passengers, too, were from around the world. They were mostly discreet, although there was a bit of subtle inquiry aimed at determining how the other guests could afford a voyage on this ship.

We left Antigua in a dead calm, and the second day was also an uncharacteristically gray and calm Caribbean morning. The crew hoisted the sails and we moved along slowly until the bridge received a distress call off the island of Dominica. The sails were dropped quickly, and we motored to the aid of a 30-foot motorboat taking on water. Arriving at the same time as a vessel from the local coast guard, we stood by ready to lend a hand. The owner was rescued, and then we watched as the motorboat dropped deeper and deeper into the water and then upended and sank.

Among the highlights of the cruise was a visit to the Îles des Saintes, a group of seven very French islands in a volcanic archipelago just south of Guadeloupe. The islands are a *Département d'Outre Mer* (an Overseas Department), and the inhabitants are French citizens.

We anchored off Terre de Haut and tendered into the small village of Bourg. From there we hiked to a hilltop to visit Fort Napoleon, which was built to protect French interests. At the fort, which offers views of Guadeloupe, Marie-Galante, and Dominica, you can take in exhibits that document the single moment of military history in the area: the Battle of the Saintes, which was fought between thirty-six British and thirty-three French ships on April 12, 1782. The French ships were on their way to join Spanish troops in an invasion of Jamaica; the British victory that day prevented the invasion and essentially ended French expansion in the Caribbean.

Another port of call was Carriacou, a modest outpost of Grenada. Ship's tenders delivered us to Sandy Island National Park, a tiny coral isle that's home to many varieties of fish.

In Bequia and Grenada we anchored near the *Club Med II,* an ultramodern cruise ship whose five skyscraping aluminum masts have computer-controlled sails reefed around them. The entire sailing rig can be put into place with the push of a button. Unlike on the *Sea Cloud,* though, the masts seemed out of place, like a mistake in the shipyard. One of the *Sea Cloud* guests asked one of our crew about *Club Med II*'s sailing abilities. "The sails don't slow her down much," he responded dismissively.

CROSSING THE POND ON HOLLAND AMERICA'S
MAASDAM

We decided to pop over to London to catch a musical in the West End. The trip east across the Atlantic began with a hectic trek through steamy Boston to a hellacious scene at Logan Airport: a blocklong line of passengers waiting to drag their bags to the check-in counter of Virgin Atlantic.

The 747 jumbo jet, crammed with more than 500 passengers, took off late, of course. We spent the night crammed into narrow seats in the economy section, sandwiched between a very large woman (with four bags of oddly configured stuff at her feet) and several caterwauling babies.

Tossing and turning in our seats, we desperately tried to snatch a few moments of sleep between interruptions: a meal served at 10:00 P.M. on tiny plastic dishes perched on the uncertain support of a tray table; a forgettable movie on a minuscule screen; and the sales pitches for useless trinkets from the onboard duty-free store.

The good news was that we were moving across the Atlantic at about 500 miles per hour. Mercifully, we landed at London's Gatwick Airport at the reasonable hour of 8:00 A.M., except that it was 3:00 A.M. to us and we had tossed and turned in our clothes all night.

After dragging our bags through customs, we squeezed onto a packed train from Gatwick to downtown London. It was two more hours before we were able to make it to our London hotel, where—miracle of miracles—we were able to check in and go to our room (although most of the others in line were told they would have to wait for the arrival of the cleaning staff). The room itself was typical for a European city: very small and relatively expensive, about $200 per night for a view of a back alley in Kensington.

We fortified ourselves with coffee, tea, chocolate, and other forms of caffeine to fight off the effects of the sleepless night and the sudden five-hour change in time zones. Exhausted and jittery, we managed to stay awake through *Miss Saigon* in the West End and stroll the streets of one of our favorite cities.

The bottom line: An overnight flight to Europe is a very efficient way to get from Point A to Point B. It is, in general, not all that pleasant in between.

■ COMING HOME

Two days later, we began our trip home. We floated westward, happily ensconced in an attractive stateroom—not huge, but larger than our room in London—with a picture window looking out on the ocean. We relaxed as we were waited on by a cabin attendant, room service, and the dining room staff.

As you may have guessed, we were not on a 747 this time. Instead, we crossed the Atlantic aboard the elegant *Maasdam* of the Holland America Line, on a weeklong trip at 20 knots that would deposit us back in Boston.

Our voyage was a repositioning cruise, a special trip to move a cruise ship from one part of the world to another. The *Maasdam* had traveled through Europe and the Baltic in the summer and was being dispatched to the East Coast of the United States for a series of trips through New England to the Maritime Provinces of Canada. Later in the fall, she would move south from Boston to Florida for winter cruises in the Caribbean.

Repositioning itineraries can offer some of the best bargains in cruising because of the extended periods at sea and unusual ports; however, they're not everyone's cup of tea. A transatlantic cruise is not one I would recommend for first-timers, and certainly not for someone who is apprehensive about the prospect of being cooped up on a ship for a week.

The ship departed from Harwich, about 70 miles east of London. Harwich (pronounced *HAR-itch*) is a busy commercial port on the English Channel and is home to cruise ships, freighters from around the world, and passenger and car ferries to the Hook of Holland and other destinations in Europe. The modern cruise terminal is about 50 yards from the train station, about an hour's ride from London's Liverpool Street Station.

For the middle five days of the trip we saw nothing but ocean—no ships, no planes, no shoreline. We carried our civilization with us, like moon explorers. However, no astronaut has ever lived in the lap of luxury as we did.

ELEGANCE AFLOAT

Holland America Line (HAL) is a notch above the middle of the market. It offers much of the refinement and a bit of the service of the luxury lines at a price closer to that of the economy brands. The company was purchased by Carnival Cruise Lines in 1989 but has maintained its own identity and class.

The *Maasdam* is an elegant ship, one of four nearly identical sister ships in the HAL fleet, including the *Veendam,* about which I wrote earlier in this chapter. It's a particularly workable design, with lots of attractive public space, including a stunning show room and handsome dining room. Although hardly a tiny ship, at 720 feet long and 55,451 tons, within it feels much larger.

As I've noted in the cruise diary about the *Veendam,* one of the hallmarks of Holland America is the onboard collection of art that's spread throughout the ships. At most every turn, you're greeted by paintings, sculptures, and antiques, most with a maritime link or a connection to great Dutch explorations. A large electronic map on the upper promenade charts the ship's progress and can be programmed to display famous maritime explorations, including those of Columbus, Captain Cook, and others.

One of the prettiest public rooms is Crows Nest, up high over the bow with views ahead, to port and starboard, and toward the stern over the Sports Deck.

On this cruise without any port calls, there was something going on almost everywhere at most times of the day. In fact, we found it hard to find a place that would remain private and quiet for more than a few hours before another activity or group began. Even the attractive library on the upper promenade deck, with a wall of windows behind the reading desks, was busy much of the day.

The *Maasdam* is among the few modern ships with a covered promenade that makes a complete circuit of the ship, four laps to the mile. Another nice touch, common to many of the Holland America ships, is a movable dome over the pool deck. In warm and dry weather, the dome is retracted to leave the pool area open to the sky but still protected from winds; in cool or wet weather, the dome remakes the deck into a large indoor pool and patio area. On our crossing of the Atlantic, we greatly appreciated both the covered promenade and the dome.

■ HOW WE ALMOST MISSED THE BOAT

If I ever needed a reminder of my own advice about confirming departure times (and ports) before the start of a cruise voyage, I received one with the *Maasdam*. The published departure time—printed right on our tickets—was 6:00 P.M. We decided to get to Harwich a few hours early to walk around the port city; we arrived near noon to find a sign announcing that the gangplank would be withdrawn at 1:30 P.M., and the ship would sail an hour later.

Passengers who had purchased transfers through Holland America to deliver them from the airport or London to the port had been notified on arrival. Those of us who made our own way to Harwich nearly missed the boat; we were among the last to climb aboard.

This is not insignificant on any cruise, but especially so on a transatlantic repositioning cruise like ours. If you miss a cruise ship sailing out of Miami, for example, you should be able to fly on ahead of the vessel to meet up with the rest of your itinerary in Nassau or wherever the ship is headed next. On our cruise, though, there was to be no intermediate port in the seven days between Harwich and Boston. And so, a reminder to you and me: Confirm your departure and arrival times a week before you travel, and if you are making your own way to the port, reconfirm a day before you begin your trip.

■ CROSSING THE POND

We pulled out of Harwich on a Sunday, entering the English Channel in the company of large freighters and fishing vessels. Monday morning we continued through the channel with the south of England to starboard and France to port. We sailed past Penzance, the Scilly Islands, and the distant green shores of Ireland. And then we were out in the Atlantic.

It would be the following Friday before we saw another sign of human life, which came in the form of a huge oil rig anchored in the cold waters a few hundred miles off the coast of Labrador. And it would be Saturday before we saw distant land.

The summer of 1999 was a particularly active season for hurricanes. As we left port on Sunday we were aware of the progress of Hurricanes Cindy and Dennis, both of which were churning off the East Coast of the United States. But our course on the Great Circle Route, an arc to the northwest to above the 50th parallel, was well north of the storms—or so we thought.

In this modern age of satellites, weather radar, and in-room CNN, it's all but impossible for a ship to be caught unawares by a storm. Two days into our weeklong journey, the captain—and most everyone else on the *Maasdam*—knew that Cindy had pulled away from the coast and was moving northward toward Iceland. In other words, it was due to cross our path.

On Wednesday, the master of the ship changed our course, heading due south off the Great Circle Route to drop below the storm. And so we did, but not without experiencing a few days of fierce weather in the North Atlantic: gale winds of up to 46 knots and seas to 27 feet. That said, we found the *Maasdam* to be extraordinarily stable in very rough seas; the modern stabilizers countered much of the rolling motion, leaving just a bit of end-to-end pitching. Up top, the water in the swimming pool was almost wild enough for a surfing competition; the crew finally had to drain the pool for safety. The mostly experienced passengers handled the weather pretty well, although we noted a few victims of seasickness, including our waiter in the dining room.

By Friday the storm was gone, and we proceeded down the coast of Labrador and Newfoundland, passing within 200 nautical miles of the location of the resting place of the *Titanic,* which is a particularly empty stretch of ocean, especially at night.

■ ENTERTAINMENT AFLOAT

The 800 or so guests (out of a possible capacity of about 1,200) represented a more sophisticated than usual group of travelers, aboard for the romance of it all and not for the ports of call.

The card rooms and libraries were packed for most of the trip. By night, the lounges were filled with an unusually diverse crew of entertainers, including a big band, two comedians, an instrumentalist, a pair of tap dancers forty years too late for the Borscht Belt, a troupe of dancers and singers, and the *Maasdam*'s capable house band.

A major attraction for some was the special presence of the Harry James Orchestra, a big-band troupe that carries on the name and arrangements of the famous bandleader; James died in 1983, but the band was continued by a former member of the group, Fred Radke. The orchestra performed a half dozen times on the trip.

Also onboard was comedian Marty Brill, a veteran performer and writer. He tailored his witty shows to the mellow crowd aboard the *Maasdam;* some will remember him for the sharper edge he displayed as a cohort of Lenny Bruce. In fact, Brill portrayed Bruce on Broadway in a one-man show.

The dance troupe put on enthusiastic and capable revues, right up the middle of the road. The dancing was pretty good, especially on the small (and sometimes pitching) stage. The singing was, well, enthusiastic; a Broadway medley was the best offering. Another night we saw an uninspired salute to great performers, most of whom were dead long before the young dancers first strapped on their shoes, plus soulless recountings of Frank Sinatra, the Supremes, Sammy Davis Jr., and Elvis Presley.

And then there was the food, which was somewhat mystifying: The presentation was very good, but the preparation was disappointing. In other words, the food looked great but tasted rather ordinary. It was a commentary we heard at most every turn at dinnertime.

We found the ship's photographers a bit too much in evidence at boarding, formal dinners, and many other shipboard activities. My wife and I are not at all keen in being interrupted at dinner by a member of the cruise director's staff made up as a pirate, or as a Dutch milkmaid, each accompanied by a cameraman. But they kept coming. If you're not comfortable shooing the photographer away, do remember that you don't have to buy any photos they take.

All in all, we greatly enjoyed the pure sailing experience of a transatlantic crossing on the *Maasdam*.

PACIFIC TO ATLANTIC IN HIGH STYLE: THE *RADISSON DIAMOND* THROUGH THE PANAMA CANAL

We made a slow and deliberate passage through the Panama Canal aboard the *Radisson Diamond*, a floating island of high-tech luxury passing through what was once one of the most inhospitable places on earth. We sat on the private veranda of our stateroom, sipping cool drinks and watching the sheer rock of the Gaillard Cut and the dense jungle go by. As we passed through the locks, the walls were just inches away from the railing of our balcony, and we were able to reach out and touch the concrete, bridging the old and new worlds with our fingers.

■ A SHIP LIKE NO OTHER

The *Radisson Diamond* is one of a kind, the largest multihull cruise ship afloat; there are a handful of small catamaran ferries and cruise ships, but no others in her class of size or luxury. She has a capacity of 20,295 tons but carries no more than 320 passengers; other ships of her size carry as many as 800 guests.

You can think of the *Radisson Diamond* as a luxury hotel mounted atop a pair of submarines. Unlike high-speed catamarans that have more than one hull but very shallow drafts, the unusual *Radisson Diamond* floats on "tubes" that extend about 23 feet below the surface of the water; each contains a separate engine room.

The ship was intended as a great breakthrough in design, and on some counts it has been a success. The two hulls and their deep draft give the ship somewhat more stability than other cruise ships. The *Radisson Diamond* also presents an unusual profile and a startling head-on appearance: There's a huge open tunnel down the center of the ship. She attracts attention on the high seas and in every port. There are also some spectacular interior spaces, including a two-story lounge that has a wall of windows at the bow (the appropriately named Windows Lounge) and an open observation deck at the top that hangs over the bridge.

The ship is made up of three floors of cabins (all with outside views, and two levels with private verandas) plus an elegant dining room, an intimate lounge, and a pool deck. The design puts most of the public rooms and the sparkling atrium down the central spine of the ship, with cabins to the outside. All of this sits atop a tunnel approximately 60 feet wide and 30 feet tall that runs more than 400 feet down the full length of the ship.

The ship is relatively short, at 420 feet, but is a full 103 feet wide, a bargelike shape that just barely squeezes through the Panama Canal. Her deep draft means she must anchor offshore in many ports, sometimes a bit farther out than larger, more conventional craft.

The ship includes four stabilizers, one each at the bow and stern of each tube. Unlike every other cruise ship afloat, the stabilizers move inward from the tubes, into the tunnel between them. You can feel the ship start to roll and then correct itself in the other direction. The short swings can take a few hours to get used to, but after a while the voyage will likely be a bit more comfortable for travelers who are concerned about seasickness. The design works well at top speed but not so well at slower speeds.

The design, however, proved to be a not particularly efficient one, at least in terms of fuel usage and speed. The underwater body and decidedly nonaerodynamic shape of the front of the ship (it's hard to call it a "bow" since it is more like a ski slope than a classic narrow cake wedge) result in a top cruising speed of just 14 knots and a monumental fuel bill, as much as twice that of a more conventionally shaped vessel. The contour of the tubes results in a short, weak side wake, a wall of water the *Radisson Diamond* must plow through. And the squat design of the ship makes it somewhat susceptible to twisting in winds or seas that move across her amidships.

A single control room on Deck 6 oversees the operation of two separate engine rooms in the underwater pontoons of the ship. Down in the submarine tubes are four engines, two on each side; engineers must scurry down five flights of stairs to one or the other tube. Up and over is a trip of ten flights; there is no connection between the pontoons below the waterline.

One of the sustaining memories of our trip came when the tender boat returning us from a visit to shore made a transit down the length of the tunnel between the hulls. The white walls of the pontoons and the "roof" of the tunnel contrasted with a gorgeous iridescent Caribbean sea; at one end of the tunnel was the green jungle of San Andrés Island and at the other end the bright tropical sun.

The unusual *Radisson Diamond* sits atop a pair of submarine-like hulls. *Courtesy Radisson Seven Seas Cruises*

■ TRAVELING IN STYLE

Like every other cruise ship, the *Radisson Diamond* has a dining room and lots of food; passenger cabins with a place to sleep and a bathroom; and show rooms, bars, and lounges. But at every turn, the *Radisson Diamond* delivers it all in great style.

The Grand Dining Room is one of the most elegant rooms at sea—or on land, for that matter. The two-floor-high glass wall at the stern of the ship offers spectacular views all through the day. There are also more than enough tables for two, a relative rarity on many cruise lines. Because of the stability of the ship, and also because this is a "customer is king" operation, the tables can be moved around the dining room and rearranged to create seating for groups large or small.

There is also an open seating policy in the dining room, with guests free to arrive at any time during serving hours. The dining room staff features female servers from Europe, not all that common on cruise ships.

That's the good news about the servers. The bad news, for some cruise veterans, is that you won't have the comfort of an assigned wait staff who will learn your favorites and become your short-term best friends aboard ship. But some other good news is that the ratio of guests to staff is low and the dedication to service so high that the entire crew seems devoted to your needs. We found a section of the dining room we liked and a pair of waitresses we enjoyed; by three days into the trip, the maître d' knew our preferences.

One other nice point: Tips are included in the cruise fare on Radisson ships. This means that members of the staff are paid a decent wage and are not reliant on gratuities from guests. Put another way, you do not feel that the waitresses, the maître d', the wine steward, and the cabin attendant are calculating the size of their tip each time they greet you or offer a service.

Of course, nothing is free; the cost of higher wages is reflected in stateroom charges. But for my money, I would just as soon see all cruise lines go this route. There certainly was no lack of effort, courtesy, or attention to detail on the tipless *Radisson Diamond*. In fact, the service was as good as or better than any we have received on a cruise ship.

■ ENTERTAINMENT ABOARD: LESS IS MORE

There are no lavish production shows, no parade of waiters with flaming baked Alaska (thank goodness), and no painful guest talent shows or costume balls onboard (even more thanks).

Instead, the *Radisson Diamond* presents a very laid-back atmosphere with a less-is-more philosophy. On our cruise there was a talented piano and violin duo who gave a few recitals and performed at dinner. The cruise director, an amiable Briton who had a respectable background in theater and cabaret, sang show tunes and pop songs. Each afternoon, the staff conducted an informal trivia quiz in the lounge during tea time.

There is a short jogging and walking track on the topmost deck, along with a golf driving net. At the stern, the *Radisson Diamond* has a small marina that can be lowered into the sea to allow guests to use personal watercraft and sailboats; the marina is mostly used in Europe and was not available on our particular cruise.

The real entertainment, however, was a lovely ship with superb service and luxurious accommodations and food. This is a cruise for the self-sufficient.

■ AND NOW FOR SOMETHING COMPLETELY DIFFERENT

Lest you fear that everything aboard the *Radisson Diamond* is prim and proper, there is also "An Evening at Don Vito's," an alternative dining experience that is not to be missed. Most evenings, the casual grill on the tenth deck is transformed into a small Italian bistro. Guests are offered an eclectic evening that's a cross between a fine Italian restaurant (the food would win raves anywhere on land) and a rollicking burlesque.

The evening starts out with a talented singer and musician performing Italian songs. Sometime around the second appetizer, the waiters begin to join in on the songs, and by the salad course there's a full chorus of wisecracking, singing, and dancing clowns bringing you your dinner. On our visit, a talented singer suddenly took the stage; a young Filipino waitress who had quietly been pouring wine took the microphone and contributed a lovely song in phonetic Italian.

By the end of the night, somewhat abetted by the free-flowing wine, one matron was in a near-swoon on the dance floor with the maître d', Guiseppe, and another took over from the singer for the final chorus.

There are only about fifty seats in the restaurant, enough room on a typical cruise for every passenger to visit once. After our first visit we immediately staked out a place on the waiting list for a second pass; we happily returned to Don Vito's for the final night of our cruise.

■ A SPARKLING ITINERARY

The *Radisson Diamond* makes a grand circuit each year from the Pacific to the Caribbean and on to Europe for the summer. The ship is also regularly chartered to major corporations for special events and "incentive" rewards.

We flew to San José, Costa Rica, to meet up with the *Radisson Diamond* for a trip through the Panama Canal that would end in Fort Lauderdale, Florida. Most of the guests on our cruise began their adventure with a day trip to a Costa Rican rain forest and animal preserve; we caught up with the group on the second day for a visit to the spectacular Poás volcano. From there we traveled the mountainous countryside to a private plantation for a peasant-style lunch. Late in the day we were delivered to Puntarenas, a port on an inlet of the Pacific Ocean.

Our first full day was spent cruising south down the untouched jungle coast of Costa Rica and northern Panama. We were accompanied in the morning by several schools of dolphins; they happily played in the ship's broad wake, launching themselves a few feet into the air.

On the second day, we arrived just before dawn at Panama City. As the sun came up we found ourselves threading our way through a few dozen freighters waiting their turn to enter the Panama Canal. At our appointed time, we passed beneath the Bridge of the Americas and entered the canal.

The construction of the Panama Canal stretched over more than thirty years, beginning in 1880 with the tragic French effort and finishing in 1914 under the sheer bravado of Teddy Roosevelt, the military prowess of George Goethals, and the not-insignificant solution to the deadly malaria and yellow fever plagues by Dr. William Gorgas.

The ten-hour passage through the six locks of the canal (three up and three down) was a fascinating voyage along the border where one of mankind's greatest feats of engineering meets nature's wildest challenges. We passed through the spectacular Gaillard Cut, where thousands of men labored for decades to cut a passage; from there we moved into Gatun Lake, a body of water created by a huge earthen dam in the jungle.

As night fell, we exited the canal and entered the Caribbean Ocean, passing through another floating waiting line of freighters heading for the Pacific.

Our first stop in the Caribbean was at San Andrés Island, a somewhat obscure possession of Colombia. From there we moved on to Grand Cayman Island and Cozumel, Mexico. On the last full day of the ten-day cruise, we moved along the mountainous northern coast of Cuba, en route to disembarkation in Fort Lauderdale, Florida.

Cuba is a Holy Grail for cruise lines. Nearly every company has plans already on the shelf for trips to the large, culturally rich, and exotic island that has been off-limits to most Americans for nearly forty years. Lying just 90 miles south of Miami, Cuba will likely one day be a popular destination for ships sailing out of Florida and the Gulf of Mexico.

■ *DIAMOND* ELEGANCE

Our cabin was decorated with an arrangement of exotic live flowers, an echo of the decorations throughout the ship. The bathroom was equipped with extra-plush towels and bathrobes. A refrigerator in the room was kept filled with soda, mixers, and bottled water.

When we boarded the ship, there was a bottle of French champagne on ice set up on our table. The cabin was also stocked with a personal bar set up with more liquor than I could personally consume over the course of a ten-day voyage; if you did manage to go through the bar, additional supplies were available for purchase.

Rooms are equipped with a video player, and the ship's library has a decent collection of classic and current movies for loan.

The cabin stewardess discreetly noted our schedule each day and made at least three visits to make the beds, remake them, and turn them down.

A small pleasure: Soda and juice flows freely and without charge at any of the bars and from wandering staff members. When you return from a shore excursion in a tropical port, a uniformed waitress stands just inside the reception area with a tray of chilled champagne or juice. At dinner, the steward pours from complimentary offerings of red or white wine selected to complement the evening's fare; there is also an extensive wine cellar for those who insist on paying extra.

And then there's the food. Nearly every cruise ship does a good job of feeding guests, but the offerings sometimes emphasize quantity over quality. On the *Radisson Diamond*, however, every meal was on the level of a four-star restaurant. The plates (Villeroy and Boch china, actually) were laid out like works of art. Each afternoon, the executive chef would appear on stateroom television to describe in luscious detail the menu for dinner and to demonstrate the creation of a sauce or stock.

Menus do not repeat over the course of a cruise. Guests are discreetly encouraged to make reasonable special requests; the chef will attempt to fulfill these requests for special dishes or preparation styles. I particularly enjoyed a gazpacho one evening; I put in a word of praise to the maître d', and the next night I was offered a second chance at the soup, freshly concocted just for me in the galley.

After dinner, if you somehow find the strength to resist dessert and order "nothing," your waitress may appear with a dinner plate decorated with "Nothing"—spelled out in chocolate icing and glaze. More than a few guests end up licking the plate in utter defeat.

Every cruise ship offers a lunchtime buffet on the upper deck, but on the *Radisson Diamond* it was more of a catered picnic than a casino smorgasbord. The silver serving dishes held rich goulash or lamb chops; an outside barbecue offered grilled fish, chicken, or beef; a cheese cart held hundreds of dollars worth of sinful international offerings. And waiters and waitresses stood by to carry your plate from station to station. Our favorite lunch included shrimp, crab legs, cold lobster, and an assortment of seafood salads. On a more ordinary cruise ship, a "gala" buffet might have featured just one of these premium dishes.

What's a Knot?

One knot is equal to one nautical mile per hour; a nautical mile is about 1.15 land-based miles. Here's a conversion chart:

15 knots	=	17.25 mph
16 knots	=	18.4 mph
17 knots	=	19.55 mph
18 knots	=	20.7 mph
19 knots	=	21.85 mph
20 knots	=	23 mph
21 knots	=	24.15 mph
22 knots	=	25.3 mph
23 knots	=	26.45 mph
24 knots	=	27.6 mph
25 knots	=	28.75 mph
30 knots	=	34.5 mph

Although on most ships I spend little time in the cabin, preferring to watch the sea from the deck or from a library or lounge, when your cabin has its own balcony, everything is different. The *Radisson Diamond*'s verandas are completely private, sheltered from one another and from the wind. When we were out to sea, the large sliding door to the outside stood open all day. We happily began every morning of our trip with breakfast on the veranda, delivered with clockwork precision and served on a linen tablecloth. Each night before retiring, we toasted a day of adventure or one of blissful indolence.

Although we preferred the elegance of the Grand Dining Room, guests can also ask room service to deliver a meal ordered from the evening menu; dishes are brought course by course to your veranda or sitting room.

We toured behind the scenes with Executive Chef Peter Spörndli, who met us in the galley with a chilled bottle of wine. The bright and open workspace is blessed with an unusual feature for cruise ships: a picture window. The dining room on the *Radisson Diamond* sits high on the eighth deck; most cruise ships set their dining rooms down low. Of course, on the *Radisson Diamond,* there is no space below the seventh deck for a wide open room.

The ship's larders were like an international gourmet shop: asparagus from Guatemala, tomatoes from Costa Rica, beef from the United States, and seafood from around the world. Shelves held fresh spices, including a case of horseradish roots. We watched as a sous-chef decorated the plates for one of the night's appetizers: exquisite cold mussels from New Zealand, served with a seasoned mayonnaise concocted fresh onboard.

Another nicety for experienced cruise travelers is the low-key shipboard commerce. On many cruises, there is a drumbeat of sales pitches for shore excursions, bingo games, "sales" at the boutique, come-ons from the ship's photographers, auctions of "fine art," and sprawling, beeping, and flashing casinos. For many cruise companies, a large portion of their profits come from onboard marketing and bar tabs.

Each day the ship's golf pro offered lessons in the net on the small sports deck above the bridge; husband-and-wife bridge experts delivered talks on arcane strategies and conducted tournaments, and a visiting professor offered several lectures on history and economics. We found it quite possible to enjoy our cruise in peaceful obliviousness to all the shipboard sideshows. They are still there, but we didn't have to go out of our way to avoid them.

In fact, that was the way we looked at our entire cruise: We let the *Radisson Diamond* transport us on the path between the seas while we laid back in the lap of luxury.

A GRAND OLD LADY: THE SWINGING SS *NORWAY*

Late October on the SS *Norway* was a tale of two hurricanes. It was also a wonderful journey of more than sixty fabulous musicians—and hundreds of dedicated fans—spread nicely down the length of the world's longest cruise ship. Our trip was one of two weeklong Jazz Cruises in the Caribbean, a long-standing tradition on Norwegian Cruise Line (NCL) that attracts a loyal following each year.

The *Norway* is one of the last of the transatlantic steamships, built as the SS *France* in 1962 and lovingly restored and updated by Norwegian Cruise Line as the *Norway* for modern days and modern cruise passengers. The *Norway* had been expected to leave the NCL fleet in late 2001; the line even conducted a farewell repositioning to Europe where it was to join the fleet of parent company Star Cruises. Instead the grand old ship was recalled to Miami and assigned to sail to the Eastern Caribbean for all of 2003 and into 2004. The ship suffered a boiler explosion while at dock in May 2003, and was withdrawn from service for several months while repairs were made.

■ THE WINDS OF OCTOBER

When we caught up with her in 1999, the *Norway* was out in the western Caribbean on a seven-day cruise as Hurricane Irene suddenly arose south of Cuba. On Thursday, the storm passed over Cuba and set its aim on the Florida Keys.

We had arrived in Miami on that same Thursday to spend a few days enjoying the lively culture and scenery of the area. The skies began to darken in the afternoon though, and by evening the rain began to fall in colossal downpours. We went to bed in our hotel on the water on narrow Miami Beach, trusting the weather forecast, which predicted that the storm would head into the Gulf of Mexico, missing Miami and making landfall farther north around Tampa. We awoke to find that Irene had changed her mind and was making a hook to the east, coming onshore just outside Miami.

Throughout the day, torrents of rain fell, as much as 15 inches in parts of Miami. In the afternoon, wind gusts as high as 75 miles per hour raked the area. Funneling through some of the canyons between high-rise hotels on the beach and in downtown, the winds knocked over palm trees and brought down signs and utility poles.

We took a midday expedition from our hotel to a shopping mall, crossing one of the sea-level causeways between Miami Beach and Miami; the water lapped at the side of the road, and our little rental car vibrated wildly in the wind. After a brief and uneasy stay, we crossed back to Miami Beach and buttoned ourselves into the relative security of the hotel.

Until the cable television system at the hotel failed at nightfall, we tracked the storm as best we could. We wondered where the *Norway* had gone to avoid the storm, and we wondered where she would be the next morning at six o'clock when she was scheduled to arrive in Miami to unload her passengers and pick us up for our voyage.

▉ THE *NORWAY* IS LOCATED

It turned out that the *Norway* had more or less kept to her schedule at sea, heading east to a planned stop at Great Stirrup Cay, NCL's private island in the Bahamas, north of Nassau. Ironically, Stirrup Cay had just been reopened to NCL ships after the repair of damage caused by Hurricane Floyd a few months earlier.

In many ways, if you're going to travel in the company of hurricanes, a large, fast, and well-provisioned cruise ship is a good place to be. Hurricanes, although they are huge weather events, are nevertheless typically only 25 to 50 miles across, with strong winds extending out perhaps 100 miles from the eye. They usually move at speeds of about 10 to 15 miles per hour, and forecasters are pretty capable of predicting the general direction of travel.

Unless a ship's captain makes a very bad decision and heads directly into the path of an oncoming storm, he can instead take his moving platform away from its path. The *Norway* can make as much as 20 knots in most conditions, about 23 miles per hour, and run ahead of the storm. The rub, though, comes when the ship has to return to a particular port to unload its passengers and pick up a new group. And in this case, Hurricane Irene lay between Stirrup Cay and Miami.

As prodigious rain and winds pounded Miami Friday night, we heard the news that along with most everything else in the area, the Port of Miami was officially closed, as was the airport through which most of the arriving guests would pass.

The NCL corporate headquarters in Miami was of no use; earlier in the day, the reservations clerks were promising that the *Norway* would sail the next day without any delay. By afternoon when we called again, the main office was closed "because of hurricane conditions." That much we knew; what we didn't know was where the *Norway* would be the next day.

The *Norway* ended up circling Stirrup Cay all day Friday, unable to offload its passengers because of rough seas and uncertainty about when the U.S. Coast Guard would reopen Miami Harbor.

Saturday morning dawned clear and beautiful, with the storm moving northeast to Fort Lauderdale and then up the coast. We ventured out onto the streets of Miami, dodging downed palm trees, cautiously creeping through intersections with nonfunctioning traffic lights, and making our way to the pier. There, as we crossed the causeway from Miami Beach to Miami, we saw in the distance the unmistakable blue hull of the *Norway* just entering the harbor.

It was nearly 11:00 A.M. before the ship finally tied up at the pier on Dodge Island and 1:00 P.M. before the first passengers began to disembark. Buses were waiting to take them to airports in Miami or Fort Lauderdale, where another storm-created mess awaited. Hundreds of flights had been canceled on Friday, and many aircraft were out of position for their Saturday schedules.

When we finally were allowed to embark at nearly 3:00 P.M., there were only a few hundred of us onboard. More than a thousand guests and many of the jazz musicians who were to be the stars of the weeklong theme cruise were still in the air and not expected to arrive until late in the evening, hours after our scheduled 4:00 P.M. departure.

■ MOON OVER MIAMI

Captain Geir Lokøen advised passengers that he would wait as long as he could for late arrivals; as it turned out, that stretched to after 11:00 P.M. Saturday. The last baggage loaded by the stevedores were two huge upright basses.

We were happy to be finally at sea. As we went to bed, though, there was vague warning of another tropical disturbance deep in the Caribbean. We put our trust in the advanced technology on the bridge and the many years of experience of the captain and officers, looking forward to our arrival on Saint Martin two full days later.

And right on schedule, the *Norway* arrived at Phillipsburg, the Dutch capital of Saint Martin. There is no dock big enough or waters deep enough to permit the *Norway* to tie up at a landing pier; instead, we set anchor in the harbor. We joined a few hundred fellow passengers on the first tender to shore.

Saint Martin has long been one of our favorite islands in the Caribbean. There's a bustling commercial center on the Dutch side (Sint Maarten) around Phillipsburg, and a very French half, relatively quiet country, with its capital at Marigot. (If you're coming to stay, you'll find a wide range of hotels and condominiums on the Dutch side; the best beaches, trendiest shops, and extraordinary small restaurants and patisseries are on French territory.)

We picked up a rental car in Phillipsburg and headed out on the single road that circles the island; the road is more or less two lanes wide, mostly paved, and possessed of a few relatively gnarly switchbacks as it crosses the central spine of hills on the island.

Just over the border between the Dutch and French sides (a simple stone marks the border) are the Terres Basses (Lowlands) that include some of the loveliest beaches in all the Caribbean: Baie Longue (Long Bay), Baie aux Prunes (Plum Bay), and Baie Rouge (Red Bay). We stopped for a swim at the nearly perfect strand of Baie Longue; at the north end of the beach is the ultraexclusive resort of La Samana, regular home to Hollywood and rock stars and the otherwise well possessed; if you have to ask the price for a night's stay, you can't afford to sleep there.

On our visit the beach was all but deserted. Two other couples, dressed only in suntan lotion and sand, occupied blankets 50 yards away in each direction. There was, though, plenty of company in the crystal waters; hundreds of iridescent fish accompanied us as we swam.

Next stop was Marigot, where we picked up a peasant lunch worthy of a Provençale: a fresh-baked baguette, a wedge of exquisite Catalan cheese, and a few bottles of Ting, a Caribbean grapefruit soda. (We would have completed the picnic with a jug of wine, but there were those switchbacks ahead of us on the road.)

We continued our tour through the open plain of La Savane and then the small village of Grand Case, a refuge of haute cuisine cafes. Somewhere around the Quartier d'Orleans, we tuned the car radio to a local station to hear the mayor of Phillipsburg declare a state of emergency: Hurricane José was barreling north, heading directly for Saint Martin and the U.S. Virgin Islands of Saint John and Saint Thomas.

Returning our rental car, we headed into Phillipsburg and saw something few tourists have ever experienced in the Caribbean: shopkeepers turning away credit card–holding visitors. The town was shutting down ahead of the storm, so we took the tender back to the *Norway*.

■ A CHANGE OF PLANS

It came as no surprise at dinner to hear Captain Lokøen announce that our plans for the next day had been scrambled by the storm. The port of Saint Thomas had been closed by authorities; instead we would steam north to the Bahamas to stay ahead of Hurricane José.

The next day I met with Lokøen in his spacious office just off the bridge. We began by talking about the weather. I asked why we had not diverted westward to make an unscheduled stop at Jamaica instead of adding another day at sea to the schedule. Lokøen said he had considered Jamaica, but a visit there would have made it impossible for the ship to make its way to its planned stop at Stirrup Cay three days hence. And, he said, there was no certainty that Hurricane José wouldn't make a swing westward. The safest route was to stay ahead of the storm and be ready to move out of its way if it moved east- or westward.

A cruise in hurricane conditions, Lokøen said, is a "search for solutions." As he went on to say, a change in ports in the middle of the week does not matter as much. Some guests may be disappointed because the ship has to skip a port, but more would be upset if the *Norway* was unable to get back to its home port on time.

According to Lokøen, the *Norway* could dock in Florida at Miami, Fort Lauderdale, or Port Canaveral. In an emergency, she could offload passengers in the Bahamas, but the airport there could not easily transport them back to Miami, especially if four or five other cruise ships in the area chose to come into the Bahamas.

"We have many contingencies," Lokøen stated, "but every contingency needs a contingency."

■ A MAN IN LOVE

I left the contingency planning to the captain and his staff. Instead we talked about the ship that would take us out of José's way.

"I have always been in love with this ship . . . since I was a boy," Lokøen said. "I went to sea when this ship came out in 1962," he continued. "I was fifteen years old. I knew I could not be a captain of this ship as long as I was a Norwegian citizen because it flew a French flag."

Of course, all that changed when Norwegian Cruise Line purchased the SS *France,* which was laid up in a French dock after its career as a transatlantic liner had been ended by the advent of the jet airplane.

At the time we met, Lokøen had been with NCL for two decades, including fifteen years on the *Norway.* For nine of those years he was master of the *Norway,* making him the longest-serving captain in the history of the ship.

We talked about the changes NCL has made to the *Norway* over the years. "When she was the *France,* she was perfect," Lokøen said. "She's still very seaworthy and a nice ship to take the elements."

When the ship served as a liner, she had four engines and four propellers. She was converted to two engines and propellers; much of the original equipment remains in place deep down in the hull. Two decks of luxury staterooms were added to the top of the ship in 1990; down below, some of the former fuel tanks for the unused engines were filled with permanent ballast to balance the extra weight.

Within the ship, the Windward dining room is essentially unchanged from its days as the first-class restaurant. A sky of electric stars twinkles in a dome over the tables. The Leeward dining room, although it serves the same food, is much less impressive.

Among the unusual features of the *France* were the Provençale Villas, a set of staterooms on the original upper deck that surrounded a small private courtyard. When the ship was converted to cruising, a pool was installed to nearly fill the courtyard. Today, if you can find an obscure doorway marked PORTHOLE on the Fjord Deck, you can enter an unusual world frozen in time. The villas are still there, but instead of a view of the sky, they have a view of a porthole into the swimming pool.

One of the most important modifications to the ship was the addition of a pair of massive tenders mounted on the forward deck. The 86-foot-long vessels can deliver 450 passengers to a dock or pull up on the beach like a landing craft with a ramp that lowers from the front. Instead of soldiers with machine guns, though, defenders on the beach are assaulted by tourists rushing to the barbecue.

The tenders are necessary because the *Norway* is unable to enter many smaller ports around the world; built for stability on transatlantic crossings, she has a deep draft of 34 feet. That puts her in the same class as the *QE2,* which has a draft of 33 feet.

"Without these tenders, we would not be able to do what we do with this ship. It's the best solution to cruising in the Caribbean. The most common complaint is that the ship is difficult to find your way around on," Lokøen said. "This is because it was originally built with two classes, with gates and decks cut off from each other."

That structural problem may also present a limit to the useful life of the *Norway.* International maritime safety regulations that go into effect in 2009 will mandate all shipboard stair towers go from the lowest deck to the highest. On the *Norway,* many of the stairs serve only portions of the ship, and Lokøen said that reworking the internals of the stairs would be extremely expensive.

◼ A FLOATING JAZZ FESTIVAL

For nearly two decades, NCL has carried jazz fans out to sea with some of their favorite performers for an intense week of concerts and get-togethers.

I have to admit right up front that my wife and I are not serious jazz fans, something that made us a distinct minority among the 1,800 passengers onboard the *Norway.* In a way, though, it was a great advantage: We strolled from lounge to show room to cafe, sampling musical styles without the baggage of experience.

Among the performers aboard ship for the week were the Ray Brown Trio, the Freddy Cole Quartet, the Jimmy McGriff Quartet, the Eddie Higgins Trio, Sphere, singer Ernie Andrews, and the nineteen-piece Frank Foster and His Loud Minority Big Band.

Featured performer in the Saga Theatre was Ernestine Anderson, a classic jazz and soul singer; without a bit of expectation we took a seat. A minute or two later we were converts and made plans to attend her next three shows. It was only later that we learned her history: a spectacular debut in 1956; performances with the likes of Lionel Hampton, Quincy Jones, and Ray Brown; appearances at Carnegie Hall, Kennedy Center, and the Hollywood Bowl; and more than thirty albums. After a number of years in forced retirement, she has been enjoying something of a revival. And as she told her audience, she was making her first, somewhat wobbly appearance on the gently rolling stage of a cruise ship.

One other thing: The crowd onboard the *Norway* for the Jazz Cruise was the happiest group we have ever traveled with. We left Miami seven hours late; we missed our scheduled port call in Saint Thomas; the seas were slightly rougher than some would have preferred. We heard nary a word of complaint: The music and the clubs and the parties were just fine, thank you.

◼ ONBOARD THE *NORWAY*

Don't look for flashiness on the *Norway.* Remember instead this ship's history as the oceangoing expression of French culture. This is classic European elegance afloat.

You can check out a collection of relics from the *France* in a cabinet on International Deck port side forward. International Deck, the covered stroll that connects the shops and clubs, was originally the promenade deck of the *France*. The most attractive of the public rooms is Club Internationale, the former first-class smoking lounge of the *France*.

More so than on most ships, on the *Norway* there is a large difference between the least expensive rooms and the middle of the range. This ship was built as a two-class vessel; more than half the passengers were looking just for transportation across the Atlantic, and the lowest-echelon cabins are just that: basic transportation. The lesser staterooms are very small, and the portholes are more like peepholes. Cabins in Class A and B and suites, on the other hand, were built for cruisers and are quite nice, with large windows and sitting areas. A handful of suites include verandas.

There are also significant differences between the two dining rooms on the *Norway*. The Leeward restaurant was built for the second-class patrons, and it can most charitably be described as ordinary; there are no windows, and the low ceiling makes it feel more like a college dining hall than an eatery on a luxury cruise ship. The Windward restaurant, built for first-class diners, is much more attractive, with a central circular dome decorated with a twinkling starfield ceiling; again, though, there are no windows.

The setting aside, the food and service are the same in both dining rooms. The NCL food is a cut or two above ordinary, and you'll find some of the best menus, presentation, and quality among ships in the middle- and upper-middle range of cruise ships.

But the real star is Le Bistro. This small, very elegant restaurant comes equipped with a first-class continental menu, extremely attentive waiters, and drop-dead gorgeous appointments, including a window wall. Le Bistro is open every night for dinner; reservations are available a day in advance. There is no extra charge to dine there, although guests are asked to leave a gratuity of $5.00 per person per meal. The menu does not change from day to day, but a special chef's recommendation of one or two entrees is added each evening.

Our floating island missed the hurricanes, chauffeuring us on a music-filled, pampered excursion on an updated classic.

FROM HAWAII TO AN ALMOST UNTOUCHED SOUTH PACIFIC ISLAND ABOARD THE *NORWEGIAN DYNASTY*

Norwegian Cruise Line has found a way to sail between ports in Hawaii and deal with the cabotage requirements of the Jones Act. In 1998 NCL began sailing round-trips from Honolulu with an extended five-day side trip to Fanning Island in the tiny Republic of Kiribati near the equator.

We sailed that itinerary on the *Norwegian Dynasty* in late fall 1998; that ship has since left the fleet. In 2001 NCL sent its new *Norwegian Star* to Hawaii for a similar itinerary. The *Norwegian Star* is a 91,000-ton Megaship, accommodating

2,200 passengers. The ship is the fastest ship in the NCL fleet, capable of a top speed of 25 knots, which will help with the long haul from Hawaii to Kiribati.

■ CRUISING BACK IN TIME

On our cruise on the *Norwegian Dynasty*, we left Honolulu and sailed to Kailua on the Kona Coast on the Big Island of Hawaii. Kona, which means "leeward" or sheltered side, lives up to its name. This is the calm, sunny side of the island, home to some relatively isolated luxury resorts, golf courses, and tons of gift shops.

Then we headed south from Kona toward the Republic of Kiribati, a two-and-a-half-day, full-steam cruise toward the equator and a place back in time. We approached Fanning Island (Tabuaeran to the locals) just after breakfast and were greeted by a native in a wooden sailboat who paralleled us the last few miles to the entrance to the inner harbor.

Fanning is a broken Cheerio of an atoll, the land only a few hundred feet wide around an inner lagoon that is actually the collapsed cone of an ancient volcano. Beaches on the ocean are somewhere between tricky and dangerous. English Harbor, the interior of the atoll, is deep enough for a major ship but not wide enough for a cruise ship to enter and turn around comfortably, and the ocean currents and soft sand bottom make it impossible to set an anchor; there are believed to be wrecks of World War II ships and planes on the bottom. Our ship was forced to cruise slowly back and forth while passengers visited the island on tenders that surfed through the waves into the harbor.

Kiribati (pronounced *KUR-a-bass*) is made up of the Gilbert, Line, and Phoenix Islands. With a population of 75,000, the thirty-three islands comprise 268 square miles of land spread over 5 million square miles of ocean. Kiribati won its independence from Great Britain in 1979. The capital is Tarawa, site of some of the bloodiest battles at the end of World War II.

Fanning Island is located 3 degrees, or 273 miles, north of the equator. A sister island, 50 miles away, is Christmas Island, which from 1954 to 1965 served as a base for American, British, and French atomic testing on more distant atolls.

Fanning Island was discovered in 1798 by Edmund Fanning, the American captain of the ship *Betsy*. A number of whaling ships visited the uninhabited island in succeeding years. Beginning in 1848, some 500 natives of other islands in the chain were moved to Fanning to operate a coconut oil plantation for a British company. A bit later in the century, the island was extensively mined for guano, and some 20,000 tons of the natural phosphate fertilizer were shipped to Honolulu.

In 1902 one of the first transoceanic telephone cables was brought ashore at Fanning. The cable stretched from near Vancouver, British Columbia, to New Zealand. During World War II, a small Japanese landing party damaged the cable station on Fanning. In another footnote to history, Fanning was one of Amelia Earhart's way points on her final voyage.

Modest plantation operations continued until midway through the twentieth century. Most of the approximately 1,600 residents of Fanning are descendants of the plantation workers who were abandoned when the company closed operations and pulled out.

■ FIRST CONTACT

NCL paid for the construction of a small pier built—like most everything else on Fanning Island—from coconut trees. Our arriving tenders were met by the town council and a band of about fifty dancers in grass skirts, along with musicians who performed continuously for the seven hours we were ashore.

We found a nearly untouched tropical paradise, where the I-Kiribati, as they call themselves, live a subsistence life of grabbing bonefish and the occasional lobster from the lagoon and harvesting taro, coconuts, and a few other crops. The local livestock includes foot-wide land crabs that make their homes in large holes in and among the coconut trees.

The island is almost untouched by modern influences, without electricity, plumbing, telephone service, and with little in the way of permanent changes to the coconut jungle. Most of the homes consist of open platforms a few feet above the ground, with thatched coconut-frond roofs. There are no doors, windows, or privacy except for the blackness of the night.

While most of the ship's passengers stayed near the pier and the pretty sand beach on the lagoon, my wife and I headed out on the packed-sand road that led from the pier. We passed some of the ruins of the old plantation and phosphate mining operations, including a few dozen feet of rusted narrow-gauge rails, and found a small overgrown cemetery that held the remains of some of the family members of the plantation people. Every few hundred feet we came to another little cluster of huts, each with its own name.

Children—and there were hundreds of them—peeked out at us from behind trees or came to the road to say hello. One group of little boys came forth to shake our hands. We walked past the atoll's primary school, listening for a while to the children reciting their numbers in math class. Once we were spotted, though, class came to a halt and dozens of heads crowded the doorway to catch a glimpse of the unusual visitors.

Alas, I expect that this island paradise will never be the same. The more visits by outsiders, the more likely the contamination of their culture. The kids will learn to stick out their hands for a dollar when they are photographed, and the native dancers will pass the hat instead of performing in welcome. And Fanning will become just another tourist island.

We were told a tragicomedy story of the ship's first visit to Fanning. It seems an intrepid American sailor had chosen Fanning as his destination for a solo journey from the West Coast of the United States. His research had told him he would be a modern-day Captain Cook, visiting a place that time had bypassed. After several weeks at sea, he arrived at the isolated speck of sand near the Equator . . . to find the *Norwegian Dynasty* pulling up with a load of 600 passengers.

■ BACK TO THE FUTURE

After our return from Fanning Island, we made port at Hilo on the other side of the Big Island. Hilo is the takeoff point for numerous helicopter tours of the Mauna Loa volcano. We chose instead to explore the island by car, renting a vehicle and driving to the extraordinary Volcano National Park. I have been to many strange places on this planet, but few exceed the peculiarity of a stroll across the miles of black lava left behind by dozens of recent flows. It's as close to a moonscape as most of us will ever experience and a scene that will stick with you forever. The lava is frozen in twisting ropes, undulating waves, and crunchy beaches of pumice.

The volcanoes of Hawaii are still very much alive, although eruptions are rarely violent explosions. Instead there are near-continuous slow flows of thick, superheated lava that bubbles out of cracks in the mountains and heads down the hillside and into the sea where it gives off clouds of steam that rise several miles into the sky.

Also in the park is the Thurston Lava Tube, a natural tunnel caused by a cooling lava flow; a walk in the long tunnel is like a journey to the center of the earth.

Lahaina, on the island of Maui, was once the royal capital of the Hawaiian kingdom and the seat of power for the Kamehameha Dynasty. In the early nineteenth century, Lahaina became the lusty port away from home for the American whaling fleet that had sailed all the way around the Horn of South America in search of "greasy luck" (whale oil). In a way, Lahaina became an extension of Nantucket, a whaling capital thousands of miles away in Massachusetts and the home of many of the ship owners and captains (and this author's home, too).

At the heyday of the whaling era, as many as 400 ships at a time were berthed in the harbor. Whalemen said there was no God west of the Horn, and they conducted themselves accordingly—at least until a band of puritanical missionaries arrived from New England to attempt to clean things up. Among the sailors was Herman Melville, who wrote about the whole scene in *Moby-Dick* and other works.

The weathered wooden buildings on Front Street now house boutiques, art galleries, and restaurants, but the sense of history in Lahaina is more intense than most anywhere else in the islands.

Lahaina also offered the most diverse collection of activities for visitors, from golf expeditions to helicopter and biplane routes to whale watching. We chose to make a visit to the floor of the harbor onboard one of the ships in the Atlantis submarine fleet; the 65-foot craft descended to a depth of 125 feet and allowed us to intrude on fish and other creatures of the sea and to view coral beds not often seen outside an aquarium. Atlantis operates similar subs at a number of ports in the Hawaiian Islands and in the Caribbean; it's a voyage worth the trip.

The last stop on our NCL tour around the fiftieth state was Nawiliwili on the lush island of Kauai, the most isolated of the major islands. Here we rented a car and drove west (there's really only one major road, and it does not quite circle the island because of the severe geography of the Na Pali Coast) and went for a visit to Waimea Canyon State Park. Waimea is called the Grand Canyon of Hawaii; just a little bit of exaggeration is involved. The steep, multicolored walls of the canyon are hidden from view until you complete a long, slow drive up the mountainside.

Kauai's scenery is unusual enough to have attracted a long line of Hollywood filmmakers who have used settings on the island for scenes in such films as *King Kong, South Pacific, Raiders of the Lost Ark,* and *Jurassic Park.*

R/B *RIVER EXPLORER*: BARGIN' ON THE MISSISSIPPI RIVER

by Valerie E. M. Forman, Econoguide Staff

The river has its own time. That's what they kept talking about during the first few days of our journey up the Mississippi River on the *River Explorer.* And they were right. By the third day of our river trip, I didn't know what day it was. Yes, we had televisions and radios in our rooms, but the peaceful movement up the river melted all sense of chronology.

I sailed in the company of Mark Twain; my literary accompaniment for the trip was a copy of *Life on the Mississippi.*

The 730-foot RiverBarge *River Explorer,* a conglomerate of two hotel barges and a towboat, first took to the water in 1998. Today the barge offers four- to ten-day excursions to seven American river regions, including the lower and upper Mississippi River, Cumberland River Valley, Atchafalaya River Basin, Ohio River Valley, Missouri River, and along the inland Texas–Louisiana Gulf Intracoastal Waterway.

Our voyage went from New Orleans to Natchez. After we first came aboard, I sat in our stateroom looking out on the yellow-green waters of the Mississippi River from the Julia Street Wharf. I watched as barges, tugboats, riverboats, and other vessels of various shapes and sizes passed by; throughout our trip the passing traffic would be one of our main sources of entertainment. We waved to the passengers on the paddle wheeler *Natchez* and the three-deck *Cajun Queen* riverboat as they passed by.

During our first dinner in the galley, we were entertained by a live New Orleans jazz band. That evening we quietly pulled away from the dock and were off on our journey.

■ MINT JULEPS BEFORE NOON

Our first stop the next morning was at a lovely antebellum home named Oak Alley. The walkway leading up to the main house was lined with perfectly spaced three-century-old oak trees. At 10:30 A.M. my husband and I sipped mint juleps as we strolled around the grounds; we never thought we'd be drinking bourbon at that hour.

Back on the ship, we spent the afternoon in the Pilot House Lounge at the bow of the barge, watching the comings and goings on the river. A map book allowed us to pinpoint our exact location on the river by reading the shore markers and matching them up to the maps; another book listed the names and histories of most of the vessels on the river. A pair of television screens marked the river's twists and turns, and radios broadcast the chatter between river barges.

The *River Explorer* under way. *Courtesy of RiverBarge Excursions*

The afternoon of the second day brought us near the town of Carville, Louisiana. We used the binoculars supplied in our stateroom to watch an egret walking in the water near the shore.

By the next morning, we were north of Baton Rouge, out of the industrial zone. A fog hung low on the river, and a flock of birds flew over the shoreline. We moved along up the river, underneath a bridge that was built under the direction of Huey Long. The clever politician had the bridge built a mere 65 feet tall to block large vessels from heading farther north, forcing them to unload their cargoes here in Louisiana.

A full day's shore excursion began in Saint Francisville; we boarded the bus, fortified with sweet pralines from a local vendor. At Myrtle's Plantation, an alleged haunted house, I was allowed to touch a tea service said to have been used by Samuel Langhorne Clemens himself, who occasionally stayed there while he was a riverboat pilot on the river—before he became Mark Twain.

Next stop was the Oakley Plantation, where John James Audubon rendered many of his wildlife paintings; for a time he served as the tutor of the plantation owner's sixteen-year-old daughter. We were unsettled to discover that Audubon would have the subjects of his paintings killed and nailed to the wall so that he could paint them. We also viewed two small slave-quarter buildings. Later on the bus, our sweet, prim-and-proper Cajun tour guide referred to the Civil War as "our recent unpleasantness."

Following our plantation tours, we shopped in downtown Saint Francisville at a shop known as Grandmother's Buttons, where I spent a whopping $1.50 and purchased a button from the 1930s that looked like an acorn, called a "twinkly" or "mirror back" because it glitters through the tiny cagelike gold metal.

When we reached Natchez, Mississippi, we traveled by trolley to three more antebellum homes: Rosalie, Stanton Hall, and Magnolia Hall. That evening, we were presented with a gospel performance by local female singers whose voices were so sweet and rich that several of us in the audience were teary-eyed.

And then we were back in New Orleans. After a morning interdenominational church service onboard, we gathered for an ice-cream social. We were given the evening to explore the sights, sounds, and smells of New Orleans, and on our last day we had a bus tour of the city that included a visit to one of the local cemeteries.

■ LIFE ABOARD A BARGE

The food—and there was so much of it—was regional American cuisine. The daily menu included fried catfish and hush puppies, pecan pie, beignets, gumbo, crab cakes, crawfish étouffée, mustard greens, black-eyed peas, grits, and a Southern barbecue complete with ribs and chicken. Seating in the dining room is open, and there's a "Raid the Fridge" area that's accessible twenty-four hours a day. My husband quickly found the location of the bottomless cookie jar!

The river barge offers recreation opportunities that include an exercise room, a jogging/walking track, shuffleboard, whirlpool tubs on the top deck, a video and book library, the Crevasse Bar, bumper pool, and card tables.

Although the cruise was billed as a family barge trip, we found ourselves the youngest people on the trip. We didn't see any guests with children (the trip took place during the school year) and we didn't meet anyone else in their forties.

Several of the retired folks who were my barge mates told me they preferred the less formal atmosphere of the river barge over that of a paddleboat or cruise ship. They enjoyed the fact that the crew was able to join the guests at the table. And several said they appreciated that the river barge fare included shore excursions and gratuities.

On the last morning, I met for breakfast with Edward Conrad Jr., founder of the company. Beginning as a freight carrier, Conrad said he was so affected by the history and people along the great muddy river that he set sharing it with the public as his goal.

Conrad travels on the barge regularly and is a great favorite with guests and crew. On the last day of our journey, the crew and some of the guests interrupted a stockholder's meeting onboard the barge to present him with a birthday cake, an unusual salute to the owner of an unusual cruise line.

CHAPTER TWELVE

ECONOGUIDE CRUISE SHIP RATINGS

SO MANY LOVELY cruise ships, so little time!

In the next chapters of the book, I'll give you a guided tour of 180 cruise ships from thirty cruise lines. This book concentrates on ships that regularly include calls at U.S. ports, the Caribbean, the Gulf of Mexico, the Mexican Riviera, and coastal Canada, as well as cruises in Europe marketed to Americans and Canadians.

Each section begins with information about the cruise line. You'll find telephone numbers and Web pages for information. Note that only a few companies accept direct reservations from travelers; in most cases you'll be referred to travel agencies or cruise specialists. If you do call directly, be sure to ask about special offers and last-minute booking.

The listings of each company's fleet are organized by the size of each ship. Sister ships are grouped together; sisters may have identical specifications, but in most cases there are slight differences in public rooms and facilities.

You'll also find a preview of new ships under construction for many major cruise lines. The names, sizes, and expected dates of maiden voyages are all subject to change.

Be aware that each year you can expect a few ships to be taken out of service or sold to another line. Most of the major lines tend to retire their ships somewhere around their early teenage years; this trend has accelerated because many of these older ships are smaller and have fewer special features, such as verandas and large show rooms, than their younger cousins. The older ships are usually sold to one of the second-tier cruise lines, which can happily operate a well-tended cruise ship for many decades.

ECONOGUIDE CRUISE CLASSIFICATIONS

Each of the cruise lines is given an overall rating, from one to six ribbons, indicating the overall quality of a cruising experience. The ratings for cruise lines are as follows:

Econoguide Cruise Line Rating

⚜	Rusty tubs
⚜⚜	Oldies but goodies
⚜⚜⚜	Middle of the fleet
⚜⚜⚜⚜	A cut above
⚜⚜⚜⚜⚜	Luxury
⚜⚜⚜⚜⚜⚜	Ultraluxury

Each of the ships in this book is given an Econoguide rating that separates the superb from the merely wonderful and the very good from the good enough.

The scale runs from 0 to 100; our minimum acceptable rating is 50, and you won't find any ships here that fall below that level. The ratings get tighter (and the points harder to come by) near the top of the scale.

Here's an explanation of the cruise ship ratings:

Econoguide Cruise Ship Rating

★	Less than 50 Not acceptable
★★	50 to 64 Budget
★★★	65 to 79 Average
★★★★	80 to 89 Above Average
★★★★★	90 to 94 Excellent
★★★★★★	95 to 100 Ultraluxury

Ship Size

Gargantuan	130,000+ gross registered tons
Colossus	100,000–129,999 GRT
Megaship	70,000–99,999 GRT
Large	40,000–69,999 GRT
Medium	10,000–39,999 GRT
Small	Less than 10,000 GRT

Category

Ultraluxury	A semiprivate yacht
Top of the Line	Best of the large cruisers
Golden Oldie	A classic older ship
Vintage	A less-than-classic older ship
Adventure	Transport to far-flung places

Price Range

Budget $	$185 per night or less
Moderate $$	$186 to $250 per night
Premium $$$	$251 to $325 per night
Opulent $$$$	$326 to $400 per night
Beyond Opulent $$$$$	More than $400 per night

Prices are based on per-person, per-day brochure prices for midrange cabins in regular season. Nearly all cruise lines offer discounts for advance booking, off-season, and special promotions. Use the price range here for comparison purposes only.

WHO OWNS WHOM?

You're not a Carnival sort of cruiser, you say. Seabourn, or maybe Cunard, sounds more like your level of luxury. That's just fine, although you might be interested to know that all three cruise lines are part of the same company.

One of the effects of the tremendous success of Carnival has been a consolidation among cruise lines into a family of brands that meet various price and luxury classes.

Here's a guide to who owns whom among the major cruise lines:

Carnival Corporation, parent company for Carnival Cruise Lines, has its headquarters in Miami and has mostly American executives. The publicly held corporation, however, is registered in Panama. Controlling interest in the company is held by the Arison family. Carnival Corporation owns Carnival Cruise Lines, Costa Cruise Line, Cunard Line, Holland America Line, Seabourn Cruise Line, and Windstar Cruises.

In 2003 Carnival completed its acquisition of Princess Cruises. Prior to the acquisition, Princess Cruises was the third-largest cruise company in the world. Its brands include Princess Cruises in the North American market, P&O Cruises for the United Kingdom and Australian market, Swan Hellenic in the United Kingdom and Europe, and Aida Cruises and A'ROSA for the German market.

All told, in early 2003 Carnival operated sixty-six ships with more than 100,000 lower berths and seventeen new ships on order for delivery by 2006.

Norwegian Cruise Line fought a hostile takeover bid by Carnival in 1999, only to find itself bought by Malaysia-based Star Cruises, the largest cruise line in Asia. Star, which also operates Orient Lines, has maintained its independence, although some observers speculate that it is a candidate for a merger or sale to a larger company.

Royal Caribbean Cruises Ltd., which also has its headquarters in Miami, is registered as a Liberian corporation. Controlling interests are held by a Bahamian partnership associated with the Pritzker family of Chicago and by a shipping company owned by the Wilhelmsen family in Norway. Royal Caribbean Cruises Ltd. owns Royal Caribbean International and Celebrity Cruises.

Radisson Seven Seas Cruises is part of Carlson Hospitality Worldwide. Its ships are owned by a variety of international companies and marketed by Radisson Hospitality Worldwide in joint ventures.

Silversea is owned by the Lefebvre family of Rome. Crystal Cruises is owned by the huge Japanese freighter company Nippon Yupen Kaiska (NYK).

ECONOGUIDE CRUISE RATINGS

ECONOGUIDE'S BEST CRUISE LINES

Celebrity Cruises. (800) 437–3111, (305) 262–6677; www.celebritycruises.com
Disney Cruise Line. (800) 326–0620; www.disneycruise.com
Holland America Line–Westours Inc. (800) 227–6482, (800) 426–0327; www. hollandamerica.com
Norwegian Cruise Line. (800) 327–7030; www.ncl.com
Princess Cruises. (800) 421–0522, (800) 774–6237; www.princess.com

ECONOGUIDE'S BEST LUXURY CRUISE LINES

Crystal Cruises. (800) 820–6663, (310) 785–9300; www.crystalcruises.com
Radisson Seven Seas Cruises. (800) 333–3333, (800) 285–1835; www.rssc.com
Sea Cloud Cruises. (888) 732–2568, (201) 227–9404; www.seacloud.com
Seabourn Cruise Line. (800) 929–9391; www.seabourn.com
Silversea Cruises. (800) 722–9955, (954) 522–4477; www.silversea.com

ECONOGUIDE'S BEST CRUISE VALUES

Celebrity Cruises. (800) 437–3111, (305) 262–6677; www.celebritycruises.com
Holland America Line. (800) 227–6482, (800) 426–0327; www.hollandamerica.com
Norwegian Cruise Line. (800) 327–7030; www.ncl.com

ECONOGUIDE'S BEST CRUISE LINES FOR FAMILIES

Disney Cruise Line. (800) 326–0620; www.disneycruise.com
Royal Caribbean International. (800) 327–6700; www.royalcaribbean.com

ECONOGUIDE'S BEST DINING AT SEA

Celebrity Cruises. (800) 437–3111, (305) 262–6677; www.celebritycruises.com
Radisson Seven Seas Cruises. (800) 333–3333, (800) 285–1835; www.rssc.com
Sea Cloud Cruises. (888) 732–2568, (201) 227–9404; www.seacloud.com

ECONOGUIDE'S BEST ADVENTURE CRUISE LINES

Delta Queen Steamboat Company. (800) 543–7637; www.deltaqueen.com
Star Clippers. (800) 442–0551; www.star-clippers.com
Windstar Cruises. (800) 258–7245, (206) 281–3535; www.windstar cruises.com

ECONOGUIDE'S BEST PARTY SHIPS

Carnival Cruise Lines. (800) 227–6482, (305) 599–2600; www.carnival.com
Costa Cruise Lines. (800) 332–6782, (305) 358–7325; www.costacruises.com

ECONOGUIDE'S BEST CRUISE LINES

� Carnival Cruise Lines	♦♦♦♦ Holland America Line
♦♦♦♦ Celebrity Cruises	♦♦♦♦ Norwegian Cruise Line
♦♦♦ Costa Cruise Lines	♦♦♦♦ Princess Cruises
♦♦♦♦♦ Cunard Line	♦♦♦ Royal Caribbean
♦♦♦♦ Disney Cruise Line	

CARNIVAL CRUISE LINES

Address: 3655 N.W. 87th Avenue
Miami, FL 33178-2428
Information: (800) 227–6482, (305) 599–2600;
www.carnival.com
Econoguide's Best Party Ships

♦ ♦ ♦

The Carnival Fleet

Carnival Valor	2004	2,974 passengers	110,000 tons
Carnival Glory	2003	2,974 passengers	110,000 tons
Carnival Conquest	2002	2,974 passengers	110,000 tons
Carnival Victory	2000	2,758 passengers	102,000 tons
Carnival Triumph	1999	2,758 passengers	102,000 tons
Carnival Destiny	1999	2,642 passengers	101,353 tons
Carnival Miracle	2004	2,124 passengers	86,000 tons
Carnival Legend	2002	2,124 passengers	86,000 tons
Carnival Pride	2002	2,112 passengers	84,000 tons
Carnival Spirit	2001	2,112 passengers	84,000 tons
Elation	1998	2,040 passengers	70,367 tons
Paradise	1998	2,040 passengers	70,367 tons
Inspiration	1996	2,040 passengers	70,367 tons

Imagination	1995	2,040 passengers	70,367 tons
Fascination	1994	2,040 passengers	70,367 tons
Sensation	1993	2,040 passengers	70,367 tons
Ecstasy	1991	2,040 passengers	70,367 tons
Fantasy	1990	2,044 passengers	70,367 tons
Celebration	1987	1,486 passengers	47,262 tons
Jubilee	1986	1,486 passengers	47,262 tons
Holiday	1985	1,452 passengers	46,052 tons

FUTURE SHIPS

Carnival Liberty	Late 2005	2,974 passengers	110,000 tons

Carnival ships offer a Mardi Gras of glitz, pizzazz, and hoopla. These are theme parks on the water, with flashing lights, polished wood and chrome, and nearly nonstop parties, contests, and lavish Las Vegas–style shows, magic, singers, and bands.

The Carnival crowd is more young, more single, more young family, and more party-seeking than the guests on most other lines; its nearest competitors are Royal Caribbean and Princess.

In other words, Carnival is not your father's Cunard . . . although Carnival now owns the separately operated Cunard Line. These are not superluxury ships like those of Seabourn (Carnival owns that line, too). And Carnival is not the Love Boat, although in 2003 the company completed a corporate merger with Princess Cruises.

On Carnival you're not likely to find an emphasis on hushed rosewood libraries and secluded deck chair hideaways; you're much more likely to hear about discos and beach blanket bingo on the pool deck.

◼ ITINERARIES

They call them the "Fun Ships," and in a typical year the fleet sails to the Bahamas, the Caribbean, the Mexican Riviera, Alaska, Hawaii, and the Panama Canal on itineraries as short as three days and as long as sixteen. In 2003 primary home ports were in Miami, San Juan, Los Angeles, Tampa, New Orleans, Port Canaveral, Galveston, Vancouver, Anchorage, New York, Charleston, and Norfolk. Secondary ports included Mobile, Alabama; Philadelphia, and Baltimore.

Carnival's ships operate primarily in the Caribbean and the Gulf of Mexico, as well as New England, Canada, Bermuda, the Bahamas, the Mexican Riviera, and Alaska. Several ships make visits to Europe and Hawaii. Primary home ports include Miami, San Juan, Tampa, Port Canaveral, New York, New Orleans, Galveston, and Vancouver. Other ports of embarkation include Seward/ Anchorage, Charleston, and Norfolk. The new 110,000-ton *Carnival Glory* became Port Canaveral's newest and largest cruise ship when it launched year-round seven-day Caribbean service from that Florida port in summer 2003.

Carnival also operated an unprecedented fifty departures from the Big Apple in 2003, including an eight-day Caribbean schedule featuring stops at San Juan, St. Thomas/St. John, and Tortola/Virgin Gorda. Also included in Carnival's 2003

New York schedule were seven-day Bermuda cruises and four- and five-day Canada voyages and seven-day "fall foliage" sailings.

The company also introduced weeklong sailings from Galveston to Belize, Cozumel, and Progreso on *Elation*. The smoke-free *Paradise* added a new program of seven-day "exotic" eastern and western Caribbean cruises from Miami, with stops at such less-visited ports as Isla Roatan, Belize, and Casa de Campo.

Carnival Pride was repositioned to Los Angeles/Long Beach to operate seven-day Mexican Riviera cruises to the resort destinations of Puerto Vallarta, Mazatlan, and Cabo San Lucas.

Carnival Conquest began sailing from New Orleans in early 2003 but was forced to shift its homeport to Gulfport, Mississippi, because of rising water levels in the Mississippi River. The high waters brought the 207-foot-tall ship uncomfortably close to low-hanging power lines at Chalmette, downriver from the Port of New Orleans. The lines may be buried below the river bed in 2004, allowing large cruise ships to call at New Orleans without concern.

■ THE CARNIVAL STORY

It all began with a small cruise charter company run by Ted Arison, an Israeli who had an air freight company in New York. In 1966, when financial difficulties by a shipowner forced the removal of a leased vessel, Arison was left with several loads of passengers but no ship. He contacted Knut Kloster, a Norwegian shipping company operator whose vessel the *Sunward* was laid up, and the two put the passengers together with a cruise ship. Thus was born Norwegian Caribbean Lines, the predecessor of today's Norwegian Cruise Line. The partnership of Arison and Kloster came to an end in 1972, and Arison went on to found Carnival.

The launch of what became the world's largest cruise company began in 1972 with just one ship, the aging classic *Empress of Canada*, renamed the *Mardi Gras*. In a much-reported example of an inauspicious start, the *Mardi Gras* ran aground off Miami Beach on her maiden voyage. But Carnival got past its beginning with a well-crafted marketing plan that turned 180 degrees away from the formal and stuffy image of the great ocean liners. Instead, Carnival's fleet was made up of the Fun Ships, featuring a near-continuous party atmosphere.

During the next twenty-five years, the line grew rapidly to become the largest cruise company in the world. In the mid-1980s Carnival launched an insistent series of television commercials that brought the cruise line into middle-class America with great success.

Carnival purchased Holland America Line and Windstar Cruises in 1989 and holds major interests in Seabourn Cruise Line, Cunard Line (including the QE2), and Costa Cruise Line.

In 1996 Carnival introduced the 2,642-passenger, 101,353-ton *Carnival Destiny*, which, for several years, was the largest passenger vessel afloat. *Carnival Conquest*, a 110,000-ton Megaship, joined the fleet in 2002; sister ship *Carnival Glory* arrived in summer 2003, and a third sister, *Carnival Valor*, is due in fall 2004. The fourth vessel in the Conquest class, *Carnival Liberty*, is due in late 2005.

The new Long Beach Cruise Terminal at the *Queen Mary,* about 25 miles south of Los Angeles, includes a single cruise berth capable of handling vessels up to 1,000 feet in length and a parking garage for approximately 1,250 vehicles. The embarkation/disembarkation facility is within a section of the existing geodesic dome, former home of Howard Hughes's *Spruce Goose* flying boat. Guests can stay in the hotel at the *Queen Mary* before and after their cruise.

Other vessels in the Carnival corporate family—Holland America Line, Costa Cruises, Cunard Line, Seabourn Cruise Line, and Windstar Cruises—may eventually use the terminal as well. Long Beach officials anticipate more than 500,000 annual departures and arrivals through the new terminal.

Guests can book one- to three-night pre- and postcruise land packages in one of 365 available Art Deco–inspired cabins within the *Queen Mary* hotel.

■ THE CARNIVAL EXPERIENCE

All Carnival vessels have at least three swimming pools, including a children's wading pool and water slide. Most staterooms can be adapted for use by families, with additional berths, rollaway beds, and cribs. There are children's playrooms on all vessels; two rooms on the six Fantasy-class vessels have toys, games, and activities for kids ages five to twelve. The *Carnival Destiny* includes a two-level 1,300-square-foot play area.

Camp Carnival has programs for four age groups: toddlers (ages two to four), intermediate (five to eight), juniors (nine to twelve), and teens (thirteen to seventeen). Kids can dine out under the stars on the lido deck with members of the youth staff.

In recent years, Carnival has introduced flexible dining on its larger ships, a combination of more assigned dining times and a wider range of alternative restaurants. You may be able to adjust your assigned time before you sail or once you are onboard the ship, or you can avail yourself of a number of alternative dining options.

For casual dining between 6:00 and 9:00 P.M., lido deck poolside eateries are converted to Seaview Bistros, where there are no assigned tables, seating times, or dress codes. Meals are served buffet-style most nights, with specialty stations serving made-to-order selections; an expanded salad bar is also offered. Full table service will occasionally be offered.

The newer ships in the Carnival fleet include a reservations-only gourmet restaurant, for which there is an additional charge.

Carnival has also adopted a prepaid gratuity system fleetwide. In 2003 a total of $9.75 per person per day was automatically posted to shipboard charge accounts; the charges break down as follows: $5.50 per day for headwaiter and waiter, $3.50 per day for cabin steward, and 75 cents per day for the assistant maître d' or hostess and the waiter and cooks in the bistro. According to the company, this system takes into account the fact that many guests are taking advantage of alternative dining and that the overall number of wait staff has been increased. Guests have the option of asking that tips be increased, decreased, or removed from their bill and can also make individual payments to staff.

According to the company, about 30 percent of its customers are under age thirty-five, 40 percent between thirty-five and fifty-five years of age, and 30 percent over fifty-five. In 2002 Carnival carried about 2.7 million travelers.

Special savings are available to members of the American Association of Retired Persons (AARP), with discounts of up to $100 per cabin for most seven-day voyages and $50 on all the line's three-, four-, or five-day cruises.

Carnival expected to host a record 400,000 kids in 2003, roughly half the number of children carried by the entire North American cruise industry (CLIA member lines). On most ships, a "teen club" for ages sixteen to eighteen offers a full schedule of supervised activities and indoor and outdoor play areas; also available is "Camp Carnival" for children ages two to fifteen.

Adults can visit a "topless" sunbathing area near the funnel on most ships; it's a popular spot for singles.

In 2003 Carnival continued its "vacation guarantee," which offers a limited escape clause to guests who board a ship and find it not to their liking. Passengers who are in any way dissatisfied with their cruise can notify the ship's purser before arrival at the first port of call. They'll be able to disembark at the first non-U.S. port of call and receive a refund of the unused portion of the cruise fare and an airline ticket back to the port of departure.

■ WEB SITE

Everything is there for a knowledgeable and adventurous traveler: descriptions of the ships, itineraries, and cabin classes. Once you register for My Carnival online booking, you can choose from specific available cabins, cross-checking location against a deck-by-deck map. You can book your cruise with a credit card or ask for a Carnival representative to call you to answer questions and proceed with booking. You can also register and wait to receive "Fun Wave" e-mails with Carnival's latest cruise specials. *Ease of use: excellent.*

Carnival Conquest, Carnival Glory, *Carnival Valor* (2004)*, Carnival Liberty* (2005) (CONQUEST CLASS)	

Econoguide rating:	★★★★ 85 points
Ship size:	Colossus
Category:	Top of the Line
Price range:	Premium $$$
Registry:	Panama
Year built:	*Carnival Conquest,* 2002; *Carnival Glory,* 2003
Future ships:	*Carnival Valor,* 2004; *Carnival Liberty,* 2005
Information:	(305) 599–2600, (800) 227–6482
Web site:	www.carnival.com
Passenger capacity:	2,974 (double occupancy)
Crew:	1,160
Passenger-to-crew ratio:	2.5:1

Tonnage:	110,000
Passenger-space ratio:	38.6
Length:	952 feet
Beam:	116 feet
Draft:	27 feet
Cruising speed:	22.5 knots
Guest decks:	13
Total cabins:	1,487
Outside:	917
Inside:	570
Suites:	42
Wheelchair cabins:	N/A
Cuisine:	Contemporary and low-fat, low-calorie Nautica spa fare
Style:	Casual, with one or two semiformal nights
Price notes:	Single-occupancy premium, 150 to 200 percent
Tipping suggestions:	$9.75 pp/pd automatically posted to bill

Stretching more than three football fields in length, each of the $500 million Conquest-class ships has twenty-two lounges, nightspots, and bars. By the end of the voyage, most passengers have found pulsating dance clubs, three-deck-high 1,500-seat theaters showcasing lavish Las Vegas–style revues, piano bars, jazz clubs, sports bars, wine and caviar bars, and cigar bars.

All the ships in this class are too wide to transit the Panama Canal and are likely to spend all their time in the Caribbean and Europe.

There are four swimming pools, including one with a 214-foot-long cascading water slide and another with a retractable dome. There is a 3,300-square-foot children's play area for the Camp Carnival program as well as a teen coffee bar and dance club and an outdoor recreation area featuring basketball and volleyball courts.

At the heart of the Camp Carnival program is "Children's World," which includes an arts and crafts center with spin and sand art and candy-making machines; an all-ages play room with a variety of toys, games, and puzzles, and kid-sized tables and chairs; a video room showing kids' favorite movies and cartoons; a children's library; a computer lab; and a set of video game machines. An onboard science education program gives children the chance to participate in science projects and experiments and a geography program focusing on the cultures and landmarks of the various ports of call.

The ships offer a golf program featuring professional instruction aboard ship and during golf excursions, along with netted driving ranges and teaching computers.

Of the 1,487 staterooms, 917 offer an ocean view and 556 feature private balconies.

Dining options begin with a pair of two-level full-service restaurants with traditional cruise ship dining for breakfast, lunch, and dinner. As an alternative, there's an expansive two-deck-high poolside eatery with full breakfast, lunch, and dinner buffets, including "Taste of the Nation," with traditional cuisine from a different country each day, a New York–style deli, a rotisserie serving broiled chicken and steak, and stations featuring traditional English-style fish-and-chips and Asian and American favorites. A twenty-four-hour pizzeria offers seven kinds of pies, calzones, Caesar salad, and garlic bread.

And then there is a patisserie featuring specialty coffees and sweets, a sushi bar, and a reservations-only steakhouse-style supper club serving prime aged beef along with crab claws from Miami Beach's famous Joe's Stone Crab Restaurant.

On the **Conquest,** the alternative restaurant is The Point, located at the top of the eleven-deck-high atrium; the eatery draws its name and design from the works of Impressionist Georges-Pierre Seurat, with colorful images inspired by his famous painting *Le Cirque* (The Circus), created in the artist's distinctive "pointillism" style, comprising thousands of tiny dots, or points. The Point comes with a hefty $25-per-person reservations fee. Specialties include large cuts of steak, broiled lobster tail, and stone crab claws.

Conquest's poolside restaurant is Restaurant Cezanne, incorporating design elements of that artist's post-Impressionist paintings. Evoking the atmosphere of a nineteenth-century French cafe, the two-level restaurant features handpainted ceramic wainscoting and authentic reproductions of the artist's works, including *Chateau Noir,* and *House of Pere Lacroix in Auvers.*

Carnival Glory takes colors as its central design theme, with each public room celebrating a different shade of the rainbow. The Conquest-class ship is scheduled to sail year-round from Port Canaveral.

It all begins in the lobby, home of the Color Bar and the main atrium, named Old Glory, featuring interpretative paintings of U.S. flags. Both the Kaleidoscope Boulevard promenade and the atrium are lit by fixtures subdivided into geometric modules that are backlit with LED lights, resulting in slow-moving kaleidoscopic effects.

Carnival Glory's main show lounge is Amber Palace. The Platinum and Golden Dining Rooms are inspired by Japanese temples; lights in concave ceiling fixtures provide color-changing effects.

The design of the White Heat Dance Club includes gigantic white candles in silver candelabra bases. The Ivory Club features replicas of elephant tusks, intricate wall coverings, and windows inset with mosaics of faux semiprecious stones. Cinn-A-Bar, a piano bar, is decorated in reddish-brown hues.

Bar Blue is the ship's jazz bar, festooned with giant peacock feathers that extend from the floor almost to the ceiling. The Ebony Cabaret has an African atmosphere, with dark ebony walls and ceilings and hand-carved and painted wooden African masks mounted in copperlike frames.

The Red Sail Restaurant, a casual poolside eatery, evokes a sailboat motif, with varnished pine masts, sails, chrome hardware, a wood-beam ceiling, teak railing, false portholes, and other touches. The reservations-only steakhouse-style supper club Emerald Room features cobalt-blue walls and lighting fixtures resembling giant emeralds.

In its first assignment, *Carnival Glory* will operate year-round from Port Canaveral in Florida, with alternating eastern and western Caribbean voyages departing every Saturday.

Carnival Valor will join the fleet in 2004, and the fourth Conquest-class ship, *Carnival Liberty,* is due in late fall 2005.

Carnival Destiny, Carnival Triumph, Carnival Victory (DESTINY CLASS)

Econoguide rating:	★★★★ 80 points
Ship size:	Colossus
Category:	Top of the Line
Price range:	Premium $$$
Registry:	Panama
Year built:	Carnival Destiny, 1999; Carnival Triumph, 1999; Carnival Victory, 2000
Information:	(305) 599–2600, (800) 227–6482
Web site:	www.carnival.com
Passenger capacity:	Carnival Destiny, 2,642; Carnival Triumph, 2,758; Carnival Victory, 2,758
Crew:	1,070
Passenger-to-crew ratio:	2.5:1
Tonnage:	Carnival Destiny, 101,353; Carnival Triumph, Carnival Victory, 102,000
Passenger-space ratio:	Carnival Destiny, 38.4; Carnival Triumph, Carnival Victory, 38.6
Length:	893 feet
Beam:	116 feet
Draft:	27 feet
Cruising speed:	22.5 knots
Guest decks:	12
Total cabins:	1,321
Outside:	758
Inside:	514
Suites:	48
Wheelchair cabins:	25
Cuisine:	Contemporary and low-fat, low-calorie Nautica spa fare
Style:	Casual, with one or two semiformal nights
Price notes:	Single-occupancy premium, 150 to 200 percent
Tipping suggestions:	$9.75 pp/pd automatically posted to bill

The **Carnival Destiny** was the first cruise ship to zoom past the 100,000-ton barrier; for a while it held the record as the largest passenger load afloat. The Destiny-class ships include the *Carnival Destiny, Carnival Triumph*, and *Carnival Victory.* Slightly smaller than the Conquest-class ships, these vessels are nevertheless also too wide to pass through the Panama Canal and will likely spend their lives sailing in the Caribbean and European waters.

The lifeboats and most other machinery are limited to Decks 3, 4, and 5, which are used for public rooms, including restaurants, lounges, and bars. This means there are hardly any outside cabins with obstructed views; the only exceptions are a scant nineteen cabins at the bow of the ship with forward-facing windows partially blocked by equipment there. More than 60 percent of the staterooms have ocean views, and 70 percent of those have private balconies.

Four upper decks offer private verandas. Up top on the Spa Deck are fourteen cabins with floor-to-ceiling windows.

These ships have an unusual feature that may appeal to extreme party animals: There are a handful of "Night Owl Staterooms" offered at deep discounts of 50 percent or more off the least-expensive rates. Of course, you'll have to be a night owl yourself, because these rooms are intended for guests who "love to party late into the night." In other words, these rooms, all inside twin/king cabins, are very close to the noisy late-night action.

At the other end of the spectrum is a set of "family staterooms" that give mom and dad a bit of privacy from the kids. Camp Carnival offers programs for children from ages five through twelve.

There are thirteen decks, numbered 1 to 14 (with an eye toward the superstitious, there's a numerical skip between the top decks). The Sky Deck contains a small observation platform and the entrance to the water slide down to the pool.

The *Triumph*'s nine-story main atrium is the Capitol, with a spectacular sky dome showing the sky above a lobby bar way down below. There is a pair of bilevel dining rooms, London and Paris; you can also dine bistro-style in the laid-back South Beach Club Restaurant.

The *Carnival Destiny* eases out of Miami. *Photo by Andy Newman/CCL*

Las Vegas–style revues are presented in the three-level Rome Lounge. Drinks and cigars can follow at a cigar bar, or cappuccino and pastry at the Vienna Cafe. Underground Tokyo is a cavernlike video arcade. Youngsters can join Camp Carnival for daily activities.

Public rooms are inspired by the world's great cities, with decorations commissioned from a crew of international artists. Among the most spectacular is a series of three-dimensional maplike murals in glass created by renowned Venetian artist Luciano Vistosi. Depicting the planet's continents, the murals are positioned along the 525-foot-long World's Way promenade. Vistosi also created *Moebius,* an expansive, tricolor glass sculpture that dominates the *Triumph's* three-deck-high aft atrium. The 8-foot-high by 8-foot-long abstract sculpture, which took nearly a year to complete, is composed of intertwining blue, green, and white glass prisms woven together in a unique free-flowing pattern.

Adorning the *Triumph's* elevator lobbies and passenger stair landings is a series of thirty-five original murals by Israeli artist Calman Shemi, whose works can also be seen aboard Carnival's *Sensation, Elation,* and *Paradise.* Citing influences ranging from Jules Vernes's *Around the World in Eighty Days* to twentieth-century French Impressionist Raoul Dufy, Shemi's vibrant, multihued murals depict such landmarks as Paris's Eiffel Tower, New York's towering skyscrapers, and India's ancient temples.

British artist Susanna Holt's four stone sculptures are located adjacent to the Universe Pool on the lido deck; the vaselike sculptures feature a variety of unique and exquisite materials from around the world, including small horn-shaped *Bullia vittata* shells from India, sea urchin spines from the Gulf of Mexico, and several varieties of star-shaped *Turritella terebra* shells from Taiwan and the Phillipines.

The centerpiece of **Carnival Victory** is Oceanic Hall, a nine-deck atrium decorated in watery hues of turquoise, green, gold, and blue. Handmade glass-tile mosaics of mermaids, the sea god Neptune, and other aqueous themes are displayed; overhead, an illuminated dome is decorated in Tiffany-style glass.

The oceanic theme is continued in the names and decor of public rooms including the Coral Sea Cafe, laid out with displays of coral.

Ecstasy, Elation, Fantasy, Fascination, Imagination, Inspiration, Paradise, Sensation (FANTASY CLASS)

Econoguide rating:	★★★ 76 points
Ship size:	Megaship
Category:	Top of the Line
Price range:	Moderate $$
Registry:	Liberia
Year built:	*Ecstasy,* 1991; *Elation,* 1998; *Fantasy,* 1990; *Fascination,* 1994; *Imagination,* 1995; *Inspiration,* 1996; *Paradise,* 1998; *Sensation,* 1993
Information:	(305) 599–2600, (800) 227–6482

Web site:	www.carnival.com
Passenger capacity:	2,044 (double occupancy)
Crew:	920
Passenger-to-crew ratio:	2.2:1
Tonnage:	70,367
Passenger-space ratio:	34.4
Length:	855 feet
Beam:	103 feet
Draft:	25.9 feet
Cruising speed:	21 knots
Guest decks:	10
Total cabins:	1,022
Outside:	566
Inside:	402
Suites:	54
Wheelchair cabins:	22
Cuisine:	Contemporary and low-fat, low-calorie Nautica spa fare
Style:	Casual during the day; on one or two nights, formal dress or dark suit suggested
Price notes:	Single-occupancy premium, 150 to 200 percent
Tipping suggestions:	$9.75 pp/pd automatically posted to bill

Members of the Fantasy class, these ships include three dining areas, ten bars and lounges, a spa and health club, casino, three swimming pools, jogging tracks, and two children's playrooms. There are few places to get away from the bustle of a lively cruise, which may or may not appeal to you.

Elation was the first company ship to include the Azipod propulsion system, which pulls instead of pushes the vessel through the water, and eliminates the need for drive shafts, rudders, and stern thrusters. The system dramatically improves maneuverability and delivers higher operating speed, all at a significant savings in fuel.

Fantasy, delivered in 1990, was the first newly built cruise liner with a diesel-electric AC propulsion and power system and joystick-controlled navigation. Of more interest to most cruisegoers, *Fantasy* was also the first cruise ship to have a seven-deck central atrium, the Grand Spectrum.

Among her more unusual decorative features is Cleopatra's Bar, a great place to get mummified; the appointments are right out of Egypt by way of Las Vegas.

In 2000 *Fantasy* underwent a major refurbishment, emerging with a new Roman-themed promenade, Via Marina, leading to many of the ship's lounges and nightspots. The promenade's design includes a faux stone floor, electric torches, Doric columns, and terra-cotta urns. Aft of the promenade is a new Formality Shop, where guests can rent tuxedos and purchase specialty items. The former aft show lounge was converted to include a large conference facility and Children's World, a high-tech play area that includes toys and games, a bank of computers loaded with educational software and games, and a new teen center with video game machines, Foosball, and pool tables.

Fascination's public rooms pay homage to Tinseltown, with public rooms that include the Tara Library, modeled after a scene from *Gone with the Wind*, the Casino Royale, the Diamonds Are Forever dance club, and the Passage to India Lounge. The ship's main drag is Hollywood Boulevard on the promenade deck.

Geared toward sixteen- to eighteen-year-old guests, *Fascination*'s "Backstreet Club" features a CD jukebox stocked with the latest rock, R&B, rap and hip-hop hits, as well as a state-of-the-art sound and lighting system and a large dance floor. The facility also houses a bank of Internet-connected Apple iMac computers, Sony PlayStation 2 video game units, and a "mocktail lounge" serving nonalcoholic versions of Carnival's popular frozen specialty drinks. A karaoke machine and a library featuring teen-oriented magazines are included as well.

Other "family-friendly" features aboard *Fascination* include three swimming pools (one with a 115-foot-long water slide), a video game room, special children's menus in the main dining rooms, and a turndown service offering chocolate chip cookies at bedtime. A nightly baby-sitting service is also available for a nominal fee.

Imagination's decor emphasizes some unusual corners of human fancy, from the Curiosity Library to the Shangri-La and Xanadu Lounges and the El Dorado Casino.

The **Inspiration**'s interior design pays tribute to the popular and fine arts, with rooms such as the Avant-Garde Lounge, featuring statues and wall designs reminiscent of the cubist art form, and the Shakespeare Library, whose ceiling is lined with some of the playwright's most famous quotations.

Paradise was the world's first smoke-free cruise ship, from cabins to dining rooms to the open decks. Carnival is pretty serious about its commitment to healthy air on this ship: According to press reports, a pair of travel agents were discovered sneaking a smoke during the ship's christening ceremonies and were made to walk the plank. Luckily, the ship was tied up in New York at the time.

Vacationers who light up onboard the ship may find it's the most expensive cigarette they've ever smoked. Guests who violate the no-smoking policy will be required to disembark at the next port of call and return home at their own expense without any refund of their cruise fare, and $250 in "liquidated damages" will be charged to the passenger's onboard charge account. The company sent out a news release when the first passenger was put off the ship because of a transgression of the rules.

Elements of the ship's design are intended to echo the legendary *Queen Mary*, one of the most famous transatlantic ocean liners of all time. Located aft on the promenade deck, the Queen Mary Lounge is used for dancing, late-night comedy shows, and other live entertainment. Funnel shapes are used throughout the room: along the walls, framing the sofas, lining the bar front, and serving as table bases. Their lower portions are veneered in Nigerian satinwood, stained bright red to match the *Queen Mary*'s celebrated smokestacks; the upper sections are finished in black gloss lacquer. Where red meets black is a strip of lacquered ebony wood inlaid with a clear polycarbonate tube of twinkling Tivoli lights. Even the distinctive ribs that segment the funnels are re-created in ebony inlays.

Set atop the large wall-mounted funnels are stylized brass-ringed "portholes," which house video monitors broadcasting vintage motion films of the celebrated *Queen Mary*, other classic liners, and life aboard the great ships of the former heyday of cruising.

Many of the vessel's interior designs are inspired by legendary ships of the past. In the case of the Rex Dance Club, the lounge takes its name from the *Rex*, a famed Italian liner of the 1930s.

Carnival plays off the name Rex, the Latin word for "king," with images of the king of the jungle and safari scenes. Floor-to-ceiling columns surrounding the lounge are stepped like the stones of ancient temples and covered with imitation animal hides that extend upward to the ceiling, creating a mosaic of zebra, leopard, and tiger skin patterns.

Paradise was assigned to Miami in 2003, sailing year-round western and eastern Caribbean cruises to ports including Isla Roatan, Honduras; Belize City, Belize; and Casa de Campo, Dominican Republic.

Sensation was one of Carnival's early breakthroughs into maritime glitz, and though it has been surpassed by more modern ships, it still has its flashy appeals, including the Roman architectural orgy of Michelangelo's Lounge and the ultracolorful Kaleidoscope Dance Club.

In July 1998 **Ecstasy** suffered a minor fire in crew areas at her stern soon after departing Miami and was forced to return. The ship has been refurbished and returned to service.

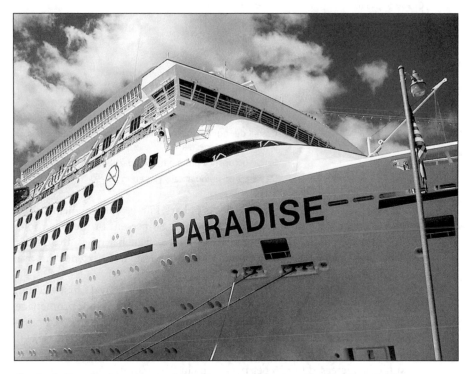

Carnival's *Paradise* in port, complete with no-smoking sign. *Photo by Corey Sandler*

Carnival Spirit, Carnival Pride, Carnival Legend, Carnival Miracle (2004) (SPIRIT CLASS)

Econoguide rating:	★★★ 79 points
Ship size:	Megaship
Category:	Top of the Line
Price range:	Budget to Moderate $–$$
Registry:	Panama
Year built:	Carnival Spirit, 2001; Carnival Pride, 2002; Carnival Legend, 2002
Future ship:	Carnival Miracle, 2004
Information:	(305) 599–2600, (800) 227–6482
Web site:	www.carnival.com
Passenger capacity:	2,124
Crew:	900
Passenger-to-crew ratio:	2.3:1
Tonnage:	86,000
Passenger-space ratio:	39.8
Length:	963 feet
Beam:	106 feet
Draft:	22 feet
Cruising speed:	22 knots
Guest decks:	12
Total cabins:	1,321
Outside:	792
Inside:	529
Suites:	None indicated
Wheelchair cabins:	None indicated
Cuisine:	Contemporary and low-fat, low-calorie Nautica spa fare
Style:	Casual during the day; on one or two nights, formal dress or dark suit suggested
Price notes:	Single-occupancy premium, 150 to 200 percent
Tipping suggestions:	$9.75 pp/pd automatically posted to bill

The Spirit-class ships include two decks of bars, lounges, and nightspots, one with an outdoor wraparound promenade. Some 80 percent of the staterooms offer ocean views; 87 percent of those cabins have private balconies. In addition to a two-level main restaurant, a topside alternative restaurant extends out over the uppermost section of the atrium.

Introduced in 2001, the Spirit class of ships included Carnival's first wedding chapel, a reservations-only supper club, and a wraparound outdoor promenade.

Carnival Spirit introduced the Nouveau Supper Club, an upscale "steakhouse–style" restaurant; soon after the ship took to the seas, Carnival announced with public relations fanfare that the restaurant was so popular that the reservations fee would be increased to $25 per person, including gratuity.

Diners are offered a choice of nine different starters and salads, prime aged beef, and stone crab claws from Miami Beach's legendary Joe's Stone Crab Restaurant, the first time the delicacies have been featured on a cruise ship menu. The claws, from crabs native to Florida waters, are traditionally served cold, accompanied by Joe's signature mustard sauce or drawn butter. The crab's hard shells are cracked with a wooden mallet immediately prior to serving.

Carnival reports serving upward of 300 pounds of stone crab claws per week. Other popular fare includes steaks, filet mignon, grilled lamb chops, broiled lobster tail with citrus butter, and Dover sole meunière.

The two-level restaurant is located at the top of a soaring nine-deck-high atrium and housed under a red-tinted glass dome that forms the forward portion of the ship's funnel. The room's design is based on the magnificent Hotel Tassel in Brussels, often cited as one of the finest examples of Art Nouveau design; there's a dance floor and nightly entertainment for diners.

The *Carnival Pride,* which joined the fleet in late 2001, introduced some elegant dining options to the fleet. The ship's main dining room, the Normandie, harkens back to the classic liner of the same name, decorated with Art Deco touches and dark wood accents. The ship's casual restaurant, Mermaids' Grille, includes Asian and American specialty areas, a pasta bar, and a twenty-four-hour pizzeria set in a world of mermaids, dolphins, and other sea creatures.

The showplace eatery is David's, an upscale New York–style steakhouse that offers steaks, chops, and seafood, including crab claws from Miami Beach's famous Joe's Stone Crab Restaurant. David's is dominated by a 12-foot replica of Michelangelo's famed statue of the same name, along with ornate wood patterns and other Renaissance-inspired touches. There's a dance floor, nightly entertainment, and $25 per person reservations fee.

Carnival Pride uses a typically eclectic cruise ship mix of decors. The lobby, atrium, and other public areas are based on the arts and craftsmanship of the

Carnival Pride departs Port Canaveral. *Photo by Corey Sandler*

Italian Renaissance in rich details of wood and bronze moldings, dominated by gold, sienna, and burnt red tones. Reproductions of murals by Botticelli, Raphael, and other Italian painters adorn the walls.

The Taj Mahal show lounge is filled with intricate Indian designs, elephant friezes, and stonework with small jewels pressed into decorative designs and illuminated from behind.

The casino salutes the atmosphere of the Jockey Club at the Kentucky Derby, with a mural of Churchill Downs and bas-relief statues of jockeys and paintings of horses in the walls and ceiling.

The Starry Night jazz club replicates Van Gogh's painting of the same name; a wall and ceiling mural are illuminated by tiny lights.

The Nobel Library, which also houses the Internet cafe, has a simple Swedish design that falls somewhere between classical and Art Deco. Portraits of Alfred Nobel and the award ceremonies conducted in his name adorn walls, which are painted Windsor blue and trimmed in light green.

At Beauties Dance Club, varicolored male and female torsos, reminiscent of *Venus de Milo,* line the walls, support the tables, and decorate the ceiling. Walls and ceilings are of antique-look one-way mirrors illuminated from behind with flashing and neon lights for a variety of effects. One wall is dominated by a two-deck-high video display that can mix live video, special effects, and prerecorded images to accompany the dance music.

The lido deck pool area features a grand mural of Botticelli's *Birth of Venus.* The pools are named after Apollo and Poseidon, and bronze sculptures of the Greek gods are on pedestals between the pools.

Included in a multimillion-dollar art collection are seventy decorative vases and candleholders by Czech glass artist Borek Sipek, who created similar works for the *Carnival Pride*'s sister ship, *Carnival Spirit.* For *Carnival Pride,* Sipek took a unique approach for his trademark glass pieces, incorporating Renaissance-inspired touches to create the ornate contemporary works, which are located in glass cases positioned in the ship's stair landings.

The classic/contemporary design concept is also carried out in a series of bronze statues of the mythical figures Venus, Apollo, and Poseidon created by Italian sculptor Katia Tasselli. These 6-foot-high figures, each of which took several months to complete due to the complexity of their design, dramatically enhance the areas surrounding the pools that bear their names.

Carnival Legend has sixteen themed bars, lounges, and nightspots, with dramatic interiors inspired by famous legends and historical figures, as well as a 14,500-square-foot health and fitness facility, four swimming pools, a cascading water slide, an Internet cafe, a wedding chapel, and a children's play area, part of the line's Camp Carnival program.

Dining options include a 1,250-seat formal dining room, a patisserie with specialty coffees and sweets, twenty-four-hour room service, and a two-level poolside restaurant offering breakfast, lunch, and dinner alternatives as well as twenty-four-hour pizza and ice cream. Also featured is an intimate steakhouse-style supper club.

Celebration, Holiday, Jubilee (HOLIDAY CLASS)

Econoguide rating:	★★★ 73 points
Ship size:	Large
Category:	Top of the Line
Price range:	Budget to Moderate $–$$
Registry:	Panama
Year built:	*Celebration,* 1987; *Holiday,* 1985; *Jubilee,* 1986
Information:	(305) 599–2600, (800) 227–6482
Web site:	www.carnival.com
Passenger capacity:	*Celebration,* 1,486; *Holiday,* 1,452; *Jubilee,* 1,486
Crew:	660 to 670
Passenger-to-crew ratio:	2.2:1
Tonnage:	*Celebration,* 47,262; *Holiday,* 46,052; *Jubilee,* 47,262
Passenger-space ratio:	31.7
Length:	727 feet
Beam:	92 feet
Draft:	24.7 feet
Cruising speed:	21 knots
Guest decks:	9
Total cabins:	726
Outside:	437
Inside:	279
Suites:	10
Wheelchair cabins:	15
Cuisine:	Contemporary and low-fat, low-calorie Nautica spa fare
Style:	Casual during the day; one or two nights, formal dress or dark suit suggested
Price notes:	Single-occupancy premium, 150 to 200 percent
Tipping suggestions:	$9.75 pp/pd automatically posted to bill

The three sisters of Carnival in the Holiday class are still pretty flashy for a trio of older women. Early examples of the Carnival flash, they introduced the broad internal "boulevard" on the promenade deck. Less than half the tonnage of Carnival's Conquest- and Fantasy-class ships, Holiday-class ships don't offer many places to escape the lively onboard activities.

On *Celebration,* Bourbon Street runs down the length of the starboard side of the ship from the Islands in the Sky Lounge to the Astoria Lounge, passing by the Galax-Z Dance Club, the Rainbow Club Casino, and the dry-docked trolley parked nearby.

Holiday's Broadway on the promenade deck features a bus parked outside the casino. The nightclub is the western-themed Doc Holiday's.

Jubilee's eclectic collection of public rooms runs from the quiet and elegant Churchill's Library, which includes a faux fireplace, wood-beamed ceilings, Ionic columns, and suits of armor, to the other extreme at Oz, a pulsating club with a checkerboard dance floor and an emerald green ceiling. Park lane emulates an old English garden, while the Speakeasy Lounge has a more raucous American theme.

On this class of ship, lifeboats sit way up high, resulting in very few obstructed views and affecting just four suites on the veranda deck.

CELEBRITY CRUISES

Address: 1050 Caribbean Way
Miami, FL 33132-2096
Information: (800) 437–3111, (305) 262–6677
www.celebritycruises.com
Econoguide's Best Cruise Lines
Econoguide's Best Cruise Values
Econoguide's Best Dining at Sea

The Celebrity Cruises Fleet

Constellation	2002	1,950 passengers	91,000 tons
Infinity	2001	1,950 passengers	91,000 tons
Millennium	2000	1,950 passengers	91,000 tons
Summit	2001	1,950 passengers	91,000 tons
Galaxy	1996	1,870 passengers	77,713 tons
Mercury	1997	1,870 passengers	77,713 tons
Century	1995	1,750 passengers	70,606 tons
Zenith	1992	1,375 passengers	47,255 tons
Horizon	1990	1,354 passengers	46,811 tons

X marks the spot for this upscale cruise line that sits somewhere between middle-of-the-market lines such as Royal Caribbean International (its parent company) and the small superluxury ships of companies such as Crystal and Seabourn.

The Celebrity *X* logo refers to the Greek character used to spell Chandris Group, the original founder of the company; Celebrity will also have you believe the symbol recalls the *X* ancient mariners used to mark their destinations.

The flagships of the line are the Millennium-class vessels. The 91,000-ton, 1,950-passenger ships, built at Chantiers de l'Atlantique in Saint-Nazaire, France, feature balconies for about 70 percent of staterooms, as well as some of the largest luxury suites afloat. Along with cousins at Royal Caribbean, they are the first cruise ships to use clean-burning gas turbines for propulsion.

The first ship in the class, *Millennium*, features a unique maritime treasure: the specialty dining room is decorated with the actual interior paneling of the RMS *Olympic*, sister ship to the RMS *Titanic.* The wood paneling in the 134-seat Olympic restaurant once graced the a la carte dining room onboard the glamorous *Olympic,* launched in 1911. The paneling was discovered in a private English residence and purchased at auction at Sotheby's.

The restaurant also offers the industry's first demonstration galley, along with a dine-in wine cellar. And speaking of wine, Celebrity was the winner of an auction at Christie's in New York for three rare bottles of 1907 Heidsieck Monopole champagne; the bottles of bubbly are displayed in the wine cellar. The champagne was salvaged in 1998 from the wreck of the *Jonkoping,* a Swedish merchant ship that was sunk in the Baltic Sea in 1916 by German sailors who believed the ship was carrying contraband: 5,000 bottles of top-quality French champagne destined for the czar of Russia. Wine experts say the champagne survived, with corks intact, in 35 degree water and total darkness. The same champagne was believed to be onboard the *Titanic* when it sank in 1912.

The Emporium is a high-tone shopping mall at sea, including outposts of DKNY, Versace, H. Stern, Fossil, La Perla, and Swarovski. The 14,460-square-foot mall also includes a shop selling cookware, kitchenware, and ingredients endorsed by chef Michel Roux.

The second ship in the class is the *Infinity,* which arrived in mid-2001. That ship includes a specialty restaurant that salutes the famed liner *United States.*

The third and fourth ships in the series are *Summit* and *Constellation.*

■ THE CELEBRITY STORY

Celebrity Cruises was founded in 1989 by the Athens-based Chandris Group as an upscale cruise line. The company's first vessel was the *Meridian,* formerly known as the *Galileo,* completely rebuilt and launched in 1990. That same year Celebrity brought onto the line a new ship, *Horizon.*

One of Celebrity's claims to fame is the quality of its food; among the company's first steps was the hiring of three-star Michelin chef and restaurateur Michel Roux to design the food service and train the executive restaurant staff. Roux continues as a consultant, sailing unannounced on the vessels and revising and updating menus every six months.

Roux also oversees the specifications for an elegant formal tea served weekly aboard all ships, elaborate midnight buffets featuring exquisite ice carvings, and theme meals.

The *Meridian* was sold to a Singapore company in 1997 when the sisters *Galaxy* and *Mercury* came on line. That same year, the Chandris family sold Celebrity to Royal Caribbean International.

Overall, Celebrity represents good value for the money, a reasonable step up in quality and price from the middle of the pack.

■ THE CELEBRITY EXPERIENCE

In the main dining room, the dress code is just a bit more formal than on other lines; jackets and ties are requested for men on formal and informal nights, with time off for good behavior on casual nights only.

At the same time, Celebrity has introduced more casual dining options most nights on every cruise, served in the Palm Springs Grill and pool area on

Mercury, at the Oasis Grill and pool area on *Galaxy,* the Coral Seas Cafe on *Horizon,* the Windsurf Cafe on *Zenith,* and in the Sky Bar on *Century.* A typical casual menu would offer lasagna, broiled salmon steak, spit-roasted chicken, and grilled sirloin steak—simpler fare than offered in the main dining rooms.

Indulgences onboard include the AquaSpa program, which offers treatments and facilities from Middle Eastern, Asian, and European sources, including a 115,000-gallon thalassotherapy pool on the *Century;* hydrotherapy spa baths of seaweed, minerals, or aromatherapy oils; and aqua meditation. There's also the Rasul treatment that includes a seaweed soap shower, medicinal mudpack, herbal steam bath, and massage. Treatments can be booked individually or as part of packages extending over the course of a voyage.

The line's Family Cruising Program serves youngsters from age three through seventeen with events that include pool Olympics, scavenger hunts, video games, arts and crafts, ship tours, and pizza and ice-cream parties.

And then there are the occasional Celebrity Escape cruises, for adults only. We're not exactly talking about an X-rating at sea, but the line does offer a Valentine's Night, late-night comedy acts including an adult-themed show, pool-side fashion shows, afternoon tea, and other entertainments. All guests on these cruises must be over the age of twenty-one.

■ ITINERARIES

Celebrity's fleet operates mostly in the Caribbean, with a limited number of seasonal cruises in Alaska, Hawaii, and Europe. Ships sailed to:

- **Caribbean** from Baltimore; Charleston, South Carolina; Fort Lauderdale; Miami; Philadelphia; San Juan; and Tampa.
- **Alaska** from San Diego; San Francisco; Seward, Alaska; and Vancouver, British Columbia.
- **Bermuda** from New York and Philadelphia.
- **California coast** from San Francisco.
- **Canada/New England** from Baltimore.
- **Europe** from Barcelona; Dover, England; Harwich, England; Stockholm; and Venice.
- **Hawaii** from Ensenada, Mexico; Honolulu; and Vancouver.
- **Mexico** from San Diego and San Francisco.
- **Panama Canal** from Fort Lauderdale, Miami, San Diego, and Tampa.
- **South America** from Buenos Aires, Argentina, and Valparaiso, Chile.

Celebrity sent *Zenith* to Jacksonville for a thirteen-week assignment from late October 2003 through late April 2004, making it the first cruise line to sail from the north Florida city. Departing from the Dames Point Marine Terminal, trips will go to the western Caribbean with visits to Roatan, the largest of Honduras's Bay Islands; a partial transit of the Panama Canal; and a visit to the company's private island, Labadee, Hispañola. The ship's southern Caribbean itinerary includes an overnight stay in Barbados, as well as visits to Tortola and Grenada.

Zenith originally was scheduled for a South America series. Instead, *Infinity,* one of Celebrity's newer Millennium-class ships, will handle that route.

■ WEB SITE

Celebrity's Web site provides a good collection of information, including a fleetwide calendar. Once you choose your trip, you can select from specific available cabins. The trip can be booked on-line, or you can hold the cabin and arrange for Celebrity to call you to complete the booking on the telephone. *Ease of use: very good.*

Millennium, Infinity, Summit, Constellation (MILLENNIUM CLASS)

Econoguide rating:	★★★★★ 93 points
Ship size:	Megaship
Category:	Top of the Line
Price range:	Premium $$$
Registry:	Liberia
Year built:	*Millennium,* 2000; *Infinity,* 2001; *Summit,* 2001; *Constellation,* 2002
Information:	(305) 262–6677
Web site:	www.celebritycruises.com
Passenger capacity:	1,950 (double occupancy)
Crew:	999
Passenger-to-crew ratio:	2:1
Tonnage:	91,000
Passenger-space ratio:	46.7
Length:	965 feet
Beam:	105.6 feet
Draft:	26.3 feet
Cruising speed:	24 knots
Guest decks:	11
Total cabins:	975
Outside:	780
Inside:	195
Suites:	50
Wheelchair cabins:	9
Cuisine:	Continental and international
Style:	Informal, with two or three formal evenings
Price notes:	Single-occupancy premium, about 125 percent
Tipping suggestions:	$9.00 pp/pd

The first of Celebrity's Millennium-class ships took to the seas in summer 2000 and was joined in coming years by three sisters.

The handsome ships employ environmentally friendly gas turbines and high-tech engine pods for maneuverability. The introduction of the cutting-edge *Millennium* was not without problems. The *Millennium* was delivered several

Celebrity's advanced *Millennium* receives an old-fashioned christening in Southampton, England.
Photo by Corey Sandler

months late, forcing the cancellation of its original maiden voyage. Then the ship had to be dry-docked for three weeks in late 2000 to alter the hull slightly because of vibration. And a few months later the ship was pulled from the water for two weeks to repair an underperforming motor in one of its engine pods. None of the problems was safety related; displaced guests were given a full refund and a 50 percent discount on a future cruise.

(You can read about a trip on the *Millennium* in Chapter 11: Cruise Diaries.)

Infinity, the second of four ships in Celebrity's Millennium class, began service in early 2001. The ship's two penthouse suites have marble floors, separate living and dining rooms, a baby grand piano, a high-tech flat-screen entertainment system, a fax machine, and a private veranda with a whirlpool for times when you absolutely need to get away from it all.

Infinity features the industry's first full conservatory at sea, created by prominent Paris-based floral designer Emilio Robba. Accenting the interior of the ship's SS United States specialty restaurant are actual glass panels from the liner *United States,* which launched in 1952 and gained fame for clocking the fastest transatlantic crossing from New York. Like the Olympic restaurant on her sister ship *Millennium,* the specialty restaurant on *Infinity* offers tableside cooking, carving, and flambé at sea. The dine-in wine cellar stocks more than 175 labels from around the world. The menu includes an entree first served in the dining room onboard the original SS *United States* in the 1950s: roast Long Island duckling à l'orange stuffed with fruit.

Like *Millennium,* the new ship presents exterior glass-enclosed elevators, offering guests panoramic ocean views as they move from deck to deck. The vessel also has an eighteen-workstation Internet cafe, accessible to all guests, and flat-screen PCs and printers in all suites. Every stateroom on the ship is also equipped with connections to the Internet for guests who bring their own computers.

Infinity is the second Celebrity ship to run on environmentally sensitive, quiet, and smokeless gas-turbine engines. The ship offers 80 percent ocean-view staterooms, 74 percent with verandas. Also on board are the industry's largest penthouse suites, encompassing nearly 3,000 square feet with veranda.

The Emporium, *Infinity*'s 14,000-square-foot shopping area, offers elegant and trendy designer labels, including Swarovski, H. Stern, Donna Karan, and La Perla, in addition to shops featuring Michel Roux gourmet delicacies and Cova Cafe Milano confections.

Summit offers the same amenities, including an upper-deck conservatory, a botanical environment of flowers, plants, trees, and fountains. The specialty restaurant onboard *Summit* features original paneling and a variety of artifacts from the *Normandie,* considered the foremost ocean liner of the 1930s. The famed *Normandie* was the industry's first 1,000-foot liner; the first French Line vessel to win the coveted Blue Riband, the North Atlantic's prize for speed; and the first to take the chic *arts decoratifs*—now known as Art Deco—design style to sea.

The $350 million *Summit* was built at Chantiers de l'Atlantique in Saint-Nazaire, France, the same shipyard that constructed the original *Normandie.*

The 134-guest specialty restaurant recalls the Art Deco design of the original *Normandie*'s scheme, with *Summit*'s dining venue divided by a circular colonnade that displays two sets of four large gold-lacquered panels from the stylish smoking room on the original *Normandie.* Celebrity obtained the panels at auction at Christie's.

The fourth sister, **Constellation,** joined the fleet in mid-2002.

Century

Econoguide rating:	★★★★★ 91 points
Ship size:	Megaship
Category:	Top of the Line
Price range:	Premium $$$
Registry:	Liberia
Year built:	1995
Information:	(305) 262–6677
Web site:	www.celebritycruises.com
Passenger capacity:	1,750 (double occupancy)
Crew:	858
Passenger-to-crew ratio:	2:1
Tonnage:	70,606
Passenger-space ratio:	40.3
Length:	815 feet
Beam:	105 feet
Draft:	25 feet
Cruising speed:	21.5 knots
Guest decks:	10
Total cabins:	875
Outside:	517
Inside:	306
Suites:	52
Wheelchair cabins:	8

Cuisine:	Continental and international
Style:	Informal, with two or three formal evenings
Price notes:	Single-occupancy premium, about 125 percent
Tipping suggestions:	$9.00 pp/pd

Celebrity's *Century* is a close sister to the handsome *Galaxy* and *Mercury* twins. The spectacular 1,080-seat two-level Grand Restaurant surrounds diners with the blue of the sea in a setting of old-world elegance.

Lifeboats on the handsome ship hang recessed into the entertainment and promenade decks, leaving very few obstructed views from passenger cabins above and below.

Galaxy, Mercury

Econoguide rating:	★★★★★ 91 points
Ship size:	Megaship
Category:	Top of the Line
Price range:	Premium $$$
Registry:	Liberia
Year built:	*Galaxy,* 1996; *Mercury,* 1997
Information:	(305) 262–6677
Web site:	www.celebritycruises.com
Passenger capacity:	1,870 (double occupancy)
Crew:	909
Passenger-to-crew ratio:	2.1:1
Tonnage:	77,713
Passenger-space ratio:	41.6
Length:	866 feet
Beam:	105.6 feet
Draft:	25.5 feet
Cruising speed:	21.5 knots
Guest decks:	10
Total cabins:	935
Outside:	419
Inside:	296
Suites:	220, with private balconies
Wheelchair cabins:	5
Cuisine:	Pacific Northwest cuisine for Alaska cruises
Style:	Informal, with two or three formal evenings
Price notes:	Single-occupancy premium, about 125 percent
Tipping suggestions:	$9.00 pp/pd

The lifeboats on **Galaxy** and **Mercury** are recessed into entertainment and promenade decks, all but eliminating obstructed views from passenger cabins that are all located above or below the boats. The promenade deck, though, does not allow a full circuit of the deck, blocked at the bow and stern by the Celebrity Theater and the Orion Restaurant, respectively.

The ships' shopping spaces resemble a European piazza. Recreation facilities include an indoor Palm Springs pool area, two outdoor La Playa pools, and four outdoor whirlpools. A sports deck offers basketball, a golf simulator, and volleyball; there's also trap shooting off the ship.

Horizon

Econoguide rating:	★★★★ 85 points
Ship size:	Large
Category:	Top of the Line
Price range:	Premium $$$
Registry:	Liberia
Year built:	1990 (refurbished 1998)
Information:	(800) 437–3111
Web site:	www.celebritycruises.com
Passenger capacity:	1,354 (double occupancy)
Crew:	642; Greek officers
Passenger-to-crew ratio:	2.1:1
Tonnage:	46,811
Passenger-space ratio:	34.6
Length:	682 feet
Beam:	95 feet
Draft:	24 feet
Cruising speed:	21.4 knots
Guest decks:	9
Total cabins:	677
Outside:	513
Inside:	144
Suites:	20
Wheelchair cabins:	4 ocean-view staterooms
Cuisine:	Continental and international
Style:	Informal, with two or three formal evenings
Price notes:	Single-occupancy premium, about 125 percent
Tipping suggestions:	$9.00 pp/pd

In relative terms, the **Horizon** is one of the more "intimate" ships in the Celebrity fleet, albeit still a rather large vessel, with more than 2,000 passengers and crew onboard most voyages. The *Horizon* is a near-twin to the *Zenith*. Most of the cabins on the Bermuda Deck have views obstructed by the lifeboats that hang outside the windows there.

In 1998 *Horizon* underwent a refurbishment that brought it up to the comfort and elegance specs of Celebrity's Century-class vessels. The Gemini Disco was gutted and redesigned to form a grand entrance area, with the intimate Michael's Club, a cigar and cognac club (complete with a high-tech fireplace). Also in the entrance area is a card room and library, complete with personal computers and printers; the former card room and library on Galaxy Deck was redesigned as a martini bar, art gallery, and boutique. A similar redesign was undertaken in late 1999 for Celebrity's *Zenith*.

Horizon's COVA Cafe, in the former Plaza Bar, is based on the famed Milan coffeehouse Pasticceria Confetteria COVA. The intimate cafe serves cappuccino, espresso, macchiato, a variety of teas, liqueurs, and chocolates.

The Fantasia bar on Sun Deck was remade as *Horizon*'s AquaSpa, including a beauty salon, five treatment rooms, and a fitness and aerobics area.

Zenith

Econoguide rating:	★★★★ 85 points
Ship size:	Large
Category:	Top of the Line
Price range:	Premium $$$
Registry:	Liberia
Year built:	1992 (refurbished 1999)
Information:	(800) 437–3111
Web site:	www.celebritycruises.com
Passenger capacity:	1,375 (double occupancy)
Crew:	670
Passenger-to-crew ratio:	2:1
Tonnage:	47,255
Passenger-space ratio:	34.4
Length:	682 feet
Beam:	95 feet
Draft:	24 feet
Cruising speed:	21.4 knots
Guest decks:	9
Total cabins:	687
Outside:	519
Inside:	146
Suites:	22
Wheelchair cabins:	4
Cuisine:	Continental and international
Style:	Informal, with two or three formal evenings
Price notes:	Single-occupancy premium, about 125 percent
Tipping suggestions:	$9.00 pp/pd

Near-twin to the *Horizon,* the **Zenith** received a major refurbishment in late 1999 along the lines of the remake of *Horizon.* The ship's observation lounge includes telescopes; the pool lies beneath a retractable sliding glass sunroof.

COSTA CRUISE LINES

Address: 80 Southwest Eighth Street
Miami, FL 33130-3097
Information: (800) 332–6782, (305) 358–7325
www.costacruises.com
Econoguide's Best Party Ships

The Costa Cruise Lines Fleet

CostaMediterranea	2003	2,154 passengers	86,000 tons
CostaAtlantica	2000	2,112 passengers	84,000 tons
CostaVictoria	1996	1,950 passengers	76,000 tons
CostaRomantica	1993	1,350 passengers	54,000 tons
CostaEuropa	1986	1,494 passengers	53,872 tons
CostaTropicale	1982	1,022 passengers	36,674 tons
CostaAllegra	1992	820 passengers	28,500 tons

FUTURE SHIPS

CostaFortuna	late 2003	2,720 passengers	105,000 tons
CostaMagica	late 2004	2,720 passengers	105,000 tons

Costa puts the emphasis on its Italian roots, even though today it is best known to Americans for Caribbean itineraries. It is operated out of Miami by a Panamanian corporation with American ownership and management and a history that dates back to an Israeli founder.

Nevertheless, its ships do have a distinctive Italian flavor in their design, cuisine, and activities. And its distinctive appearance is enhanced with bright yellow smokestacks that bear the company's C.

Costa's history can be traced back to 1860 when Giacomo Costa began an olive oil business in Genoa, Italy. In 1916 his three sons inherited the family business; in 1924 they purchased the *Ravenna,* a 1,100-ton freighter, to reduce the transportation costs for their oil empire.

By 1935 seven more freighters had joined the fleet, with two more by 1942. World War II reduced the fleet back to a single ship, but by 1948 the company had rebounded to a twelve-ship fleet.

Passenger service began in 1948 with the 12,000-ton, 850-passenger *Anna C,* carrying passengers between Genoa and South America. The service was an immediate success, and within four years Costa had added three more vessels. In the late 1950s the company constructed its first brand-new ships.

Costa's year-round North American cruise operation began in 1959 with seven-day cruises into the Caribbean from Miami on the *Franca C.* The company continued to grow in North America and Europe, introducing in 1985 its North American flagship, the 984-passenger *CostaRiviera.*

After more than a century under Costa family ownership, the company was opened to outside investors in 1989, ushering in a new era of expansion. In 1997 Costa Crociere (Costa Cruises) was purchased by Carnival Corporation and Airtours PLC. In 2000 Carnival acquired the outstanding 50 percent interest in Costa from Airtours.

The *CostaAtlantica,* a handsome 84,000-ton, 2,112-passenger ship, joined the fleet in spring 2000. Sister ship *CostaMediterranea* arrived in 2002. Both are similar to Carnival's Spirit-class vessels.

In 2002 *CostaEuropa* was added to the fleet; the ship is the renovated and rebuilt *Westerdam,* formerly operated by sister company Holland America Line. The *CostaTropicale,* formerly Carnival's *Tropicale,* began sailing from Venice in mid-2002.

CostaFortuna and *CostaMagica* will enter service at the end of 2003 and 2004, respectively. Costa's largest ships, at 105,000 tons and carrying 2,720 passengers, these two are expected to sail in Europe for the summer and move to the Caribbean for the winter.

Costa Cruises launched a new cruise product aimed at the German market in spring 2002. Costa Kreuzfahrten will operate year-round European and Caribbean sailings aboard the 760-passenger *CostaMarina.*

The venerable *CostaRiviera,* one of the oldest steamships still in use, was retired in early 2002 and sent to India for scrapping.

■ ITINERARIES

Costa operates in the Caribbean, the Mediterranean, and northern Europe. In a typical year, European cruises are concentrated from March through November, with most of the ships repositioning to the Caribbean for the winter months.

In the Caribbean, Costa's primary port of embarkation is Fort Lauderdale, with cruises to eastern and western parts of the basin.

Mediterranean ports of call typically include Spain, Portugal, Morocco, Greece, Croatia, Turkey, Tunisia, and Malta.

Costa operates transatlantic repositioning cruises from Europe late in the year and to Europe in the spring.

■ THE COSTA EXPERIENCE

Costa promotes "cruising Italian-style" with Italian theme nights, Italian language lessons, cooking lessons, and its famously quirky entertainments, including the Festa Italiana, which is billed as an Italian street festival at sea, with boccie ball tournaments, tarantella dance lessons, pizza dough–tossing contests, Italian karaoke, and the like.

Another theme night is Notte Tropical, when the evening's activities, which take place out on deck, include ice-carving demonstrations and a sumptuous midnight alfresco buffet.

But Costa is most famous for the "Roman Bacchanal" toga party on the last night of its Caribbean cruises; for the evening, passengers don togas and enjoy a bacchanal parade and other such preplanned debauchery. (By the way, passengers no longer have to create their own togas from bedsheets; ready-made off-the-shoulder models are available from the cruise staff.)

Costa added Ristorante Magnifico by Zeffirino to the *CostaVictoria* and *Costa-Atlantica*. Zeffirino has been a favorite restaurant in Genoa since 1939. Seating is by reservation, and a service charge of about $20 per person is applied.

The *CostaRomantica* and *CostaVictoria* offer the Golf Academy at Sea, with onboard golf clinics and seminars conducted by a PGA member golf instructor. Guests can also be accompanied by a PGA instructor as they play on some of the Caribbean's best golf courses, such as Mahogany Run in Saint Thomas, the Links at Safe Haven in Grand Cayman, Runaway Bay and Sandals Golf Resorts in Ocho Rios, Cable Beach Golf Course in Nassau, Key West Golf Course in Key West, and Teeth of the Dog or The Links at the Casa de Campo Resort in the Dominican Republic.

Costa's private beach is Catalina Island just off the coast of the Dominican Republic. Entertainment includes a beach barbecue, chaise longues, water floats, and land and water sports.

CostaMediterranea, an 86,000-ton sister ship to the *CostaAtlantica,* entered the fleet in June of 2003.

■ SPECIAL DEALS

Passengers who book at least 120 days in advance can take advantage of Costa's "Andiamo Rates" of about $500, which can work out to as much as one-third off per person on the less expensive cabins and still a decent break on more expensive accommodations.

Costa Cruise Savers offer additional savings for senior citizens, children, and single parents on selected ships and sailing dates. Savings are also available for passengers who combine two seven-night cruises.

■ WEB SITE

Costa provides a confusing and minimal site. Each of the ships in the fleet carries Web cams, and you can see the fore-aft views, current position, and speed of each ship. In mid-2003, there was no on-line booking capability, although the Web site appears to be set up to eventually permit reservations. ***Ease of use: poor.***

CostaFortuna, CostaMagica (2004)

Econoguide rating:	★★★ 79 points
Ship size:	Colossus
Category:	Top of the Line
Price range:	Moderate to Premium $$–$$$
Registry:	Liberia

Year built:	CostaFortuna, 2003; CostaMagica, 2004
Information:	(800) 332–6782
Web site:	www.costacruises.com
Passenger capacity:	2,720 (double occupancy)
Crew:	1,100 (estimated)
Passenger-to-crew ratio:	2.5:1 (estimated)
Tonnage:	105,000
Passenger-space ratio:	38.6
Length:	885 feet
Beam:	123 feet
Draft:	27 feet (estimated)
Cruising speed:	19.5 knots
Guest decks:	14
Total cabins:	1,359
Cuisine:	Italian/continental
Style:	Informal, with two formal nights per cruise; one casual night is a Roman Bacchanal, with guests invited to wear togas
Price notes:	Single-occupancy premium, 150 to 200 percent
Tipping suggestions:	$8.50 pp/pd
Best deal:	Andiamo advance rates, Costa Cruise Savers for seniors and singles

CostaAtlantica, CostaMediterranea

Econoguide rating:	★★★ 79 points
Ship size:	Megaship
Category:	Top of the Line
Price range:	Moderate to Premium $$–$$$
Registry:	Liberia
Year built:	CostaAtlantica, 2000; CostaMediterranea, 2003
Information:	(800) 332–6782
Web site:	www.costacruises.com
Passenger capacity:	2,112 (double occupancy)
Crew:	900
Passenger-to-crew ratio:	2.4:1
Tonnage:	86,000
Passenger-space ratio:	39.8
Length:	951 feet
Beam:	105 feet
Draft:	25 feet
Cruising speed:	24 knots
Guest decks:	12
Total cabins:	1,057

Outside:	787
Inside:	212
Suites:	58
Cuisine:	Italian/continental
Style:	Informal, with two formal nights per cruise; one casual night is a Roman Bacchanal, with guests invited to wear togas
Price notes:	Single-occupancy premium, 150 to 200 percent
Tipping suggestions:	$8.50 pp/pd
Best deal:	Andiamo advance rates, Costa Cruise Savers for seniors and singles

The fast and splashy *CostaAtlantica* joined the fleet in summer 2000. Sister ship *CostaMediterranea* arrived three years later. Nearly three-quarters of the cabins on the $400 million ships have verandas. There are three pools, including one with a retractable magrodome, which allows swimming in all weather.

The twelve passenger decks of *CostaAtlantica* are named after motion pictures by famed Italian director Federico Fellini; deck names include La Dolce Vita, Amarcord, I Clowns, and La Strada.

The *CostaAtlantica* features a replica of the famed Caffé Florian, the landmark cafe located under the arcades of the Procuratie Nuove in Saint Mark's Square in Venice. The original cafe opened in 1720 and became the most famous *botega da caffé* of its time. Along the years, the Caffé Florian has entertained such notables as Casanova, who hung out there in search of beautiful women; composers Antonio Vivaldi and Igor Stravinsky; and author Charles Dickens.

In addition to the two-level Tiziano main restaurant, the Botticelli Buffet, and the Napoli Pizzeria, guests can also opt for an alternative dining experience at the Ristorante Magnifico by Zeffirino.

CostaClassica, CostaRomantica

Econoguide rating:	★★★ 75 points
Ship size:	Large
Category:	Top of the Line
Price range:	Moderate $$
Registry:	Liberia
Year built:	*CostaClassica,* 1991; *CostaRomantica,* 1993
Information:	(800) 332–6782
Web site:	www.costacruises.com
Passenger capacity:	*CostaClassica,* 1,308; *CostaRomantica,* 1,350
Crew:	610
Passenger-to-crew ratio:	2.2:1
Tonnage:	*CostaClassica,* 53,000; *CostaRomantica,* 54,000
Passenger-space ratio:	39

Length:	722 feet
Beam:	102 feet
Draft:	25 feet
Cruising speed:	18.5 knots
Guest decks:	10
Total cabins:	678
Outside:	428
Inside:	216
Suites:	34
Wheelchair cabins:	6
Cuisine:	Italian/continental
Style:	Informal, with two formal nights per cruise
Price notes:	Single-occupancy premium, 150 to 200 percent; single cabins available
Tipping suggestions:	$4.50 pp/pd
Best deal:	Andiamo advance rates, Costa Cruise Savers for seniors and singles

CostaRomantica offers a bit of European sophistication at sea, showcasing almost $20 million in works of art, including sculptures, paintings, murals, and wall hangings. There's a primarily Italian and international hotel and dining staff, and within is the Via Condotti, an elegant European shopping promenade.

The ship's decks are named after great cities of Europe: Monte Carlo, Madrid, Vienna, Verona, Paris, London, Copenhagen, and Amsterdam.

The Piazza Italia Grand Bar on the Verona Deck is one of the largest lounges afloat, with a capacity of 300; it has a teak dance floor and offers live entertainment. L'Opera Theatre is a 630-seat Renaissance-style amphitheater setting, extending to the Vienna Deck above. A disco atop the ship offers 360-degree views.

Oversize staterooms average 200 square feet, and thirty-four luxurious suites have as much as 580 square feet; there are only ten verandas, though. An inside standard room is a still-spacious 175 square feet.

CostaClassica is a near-twin sister.

CostaVictoria

Econoguide rating:	★★★ 77 points
Ship size:	Megaship
Category:	Top of the Line
Price range:	Moderate $$
Registry:	Liberia
Year built:	1996
Information:	(800) 332–6782
Web site:	www.costacruises.com

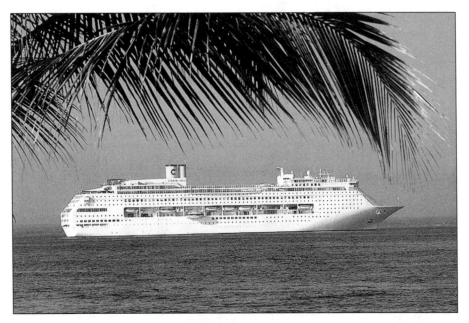

CostaVictoria under sail. *Courtesy Costa Cruise Lines*

Passenger capacity:	1,928 (double occupancy)
Crew:	800
Passenger-to-crew ratio:	2.4:1
Tonnage:	76,000
Passenger-space ratio:	39
Length:	828 feet
Beam:	105.5 feet
Draft:	26 feet
Cruising speed:	23 knots
Guest decks:	10
Total cabins:	964
Outside:	555
Inside:	389
Suites:	20
Wheelchair cabins:	6
Cuisine:	Italian/continental
Style:	Informal, with two formal nights per cruise; one casual night is a Roman Bacchanal, with guests invited to wear togas
Price notes:	Single-occupancy premium, 150 to 200 percent
Tipping suggestions:	$8.50 pp/pd
Best deal:	Andiamo advance rates, Costa Cruise Savers for seniors and singles

An unusual design in this day of Megaships; the **CostaVictoria** is almost squared off at the stern and pinched like a pumpkin seed at the bow, with a very steep forward slope. From the side it looks like a horizontal skyscraper.

Inside is the central Planetarium Atrium, seven decks high and covered by a large glass dome. Four panoramic elevators take passengers to the upper deck. The decks, named after classic operas, include Madame Butterfly, Rigoletto, Norma, Tosca, Othello, Carmen, Traviata, and Boheme.

CostaTropicale

Econoguide rating:	★★★ 68 points
Ship size:	Medium
Category:	Vintage
Price range:	Budget to Moderate $–$$
Registry:	Liberia
Year built:	1982
Information:	(800) 332–6782
Web site:	www.costacruises.com
Passenger capacity:	1,022 (double occupancy)
Crew:	550
Passenger-to-crew ratio:	1.9:1
Tonnage:	36,674
Passenger-space ratio:	35.9
Length:	660 feet
Beam:	85 feet
Draft:	23 feet
Cruising speed:	20 knots
Guest decks:	10
Total cabins:	511
Outside:	312
Inside:	187
Suites:	12
Wheelchair cabins:	11
Cuisine:	Contemporary and low-fat, low-calorie Nautica spa fare
Style:	Casual, with one or two semiformal nights
Price notes:	Single-occupancy premium, 150 to 200 percent
Tipping suggestions:	$9.00 pp/pd
Best deal:	Andiamo advance rates, Costa Cruise Savers for seniors and singles

New to the Costa fleet in 2001, **CostaTropicale** had been the oldest and smallest ship in the Carnival fleet before it was transferred within the corporation.

The ship, formerly named *Tropicale,* underwent extensive refurbishment in Genoa before reemerging under Costa's colors. In addition to a refurbishment of all public areas and staterooms, the signature Carnival funnel was replaced with an upright yellow stack in Costa's style.

CostaTropicale is marketed as part of Costa's Best Value Collection, sailing mostly in the Mediterranean.

When the ship was commissioned in 1978, industry experts declared that she was too big and too expensive to ever make a profit; instead, the *Tropicale* blazed a path for the birth of the cruising industry and helped make Carnival a major success.

Tropicale entered service in 1982 as the first new cruise ship built in nearly a decade and served as the prototype on which Carnival's Holiday-class vessels were based.

CostaEuropa

Econoguide rating:	★★★ 76 points
Ship size:	Large
Category:	Top of the Line
Price range:	Premium $$$
Registry:	Liberia
Year built:	1986 (built as *Homeric,* lengthened by 130 feet in 1989, formerly *Westerdam* of Holland America Line)
Information:	(800) 332–6782
Web site:	www.costacruises.com
Passenger capacity:	1,494 (double occupancy)
Crew:	642
Passenger-to-crew ratio:	1:2.33
Tonnage:	53,872
Passenger-space ratio:	36
Length:	798 feet
Beam:	95 feet
Draft:	23.6 feet
Cruising speed:	20.5 knots
Guest decks:	9
Total cabins:	747
Outside:	489
Inside:	252
Suites:	6
Wheelchair cabins:	4
Cuisine:	Contemporary and low-fat, low-calorie Nautica spa fare
Style:	Casual, with one or two semiformal nights

Price notes:	Single-occupancy premium, 150 to 200 percent
Tipping suggestions:	$9.00 pp/pd
Best deal:	Andiamo advance rates, Costa Cruise Savers for seniors and singles

New to the Costa fleet in 2002, *CostaEuropa* sailed for more than a decade as the *Westerdam* of Holland America Line. She changed her attitude from Dutch reserve to Italian *dolce vita* with a multimillion-dollar makeover that included the creation of the 450-seat Medusa Ball Room, the Delo Bar, and the Squok Club, reserved for Costa's youngest guests. An upright yellow Costa funnel was also installed.

One of the ships' two swimming pools is beneath a sliding roof for protection from the elements.

CostaEuropa was originally built in 1986 in West Germany as the *Homeric*, with a capacity of 1,000 passengers. After Holland America bought the ship in 1988, it was renamed as the *Westerdam* and sent back to the shipyard for an $84 million expansion and redesign. The project included the insertion of a 130-foot section, increasing the ship's size by 13,872 tons. The capacity was increased to 1,494 passengers and the ship's length from 668 to 798 feet.

CostaAllegra, CostaMarina

Econoguide rating:	★★★ 66 points
Ship size:	Medium
Category:	Vintage
Price range:	Budget $

Costa operates two other ships, *CostaAllegra* and *CostaMarina,* primarily marketed in Europe and South America. Travel agents may be able to book space through international contacts, sometimes taking advantage of favorable international exchange rates for bookings made in a European currency. However, if you sail on one of these older, budget-priced ships, you might be the only English-speaking clientele.

Costa Cruises launched a new cruise product aimed at the German market in spring 2002. Costa Kreuzfahrten will operate year-round European and Caribbean sailings aboard the 760-passenger *CostaMarina*.

While the *CostaMarina* will maintain its Mediterranean-style decor and Italian dining experiences, the ship will have a German-speaking crew with German the vessel's official language. Entertainment and onboard activities will also be geared toward German audiences.

CostaAllegra, refurbished in 2002, is an elegant smaller ship marketed mostly to French and Italian travelers. She sailed in the Mediterranean and the Greek Isles for the year.

CUNARD LINE

Address: 6100 Blue Lagoon Drive, Suite 400
Miami, FL 33126
Information: (800) 528–6273, (305) 463–3000
www.cunard.com

The Cunard Fleet

Queen Mary 2	2004	2,620 passengers	150,000 tons
Queen Elizabeth 2	1969	1,715 passengers	70,326 tons
Caronia (formerly *Vistafjord*)	1973	677 passengers	24,492 tons

FUTURE SHIPS

Queen Victoria	early 2005	1,968 passengers	85,000 tons

Cunard is one of the most storied of passenger lines, dating back to 1839, when Samuel Cunard of Halifax, Nova Scotia, won the contract to deliver the mail across the Atlantic from Great Britain to North America. Today Cunard operates one of the best-known ships afloat, the *Queen Elizabeth 2,* as well as another fine old ship that carries on the name of another classic vessel, *Caronia.*

In early 2004 Cunard Line will reintroduce another great name with a fabulous vessel, the *Queen Mary 2.* Superlatives begin here: It will be the longest and widest cruise ship afloat, with claims as the most technologically advanced and most luxurious. The massive vessel will be 150,000 tons in size and 1,132 feet in length, with a beam of 135 feet. The Gargantuan ship will carry a relatively small passenger load of 2,620. This longest and widest cruise ship is too big to fit through the Panama Canal.

In April 2004 the new *Queen Mary 2* is expected to sail eastbound from New York to Southampton along with the *Queen Elizabeth 2,* which will be making her last regular transatlantic crossing. The QE2 is expected to become a full-time cruise ship, based in Southampton but continuing with her annual world cruises.

About a year later, in early 2005, Cunard will add *Queen Victoria,* an 85,000-ton vessel dedicated to the British cruise market. The second-largest Cunard ship ever built will carry 1,968 passengers and will mark the first time ever that the line's fleet includes three Queens.

Under construction at the Fincantieri shipyard in Italy, *Queen Victoria* will operate round-trip Southampton cruises to the Mediterranean, Canary Islands, and northern Europe and make seasonal cruises to the Caribbean.

The onboard menus, entertainment, and lecture programming will be geared toward British tastes, and the currency will be sterling. The vessel will feature a covered wraparound promenade deck, a forward-facing observation lounge, and a large lido pool with a retractable magrodome. Exterior elevators with glass walls tower ten decks high on both sides of the vessel. Like *QE2* and *QM2,* the liner will have a Queens Grill offering single-seating gourmet dining.

The vessel is based on the same design used by Holland America Line's Vista class (*Zuiderdam, Oosterdam,* and *Westerdam*).

■ THE CUNARD STORY

Cunard, originally known as the British and North American Royal Mail Steam Packet Company, began service in 1840 with the 1,154-ton paddle-wheel steamer *Britannia* and three near-sister ships: *Arcadia, Caledonia,* and *Columbia.*

Cunard's ships could cross the Atlantic in fourteen days, and the four ships permitted weekly departures from Liverpool. Novelist Charles Dickens was an early passenger on the *Britannia;* his description of the sleeping and eating facilities was not of the sort that would be reprinted in a sales brochure.

From that beginning, Cunard went on to become one of the most successful transatlantic lines. Among its most famous liners were the *Lusitania* and the *Mauretania,* launched in 1906 and 1907; the *Mauretania* held the Blue Riband for twenty-two years.

Cunard carried more than a million troops and ten million tons of cargo during World War I; twenty vessels, including the *Lusitania,* were lost.

The *Queen Mary* and the *Queen Elizabeth* were requisitioned for use in World War II, carrying more than 1.5 million troops. From 1940 until 1996 the *Queen Elizabeth* held the title as the largest passenger ship ever built.

By the 1950s Cunard had twelve liners in service, carrying one-third of all transatlantic passengers. But after the first jet plane crossed the pond in 1959, the liners went into decline. When Cunard launched the *Queen Elizabeth 2* in 1969, it was the first major liner designed for both transatlantic and cruise service.

Today Cunard is the only cruise line to sail a regular schedule of transatlantic service, with nearly twenty crossings each year; at other times the company's fleet takes spectacular world cruises and special cruises in Europe, the Americas, and the Caribbean.

In recent years, Cunard has gone through a number of incarnations; in 1998 the company was acquired by Carnival Corporation and a group of Norwegian investors. Carnival then merged Cunard into its Seabourn Cruise Line division.

Cunard's *Vistafjord* was renamed *Caronia* in 2000, harkening back to one of the classic old liners of the heyday of the transatlantic ferry.

In early 2005 Cunard plans to unveil a new ship to be based in Southampton that will primarily serve the British market. The 85,000-ton ship will accommodate 1,968 passengers. The ship is a version of the "Project Vista" ships that debuted at sister line Holland America in 2002.

In the Cunard tradition, the new ship will boast a covered promenade deck encircling its entire exterior, a forward-facing observation lounge, and a large lido pool with a retractable magradome for inclement weather. Exterior elevators with glass walls will tower ten decks high on both sides of the vessel. A wide range of accommodations will be available, with 67 percent of outside staterooms and suites offering private balconies.

Like *Queen Elizabeth 2* and *Queen Mary 2,* plans call for the new liner to have a Queens Grill, which offers single-seating, gourmet dining for passengers in upper-level staterooms.

The original *Queen Mary* of Cunard White Star Line entered transatlantic service in May 1936, first winning the Blue Riband for the fastest crossing in August of that year. In 1938 the ship won the Blue Riband again and held the award until 1952.

After serving as a troop transport during World War II, the *Queen Mary* was refitted and reentered the transatlantic liner service. But as air travel increased, that trade declined. In 1967 the ship was sold to the city of Long Beach, California, where she serves today as a floating hotel and conference center.

■ THE CUNARD EXPERIENCE

Travelers will find Cunard a bit more formal than some other cruise lines. On most transatlantic crossings, every night except the first and last calls for formal dress, and the guests like it that way very much, thank you.

The *Queen Mary 2*'s maiden voyage in 2004 is a fourteen-day cruise from Southampton in Great Britain to Fort Lauderdale, calling at Madeira, Tenerife, and Las Palmas in the Canary Islands; Barbados; and St. Thomas en route. Other inaugural-season itineraries include Caribbean cruises from New York, Rio de Janeiro sailings at Carnival time, summer voyages to Europe and New England/Canada, and fifteen crossings between Southampton and New York. QM2 will be positioned in the Greek port of Piraeus to serve as a floating hotel for the 2004 Athens Olympic Games, to be held the last two weeks of August.

The 2004 World Cruise on *Queen Elizabeth 2* celebrates the travels of the great explorers, departing New York on January 5, 2004, on a 110-day voyage around the globe. From New York QE2 sails through the Panama Canal to Los Angeles, across the Southern Seas to New Zealand and Australia, then through Southeast Asia to India, Africa, and Europe before heading back to New York. The least-expensive inside stateroom was priced at $23,999 per person; Grand Suites cost $299,999 per person for double occupancy.

For travelers not prepared to spend nearly four months at sea, Cunard offers fourteen segments, ranging from as few as 12 to as many as 108 days.

Caronia operates mostly in the Mediterannean, with seasonal forays to northern Europe and the Arctic. In recent years, the ship has also visited the Middle East and Africa.

■ WEB SITE

Cunard's attractive Web site includes a great deal of information about Cunard and its ships, as well as destinations around the world. Cruising aficionados will appreciate a section that describes the history of dozens of ships that have sailed under the company's colors.

There is currently no provision for on-line booking, but visitors can fill out a form with their interests and request a phone call from a Cunard booking agent. *Ease of use: very good.*

Queen Mary 2 (2004)

Econoguide rating:	★★★★★★ 95 points (estimated)
Ship size:	Gargantuan
Category:	Luxury
Price range:	Premium $$$$
Registry:	Great Britain
Year built:	2004
Information:	(305) 463–3000
Web site:	www.cunard.com
Passenger capacity:	2,620 (double occupancy)
Crew:	1,250
Passenger-to-crew ratio:	2.1:1
Tonnage:	150,000
Passenger-space ratio:	57.25
Length:	1,131 feet
Beam:	131 feet
Draft:	32.6 feet
Cruising speed:	30 knots maximum
Guest decks:	17
Total cabins:	1,310
Outside:	1,010
Inside:	300
Suites:	93
Wheelchair cabins:	30
Cuisine:	International
Style:	Informal, with several formal nights per cruise
Price notes:	Single cabins available
Tipping suggestions:	$10–$13 pp/pd

Her Majesty's a pretty nice girl. The **Queen Mary 2,** the first liner to be built in more than three decades, is by most descriptions the longest, widest, tallest, most technologically advanced, and most luxurious passenger vessel afloat.

"We believe there is an eager and growing audience for the drama, elegance, and shipboard ambience exemplified by sailing aboard a true Atlantic ocean liner," said a company spokesman. "No one has built a true ocean liner in more than thirty years. It is nearly a lost art. We are re-creating history."

Harkening back to the designs of the grand liners, a promenade deck with a one-third-mile walkway completely circles the ship. Onboard are five swimming pools, including one beneath a retractable roof, as well as a large indoor pool in the spa.

A pair of exterior glass-walled elevators take passengers to the bridge deck, where they can look through windows at the operations of the ship's bridge.

In the style of the dining salons of classic grand liners, the 1,300-seat

Britannia Restaurant, a three-deck-high main dining room, spans the full width of the ship. Guests can choose to make a grand entrance on a sweeping central staircase. The room is decorated with a large painting of the original *Queen Mary* and the skyline of Manhattan.

Although there is no formal class structure for dining rooms, assignments within the rooms are based on the class of guests' cabins.

Smaller, more intimate dining areas including buffets, are located elsewhere on the ship. Included are Cunard's traditional Grill Rooms, reserved for the higher stateroom categories.

The Golden Lion Pub is a British pub with its own onboard microbrewery, a wine bar, a cocktail bar, and a wood-paneled smoking room.

Celebrity chef Todd English is responsible for an alternative restaurant, Todd English, that highlights his Mediterranean-style cuisine. The 216-seat room offers both indoor and poolside seating. Passengers must make advance reservations, but there is no additional gratuity or surcharge.

Chef's Galley, located in the ship's innovative King's Court dining pavilion, includes a mirrored workstation to allow diners to view meal preparation. Three other dining venues make up the King's Court, which by day serves as a casual-dining venue for breakfast and lunch but at night is transformed, through lighting and special screens, into four individual sit-down restaurants with distinctive china, menus, wine lists, and server uniforms. The smaller eateries include Lotus, serving Asian cuisine, including Chinese, Thai, Japanese and Indian fare; La Piazza, a twenty-four-hour restaurant serving pasta, pizza, and other Italian specialities; and The Carvery, a nod to Cunard's rich British heritage. Here diners can enjoy carved beef, lamb, pork, and poultry.

A proper British afternoon tea can be taken in the Winter Garden or Queens Grill Lounge. The tea, of course, is freshly brewed (no tea bags in sight), complete with scones, clotted cream, fresh pastries, finger sandwiches, and white-glove service.

And if you bring the kids, you can deposit them with real English nannies at the Play Zone (for children two to seven years old) or the Zone (for kids eight to twelve).

Illuminations, the full-scale onboard planetarium, offers an opportunity to view the stars, take a virtual ride into outer space, or take a course on celestial navigation. The facility also serves as a grand cinema, a 500-seat lecture hall, and even a broadcasting studio.

Cunard has engaged the London-based Royal Academy of Dramatic Art (RADA) to provide a company of actors to perform plays and lead onboard acting workshops. RADA, established in 1904, is one of the foremost acting training programs in the world. Graduates include a "who's who" of British actors, from Sir John Gielgud and Vivien Leigh to Anthony Hopkins, Joan Collins, Glenda Jackson, Peter O'Toole, Kenneth Branagh, and Ralph Fiennes. In addition to seminars led by graduate students, *Queen Mary 2* passengers will have the opportunity to see talented performers on the thresholds of their careers in plays seldom performed in the commercial theater.

An educational center is used for Cunard's College at Sea enrichment programs, offering classes in such subjects as computers, seamanship, cooking, wine, and art. The seven classrooms can be joined together for classes of as many as 230 persons.

A language program includes the option of total immersion in a foreign language, with instructors, waiters, butlers, and menus held to a particular language.

Satellite communications bring high-speed Internet connections to every stateroom as well as to an Internet cafe.

Standard cabins are about 194 square feet; suites are twice that size. Six 570-square-foot penthouses include butler and concierge services. Four deluxe penthouses, overlooking the bow, measure between 861 and 1,076 square feet and can be combined to create a luxurious living space of more than 5,000 square feet.

Finally, there are five duplex apartments overlooking the stern; the two-story spaces encompass more than 1,650 square feet and include a two-story glass wall, their own gymnasium, and butler and concierge services. And if that's not large enough, the duplexes can be combined and connected with two of the suites to create a private apartment of more than 5,000 square feet occupying the entire stern of the vessel.

With a passenger capacity of 2,620 (lower berths), *Queen Mary 2* boasts a space ratio per passenger of 57.25, making her among the roomiest of the world's larger passenger ships. Nearly three-quarters of the staterooms have a private balcony.

An unusual combination of four smokeless diesel engines and two gas turbines power the electrical plant of the ship to drive the motors of four podded propellers extending beneath the hull. The two forward pods are fixed; the two aft pods are steerable.

Constructed as a liner with a deep draft and more speed than most other cruise ships, the *Queen Mary 2* has a dramatic raked prow, with the hull painted matte black, a Cunard tradition dating back nearly 160 years. The ship's whistle is an exact replica of the one on the original *Queen Mary*. A giant single smokestack is painted in the historic Cunard red with black bands.

The ship was built at Chantiers de l'Atlantique in Saint-Nazaire, France, birthplace of such famous liners as *Normandie, France* (now Norway) and *Île de France.*

The ship includes seventeen decks, towering 200 feet above the waterline and just barely able to pass beneath the roadway of the Verrazano Narrows Bridge at the entrance to New York harbor. Her length and width make her too large to pass through the Panama Canal.

From the bottom of the keel to the top of the funnel, *Queen Mary 2* stands 236 feet tall. (By comparison, the same measure on the original *Queen Mary* is 181 feet, and the *Titanic* was 175 feet.) There are longer commercial ships, including the 1,513-foot supertanker *Jahre Viking.*

The ship is about 10 percent larger than Royal Caribbean's *Voyager of the Seas,* the previous holder of the largest passenger vessel record. The design of the ship takes into consideration the sometimes wild seas and weather of the North Atlantic, limiting the use of balconies at the front of the vessel and including an enclosed walkway at the bow for the promenade deck that circles the ship. The ship's hull is highly streamlined and angular, with a rounded stern, allowing for high speed through the water.

After maiden voyages from Southampton, the *Queen Mary 2* was due to sail from Fort Lauderdale to the Caribbean in winter 2004. In 2004 the schedule calls for a set of six-night transatlantic crossings between New York and Southampton, replacing the *Queen Elizabeth 2* on that route.

In August 2004 the new ship will take up residence in the Greek port of Piraeus for two weeks to serve as a floating hotel for the 2004 Athens Olympic Games.

Queen Elizabeth 2

Econoguide rating:	★★★★★ 90 points (ratings vary by class)
Ship size:	Megaship
Category:	Vintage/Luxury
Price range:	Premium $$$
Registry:	Great Britain
Year built:	1969 (changed from steam to diesel electric engines, 1987; refurbished in 1994, 1996, 1999)
Information:	(305) 463–3000
Web site:	www.cunard.com
Passenger capacity:	1,778 (double occupancy)
Crew:	921
Passenger-to-crew ratio:	1.9:1
Tonnage:	70,327
Passenger-space ratio:	39.5
Length:	963 feet
Beam:	105 feet
Draft:	32 feet
Cruising speed:	28.5 knots; 32.5 knots maximum
Guest decks:	12
Total cabins:	950
Outside:	671
Inside:	279
Suites:	187
Wheelchair cabins:	4
Cuisine:	International
Style:	Informal, with several formal nights per cruise
Price notes:	Single cabins available
Tipping suggestions:	$10–$13 pp/pd

With apologies to Her Majesty, the **QE2** is one of the grand old ladies of the sea. As she moves into her fourth decade, she's still an elegant, luxurious way to travel. She also offers one of the best glimpses back to the days of the great transatlantic liners; the *QE2* was one of the last of the breed, launched after jets began flying over the route of the Atlantic Ferry.

The ship was designed as a replacement for the *Queen Mary* and *Queen Elizabeth*. In the face of competition from the jets, the designers chose to build a slightly smaller liner that could pass through the Panama and Suez Canals and combine service as a liner and as a cruise ship. She was originally intended to spend half the year on the Atlantic Ferry route between Southampton and New York and the other half in cruising. Today the *QE2* still sails a dozen or more crossings, cruises in the Caribbean, and conducts one major around-the-world voyage each year.

The ship's impressive offerings include a thirteen-car garage, a florist, kennels, seven restaurants, a foreign exchange bank, twenty-channel television, e-mail, and financial fax service. The engines can deliver a top speed of 32.5 knots.

When the *QE2* was requisitioned for service in the Falklands War in 1982, helicopter flight decks and a modern communications system were hurriedly added. In May of that year, the ship left Southampton for the Falklands with an infantry brigade of Scots and Welsh Guards and Gurkhas aboard. Arriving two weeks later, the ship took onboard the survivors of a sunken Royal Navy ship and quickly steamed out of harm's way.

The ship was out of service for approximately six months in 1986 and 1987 for the installation of modern diesel electric engines and propellers. Passenger accommodations were also upgraded at that time.

A major interior redesign was accomplished in 1994. Among the changes was a reduction in passenger cabins from 1,750 to 1,500, and a changeover of all restaurants to permit single seatings.

In late 1999 the ship emerged from a monthlong $18 million refurbishment program at Lloyd Werft Shipyard in Bremerhaven, Germany. From the Grand Lounge and the Queens Room to the renowned restaurants and the Golden Lion Pub, there were new furnishings, draperies, carpeting, and woodworking throughout. In addition, *QE2* added Harrods, the London-based luxury department store, to the shops of its Royal Promenade.

The Queens Grill received new furniture, carpeting, upholstery, and lighting, as well as etched-glass doors and a completely new galley. Following a complete makeover, the Caronia Restaurant displays the elegance and luster of an English country house, with rich mahogany paneling, new table lighting, crystal chandeliers, carpeting, curtains, and chairs, as well as a new stereo system. New etched-glass doors and a "rainfall" pattern air-conditioning system eliminate drafts.

The Queens Room received major treatment, including all new furniture and new royal blue carpeting interwoven with gold Tudor roses. The walls were repaneled in mahogany, and the famed bust of Her Majesty the Queen was relocated to the most prominent position within the room.

The 575-square-foot Caledonia Suite on the port side of Boat Deck, directly adjacent to and forward of the Queens Grill, features marble master and guest bathrooms, a separate dining area, and large picture windows. The 777-square-foot Aquitania Suite, forward of the midships lobby on the starboard side of Two Deck, offers similar luxury appointments.

Caronia

Econoguide rating:	★★★★ 83 points
Ship size:	Medium
Category:	Vintage/Luxury
Price range:	Premium $$$
Registry:	Great Britain
Year built:	1973 (formerly *Vistafjord*; refurbished 1997, 1999)
Information:	(305) 463–3000
Web site:	www.cunard.com
Passenger capacity:	677
Crew:	379 British
Passenger-to-crew ratio:	1.8:1
Tonnage:	24,492
Passenger-space ratio:	36.2
Length:	627 feet
Beam:	82 feet
Draft:	27 feet
Cruising speed:	20 knots
Guest decks:	9
Total cabins:	379
Outside:	325
Inside:	54
Suites:	13
Wheelchair cabins:	6
Cuisine:	International
Style:	Semiformal, with several formal nights per cruise
Price notes:	Single cabins available
Tipping suggestions:	$10–$13 pp/pd

The *Vistafjord* was renamed ***Caronia*** and reflagged under the Union Jack in Liverpool in 1999. In keeping with Cunard tradition, the ceremony was carried out not with champagne but with wine. Unlike the *Queen Mary, Queen Elizabeth,* and *QE2,* though, the *Caronia* was ceremonially doused not with Australian wine but with a bottle from the British Isle of Wight.

Prior to the ceremony, the ship underwent a multimillion dollar refurbishing. Today she's a well-kept middle-aged lady with some touches of Scandinavian elegance. The enlarged and redesigned dining room can accommodate all passengers in a single seating. Unusually large windows offer views of the sea from nearly all tables. There's also Tivoli, a forty-seat alternative Italian restaurant.

In an earlier update, two lavish penthouses were added forward; the bilevel suites include a large private veranda and a seaside whirlpool.

DISNEY CRUISE LINE

Address: 210 Celebration Place, Suite 400
    Celebration, FL 34747-4600
Information: (800) 326–0620
    www.disneycruise.com
Econoguide's Best Cruise Lines
Econoguide's Best Cruise Lines for Families

The Disney Cruise Line Fleet

Disney Wonder	1999	1,750 passengers	85,000 tons
Disney Magic	1998	1,750 passengers	85,000 tons

OK, let's get this out of the way right now: The Disney Cruise Line is a Mickey Mouse operation.

But this is the Mickey Mouse of *Fantasia,* the cultured gentleman in tuxedo and tails. The *Disney Magic* and her nearly identical sister ship, *Disney Wonder,* are two of the most stunning, beautifully realized cruise ships on the water today. From the moment they welcomed their first paying passengers in mid-1998 and summer 1999, respectively, the ships were instant classics.

Kids of all ages will love these ships, and adults will find an above-average cruise line that pays respects to the great ocean liners . . . and the world of Disney. (See Chapter 11 for a cruise diary about a voyage on the *Disney Magic.*)

Now let me say right up front that I had my misgivings about sailing on a Disney ship before I crossed the gangplank. I spend an inordinate amount of my time with Mickey Mouse and friends each year in keeping my travel books on Orlando and Anaheim up to date. It's not that I don't like Disneyland or Walt Disney World; it's just that I had a fear that too many parts of my world were coming together. I wanted the glamour, excitement, and sublime relaxation of a cruise, not the oh-too-popular hubbub of a theme park.

Well, I was 90 percent wrong—and 100 percent satisfied. Disney has done a wonderful job of creating a pair of cruise ships that, like a classic Disney film, bring together our dearest fantasies, an impressive display of artistry, and some welcome touches of the real world.

I have come to realize the following: Every other cruise line starts with the ship and tries to find the right mix of entertainment to help guests fill out their time. But Disney starts as one of the most successful entertainment companies of all time, adding a pair of handsome ships as home to their floating theme park.

Disney chose as its initial target the 90 percent or so of travelers who have never taken a cruise before, but even the most experienced cruise veteran will recognize how Disney has paid loving homage to the great ocean liners of the past. Today you're likely to find many Disneyphiles on their fourth or fifth or tenth sailing.

■ FANTASY AFLOAT

The fantasy begins with the exterior design of the twin ships, which consciously evokes the memory of the classic transatlantic liners of the prejet era, vessels like the *Queen Mary*. Their long, sleek hulls are painted jet black; atop the white upper half sit a pair of bright-red smokestacks. They look just about the way a child (of any age) would draw an ocean liner.

The black, white, and red colors of the ships, together with bright-yellow lifeboats, not only evoke the colors of the great liners but also match the color scheme for the admiral of the fleet, Mickey Mouse.

These are true Megaships, more than three football fields long, at 964 feet, from stem to stern; eleven decks tall; and 85,000 tons in size.

The artistry begins with those two smokestacks. The ultramodern power plant for the ships requires only one set of pipes, and those pipes run through the stack toward the stern. The forward smokestack is there because the ship looks better with one. And as long as you've got this big stack, why not make use of it? Disney's "Imagineers" installed a funky sports bar way up high and a dream-world club for teenagers (no adults allowed) at its base.

The Imagineers also took hold of the ships' design in myriad other wondrous ways—things like a truly spectacular central atrium with glass-walled elevators; a quartet of extraordinary and quirky restaurants that deliver fine food and more than a bit of Disney magic; a Broadway-quality theater that offers a different show every night; and a floor full of nightclubs for adults, including a comedy club, a country-western bar, a jazz club, and a sophisticated chrome-and-glass piano bar where Noel Coward would have felt right at home.

The interior design of the *Disney Magic* is based on an Art Deco vocabulary, with rounded chrome and brass, carved-wood details, and lovely oversize portholes along some of the interior promenade decks. The *Disney Wonder* is based on slightly different Art Nouveau flourishes.

The real world lies in the modern-day amenities, such as private verandas, relatively spacious family cabins that have nice touches like privacy curtains to separate the kids from the parents, and an overall sense of elegance. Disney has left neon flash to Royal Caribbean, Carnival, and others; the real competition to these ships, at least in terms of design, are the *Queens* of Cunard, present and past.

And finally, back to the fantasy. What kid wouldn't add a spiraling water slide to the top-deck kids-only swimming pool? (Adults have their own pond, and there's a third pool for families.) And how about nearly a full deck devoted to a kids' world of games, entertainment, and exploration, as well as a teens-only club up top and a state-of-the-art video arcade at sea?

And then there's Mickey. Disney is always quick to admit that it all started with a mouse. Mickey and his friends are there, making cameo appearances at the children's clubs and an occasional visit to the pools and restaurants. Goofy will sometimes appear on the dance floor in one of the clubs, or Minnie may visit the shopping district. But, in truth, the Disney characters have a relatively low-key presence aboard ship.

Within the massive ship are no fewer than four separate and distinct dining rooms, a huge theater for live productions, and an entire entertainment district for adults. The quality and presentation of the food is excellent, although some guests may find the offerings a bit on the safe side. There are a few adult touches if you want to amaze or frighten younger guests: escargots one night and an unusual side dish of braised parsnips in orange sauce.

Disney says its marketing target is the vast majority of Americans who have never taken a cruise. But experienced cruisers are likely to enjoy the many lovely touches onboard this elegant ship. A good deal of Disney's marketing is also aimed at tying a cruise into a visit to Walt Disney World; you can purchase a four-night cruise and a three-night stay at the park or a three-night cruise and a four-night stay. Or you can book a three-, four-, or seven-day cruise by itself.

Although Mickey, Minnie, Goofy, and others can be found onboard the ship, and the entertainment package features Disney characters in most productions, it is also possible to avoid most things Disney. The company offers Palo, a lovely adults-only restaurant, and also tries to place most families who have children in the early dining seating for the other restaurants. Then there is Beat Street, the nightclub area onboard *Disney Magic,* where there are lively jazz, comedy, and country-western clubs . . . and neither kids nor cartoon characters are expected after 9:00 P.M. The equivalent on the *Disney Wonder* is Route 66.

Only on a ship of this size owned by a company like Walt Disney would you reasonably expect to find most of an entire deck devoted to supervised children's activities: Disney's Oceaneer Lab and Disney's Oceaneer Club. There's even a kids-only buffet. And up top on the pool deck is Common Grounds, a coffee bar and hangout place just for teenagers; adults are carded at the door and asked to step outside.

Disney's seven-day cruises include some special Disney magic with nightly shows and special presentations. The tony Palo restaurant is open during the day for a champagne brunch and afternoon tea.

Guests can take backstage peeks at the extensive theater facilities on the ship, as well as tours of the bridge, galley, and other places not ordinarily open to the public. There is also a program that focuses on sea lore, from the days of the pirates to modern cruise ships.

■ THE DISNEY EXPERIENCE

Disney is a young cruise line without a grand history on the seas, and some purists will find fault with Goofy hanging on the stern or Mickey and Minnie lounging by the pool. But in some ways Disney has come up with a ship that is more true to our memories or dreams of grand ocean liners than are many of the larger vessels now being launched, ships that are more like floating vacation resorts or shopping malls.

Blessed with the deep pockets of Walt Disney Company, the Disney Cruise Line purchased a pair of stunning ships from one of the most advanced shipyards. Its ships are among the most elegant and polished afloat.

Among Disney's innovations is "rotation dining": Guests are assigned to one of the three main restaurants each day, and their servers and tablemates move with them from dining room to dining room.

Disney Magic tied up at Disney's private island, Castaway Cay. *Photo by Corey Sandler*

Onboard the *Disney Magic,* the elegant continental Lumière's restaurant mixes a grand dining room of a classic ocean liner with chandeliers and candlesticks whimsically derived from Disney's *Beauty and the Beast.* The equivalent dining room on the *Wonder* is Triton's, based on *The Little Mermaid.* Parrot Cay, on both ships, is an informal eatery bedecked with palms and flowers and gingerbread-trimmed verandas—a Disney magnification of the mind's-eye perception of the Bahamas and the Caribbean.

Also on both ships is Animator's Palette, one of the most unusual settings for a restaurant at sea or on land. The very room itself is an actor in the evening's entertainment. The meal begins in a room that is entirely outlined in black and white—from the linens on the table and the uniforms on the serving staff to the line art sketches on the wall. As the meal progresses, dabs of color work their way into the drawings and onto the uniforms.

The fourth restaurant is Palo, an adults-only sophisticated Italian bistro perched high in the second smokestack. You'll need a reservation; Disney assesses a reasonable $5.00 service charge for dinner or $10.00 for the brunch, which includes a glass of bubbly.

About three-quarters of the 875 staterooms have outside views, and nearly half have verandas, a welcome modern touch. Most of the cabins offer a bath-and-a-half design; one bathroom holds a sink and toilet, the other a sink and bathtub/shower.

Disney's attention to detail begins at the handsome Art Deco–style terminal it constructed in Port Canaveral; it's all part of the company's packaging of its ships as a return to the golden era of cruising. Many guests arrive at the terminal by bus from Disney World, about an hour away; even the buses have been molded and painted in an artist's vision of a streamlined conveyance of the 1930s and 1940s.

■ DISNEY ENTERTAINMENT AT SEA

The Walt Disney Theatre is a 975-seat showplace that would be the envy of most Broadway producers. The stage is used for nightly performances of Disney-produced shows that are entertaining, but not to be confused with *Les Misérables*. Facilities include three elevators for special effects, indoor fireworks, and lasers.

On no other cruise line does the captain magically appear on stage in a cloud of fog, popping up on a hidden stage elevator.

Also onboard is the Buena Vista Theatre, a full-screen, 270-seat cinema that presents Disney classics and first-run films, including an occasional premiere at sea. Disney has offered theme cruises from time to time, such as a focus on movies, with appearances by noted critics.

There are no casinos onboard the ships, which Disney executives said would be at odds with the corporate mission. They point out, however, that if you've got the itch to gamble, the proprietors of the casinos in Nassau and Saint Martin will be happy to take your money.

Disney claims the largest dedicated area of children's space on any ship. Children ages three through eight have Disney's Oceaneer Club, a supervised playroom. Older youngsters through age twelve can spend their time at Disney's Oceaneer Lab, which includes giant video walls and computer activities. Parents can borrow a pager so that they can head off on their own while staying in touch aboard ship.

Our teenagers were thrilled to be granted admission to Common Grounds, a trendy coffee-bar setting where they could dance, listen to music, play video games, and generally hang out in a place that adults were politely encouraged not to visit.

■ ITINERARIES

Disney Wonder sails from Port Canaveral on three- or four-day cruises to Nassau and Castaway Cay, Disney's private Bahamas beach. On alternate four-day cruises, the itinerary trades a day at sea for a second stop in the Bahamas, at Freeport, Grand Bahama Island.

Disney Magic sails alternating weeklong itineraries to the eastern and western Caribbean. The eastern Caribbean trip departs each Saturday from Port Canaveral for Saint Martin, Saint Thomas, and Castaway Cay and includes three days at sea. The western trip departs on Saturday for Key West, Grand Cayman Island, Cozumel, and Castaway Cay, with two full days at sea.

In late 2004, Disney will experiment with six special itineraries. Three cruises in August and early September will visit St. Thomas and San Juan. A pair of cruises in mid-September and early October will make stops in St. Thomas and Antigua. And one mid-December cruise will extend to ten days with port calls at Key West, St. Maarten, St. Lucia, and Antigua.

Guests with confirmed reservations can reserve shore excursions in advance through the cruise line.

Disney promotes its shorter cruises as part of a weeklong vacation that includes a few days at Walt Disney World in Orlando. You can, however, choose to book just a cruise.

■ DISNEY'S BAHAMIAN THEME PARK

Although the Walt Disney Company has created its own worlds in California, Florida, Japan, and France, the creation of the Disney Cruise Line offered the first opportunity for the Imagineers to design their own little country. In typical Disney style, they ended up creating a place that is more real than the real thing, an idealized island paradise with perfect white sand beaches, palm trees, and a huge Megaship parked at a dock around the corner.

Castaway Cay, a 1,000-acre island 50 miles north of Nassau and near Abaco, was reworked by Disney Imagineers in a massive $25 million effort that included construction of a dock for the ships and creation of beaches with some 50,000 truckloads of sand dredged from the floor of the Atlantic when the channel was dug.

In an interesting irony, Disney's island, formerly known as Gorda Cay, is reputed to have been used in recent years as a hideaway for drug smugglers. A short World War II–era runway on the island was believed to have been used by the smugglers.

Only about fifty-five acres of the island have been developed, with the remainder mostly open for hiking and biking paths. Saltwater desalination and sewage treatment plants, as well as a small village of housing for staff members, are well hidden from view.

The main beach is the snorkeling and swimming lagoon, which features a snorkeling "track" with underwater and marine objects to explore (you'll need to rent snorkels and a flotation vest). Nearby are Scuttle's Cove, a supervised children's water area, and the Teen Beach. Again, in keeping with Disney's promise to offer grown-ups an escape, the north side of the island has a somewhat isolated "quiet" beach for adults only.

Recent additions include parasailing on the open waters beyond the lagoon, wet and high-speed tours on a "banana boat," and tours of the surrounding reef on a glass-bottom boat.

■ THE BOTTOM LINE

All of this does not come cheap. Disney's list prices for cruises are approximately 15 to 30 percent higher than those for similar operations, placing the cruise line somewhere between moderate- and premium-priced classes. As with most other cruise lines, however, cruises with Disney are often available at deep discounts from travel agencies; Disney also books its cruises directly. There are advance booking discounts, and guests onboard one of the ships are offered substantial cuts for cruises engaged at sea.

■ WEB SITE

Disney offers a polished and informative Web site with details about the ships, itineraries, and onboard activities. You can check availability of cabins for individual cruises and make reservations on-line. *Ease of use: excellent.*

Disney Magic, *Disney Wonder*	
Econoguide rating:	★★★★ 86 points
Ship size:	Megaship
Category:	Top of the Line
Price range:	Premium $$$
Registry:	Bahamas
Year built:	*Disney Magic,* 1998; *Disney Wonder,* 1999
Information:	(800) 326–0620
Web site:	www.disneycruise.com
Passenger capacity:	1,750 (double occupancy)
Crew:	915; European and American staff
Passenger-to-crew ratio:	1.9:1
Tonnage:	85,000
Passenger-space ratio:	48.6
Length:	964 feet
Beam:	106 feet
Draft:	25.3 feet
Cruising speed:	21.5 knots
Guest decks:	11
Total cabins:	875
Outside:	547
Inside:	246
Suites:	82
Wheelchair cabins:	14
Cuisine:	Continental, American; three restaurants in rotation
Style:	Casual, informal resort atmosphere
Price notes:	Single-occupancy premium, 175 to 200 percent; reduced rates for third through seventh occupant of cabins or suites
Tipping suggestions:	$11 pp/pd

The *Disney Magic* and *Disney Wonder* are spectacular ships that look back fondly on the grand old liners of the past. Disney's Imagineers worked with Italian designers to create a pair of thoroughly modern Megaships that come very close to our mind's-eye view of what a cruise ship should look like.

Disney's attention to detail includes wondrous parallel worlds for children and adults. There's an adults-only restaurant and an adults-only swimming pool and a kids-only buffet and pool. Most of an entire deck of the huge ship is devoted to kids' programs, and an adult entertainment district has a set of swinging nightspots.

The Walt Disney Theatre is a tribute to grand theatrical palaces, with a different live musical stage show each night of the cruise.

The art theme for *Disney Wonder* is Art Nouveau, differing from the *Disney Magic*'s Art Deco concept.

The showplace dining room on the *Wonder* is Triton's, derived from *The Little Mermaid* story. The menu, of course, emphasizes seafood. Animator's Palette and Parrot Cay are alternative restaurants on both ships.

The adult entertainment district on the *Wonder* is Route 66, and includes Cadillac's dance club, the Brew Ha Ha (themed like a brewpub) comedy club, and the Wave Bands jazz club.

HOLLAND AMERICA LINE

Address: 300 Elliott Avenue West
   Seattle, WA 98119

♛ ♛ ♛ ♛

Information: (800) 227–6482, (800) 426–0327
   www.hollandamerica.com
Econoguide's Best Cruise Lines
Econoguide's Best Cruise Values

Holland America Fleet

Westerdam	April 2004	1,848 passengers	85,000 tons
Oosterdam	2003	1,848 passengers	85,000 tons
Zuiderdam	2002	1,848 passengers	85,000 tons
Zaandam	2000	1,440 passengers	63,000 tons
Volendam	1999	1,440 passengers	63,000 tons
Amsterdam	2000	1,380 passengers	61,000 tons
Rotterdam	1997	1,316 passengers	60,000 tons
Veendam	1996	1,266 passengers	55,451 tons
Ryndam	1994	1,266 passengers	55,451 tons
Maasdam	1993	1,266 passengers	55,451 tons
Statendam	1993	1,266 passengers	55,451 tons
Prinsendam	1988	758 passengers	37,845 tons
Noordam	1984	1,214 passengers	33,930 tons

FUTURE SHIPS

Unnamed	February 2006	1,848 passengers	85,000 tons

Holland America was the floating highway for nearly a million European immigrants who traveled to the New World in the late nineteenth and early twentieth centuries. Today it continues as one of the premier cruise lines, carrying

Americans and others to holidays in the Caribbean, Alaska, and through the Panama Canal.

■ THE HOLLAND AMERICA STORY

The company was founded in 1873 as the Netherlands-America Steamship Company for shipping and passenger service. Because it provided service to the Americas, it became known as Holland America Line (HAL).

The company's first liner was the original *Rotterdam,* which made its maiden voyage from the Netherlands to New York in 1872. Within twenty-five years the company owned a fleet of six ships and also provided service between Holland and the Dutch East Indies via the newly constructed Suez Canal.

Today the company's Holland America–Westours is the largest cruise tour operator in Alaska and Canada's Yukon, with a fleet of 176 buses and several dozen tourism railroad cars. Westours owns Gray Line of Alaska, Gray Line of Seattle, and the Westmark Hotels and Inns group, with more than a dozen hotels in Alaska and the Yukon Territory. The company also owns both the *Ptarmigan,* a small ship that operates tours to the face of Portage Glacier, and the *Yukon Queen,* which travels the Yukon River between Dawson City in the Yukon Territory and Eagle, Alaska.

In January 1989 Holland America Line–Westours, Inc., became a wholly owned subsidiary of The Carnival Corporation. Holland America also owns Windstar Cruises, which operates four computer-directed luxury sailing cruise ships in the Mediterranean, the Caribbean, and Costa Rica.

Many Caribbean cruises include a stop at Half Moon Cay, a 2,500-acre private Bahamian island purchased in 1997 and lightly developed by Holland America Line. The crescent-shaped isle, just 2 miles long and a third of a mile across, was an uninhabited cay known as Little San Salvador. The nation of the Bahamas honored the tourist dollars of HAL guests with a special postage stamp that has an image of the *Ryndam* and a small Holland America Line logo.

■ NEW SHIPS

Three new "Project Vista" ships will be added to the fleet between 2003 and 2006. The 85,000-ton, 951-foot-long, 1,848-passenger ships mark the beginning of a new class of vessels for Holland America, introducing new features, including the first "exterior elevators" on a cruise ship. The lifts, located on the port and starboard sides, connect ten decks of the ship, offering panoramic sea views through glass walls. About 85 percent of the cabins on the new ships are outside; about 80 percent of those have private verandas. The first three ships are *Zuiderdam* (pronounced *ZOO-der-dam*), *Oosterdam* (*OH-ster-dam*), and, returning to the fleet, the *Westerdam.*

Other features include two interior promenade decks, an exterior covered promenade deck encircling the entire ship, and HAL's trademark lido area pool with a retractable dome. The ships also offer a new cabaret-style show lounge complementing a new three-deck main show lounge. Other new features include a sophisticated nightclub, the largest spa facilities in the fleet, Internet/e-mail dataports in all staterooms, an extensive Club HAL children's facility with inside and outside play areas, a concierge lounge for the exclusive use of Penthouse and Deluxe Verandah Suite guests, and two interior promenade decks.

The new vessels' propulsion system includes a full-scale diesel-electric power plant, backed up by a gas turbine as an additional power source. The ships also will use the Azipod propulsion system, allowing for greater maneuverability.

In April 2002 the sumptuous *Seabourn Sun* was transferred to Holland America Line from Seabourn Cruise Line. The ship was refurbished and re-named *Prinsendam* and is billed as the most luxurious vessel in the HAL fleet.

HAL's former *Nieuw Amsterdam* came back into the corporate portfolio in mid-2002 with the bankruptcy of American Classic Voyages, which had been operating the ship as the *Patriot* in Hawaii. At press time, it was unclear whether the ship would sail again for Holland America or another part of the Carnival family, or whether it would be sold.

ITINERARIES

Holland America Line ships sail around the world on cruises and a global tour. The twelve-ship fleet offers 449 cruises ranging from 3 to 108 days, visiting all seven continents.

The largest percentage of itineraries are in the Caribbean and Alaska.

In 2003 *Zuiderdam* was positioned year-round in the Caribbean. *Maasdam, Veendam, Volendam,* and *Zaandam* sailed in the Caribbean during the winter, passing through the Panama Canal for summer in Alaska, and returning to the Caribbean in the fall.

Noordam split its time between winter in the Caribbean and spring and summer in Europe. The new *Oosterdam* was scheduled to begin service in Europe and transition to the Caribbean for winter 2003–2004.

Rotterdam had an ambitious schedule that included back-and-forth transits of the Panama Canal in the early part of the year, a reposition to New York for cruises in New England and Canada in spring, and a transatlantic crossing to Europe for the summer before returning to the Caribbean in late 2003.

Ryndam was scheduled to sail in South America in the early part of the year, moving on to Alaska for the summer, and then sailing between Mexico and Hawaii late in the year. *Statendam* sailed from Mexico to Hawaii in the colder months, moving to Alaska for the summer.

Prinsendam moved from Asia to Australia and the South Pacific in the first half of the year, continuing on to Alaska for part of the summer before returning to Europe and Asia.

Amsterdam conducted a world tour from January through April, moving on to Alaska in the summer and South America at the end of the year.

THE HOLLAND AMERICA EXPERIENCE

Holland America cultivates an air of refinement aboard its ships, and its clientele has historically been slightly older and more experienced than that of other cruise lines. Fresh flowers, in some cases flown in from Holland, decorate the ship. An art and history tour is scheduled on each cruise to inform guests about the $2 million worth of art and artifacts aboard each ship.

For families traveling with children, Holland America's Club HAL youth program provides activities for youngsters ages five through seventeen. Additional youth counselors are onboard for Christmas and Easter cruises.

The ships also offer more traditional cruise activities: dance lessons, bingo, "horse" racing, trap shooting, a mileage pool, a passenger talent show, and karaoke. The show lounge features a Broadway or Las Vegas–style revue or variety entertainment.

Harking back to its Dutch roots, HAL employs mostly Indonesian and Filipino crew members, training them in its own school in Jakarta. Holland America promotes a "no tipping required" policy, which means just what it says; however, most guests do leave a gratuity in the same range as those offered on ships that encourage tipping.

Guests aboard all Holland America Line cruise ships are now offered a casual lido dining option for dinner on several nights of their cruise. Serenaded by a pianist, diners order from a set menu with choices including Caesar salad, shrimp cocktail, and such entrees as fillet of salmon, sirloin steak, roast chicken, and lasagna.

The sister ships *Volendam* and *Zaandam* are the first of a new generation of luxury cruise ships. The interior decor of the *Volendam* features a flower theme, while the *Zaandam* is based around musical themes. The two ships have the same length and width as the *Rotterdam*, but their gross tonnage is larger (about 63,000 tons versus 59,652 tons) because they have more passenger staterooms.

In 2000 Holland America added a new ship with an old name. The *Amsterdam* also has the same length and beam as the *Rotterdam* but has a slightly larger gross tonnage (61,000 gross tons) because of an increase in the number of staterooms to 690. The new ship's all-suite deck was extended, and the number of suites that have verandas increased. The new ship also features 120 deluxe minisuites with verandas, 385 large outside staterooms, and 133 large inside staterooms, for a total of 690 staterooms.

In early 2002 Holland America began implementing a new ban against smoking in all dining areas, including main dining rooms and the enclosed portion of lido restaurants. Alternative restaurants have been nonsmoking since their introduction and continue as such under the new policy. All ships will continue to have designated smoking areas in public spaces.

Holland America offers early booking fares at a 25 percent discount for a limited number of staterooms.

■ WEB SITE

Holland America's Web site includes full information about ships and itineraries and offers the option to book a cruise on-line or request a call from the company's reservations department to answer questions and make reservations. Although the organization of the Web site is a bit confusing, a strong point is the cruise calendar, which makes it easy to see where the ships are at any time of the year. *Ease of use: good.*

Zuiderdam, Oosterdam, Westerdam (2004)

Econoguide rating:	★★★★ 86 points
Ship size:	Megaship
Category:	Top of the Line
Price range:	Premium $$$
Registry:	Netherlands
Year built:	*Zuiderdam,* 2002; *Oosterdam,* 2003; *Westerdam,* 2004
Information:	(206) 283–2687, (800) 426–0327
Web site:	www.hollandamerica.com
Passenger capacity:	1,848 (double occupancy)
Crew:	800
Passenger-to-crew ratio:	2.3:1
Tonnage:	85,000
Passenger-space ratio:	46
Length:	951 feet
Beam:	105.8 feet
Draft:	22 feet
Cruising speed:	23 knots
Guest decks:	10
Total cabins:	720
Outside:	552
Inside:	139
Suites:	29
Wheelchair cabins:	23
Cuisine:	International
Style:	Elegantly casual to formal in the evening
Price notes:	Single-occupancy premium, 150 to 190 percent; Single Partners Program (agree to share a stateroom with another nonsmoking guest of the same gender, and pay only the per-person, double-occupancy rate)
Tipping suggestions:	No tipping required
Best deal:	Early-booking savings

Zuiderdam, Oosterdam, and **Westerdam,** named for the southern, eastern, and western points of the Dutch compass, are technologically advanced ships, each powered by a full-scale diesel-electric power plant backed up by a gas turbine as an additional power source. The turbines reduce exhaust emissions and can be used together with the diesels when cruising in particularly sensitive environments such as Glacier Bay in Alaska or the Baltic Sea. Azipods also reduce consumption—and therefore emissions—by as much as forty tons of fuel per week.

Fully 85 percent of the staterooms have an ocean view, with 80 percent of those offering private verandas. Two interior promenade decks and a covered exterior promenade deck circle the ship.

Exterior elevators traverse ten decks, with panoramic views out over the water. Other features include a Cabaret-style show lounge and a three-level main show lounge. Computer users will find an Internet cafe and data ports in all staterooms.

The ships include extensive facilities for children. The Club HAL program features KidZone for younger cruisers ages five to twelve, with inside play areas with safety matting. Professional youth coordinators supervise daily activities such as games, arts and crafts, computer fun, candy-bar bingo, movies, and special kids-only parties.

WaveRunner is a place for teenagers, complete with a dance floor where they can dance to a booming sound system and special lighting effects. There is also a video game room and large-screen TV.

The third ship in the Vista class, due for delivery in spring 2004, will be named *Westerdam*, the third ship in Holland America Line's history with that name. Two additional ships in the class are due in 2005 and 2006. Another Vista-class ship will be added to fleet of sister cruise line Cunard in 2005, sailing as the *Queen Victoria*.

Vista ships also feature a new stateroom category, Deluxe Veranda Outside, which feature verandas approximately twice the size of the regular verandas for the category. A concierge lounge is for the exclusive use of Penthouse and Deluxe Veranda Suite guests. The *Oosterdam* offers 461 of these staterooms.

Volendam, Zaandam

Econoguide rating:	★★★★ 85 points
Ship size:	Large
Category:	Top of the Line
Price range:	Premium $$$
Registry:	Netherlands
Year built:	*Volendam,* 1999; *Zaandam,* 2000
Information:	(206) 283–2687, (800) 426–0327
Web site:	www.hollandamerica.com
Passenger capacity:	1,440 (double occupancy)
Crew:	561
Passenger-to-crew ratio:	2.6:1
Tonnage:	63,000
Passenger-space ratio:	43.8
Length:	781 feet
Beam:	105.8 feet

Draft:	23 feet
Cruising speed:	23 knots
Guest decks:	10
Total cabins:	720
Outside:	552
Inside:	139
Suites:	29
Wheelchair cabins:	23
Cuisine:	International
Style:	Elegantly casual to formal in the evening
Price notes:	Single-occupancy premium, 150 to 190 percent; Single Partners Program (agree to share a stateroom with another nonsmoking guest of the same gender, and pay only the per-person, double-occupancy rate)
Tipping suggestions:	No tipping required
Best deal:	Early-booking savings

Sister ships **Volendam** and **Zaandam** have the same basic layout as *Rotterdam*. Slightly larger, the new design moves the oudoor swimming pool one deck higher to the lido deck and extends the navigation deck aft to accommodate forty-eight additional minisuites with verandas.

Volendam, the third ship in the company's 125-year history to bear that name, cruises in the winter in the Caribbean out of Fort Lauderdale. In spring she repositions to Vancouver, British Columbia, via the Panama Canal, for a season of sailings in Alaska's Inside Passage before returning to Florida for the winter.

The predominant theme of *Volendam*'s interior decor is flowers, from the seventeenth to the twenty-first centuries. Flowers are featured in the ship's artwork,

Holland America's *Volendam. Courtesy Holland America Line*

doors, and other design elements. The three-deck-high central atrium features a monumental crystal sculpture titled *Caleido* by Italian artist Lucian Vistosi, who also created the towering glass sculptures onboard the *Maasdam* and *Veendam.*

The *Volendam*'s Marco Polo Restaurant, an alternative to the dining room, is a re-creation of a classic European "artist's bistro," a place where the walls are lined with works of art traded by artists for plates of spaghetti. The walls are a pastiche across time, with works by unknown contemporary artists as well as etchings by Rubens and Rembrandt and works by Henry Moore, Matisse, and Picasso.

Diners at the eighty-eight-seat restaurant are offered "California-style" Italian cuisine for lunch or dinner; there is no extra charge, but advance reservations are required. Typical pasta menu items include fettuccine with rock shrimp, chopped tomato, spinach, garlic, and toasted pine nuts; and linguine with Italian sausage, peppers, onions, tomato, and sangiovese wine sauce. Entrees include marinated chicken breast in garlic puree and rosemary, veal chop grilled with sage and rosemary, and pan-roasted lamb loin with red wine sauce.

Luncheon offerings include pizza rustica with goat cheese, salami, mushrooms, kalamata olives, crisp pancetta, tomato sauce, fontina cheese, and oregano; and a poached salmon niçoise salad with potatoes, eggs, green beans, tomato, red onions, cucumber, capers, and a light mustard dressing.

The casino bar, in addition to being the ship's sports bar, features such cinematic memorabilia as costumes, props, photos, and posters of movies and the stars who made them.

The ship's main show lounge features colorful colonnades against satiny dark wood walls, harkening back to the Art Deco era, with a design inspired by the famed Tuschinski Theater in Amsterdam.

On both the *Volendam* and *Zaandam,* the navigation deck was extended aft to accommodate the additional staterooms, moving the outdoor swimming pool to the lido deck, one level above its location on the Rotterdam- and Statendam-class ships. This design change permits direct access between the indoor and outdoor swimming pools and the Lido Restaurant.

Zaandam joined the Holland America fleet in spring 2000. The interior theme is music, featured throughout public rooms but most prominently in the Casino Bar, which showcases music memorabilia from jazz and blues to rock and roll and the classics. The centerpiece of the *Zaandam*'s grand atrium is a towering pipe organ that has mechanical figures of dancing musicians.

Amsterdam, Rotterdam

Econoguide rating:	★★★★ 85 points
Ship size:	Large
Category:	Top of the Line
Price range:	Premium $$$
Registry:	Netherlands

Year built:	*Amsterdam,* 2000; *Rotterdam,* 1997
Information:	(206) 283–2687, (800) 426–0327
Web site:	www.hollandamerica.com
Passenger capacity:	*Amsterdam,* 1,380; *Rotterdam,* 1,316 (double occupancy)
Crew:	644
Passenger-to-crew ratio:	2.1:1
Tonnage:	*Amsterdam,* 61,000; *Rotterdam,* 60,000
Passenger-space ratio:	47.1
Length:	*Amsterdam,* 780 feet; *Rotterdam,* 778 feet
Beam:	105.8 feet
Draft:	25.5 feet
Cruising speed:	25 knots
Guest decks:	10
Total cabins:	658
Outside:	381
Inside:	117
Suites:	160
Wheelchair cabins:	20
Cuisine:	International
Style:	Elegantly casual to formal in the evening
Price notes:	Single-occupancy premium, 150 to 190 percent; Single Partners Program (agree to share a stateroom with another nonsmoking guest of the same gender, and pay only the per-person, double-occupancy rate)
Tipping suggestions:	No tipping required
Best deal:	Early-booking savings

The **Rotterdam** is the sixth company ship to bear the name. The onboard art collection includes artifacts related to the voyages of seventeenth-century mariners for the Dutch East and West Indies Companies.

The two-deck, 747-seat La Fontaine Dining Room features a giant mural reminiscent of the wall treatment of the previous *Rotterdam*'s much loved Ritz Carlton room.

The **Amsterdam** is slightly larger than her sister. HAL quietly reintroduced a bit of the old class system with the Neptune Lounge on the *Amsterdam;* the room is open only to guests in suites. The flashy star of the lobby is the Astrolabe Clock, a three-story thingamabob. One of the four faces of the clock displays twenty-four-hour ship's time; a second is a calendar with a zodiac. Another face shows the constellations as they appear in the night sky of Amsterdam, and a fourth shows the time in cities around the world.

The ship's eighty-eight-seat alternative restaurant, Odyssey, features Italian cuisine. Typical entrees may include *costelleta di vitello al carbone,* a sage and rosemary broiled veal chop served on sautéed eggplant and peppers; *petto de pollo rustico,* grilled chicken breast with mushroom, tomato concasse, and Gorgonzola; and *osso buco alla Milanese,* braised veal shank in red wine sauce with saffron risotto and asparagus.

Maasdam, Ryndam, Statendam, Veendam

Econoguide rating:	★★★★ 84 points
Ship size:	Large
Category:	Top of the Line
Price range:	Premium $$$
Registry:	Netherlands
Year built:	*Maasdam,* 1993; *Ryndam,* 1994; *Statendam,* 1993; *Veendam,* 1996
Information:	(206) 283–2687, (800) 426–0327
Web site:	www.hollandamerica.com
Passenger capacity:	1,266 (double occupancy)
Crew:	588
Passenger-to-crew ratio:	2.2:1
Tonnage:	55,451
Passenger-space ratio:	43.8
Length:	720 feet
Beam:	101 feet
Draft:	24.6 feet
Cruising speed:	22 knots
Guest decks:	10
Total cabins:	633
Outside:	336
Inside:	148
Suites:	149
Wheelchair cabins:	6
Cuisine:	International
Style:	Elegantly casual to formal in the evening
Price notes:	Single-occupancy premium, 150 to 190 percent; Single Partners Program (agree to share a stateroom with another nonsmoking guest of the same gender, and pay only the per-person, double-occupancy rate)
Tipping suggestions:	No tipping required
Best deal:	Early-booking savings

The fifth Holland America Line ship to carry the name, the **Maasdam** features a $2 million collection of art and artifacts, a company trademark. A three-deck grand atrium, featuring a monumental glass sculpture by Italian artist Luciano Vistosi, extends from lower promenade deck to upper promenade. An escalator provides access upward from the main deck to staterooms on lower promenade deck.

Located on promenade and upper promenade decks, the Rotterdam Dining Room seats 657 on two levels connected by a pair of grand curved staircases. An antique marble fountain from Argentina is the centerpiece of the lower level. Windows on two sides and at the stern offer panoramic views of the sea, accented by murals by Danish ceramic artist Bjorn Wiinblad.

At the opposite end of the ship, the two-deck, 600-seat Rembrandt Show Lounge features Broadway-style entertainment. The room is decorated with delft ceramic tiles from Holland as well as plush brocaded fabrics, gold-tinted mirrors, and mahogany panels to recall the era of seventeenth-century Dutch master Rembrandt van Rijn, whose portrait is etched into the glass doors. (A cruise diary about a trip on the *Maasdam* is included in Chapter 11.)

The **Ryndam,** third in the company's history to carry the name, shares most of the same interior features. The Rotterdam Dining Room, with side and stern windows, is decorated with four large murals by a Dutch artist depicting elaborately costumed seventeenth-century Dutch noblemen against a backdrop of period sailing ships. The Vermeer Show Lounge has a tulip motif throughout, in light fixtures, wall panels, and carpeting.

On the **Statendam,** the atrium features the ornate, 26-foot-high *Fountain of the Sirens,* extending from the lower promenade deck to upper promenade. At the opposite end of the ship, the two-deck, 600-seat Van Gogh Show Lounge presents Broadway-style entertainment. The show room is themed to Dutch artist Vincent van Gogh's paintings *The Starry Night* and *Irises.*

On the **Veendam,** the Rotterdam Dining Room, seating 657 on two levels connected by a pair of grand curved staircases, is decorated with enormous paintings of flowers based on details from seventeenth-century Dutch still lifes. The Rubens Show Lounge, named for Flemish master painter Peter Paul Rubens, is done in copper brown and gray tones with accents of gold leaf and brass. Glass cutouts of dancers' forms radiate from large columns. (You can read a cruise diary about the *Veendam* in Chapter 11.)

Noordam

Econoguide rating:	★★★ 74 points
Ship size:	Medium
Category:	Top of the Line
Price range:	Premium $$$
Registry:	Netherlands
Year built:	1984
Information:	(206) 283–2687, (800) 426–0327
Web site:	www.hollandamerica.com
Passenger capacity:	1,214 (double occupancy)
Crew:	605
Passenger-to-crew ratio:	2:1
Tonnage:	33,930
Passenger-space ratio:	27.9
Length:	704.2 feet

Beam:	89.4 feet
Draft:	24.2 feet
Cruising speed:	21 knots
Guest decks:	10
Total cabins:	605
Outside:	391
Inside:	194
Suites:	20
Wheelchair cabins:	4
Cuisine:	International
Style:	Elegantly casual to formal in the evening
Price notes:	Single-occupancy premium, 150 to 190 percent; Single Partners Program (agree to share a stateroom with another nonsmoking guest of the same gender, and pay only the per-person, double-occupancy rate)
Tipping suggestions:	No tipping required
Best deal:	Early-booking savings

The **Noordam**'s theme is the Dutch East India Company, established in Amsterdam in 1603 for trade between Holland and the Far East and East Indies. The art collection comprises priceless vases and statues from China, Japan, and Indonesia.

She is sister ship to the *Nieuw Amsterdam,* which left the HAL fleet in 2001 to sail as the *Patriot* of United States Lines. In 2001 that line went into bankruptcy and the future of the *Nieuw Amsterdam* was uncertain.

Although she is a favorite of some guests, as the oldest ship in the fleet, *Noordam*'s days would seem to be numbered.

Prinsendam

Econoguide rating:	★★★★★ 91 points
Ship size:	Medium
Category:	Ultraluxury
Price range:	Beyond Opulent $$$$$
Registry:	Netherlands
Year built:	1988 (formerly *Royal Viking Sun, Seabourn Sun;* refurbished 1995, 1999, 2002)
Information:	(206) 283–2687, (800) 426–0327
Web site:	www.hollandamerica.com
Passenger capacity:	794 (double occupancy)
Crew:	460
Passenger-to-crew ratio:	1.6:1
Tonnage:	37,845
Passenger-space ratio:	48.5

Length:	669 feet
Beam:	95 feet
Draft:	23 feet
Cruising speed:	21.4 knots
Guest decks:	9
Total cabins:	397
Outside:	372
Inside:	25
Suites:	19
Wheelchair cabins:	4
Cuisine:	International
Style:	Elegantly casual to formal in the evening
Price notes:	Single-occupancy premium, 150 to 190 percent; Single Partners Program (agree to share a stateroom with another nonsmoking guest of the same gender, and pay only the per-person, double-occupancy rate)
Tipping suggestions:	No tipping required
Best deal:	Early-booking savings

The **Prinsendam** is an understatedly elegant ship, designed for the Royal Viking Line, then part of the Cunard fleet. She was transferred to Seabourn as the *Seabourn Sun* in 2000 and, most recently, to Holland America in 2002. The line plans to promote her as the "Elegant Explorer."

The ship's public rooms were completely refitted in 1999, and a Roman-style health spa and expanded golf facilities were added. Improvements to the spa on the Scandinavia Deck began at the entrance to the beauty salon, which was enlarged to add a reception area; an outdoor pool there was covered and enclosed to become a gymnasium. The center of the deck was extended to accommodate a new lap pool and two whirlpools.

The ship's two pools are filled with heated salt water; the pool on the Bridge Deck includes a swim-up bar. Four modern catamaran tenders have sloping bows for beach landings.

Renaming the ship *Prinsendam* brings back one of the cherished names of HAL's history. The original ship of that name sailed Far East and Alaska itineraries from 1973 through 1980. The name translates to "prince's" ship, with "dam" being the familiar Holland America passenger ship name suffix.

One of the most spacious larger ships in the cruise industry, the *Prinsendam* offers eight passenger decks plus fifteen public rooms and boutiques. Among Holland America's classic Dutch art and ambience, passengers will discover an Explorer's Lounge, Crow's Nest, Java Cafe, Rotterdam Dining Room, an Italian alternative restaurant, and other familiar features.

Starting from the thirteenth deck, the passenger decks were renamed Sky, Sports, Lido, Verandah, Upper Promenade, Promenade, Lower Promenade, Main, and Dolphin. Other enhancements include a reconfigured La Fontaine dining room to accommodate two dinner sittings, a new concierge lounge for the exclusive use of suite guests, conversion of the Compass Rose Room to an

Explorer's Lounge, upgraded furnishings in the Wajang movie theater, a new windscreen at the bow, and a specially commissioned sculpture for the central atrium.

The Sky Deck houses a Holland America trademark Crow's Nest lounge. The intimate lounge has floor-to-ceiling windows, a piano, and spectacular views from high atop the ship.

The *Prinsendam* introduces a new type of stateroom with its ten "lanai" cabins. These staterooms, constructed in space formerly used as a lounge on promenade deck aft, have private lanais and share a private covered deck and a hot tub.

The Queen's Lounge show room on promenade deck forward was redesigned for Holland America's customary two nightly shows with state-of-the-art lighting and sound equipment.

The port side of the forward portion of the dining room was converted into an alternative Odyssey Restaurant, featuring Italian cuisine and Mediterranean decor. Opposite the Odyssey is a traditional Ocean Bar, with bandstand and dance floor.

The ship also has a golf simulation center on the main deck. This virtual-reality golf game allows golfers to "play" several famous courses around the world as well as practice their golf swing and putting stroke. It is identical to simulators to be installed on Holland America's new Vista series of ships.

During its first year under the HAL flag, the 38,000-ton, 794-passenger *Prinsendam* sailed on twenty-three cruises ranging in length from ten to twenty-two days.

NORWEGIAN CRUISE LINE

NORWEGIAN CRUISE LINE

Address: 7665 Corporate Center Drive
Miami, FL 33126
Information: (800) 327–7030
www.ncl.com
Econoguide's Best Cruise Lines
Econoguide's Best Cruise Values

The Norwegian Cruise Line Fleet

Norwegian Dawn	2002	2,200 passengers	91,000 tons
Norwegian Star	2001	2,200 passengers	91,000 tons
Norwegian Sun	2001	2,400 passengers	77,104 tons
Norwegian Sky	1999	2,400 passengers	77,104 tons
Norway	1962, rebuilt 1980	2,032 passengers	76,049 tons
Norwegian Wind	1993	1,748 passengers	50,760 tons
Norwegian Dream	1992	1,748 passengers	46,000 tons

Norwegian Sea	1988	1,518 passengers	42,000 tons
Norwegian Majesty	1992, to NCL in 1997	1,460 passengers	38,000 tons
Norwegian Crown	1988	1,050 passengers	34,250 tons

FUTURE SHIPS

| Pride of America | July 2004 | Estimated 1,900 passengers | About 72,000 tons |
| Pride of Aloha (Formerly Norwegian Sky) | September 2004 | 2,400 passengers | 77,104 tons |

Norwegian Cruise Line is a fleet on the move, growing rapidly and expanding its reach from its Caribbean roots to include Alaska, Hawaii, the Mexican Riviera, and a subsidiary operation out of Australia. In 2003 the line positioned its newest vessel year-round in New York for round-trip cruises to Port Canaveral and Miami in Florida and the Bahamas.

Now owned by Star Cruises, a growing Asian line, NCL added three large ships in recent years. The first was the *Norwegian Sun*, a near-twin to the popular *Norwegian Sky*. It was followed by the *Norwegian Star*, a huge new ship originally planned for Star Cruises. *Norwegian Dawn*, a sister to *Norwegian Star*, arrived at the end of 2002. *Crown Odyssey*, an older, smaller vessel, returned to NCL from its previous assignment to Star and resumed its former NCL name of *Norwegian Crown*.

Norwegian Sky will be renamed as *Pride of Aloha* and reflagged to sail as part of NCL's Project America fleet, beginning in September 2004.

■ THE NORWEGIAN STORY

NCL, originally named Norwegian Caribbean Lines, began in 1966 as a partnership between the Norwegian shipping company Klosters and entrepreneur Ted Arison. That arrangement lasted until 1972 when Arison left to form Carnival Cruise Lines.

NCL's first vessel was the *Sunward*. Part ocean liner and part ferryboat, the ship was built to take British vacationers and their cars to Spain. That itinerary became less attractive because of political issues, and the ship was transferred to the then obscure port of Miami. A company named Norwegian Caribbean Lines was formed.

The *Sunward* was an instant success, contributing to Miami's tremendous growth as a cruise ship port. NCL brought out a line of new "white ships," beginning with the *Starward* in 1968.

In 1979 NCL rescued the nearly forgotten *France* from retirement for $18 million; the ship was towed to Bremerhaven, Germany, and rebuilt for Caribbean cruising at a cost of $130 million. The flagship of the NCL fleet, renamed the *Norway*, it is the longest cruise ship afloat. The *Norway* was scheduled to sail for NCL through at least April 2004.

In 1984 the line's parent company purchased another Norwegian company, the Royal Viking Line, integrating it into NCL operations. Five years later, Royal Cruise Line was also brought into NCL.

In 1997 and 1998 the *Windward* and *Dreamward* were stretched, with the insertion of a 130-foot midsection, increasing each vessel's capacity by 40 percent. The ships were reborn as the *Norwegian Wind* and *Norwegian Dream.*

In summer 1998, NCL completed the acquisition of Orient Lines, including the 845-guest cruise ship *Marco Polo.* Orient Lines continues as an independent premium brand, offering five- to twenty-five-day itineraries onboard the *Marco Polo* to exotic destinations in Africa, Antarctica, Australia, Egypt, India, Southeast Asia, and the Mediterranean, including the Greek Isles. In summer 2002, Star Cruises transferred *SuperStarAries* to Orient Lines, renaming her *Ocean Voyager.*

In 1999 the *Norwegian Majesty* received a 100-foot stretch, with the new midsection adding 202 new staterooms and increasing capacity from 1,056 to 1,460 guests.

The *Norwegian Sky* joined the fleet in summer 1999. NCL acquired the unfinished hull of the *CostaOlympia* in 1997 when a German shipyard went bankrupt; the hull was towed to another shipyard and recast as the *Norwegian Sky,* allowing completion within a speedy twenty months.

The *Norwegian Sun,* sister ship to the *Norwegian Sky,* joined the fleet in 2001.

■ ITINERARIES

NCL stakes the claim to offering regularly scheduled round-trip cruises from more U.S. and Canadian ports than any other cruise line, emphasizing "homeland cruising." With the addition of *Norwegian Dawn* and the return of *Crown Odyssey,* NCL has a hold on first place on itineraries in Hawaii, the Northeast, Alaska's Inside Passage, and Bermuda.

In 2003 NCL ships sailed itineraries departing seasonally from Baltimore, Boston, New Orleans, Philadelphia, Port Canaveral, San Juan, Seattle, and Vancouver and year-round sailings from New York, Miami, Houston, and Honolulu. The line added Charleston, South Carolina, sailings by *Norwegian Majesty* to the western Caribbean from November 2003 through April 2004. The ship was due to reposition to Boston for a summer of sailings to Bermuda.

Crown Odyssey was transferred to NCL from the company's Orient Lines in September 2003; resuming its former name of *Norwegian Crown,* it was due to undertake a series of eleven-day Canada/New England sailings from Baltimore before moving on to South America for winter and spring 2003–2004. In May 2004 *Norwegian Crown* was due to sail from Philadelphia and New York to Bermuda through October before heading to South America again for the winter.

Norwegian Sea was moved to Houston in November 2003 to begin year-round seven-day western Caribbean itineraries. At the same time, *Norwegian Dream* began service from New Orleans for western Caribbean itineraries through the winter. In April 2004 the ship was due to reposition to sail in Europe to Scandinavia and Russia, returning in the fall to sail to New England and Canada from Boston.

■ PROJECT AMERICA

Sometime in summer 2004, NCL hopes to be the first company in nearly fifty years to hoist the Stars and Stripes above a new oceangoing passenger ship. This represents no easy accomplishment: It took an act of Congress and—truth be told—the failure of another company's effort to bring it about.

In late 2002 NCL purchased from Northrup Grumman Ship Systems the partially completed hull of the first Project America ship, which had been under way for United States Line, an offshoot of the former owner of Delta Queen Steamboat Company. United States Line had planned to build and launch a pair of 1,900-passenger vessels that would have been the first new American-built and -operated cruise ships in half a century. Unfortunately the company went out of business and the ships were never completed.

NCL arranged for the towing of one hull and associated materials for a second vessel from the Northrup shipyard in Pascagoula, Mississippi, to a shipyard in Bremerhaven, Germany. The company also successfully managed to get some fancy legal language into the 2003 federal appropriations act that allows NCL to use the two Project America vessels and one existing cruise ship in the Hawaiian Islands for interisland cruise service. The vessels will be U.S. flagged and 100 percent U.S. crewed, allowing NCL to avoid the necessity of visiting a foreign port, such as the long haul from Hawaii to Fanning Island in the Republic of Kiribati. The exemption also gives NCL an exclusive license for interisland cruising. Congress did add a requirement that the Hawaii ships could not be repositioned for revenue service in Alaska or the Gulf of Mexico.

The ships will be modified in Germany for freestyle cruising as well as to upgrade safety and environmental specifications for offshore operations. Plans call for *Pride of America* to begin service in July 2004, followed by *Pride of Aloha* (formerly *Norwegian Sky*) in September 2004.

Pride of America will offer open-seating main dining rooms, multiple dining choices at eight restaurants, three pools, an expansive spa and health and fitness center, and extensive children's facilities. Eighty percent of the staterooms will have an ocean view, with 85 percent of those including private balconies.

■ WEB SITE

The NCL Web site includes all you need to know about ships and itineraries, and its on-line booking engine permits you to view the location of available cabins. You can also select pre- and postcruise accommodations and tours and selected shore excursions. Travelers have the option to book on-line, direct their information to a travel agent of their choice, or seek the assistance of an NCL reservationist. ***Ease of use: excellent.***

Norwegian Star, ***Norwegian Dawn***		

Econoguide rating:	★★★★ 84 points
Ship size:	Megaship
Category:	Top of the Line
Price range:	Premium to Opulent $$$–$$$$
Registry:	Bahamas

Year built:	*Norwegian Star,* 2001; *Norwegian Dawn,* 2002
Information:	(800) 327–7030
Web site:	www.ncl.com
Passenger capacity:	2,200 (double occupancy)
Crew:	1,122
Passenger-to-crew ratio:	2:1
Tonnage:	91,000
Passenger-space ratio:	41.4
Length:	965 feet
Beam:	105 feet
Draft:	23 feet
Cruising speed:	25 knots
Guest decks:	15
Total cabins:	1,122
Outside:	761
Inside:	361
Suites:	147
Wheelchair cabins:	20
Cuisine:	Italian, Asian, continental
Style:	Informal, with two formal nights per cruise
Price notes:	Single surcharge, 150 to 200 percent
Tipping suggestions:	$10 pp/pd
Best deal:	Early-bird fares; group discounts with minimum of eight guests

NCL's fastest and largest ships, **Norwegian Star** and **Norwegian Dawn** were originally planned for Star Cruises, but the parent company transferred them as they were being built.

Designed with the freestyle cruising concept in mind, there are ten different restaurants aboard. On the *Norwegian Star,* Versailles is an ornate main restaurant with a French-inspired design offering traditional six-course dining. Aqua is a contemporary-styled main restaurant featuring a lighter, modern menu. It has an open galley displaying the preparation of pastries and desserts. Ginza, a Japanese/Chinese/Thai restaurant, includes a sushi tempura bar, a teppanyaki room, and a sake bar. The show kitchen in the entrance area introduces passengers to the traditional styles of Asian preparation.

The Soho Room, a Pacific Rim restaurant, serves a fusion of a la carte Californian, Hawaiian, and Asian dishes. The restaurant has a modern art gallery with a collection of pop art. Passengers can pick a lobster from a large tank. Le Bistro is an upscale French Mediterranean restaurant with an a la carte menu of traditional gourmet French cuisine in Art Nouveau style. Market Cafe has buffet-styled "food action stations" with prepared-to-order breakfast, lunch, and themed dinners. Endless Summer is a Hawaiian-themed restaurant offering such delicacies as roast suckling pig and Lomi Lomi salmon.

Las Ramblas Tapas Bar and Restaurant contains a Spanish tapas bar along with a full selection of hot and cold dishes and authentic Spanish entertainment. La Trattoria is an evening-only offering at the Market Cafe serving pasta, pizza, and other traditional Italian fare, and Blue Lagoon is an indoor/outdoor food court featuring hamburgers, hot dogs, stir-fry dishes, and traditional fish-and-chips with malt vinegar.

The artwork of *Norwegian Dawn* begins on the hull. Paintings on the starboard side feature dolphins playing in colorful waves, a salute to Caribbean itineraries. The port side shows New York's Statue of Liberty, signifying the ship's Bahamas and Florida itinerary from the port of New York. The ship's hull also features reproduced signatures of nineteenth- and twentieth-century masters Renoir, Matisse, Van Gogh, and Monet and pop icon Andy Warhol. NCL installed a collection of original oil paintings by Impressionist artists in its signature Le Bistro restaurant and a collection of original signed works by Warhol around the ship. The interior paintings are on loan from the personal collection of the chairman of Star Cruises, parent company of Norwegian Cruise Line.

Norwegian Dawn was due to begin year-round operations from New York in fall 2003, sailing seven-day round-trip cruises to Port Canaveral, Miami, and the Bahamas.

Norway

Econoguide rating:	★★★ 76 points
Ship size:	Megaship
Category:	Vintage
Price range:	Premium $$$
Registry:	Bahamas
Year built:	1962 (formerly *France*; rebuilt 1980)
Information:	(800) 327–7030
Web site:	www.ncl.com
Passenger capacity:	2,032 (double occupancy)
Crew:	920
Passenger-to-crew ratio:	2.2:1
Tonnage:	76,049
Passenger-space ratio:	37.4
Length:	1,035 feet
Beam:	110 feet
Draft:	35 feet
Cruising speed:	20 knots
Guest decks:	12
Total cabins:	1,016
Outside:	584

Inside:	291
Suites:	130
Wheelchair cabins:	11
Cuisine:	Italian, continental, international
Style:	Informal, with two formal nights per cruise
Price notes:	Single surcharge, 150 to 200 percent
Tipping suggestions:	$10 pp/pd
Best deal:	Early-bird fares; group discounts with minimum of eight guests

A grand classic, remade and maintained for the modern era, the **Norway,** born as the *France,* is the longest ship now afloat. She is just a bit too long to squeeze through the Panama Canal; in 2001 she was assigned to year-round patrol in the Caribbean, operating out of Miami.

Norway suffered a disastrous accident while at dock in Miami in May 2003; one of the four boilers on the steamship exploded, killing seven crewmen. No passengers were injured. NCL announced plans to repair and upgrade the ship, although the reconstruction process for the classic vessel proved to be very complex. Furthermore, the vessel is not in full compliance with all the current provisions of the SOLAS safety regulations. The company says the ship will return to the fleet no earlier than the spring of 2004 and perhaps later

The great ocean liner *France* was rescued from oblivion by Norwegian Cruise Line and rebuilt for cruising. Her public rooms are old-world elegant, and other remnants of her original incarnation include the two separate (but now equal) dining rooms, a holdover from the days of cabin classes.

The ship's deep draft may make the *Norway* more stable in high seas, although that same draft often requires the ship to anchor out in the harbor instead of pulling into a dock in shallow waters.

Notable public rooms include the Saga Theatre, a two-story show room with a proscenium stage. The room is used for full-scale Broadway productions and special events. The large Monte Carlo Casino on the pool deck includes 236 slot and poker machines as well as gaming tables.

Kids can romp in the Trolland playroom and the Port Hole activity center. The Kids Crew program is open to youngsters ages three to seventeen.

Norwegian Sky, Norwegian Sun

Econoguide rating:	★★★★ 82 points
Ship size:	Megaship
Category:	Top of the Line
Price range:	Premium to Opulent $$$–$$$$
Registry:	Bahamas
Year built:	*Norwegian Sun,* 2001; *Norwegian Sky,* 1999

Information:	(800) 327–7030
Web site:	www.ncl.com
Passenger capacity:	2,002 (double occupancy)
Crew:	800
Passenger-to-crew ratio:	2.5:1
Tonnage:	77,104
Passenger-space ratio:	39
Length:	853 feet
Beam:	108 feet
Draft:	26 feet
Cruising speed:	23 knots
Guest decks:	12
Total cabins:	1,001
Outside:	574
Inside:	407
Suites:	14
Wheelchair cabins:	6
Cuisine:	French, Italian, Chinese, continental
Style:	Resort casual
Price notes:	Single supplement, 150 to 200 percent
Tipping suggestions:	$10 pp/pd
Best deal:	Early-bird fares; group discounts with minimum of eight guests

The *Norwegian Sun* and her near-twin the *Norwegian Sky* are the flagships of the NCL fleet, elegant and comfortable Megaships. The **Norwegian Sky** entered service in August 1999, sailing from the shipyard to Boston to begin her service with a series of cruises to Canada. Unfortunately, the spectacular new ship made a most spectacular debut on her first passage in the Saint Lawrence River—running aground at the juncture with the Saguenay River. The mishap damaged one of the rudders and a propeller and cut a large gash in her side. There were no reported injuries (except perhaps to the résumé of the captain and the two river pilots aboard), but the brand-spanking-new ship had to limp back to Quebec City and enter into dry dock for more than a month of repairs.

NCL acquired an unfinished hull in 1997 when the Bremer Vulkan shipyard in Germany went bankrupt. Intended as the *CostaOlympia* flagship of the Costa line, the ship was recast as the *Norwegian Sky.* Most of the cabins are on Decks 8, 9, and 10, well above the lifeboats on Deck 7; a bit more than 200 others are spread among the lower decks. About a quarter of the ship's staterooms have a private teak-floored balcony; four owners' suites also have private outdoor hot tubs. Up top are three pools, including one with a waterfall.

The focus of the interior is a pair of glass-domed atria. Aft, there's Neptune's Court with a grand stair tower; midships is the Atrium, eight decks high with four panoramic lifts.

There are two major restaurants on the Atlantic Deck: the Four Seasons and

NCL's *Norwegian Sky* docked in Haines, Alaska. *Photo by Corey Sandler*

Seven Seas dining rooms. The Horizons Restaurant on the Atlantic Deck offers intimate dining for eighty-four. The Stardust Lounge on the promenade and international decks seats about 1,000 guests in a two-story show lounge that has a proscenium stage. The Sports Bar on the pool deck serves as a teen disco during the day; also onboard is The Zone teenage disco, which has a soft-drink bar.

In September 2004, *Norwegian Sky* will be recast once more, this time as *Pride of Aloha* as part of NCL's Project America fleet.

The ship will join the new *Pride of America* with an all-American crew sailing among the islands of Hawaii. Operating under U.S. registry, *Pride of Aloha* will be able to sail between domestic ports without the need for a visit to a foreign country.

Norwegian Sun was based on the same hull design, but NCL modified its internal design to work with the freestyle cruising concept. Among the many new features on the ship are no less than nine different restaurants and slightly larger staterooms than those on her near-sister. Dining choices include two main dining rooms; a formal Italian restaurant; Le Bistro gourmet French cafe; a Pacific Rim restaurant complex featuring a sushi bar, teppanyaki room, and a California/Hawaii/Asian fusion restaurant; a tapas bar; a twenty-four-hour indoor-outdoor cafe; and a "healthy living" restaurant with spa menus.

The *Norwegian Sun* offers more than a hundred additional outside staterooms than the *Norwegian Sky,* and cabins with verandas are slightly larger. You can read a cruise diary about the *Norwegian Sky* in chapter 11.

Norwegian Dream

Econoguide rating:	★★★ 76 points
Ship size:	Large
Category:	Top of the Line
Price range:	Premium to Opulent $$$–$$$$
Registry:	Bahamas
Year built:	1992 (as *Dreamward;* stretched by 130 feet in 1998 and renamed)
Information:	(800) 327–7030
Web site:	www.ncl.com
Passenger capacity:	1,760 (double occupancy)
Crew:	614
Passenger-to-crew ratio:	2.9:1
Tonnage:	50,760
Passenger-space ratio:	26.1
Length:	754 feet
Beam:	94 feet
Draft:	22 feet
Cruising speed:	18 knots
Guest decks:	10
Total cabins:	874
Outside:	585
Inside:	158
Suites:	118
Wheelchair cabins:	13
Cuisine:	Italian, continental, French, international
Style:	Resort casual
Price notes:	Single supplement, 150 to 200 percent
Tipping suggestions:	$10 pp/pd
Best deal:	Early-bird fares; group discounts with minimum of eight guests

The **Norwegian Dream** and her sister ship *Norwegian Wind* were reborn in 1998 after they were stretched and refurbished, growing from nice Medium-size vessels to even nicer Large ships.

You don't really "stretch" a ship. Instead, each ship was cut in half and a matching 130-foot midsection was installed. As a result, passenger capacity was increased by 40 percent, with the addition of 502 new berths, several new public rooms, and a few interesting amenities, including a swim-up pool bar.

On the *Dream,* the Stardust Lounge is a two-story main show lounge that has a proscenium stage, used for a full production of Broadway shows.

In August 1999 the *Norwegian Dream* inexplicably collided with a large freighter in the English Channel, sustaining major damage and shaking up passengers, though none was seriously injured. The ship continued to England under her own power but was disabled for more than a month.

Norwegian Wind

Econoguide rating:	★★★ 76 points
Ship size:	Large
Category:	Top of the Line
Price range:	Moderate to Premium $$–$$$
Registry:	Bahamas
Year built:	1992 (as *Windward*; stretched by 130 feet and renamed in 1998)
Information:	(800) 327–7030
Web site:	www.ncl.com
Passenger capacity:	1,760 (double occupancy)
Crew:	689
Passenger-to-crew ratio:	2.6:1
Tonnage:	50,760
Passenger-space ratio:	28.8
Length:	754 feet
Beam:	94 feet
Draft:	23 feet
Cruising speed:	21 knots
Guest decks:	10
Total cabins:	874
Outside:	623
Inside:	139
Suites:	101
Wheelchair cabins:	11
Cuisine:	Italian, continental, French, international
Style:	Resort casual
Price notes:	Single supplement, 150 to 200 percent
Tipping suggestions:	$10 pp/pd
Best deal:	Early-bird fares; group discounts with minimum of eight guests

As with the *Norwegian Dream,* the *Windward* was stretched by 130 feet in 1998 and renamed the **Norwegian Wind.** The two sisters are now nearly identical.

In 2001 the ship underwent another renovation, resulting in the enlargement of the Sports Bar and Grill and a remodeling of the casino. Open, restaurant-style seating and extended hours are now offered in the ship's dining rooms and alternative restaurants. *Norwegian Wind* has five dining venues each night: two main dining rooms; the Sun Terraces, converted to an Italian Trattoria offering traditional Italian fare; Le Bistro; and the Sports Bar and Grill, serving buffet-style breakfast, lunch, dinner, and snacks throughout the day. In addition to the five permanent full-service restaurants, *Norwegian Wind* also has an on-deck Caribbean Night barbecue with jerk chicken, pork, ribs, and fish.

The Sports Bar and Grill on the Sports Deck contains a wall of multiple televisions that display videotaped and live broadcasts of major sports events. The Stardust Lounge on the Star Deck is a two-story main show lounge used for full-scale productions of Broadway shows.

Norwegian Sea

Econoguide rating:	★★★ 76 points
Ship size:	Large
Category:	Vintage
Price range:	Premium $$$
Registry:	Bahamas
Year built:	1988 (formerly the *Seaward*)
Information:	(800) 327–7030
Web site:	www.ncl.com
Passenger capacity:	1,518 (double occupancy)
Crew:	630
Passenger-to-crew ratio:	2.4:1
Tonnage:	42,000
Passenger-space ratio:	27.7
Length:	700 feet
Beam:	93 feet
Draft:	22 feet
Cruising speed:	20 knots
Guest decks:	9
Total cabins:	759
Outside:	536
Inside:	212
Suites:	7
Wheelchair cabins:	4
Cuisine:	Italian, continental, French, international
Style:	Resort casual
Price notes:	Single supplement, 150 to 200 percent
Tipping suggestions:	$10 pp/pd
Best deal:	Early-bird fares; group discounts with minimum of eight guests

A veteran of the Caribbean (and on a comparative basis, a relatively homely member of the NCL fleet), the **Norwegian Sea** nevertheless has some nice touches in public areas, enhanced by redecoration. The ship's name was changed from *Seaward* to add a reference to its owner's Scandinavian heritage. The

Cabaret Lounge is used for full-scale Broadway productions.

The ship underwent another round of refurbishment in early 2003, adding a new restaurant and upgrades to public rooms. The forty-seat Pasta Cafe serves traditional Italian fare. The refurbished Stardust Lounge features a rich burgundy-and-gold theme with new carpet, drapes, and upholstery. Le Bistro, NCL's signature restaurant, was also redecorated.

Junior cruisers have their own playroom, The Porthole, for NCL's "Kids Crew" activities.

Norwegian Majesty

Econoguide rating:	★★★ 76 points
Ship size:	Large
Category:	Top of the Line
Price range:	Moderate to Premium $$–$$$
Registry:	Bahamas
Year built:	1992 (formerly *Royal Majesty*; stretched by 112 feet in 1999)
Information:	(800) 327–7030
Web site:	www.ncl.com
Passenger capacity:	1,462 (double occupancy)
Crew:	550
Passenger-to-crew ratio:	2.65:1
Tonnage:	40,876
Passenger-space ratio:	26
Length:	680 feet
Beam:	91 feet
Draft:	20 feet
Cruising speed:	20 knots
Guest decks:	9
Total cabins:	731
Outside:	466
Inside:	239
Suites:	22
Wheelchair cabins:	4
Cuisine:	Italian, continental, French, international
Style:	Resort casual
Price notes:	Single supplement, 150 to 200 percent
Tipping suggestions:	$10 pp/pd
Best deal:	Early-bird fares; group discounts with minimum of eight guests

The **Norwegian Majesty** was stretched by 112 feet in early 1999; addition of the new midsection increased the capacity from 1,056 to 1,462 guests and boosted the crew size by 25 percent.

The new midsection contains a second swimming pool and dining room, a new casino, the intimate fifty-eight-seat Le Bistro restaurant, more deck space, and 203 new staterooms. Also included in the section were two new elevators and a third set of stairs to improve movement throughout the ship.

An entirely new space, the Sky Deck, was added above the lengthened Sun Deck to add sunning areas and to create a ring of shaded areas around the two pools and whirlpools below.

Existing staterooms on the ship will be upgraded to match the new staterooms in upcoming refurbishments.

Installation of the new midsection took about three months. According to engineers, the new midsection actually helped the ship's underwater profile, allowing it to maintain its 21 knot speed without changes to the power plant. And added buoyancy from the new midsection reduced the vessel's draft about 18 inches.

Norwegian Crown

Econoguide rating:	★★★ 79 points
Ship size:	Medium
Category:	Vintage
Price range:	Premium $$$
Registry:	Bahamas
Year built:	1988 (As the *Crown Odyssey* of the Royal Viking Line and Royal Cruise Line; renamed *Norwegian Crown* for NCL in 1996; renamed *Crown Odyssey* in 2000 for Orient Lines; renamed again as *Norwegian Crown* for NCL in 2003.)
Information:	(800) 327–7030
Web site:	www.ncl.com
Passenger capacity:	1,050 (double occupancy)
Crew:	470
Passenger-to-crew ratio:	2.3:1
Tonnage:	34,250
Passenger-space ratio:	32.6
Length:	614 feet
Beam:	92.5 feet
Draft:	24 feet
Cruising speed:	22 knots
Guest decks:	10
Total cabins:	526
Outside:	322
Inside:	114
Suites:	90
Wheelchair cabins:	4
Cuisine:	Contemporary
Style:	Informal with two formal nights per cruise

Price notes:	Single supplement, 150 to 200 percent
Tipping suggestions:	$10 pp/pd
Best deal:	Early-bird fares; group discounts with minimum of eight guests

Built as an upper-ranks cruise ship, the **Norwegian Crown** has held up well over the years through several reinventions. She was transferred from NCL to sister company Orient Lines in 2000 but was brought back to NCL for 2003 and beyond.

In anticipation of her return to NCL, the ship was remodeled in 2003 in keeping with the line's freestyle cruising scheme for dining. The Seven Seas Restaurant is built on two levels, with a central sunken section beneath a domed Tiffany-style glass ceiling. New eateries added during the remodeling include Cafe Italia, an alfresco Italian kitchen; Le Bistro, an upscale French restaurant; Pasta Cafe, an informal pasta restaurant; and Chopsticks, a modern combination of Pacific Rim and Asian fusion offerings.

The ship also gained a state-of-the-art fitness center and children's activity area.

PRINCESS CRUISES

PRINCESS CRUISES 🐾.

Address: 24844 Avenue Rockefeller
Santa Clarita, CA 91355
Information: (800) 421–0522, (800) 774–6237
www.princess.com
Econoguide's Best Cruise Lines

❀ ❀ ❀ ❀

Princess Cruises Fleet

Star Princess	2002	2,600 passengers	110,000 tons
Golden Princess	2001	2,600 passengers	110,000 tons
Grand Princess	1998	2,600 passengers	109,000 tons
Island Princess	2003	1,970 passengers	88,000 tons
Coral Princess	2003	1,970 passengers	88,000 tons
Dawn Princess	1997	1,950 passengers	77,000 tons
Sun Princess	1995	1,950 passengers	77,000 tons
Regal Princess	1991	1,590 passengers	70,000 tons
Royal Princess	1984	1,200 passengers	45,000 tons
Pacific Princess	1997	680 passengers	30,277 tons
Tahitian Princess	1997	680 passengers	30,277 tons

FUTURE SHIPS			
Diamond Princess	March 2004	2,600 passengers	113,000 tons
Sapphire Princess	May 2004	2,600 passengers	113,000 tons
Caribbean Princess	April 2004	3,110 passengers	116,000 tons
Unnamed	May 2006	3,110 passengers	116,000 tons

No other cruise line has undergone as many changes in the past year: Princess introduced three ships (one new and two slightly used modern gems) and prepared to add three more Megaships in the coming year. Along the way, the company was gobbled up by Carnival Corporation—victor in a battle of the giants with Royal Caribbean.

Princess is expected to keep its own identity and its interesting fleet of ships. The first move by the new ownership was to announce an order for a sister ship to the new *Caribbean Princess,* due to enter service in May 2006 and, like its sister, to sail year-round in the Caribbean.

Princess, of course, is the cruise line that made its name as the home of "The Love Boat." Today Princess sails to six continents and calls at more than 260 ports around the world. Princess owns a big piece of Alaska, too, dispatching at least six cruise ships to those waters and operating four riverside wilderness lodges, a fleet of deluxe motor coaches, and an armada of Midnight Sun Express luxury railcars.

The flagships of the fleet are the *Grand Princess, Golden Princess,* and *Star Princess* sisters. They are due to be joined by the slightly larger *Diamond Princess* and *Sapphire Princess* in 2004. The 2,600-passenger ships are 951 feet long and 118 feet wide, a few feet wider than the Panama Canal.

The new *Coral Princess* arrived in 2003, and the line added *Pacific Princess* and *Tahitian Princess,* newly repolished gems purchased from the assets of much-loved but very bankrupt Renaissance Cruises.

■ THE PRINCESS STORY

Princess itself was founded in 1965 with a single chartered ship cruising from Los Angeles to Mexico; within a few years, Princess Cruises had a small fleet of ships on the West Coast. London-based Peninsular and Orient Steam Navigation Company (P&O) came to the same waters in the early 1970s; although it could not compete against Princess's head start, P&O later purchased the cruise line.

P&O dates back to 1822 to a fleet of small sailing ships; among their destinations was a link between Great Britain and Spain and Portugal, the Iberian Peninsula. To demonstrate their appreciation for the services provided during the Portuguese and Spanish civil wars of the early 1830s, the Royal Houses of both countries granted the company the right to fly their colors: the Portuguese blue and white, and the Spanish red and gold. Those colors continue to this day in the P&O flag.

In 1836 the company began a regular steamer service to the Iberian Peninsula under the name Peninsular Steam Navigation Company. Within a few years, the steamer company added routes to India and Egypt (with an overland route across Egypt until the opening of the Suez Canal in 1869). P&O began offering leisure cruises in 1844 and eventually became known for its "big white ships." By 1845 the steamers reached to Malay and China, and *Orient* was added to the company's name.

P&O purchased Princess in 1974. A year later, a television producer approached Princess Cruises with an idea for a series about cruising; *The Love Boat* was the result. The successful show became a weekly prime-time advertisement for cruising in general, and Princess in particular. The cruise company continued to market itself as The Love Boat well after the original series left the airwaves. *Pacific Princess,* the original Love Boat of the TV series, was retired from the Princess fleet at the end of 2002 after more than three decades of service.

In 1988 P&O bought out another competitor, Sitmar Cruises of Los Angeles, and merged its operations and ships into the Princess fleet. Today P&O Princess Cruises operates Princess Cruises; P&O Cruises and Swan Hellenic in the United Kingdom; Aida Cruises, A'ROSA, and Seetours, which offer vacations for the German market; and P&O Cruises in Australia. The new *Ocean Princess* left the Princess Cruises fleet in late 2002 to join P&O, sailing as the *Oceana* in Europe. The A'ROSA line was formed in 2002; her first ship was *A'Rosa Blu,* the former *Crown Princess.* A'ROSA operates a pair of river cruise boats on the Danube and elsewhere in Europe.

■ THE PRINCESS EXPERIENCE

The Love Boat lives on in the hearts and minds of Princess executives and many of the company's passengers. In 1998 another go-round of the television show took to the airwaves. *Love Boat: The Next Wave* was filmed in part aboard the $300 million 77,000-ton *Sun Princess.*

The original *Love Boat* series was set aboard the smaller 20,000-ton *Pacific Princess,* which left the fleet in 2002; its twin sister, the *Island Princess,* departed in 1999. Both names have since returned to the fleet on new ships.

Love Boat aside, Princess actually offers a pretty refined experience, with continental cuisine and a mostly Italian dining room staff. There are sushi restaurants on all ships in the fleet during lunch hours, and you can expect a full regime of parties, games, and other cruise entertainment.

The company operates the 353-room Denali Princess Wilderness Lodge just outside Denali National Park in Alaska. The company also owns the Kenai Princess Wilderness Lodge, the Mount McKinley Princess Wilderness Lodge, and the Fairbanks Princess Lodge.

Princess also has the eighty-four-room Copper River Princess Wilderness Lodge on land bordering Wrangell–Saint Elias National Park and Preserve in south-central Alaska. Public areas include a signature two-story Great Room featuring a stone fireplace, 25-foot ceilings, and stunning views of awe-inspiring Mounts Wrangell, Drum, and Blackburn.

Tours include an opportunity to fly over Wrangell–Saint Elias National Park en route to the historic towns of McCarthy and Kennicott. A guide takes participants on a tour of main street Kennicott and tells the incredible story of this mining boomtown. This is followed by a short trip to McCarthy, which served as a supply post for prospectors, hunters, and trappers. Also offered is an airplane tour to view three of the tallest peaks in Wrangell–Saint Elias National Park and one of the tallest in North America, Mount Sanford, with its 9,000-foot vertical rock wall. The Klutina River Whitewater Adventure offers Class III rapids and continuous splashy white water as it cascades over large boulders left behind from the last major glaciation period.

Personal Choice Dining on Princess ships allows travelers to choose from a traditional two-seating, fixed-time dining schedule with assigned seats and tablemates, or a flexible option to choose when, where, and with whom to dine during an expanded dining period from 5:30 P.M. to midnight. A special dining desk is open throughout the day to accept reservations; guests can also dine without reservations.

Partly to deal with the fact that guests may not have the same servers through the course of a trip, the line now includes an automatic gratuity program to cover all service staff; a daily charge of $10 per person is placed on the passenger's shipboard account. The tip can be adjusted up or down or removed by request.

Princess struck a blow for the environment with a program to turn off the engines of its ships when they dock in Juneau. Instead they use surplus hydroelectric power supplied by the local utility to run the ship's systems while it is in port.

Princess Kids, the line's expanded children's program, includes activities for three age groups as well as complimentary in-port programming. The program also includes activities developed with the California Science Center and the National Wildlife Federation. Activity groups are Princess Pelicans (ages three to seven), Princess Pirateers (ages eight to twelve), and Off Limits (ages thirteen to seventeen). Group baby-sitting services for children ages three to twelve are also available for $5.00 per hour per child. Junior cruisers can participate in two special dinner evenings designed for each age group. Teens can also take advantage of Princess's new Teen Spa program, which has an exclusive selection of specialized spa packages.

■ ITINERARIES

Princess, which has its roots in Europe and Asia but most of its customers in the United States, has concentrated on the Caribbean and Alaska for the past few years. In 2003, as the international situation turned threatening, the company reduced its plans for cruises in the Mediterranean, boosting its capacity in the Caribbean.

Four huge Princess ships sailed in the Caribbean for the 2003–04 season. *Grand Princess, Golden Princess, Dawn Princess,* and *Sun Princess* offered 111 departures on six itineraries ranging from seven to ten days through April or May 2004.

Grand Princess sailed to the western Caribbean from Fort Lauderdale, including calls at Cozumel, Grand Cayman, Costa Maya, and Princess Cays. *Golden Princess* ventured to the eastern Caribbean from Fort Lauderdale, with calls at St. Thomas, St. Martin, and Princess Cays. *Dawn Princess* offered alternating seven-day itineraries in the southern Caribbean from San Juan, including visits to Grenada, Caracas, and Aruba. *Sun Princess* alternated ten-day cruises to the eastern and southern Caribbean from Fort Lauderdale: The Eastern Caribbean Islander route featured calls at St. Vincent, Antigua, Barbados, St. Martin, St. Thomas, and Princess Cays; the Southern Caribbean Medley featured Curacao, Isla Margarita, Barbados, Dominica, St. Thomas, and Princess Cays.

(Princess moved the *Grand Princess* out of Europe in 2003 due to what the line said was lower than expected demand for Mediterranean vacations.)

The new *Caribbean Princess* will be assigned year-round to its namesake waters beginning in summer 2004. The *Golden Princess* will also sail in the Caribbean for the summer, marking the first time the company has had two ships in the area during that time of the year. Together the two ships will offer four different itineraries. *Caribbean Princess* will alternate seven-day Classic Eastern and Western Caribbean sailings. *Golden Princess* will offer alternating seven-day Southern Classic and Southern Explorer Caribbean itineraries.

Royal Princess sailed to new waters for Princess in late 2003, as Princess unveiled its first Antarctic itinerary. The cruise was part of the ship's extensive Exotics program for 2003–04, featuring South America and Africa. The twenty-four-day South Atlantic/Antarctica/South America cruise travels between Cape Town and Santiago, Chile, taking in some of the least-visited areas in the Atlantic and Southern Oceans along the way, with two days of cruising among the islands and channels of the southernmost continent.

For summer 2003, Princess dispatched four ships to sail from Vancouver up the Inside Passage to Alaska: *Coral Princess, Dawn Princess, Island Princess,* and *Sun Princess.* From San Francisco, *Pacific Princess* also sailed north to Alaska.

Tahitian Princess sails year-round from Papeete, joined for part of the year by *Pacific Princess.*

Regal Princess ventured to New England and Canada on one-way itineraries from New York or Montreal in fall 2003; *Golden Princess* also sailed a number of itineraries from New York.

Princess's reduced European offerings were led by *Regal Princess* and *Royal Princess* in 2003.

Diamond Princess is due to begin service in March 2004, with weekly sailings to Mexico round-trip from Los Angeles. After the Mexico season, the ship is due to reposition to Seattle and be joined by *Sapphire Princess,* placing the two newest and largest Princess ships together in Seattle for seven-day round-trip Alaska Inside Passage sailings.

■ WEB SITE

Visitors to the Princess Web site can find information about the ships and itineraries but can not book staterooms directly. Princess was the first major cruise line to add live bridgecams on most of its ships. ***Ease of use: very good.***

Grand Princess, Golden Princess, Star Princess, Diamond Princess, Sapphire Princess (2004), Caribbean Princess (2004)

Econoguide rating:	★★★★ 85 points
Ship size:	Colossus
Category:	Top of the Line
Price range:	Opulent $$$$
Registry:	Bermuda
Year built:	*Caribbean Princess,* 2004; *Sapphire Princess,* 2004; *Diamond Princess,* 2003; *Star Princess,* 2002; *Golden Princess,* 2001; *Grand Princess,* 1998

Information:	(800) 774–6237
Web site:	www.princess.com
Passenger capacity:	2,600 to 2,670 (double occupancy)
Crew:	1,100
Passenger-to-crew ratio:	2.4:1
Tonnage:	*Diamond Princess,* 113,000; *Sapphire Princess,* 113,000; *Golden Princess,* 110,000; *Star Princess,* 110,000; *Grand Princess,* 109,000; *Caribbean Princess,* 116,000
Passenger-space ratio:	41.9
Length:	951 feet
Beam:	118 to 123 feet; 159 feet including bridge wing
Draft:	26 to 28 feet
Cruising speed:	22 knots; 24 knots maximum
Guest decks:	18
Total cabins:	1,300 to 1,337
Outside:	928 to 960
Inside:	372 to 377
Suites:	208 to 216
Wheelchair cabins:	28 (18 outside, 10 inside)
Cuisine:	International
Style:	Formal, semiformal, and casual
Price notes:	Single-occupancy premium, 160 to 200 percent
Tipping suggestions:	$10 pp/pd
Best deals:	Advance-booking "Love Boat Savers" fares

For a short time, the **Grand Princess** was the Colossus of the Oceans, the largest cruise ship afloat. (She was trumped by Royal Caribbean's *Voyager of the Seas* and her sisters.) Her sister ships, *Golden Princess* and *Star Princess,* squeeze

The *Grand Princess* arrives in New York City. *Courtesy Princess Cruises*

an extra thousand tons of space aboard, and the *Diamond Princess* and *Sapphire Princess* will be 3,000 tons larger.

How big are these ships? More than three football fields long, they're too wide to fit through the Panama Canal; and at 201 feet tall, the ships are 50 feet taller than the Statue of Liberty and higher than Niagara Falls. They're home to 3,700 or so close friends and crew members. The *Pacific Princess,* the original "Love Boat," could fit within the *Grand Princess*'s Horizon Court dining and lido areas.

As befits the queen of the Love Boat line, the *Grand Princess* featured the first oceangoing wedding chapel, including a program that allows passengers to be married by the ship's captain—something that despite the common conception is not often permitted. On the **Golden Princess,** a live "Wedding Cam" will allow friends, relatives, and complete strangers to observe the goings-on in the chapel while the ship is at sea, if the participants desire; a similar camera will later be added to the *Grand Princess.*

The ships sport five swimming pools, including a lap pool that allows you to swim against the current. Princess Links offers simulated play on the world's greatest courses as well as a nine-hole putting green.

Skywalker's Disco is suspended 150 feet above the water at the stern of the ship, accessible by a glass-enclosed, moving "skywalk." There's also an oceangoing virtual-reality game center and a blue-screen digital studio to permit guests to star in their own shipboard epics.

The *Grand Princess* boasts the greatest number of cabins with private balconies (710 total) of any ship, and it has the largest casino at sea. It was also the first major commercial ship built with fully redundant operational and technical systems. There are two separate engine rooms. Power supplies are duplicated, and cooling systems are split into two separate circuits, with pumps and coolers in separate spaces.

The Horizon Court on the lido deck is a twenty-four-hour cafe with 620 seats. On the promenade deck are two of the three main dining rooms, the Da Vinci, with 486 seats, and the Botticelli, with 508 seats. Nearby is the Painted Desert, a ninety-two-seat Southwestern-themed restaurant.

The Plaza Deck is home to the third major restaurant, the 486-seat Michelangelo Dining Room. Nearby is Sabatini's Trattoria, a ninety-seat bistro for casual Italian dining. Sabatini's, one of two specialty restaurants aboard *Grand Princess,* serves informal Italian fare, specializing in seafood. A selection of Italian antipasti, Sevruga caviar, fresh-baked pizza, pastas, soups, and breads are offered. Entrees include lobster, langoustines, tiger prawns, Chilean sea bass, scallops, and meat dishes. Beginning in 2002, an additional charge of $15 per person was levied.

On the health front, the ship includes a "telemedicine" setup that allows the ship's doctors to consult electronically with emergency physicians at Cedars-Sinai Medical Center in Los Angeles.

In early 2002 the new **Star Princess** transited the Suez Canal, becoming the largest cruise ship ever to have made this passage. The ship was on her way to Singapore to pick up her first passengers and begin an inaugural twenty-six-day Pacific cruise to Los Angeles. The ship later began sailing on its regular itinerary,

Golden Princess docked in St. Martin. *Photo by Corey Sandler*

a seven-day round-trip voyage to the Mexican Riviera; at press time, *Star Princess* was the largest cruise ship ever to be based on the West Coast. The Grand-class ship draws her name from one of the line's former vessels. The original *Star Princess* debuted in 1989, just after Princess merged with Sitmar Cruises. The ship was transferred to P&O Cruises in 1997 to sail as *Arcadia*.

The ship that was to have been christened the *Diamond Princess* was severely damaged in a shipyard fire in Japan in late 2002. According to investigators, welders set afire wooden furniture in a neighboring cabin. The fire burned for thirty-six hours before being extinguished. The shipyard arranged to move forward the completion of *Sapphire Princess,* under construction nearby, and the two ships swapped names in the shipyard.

In spring 2004 the *Caribbean Princess* will arrive. (Plans had originally called for that ship to be named *Crown Princess,* a venerable name in the fleet.) That new ship—built at the Fincantieri shipyard in Italy—will be assigned year-round to her namesake waters, alternating between the eastern and western Caribbean.

One interesting new feature of the *Caribbean Princess* is Dive-In Movies, a splashy way for passengers to enjoy the latest movies under the sun—or stars— as they relax on deck. Films are played on a giant Times Square–style screen built into the superstructure of the vessel at the midship pool. The screen will also be used to present special sports events and for Caribbean Island Night parties held on each cruise.

Other features of the ship will be a new Caribbean-themed alternative restaurant, plus Princess's trademark Italian trattoria, four pools, three separate show lounges, and nearly 900 cabins with balconies, more than on any other cruise ship.

Coral Princess, Island Princess

Econoguide rating:	★★★★ 85 points
Ship size:	Megaship
Category:	Top of the Line
Price range:	Opulent $$$$
Registry:	Bermuda
Year built:	*Coral Princess,* 2003; *Island Princess,* 2003
Information:	(800) 774–6237
Web site:	www.princess.com
Passenger capacity:	1,970 (double occupancy)
Crew:	900
Passenger-to-crew ratio:	2.2:1
Tonnage:	88,000
Passenger-space ratio:	44.6
Length:	964 feet
Beam:	106 feet; 122 feet including bridge wing
Draft:	27 feet
Cruising speed:	22 knots; 24 knots maximum
Guest decks:	11
Total cabins:	987
Outside:	879
Inside:	108
Suites:	208
Wheelchair cabins:	28 (18 outside, 10 inside)
Cuisine:	International
Style:	Formal, semiformal, and casual
Price notes:	Single-occupancy premium, 160 to 200 percent
Tipping suggestions:	$10 pp/pd
Best deals:	Advance-booking "Love Boat Savers" fares

Coral Princess, the line's first 88,000-ton 1,950-passenger ship from French builder Chantiers de l'Atlantique, launched in January 2003. Sister ship **Island Princess** arrived in July 2003, reprising the name of one of the original "Love Boats." The ships use diesel and gas turbine engines, and the design will have only 10 percent of staterooms inside; 80 percent of the outside cabins will have balconies. There are three pools, three show rooms, and five restaurants onboard.

The two ships are the largest of the line's ships to be able to transit the Panama Canal.

Both ships offer a pair of main dining rooms, Provence and Bordeaus, as well as Sabatini's Trattoria, the Bayou Cafe New Orleans Restaurant, and the Princess Theater main show room. The two-story interactive aft lounge is equipped to offer full television production capabilities and high-definition projection. Known as the Universe Lounge, this special area features decor inspired by Jules Verne's classic tale *20,000 Leagues Under the Sea,* and offers three revolving stages. The lounge will also be home to a new "ScholarShip at Sea" program, including enrichment courses on cooking, photography, ceramics, visual arts, computers, and other fun and informative classes.

The Bayou Cafe—the $10 lunch and dinner cover charge includes a complimentary Hurricane cocktail—offers platters of Mardi Gras shrimp piquante, sausage grillades, oysters Sieur de Bienville, and crawfish "mud bug" bisque as entrees. Traditional Creole favorites include Seafood Gumbo Ya-Ya, Toulouse chicken, and chorizo jambalaya. Grill options feature such spicy delicacies as smothered gator ribs, flambeaux grilled jumbo prawns, cornmeal-fried catfish, blackened chicken brochette, Carpetbagger's Trinity Smothered Filet of Beef, and red pepper–butter broiled lobster. If you've got room left for dessert, consider buttermilk bread pudding, sweet potato pie, fried yellow peach pie, or banana whiskey pound cake.

Both vessels use innovative power generation technology: a gas turbine/diesel engine combination, with the gas turbines placed in the ships' funnels. This configuration is not only environmentally advantageous but also allows for additional space inside the ships for passenger facilities.

Pacific Princess, Tahitian Princess

Econoguide rating:	★★★★ 83 points
Ship size:	Medium
Category:	Top of the Line
Price range:	Premium $$$
Registry:	Gibraltar
Year built:	*Pacific Princess* (built as *Renaissance R3* in 1999); *Tahitian Princess* (built as *Renaissance R4* in 1999)
Information:	(800) 774–6237
Web site:	www.princess.com
Passenger capacity:	680 (double occupancy)
Crew:	373
Passenger-to-crew ratio:	1.8:1
Tonnage:	30,277
Passenger-space ratio:	44.1
Length:	592 feet
Beam:	83.5
Draft:	19.5 feet
Cruising speed:	20 knots maximum

Guest decks:	9
Total cabins:	342
Outside:	317
Inside:	25
Suites:	10
Wheelchair cabins:	14
Cuisine:	International
Style:	Formal, semiformal, and casual
Price notes:	Single-occupancy premium, 160 to 200 percent
Tipping suggestions:	$10 pp/pd
Best deals:	Advance-booking "Love Boat Savers" fares

Renaissance Cruise Lines had a devoted following for its eight medium-size cruise ships, vessels that bridged the gap between the best of the major ships and the small boutique luxury vessels. When Renaissance went out of business in late 2001, most of the company's young fleet of nearly identical ships were purchased by existing or new companies.

Princess added *R3* and *R4* to its fleet, renaming them *Pacific Princess* and *Tahitian Princess*, respectively. The ships will offer sailings in Tahiti and the wider Pacific Ocean region. The vessels include a wide variety of dining options, including a twenty-four-hour Lido and alternative dining programs with both an Italian restaurant (Sabatini's Trattoria) and an American steakhouse (Sterling Steakhouse). Ninety-two percent of the staterooms offer outside views, with more than two-thirds of these having a private balcony.

Plans call for the **Tahitian Princess** to sail year-round in Tahiti and the South Pacific. Three unique itineraries, with a total of fifty round-trip departures from Papeete, Tahiti, include calls at the tropical paradises of Bora Bora, Moorea, and Raiatea. Passengers can choose one of the thirty-four French Polynesia/Cook Islands sailings that explore such ports as mystic Huahine and Raratonga, trips with stops at Pago Pago and Apia, or Marquesas islands such as Nuku Hiva and Hiva Oa.

The **Pacific Princess** will operate on a split deployment, sailing half the year throughout French Polynesia and the wider Pacific region for Princess Cruises and the other half for the P&O Cruises Australia brand, serving the growing Australian market in the South Pacific region.

Dawn Princess, Sun Princess

Econoguide rating:	★★★★ 85 points
Ship size:	Megaship
Category:	Top of the Line
Price range:	Premium to Opulent $$$–$$$$
Registry:	Great Britain
Year built:	*Sun Princess,* 1995; *Dawn Princess,* 1997

Information:	(800) 774–6237
Web site:	www.princess.com
Passenger capacity:	1,950 (double occupancy)
Crew:	900; Italian officers
Passenger-to-crew ratio:	2.2:1
Tonnage:	77,000
Passenger-space ratio:	39.5
Length:	856 feet
Beam:	106 feet
Draft:	26 feet
Cruising speed:	21 knots
Guest decks:	14
Total cabins:	975
Outside:	603
Inside:	372
Suites:	38
Wheelchair cabins:	19
Cuisine:	International
Style:	Formal, semiformal, and casual nights
Price notes:	Single-occupancy premium, 160 to 200 percent
Tipping suggestions:	$10 pp/pd
Best deals:	Advance-booking "Love Boat Savers" fares

The ships in the Grand class are modern favorites, with more than 400 veranda staterooms and high-tech theaters. A teak promenade deck encircles the entire ship. Within is a $2.5 million art collection.

Two of the sister ships in this class left the Princess fleet in 2002 and 2003. *Ocean Princess* was transferred to P&O Cruises and renamed *Oceana* to serve the growing cruise market in the United Kingdom. *Sea Princess* made the same move in 2003, renamed *Adonia* and replacing the *Arcadia,* which was moved to a new, informal P&O line, Ocean Village.

Regal Princess

Econoguide rating:	★★★★ 80 points
Ship size:	Megaship
Category:	Top of the Line
Price range:	Premium to Opulent $$$–$$$$
Registry:	Great Britain
Year built:	1991
Information:	(800) 774–6237
Web site:	www.princess.com
Passenger capacity:	1,590 (double occupancy)
Crew:	696

Passenger-to-crew ratio:	2.3:1
Tonnage:	70,000
Passenger-space ratio:	44
Length:	811 feet
Beam:	105.8 feet
Draft:	26.5 feet
Cruising speed:	21 knots
Guest decks:	12
Total cabins:	795
Outside:	624
Inside:	171
Suites:	50
Wheelchair cabins:	10
Cuisine:	International
Style:	Formal, semiformal, and casual nights
Price notes:	Single-occupancy premium, 160 to 200 percent
Tipping suggestions:	$10 pp/pd
Best deals:	Advance-booking "Love Boat Savers" fares

Older but still elaborate and elegant, with her original dolphin profile intact, the **Regal Princess** received a "Millennium Makeover" in 2000, with new decor in public rooms, a new children's and teens' center, and an expanded twenty-four-hour bistro in addition to a pizzeria and patisserie. The ship now sports the Bacchus Bar, a handsome wine-and-caviar watering hole.

Near-identical sister *Crown Princess* left the line in early 2002 to join the fleet of A'ROSA, renamed *A'rosa Blu* and catering to the German market.

Royal Princess

Econoguide rating:	★★★★ 84 points
Ship size:	Large
Category:	Golden Oldie
Price range:	Moderate $$
Registry:	Great Britain
Year built:	1984
Information:	(800) 774–6237
Web site:	www.princess.com
Passenger capacity:	1,200 (double occupancy)
Crew:	520; British officers
Passenger-to-crew ratio:	2.3:1
Tonnage:	45,000
Passenger-space ratio:	38.3
Length:	757 feet
Beam:	106 feet

Draft:	26 feet
Cruising speed:	20 knots
Guest decks:	9
Total cabins:	600
Outside:	600
Inside:	0
Suites:	66
Wheelchair cabins:	4
Cuisine:	International
Style:	Formal, semiformal, and casual nights
Price notes:	Single-occupancy premium, 160 to 200 percent
Tipping suggestions:	$10 pp/pd
Best deals:	Advance-booking "Love Boat Savers" fares

A gracefully aging pioneer of cruising, **Royal Princess** earned her name when she was christened by Princess Diana. Among the first ships to offer verandas on many of her cabins, her 600 staterooms are in prime outside, upper-deck locations; public rooms are located on lower decks. (Some of the outside cabins, however, have restricted views because of low-hanging lifeboats.)

ROYAL CARIBBEAN INTERNATIONAL

Address: 1050 Caribbean Way
Miami, FL 33132-2096
Information: (800) 327–6700
www.royalcaribbean.com
Econoguide's Best Cruise Lines for Families

The Royal Caribbean Fleet

Mariner of the Seas	2003	3,114 passengers	142,000 tons
Navigator of the Seas	2003	3,114 passengers	142,000 tons
Adventure of the Seas	2001	3,114 passengers	142,000 tons
Explorer of the Seas	2000	3,114 passengers	142,000 tons
Voyager of the Seas	1999	3,114 passengers	142,000 tons
Serenade of the Sea	2003	2,100 passengers	88,000 tons
Brilliance of the Seas	2002	2,100 passengers	88,000 tons
Radiance of the Seas	2001	2,100 passengers	88,000 tons
Vision of the Seas	1998	2,435 passengers	78,491 tons
Rhapsody of the Seas	1997	2,435 passengers	78,491 tons
Enchantment of the Seas	1997	2,446 passengers	74,140 tons
Grandeur of the Seas	1996	2,446 passengers	74,140 tons
Majesty of the Seas	1992	2,744 passengers	73,941 tons
Monarch of the Seas	1991	2,744 passengers	73,941 tons

Sovereign of the Seas	1988	2,850 passengers	73,192 tons
Splendour of the Seas	1996	2,076 passengers	69,130 tons
Legend of the Seas	1995	2,076 passengers	69,130 tons
Nordic Empress	1990	2,020 passengers	48,563 tons

FUTURE SHIPS

Jewel of the Seas	2004	2,100 passengers	88,000 tons

Think Royal Caribbean and think large. The line owns and operates five of the largest cruise ships afloat: the 142,000-ton *Adventure of the Seas, Explorer of the Seas, Mariner of the Seas, Navigator of the Seas,* and *Voyager of the Seas.* Each of these ships is about twice the size of the average cruise ship. The ships will cede their place as the hugest of the huge in 2004 with the arrival of Cunard's *Queen Mary 2,* which will put 150,000 tons afloat.

Radiance of the Seas joined the fleet in mid-2001, the first of a new line of 88,000-ton Radiance-class ships. *Brilliance of the Seas* arrived in mid-2002. *Serenade of the Seas* arrived in 2003, with *Jewel of the Seas* due in 2004. These ships are powered by gas turbines, claimed to reduce airborne emissions, noise, and vibration. The turbines provide power to electric propulsion motors that turn the propellers mounted in rotating pods beneath the ship's hull. Exhaust heat from the turbines is captured to spin turbines for lighting, air-conditioning, and water heating.

Six older ships in the fleet are members of the Vision class: *Vision of the Seas, Enchantment, Grandeur, Legend, Rhapsody,* and *Splendour.* They were among the first cruise ships to open up large portions of the public areas with glass windows and skylights.

The venerable *Viking Serenade* left the fleet in early 2002, beginning a new role with the launch of a new cruise brand in Europe in a partnership beween First Choice Holidays and Royal Caribbean. The ship, renamed *Island Escape,* will sail seven-night Mediterranean cruises in the summer and seven-night Caribbean cruises in the winter.

Royal Celebrity Tours, the land-tour company of Royal Caribbean Cruises, added two new Wilderness Express train cars to its fleet in 2002 to expand offerings in Alaska. The coaches boast the most dome glass of any double-deck train cars in the world, outdoor 360-degree viewing platforms, extra-wide seats that recline and rotate, and onboard dining. The cars are also equipped with dome-level ADA-compliant seating, allowing physically challenged travelers to access both levels. Royal Celebrity Tours has also expanded operations into the Canadian Rockies, in conjunction with Rocky Mountaineer Railtours.

Guests on Celebrity Cruises' and Royal Caribbean International's Alaska sailings can select pre- or postcruise land packages, ranging from two to six nights and featuring cities such as Talkeetna, Fairbanks, the Alyeska resort, Denali, and Anchorage.

■ THE RCI STORY

Royal Caribbean Cruise Line was founded in 1969 by three Norwegian shipping companies: Anders Wilhelmsen and Company, I. M. Skaugen and Company, and later, Gotaas Larsen. The cruise company pioneered air/sea vacations, flying cruise guests to meet the ships in their first port, Miami.

The company's first ship, *Song of Norway,* entered service in 1970; the *Nordic Prince* followed the next year and the *Sun Viking* a year later. Promoted as the first passenger ship built specifically for warm-weather cruising rather than point-to-point transport, the *Song of Norway* was also the first ship to have a cocktail lounge cantilevered from its smokestack; the Viking Crown Lounge has since become the hallmark of every Royal Caribbean vessel.

In 1978 the *Song of Norway* became the first major passenger cruise ship to be "stretched"; it was cut in two and an 85-foot midsection was added, increasing guest capacity from 700 to just over 1,000. The *Nordic Prince* underwent a similar conversion in 1980. The *Nordic Prince* and the *Song of Norway* were sold in 1995 and 1997, respectively, to the British leisure company Airtours PLC.

In 1988 Royal Caribbean merged its operations with Admiral Cruises, and Anders Wilhelmsen and Company bought out its original partners. That same year the massive *Sovereign of the Seas* debuted, introducing a five-deck atrium—the Centrum—with glass elevators, sweeping staircases, and fountains in marble pools; this marked the first time such a central atrium had been constructed on a passenger ship.

Royal Caribbean became a publicly traded company in 1993. The line sold *Song of America* in early 1999 to Airtours. The 1,400-passenger ship, introduced in 1982, most recently sailed seven-night Mexican Riviera cruises in the winter and Bermuda itineraries in the summer.

■ THE RCI EXPERIENCE

Royal Caribbean goes for headlines: an ice-skating rink on *Voyager of the Seas,* an eighteen-hole miniature golf course on *Splendour of the Seas* and *Legend of the Seas,* and cantilevered cocktail lounges up high on the smokestacks.

In 2003 the company committed to installing rock-climbing walls on all of its ships by the end of the year. First introduced on *Voyager of the Seas,* the climbing walls have proven very popular—and distinctive. Designed for both beginners and advanced climbers, the walls are perched on the top decks; participants are rewarded with an unparalleled bird's-eye view of the ship, sea, and sky. On Voyager-class vessels, the top of the walls are nearly 200 feet above the ocean. Lessons are offered.

RCI delivers a high-quality product aimed at the middle of the cruise market. A corporate goal is to make the experience pretty much the same on all of its ships, even though they may differ in size and configuration.

Royal Caribbean offers two private spots just for its guests in the Caribbean and the Bahamas. Labadee is a 260-acre wooded peninsula at Pointe Sainte Honore, about 6 miles from Cap Haitien on the mountainous and secluded north coast of Haiti. There are five beaches, an outdoor performance area, an open-air dining area, nature trails, shaded hammocks, and a coral reef that includes a sunken airplane. Recreational highlights include paddleboats, water cycles, parasailing, sailboats, and snorkeling with underwater cameras. CocoCay is a 140-acre island in the Bahamas' Berry Island chain between Freeport and

Nassau; its offerings are similar to those of Labadee.

Renovations in 2003 at CocoCay added new facilities for snorkeling and personal watercraft. With equipment from the Snorkel Shack, guests can check out a sunken plane wreck, explore the coral reef, or attend a fish-feeding frenzy. For deeper explorations, the Diver's Den offers certified divers an opportunity to experience the crystal-clear waters of the Bahamas on a one-tank, shallow-water beach dive that takes them 40 feet below, where a PADI scuba instructor will help identify the varied marine life and coral formations.

Guests can also rent a personal watercraft to head out on a guided, fifty-minute tour of Great Stirrup Cay Lighthouse, Slaughter Harbor, Star Fish Alley, and the abandoned island community of Cistern Cay. Back on land, guests can explore the island's attractions on a new 3-mile-long nature trail.

The Adventure Ocean children's program organizes activities for Aquanauts (ages three to five), Explorers (six to eight), Voyagers (nine to twelve), and Navigators (thirteen to seventeen). Programs include finger painting and dress-up for the very young, arts and crafts, sports and pool activities, karaoke, talent shows, and special parties. Island activities include beach parties and games, sand castle building, seashell collecting, and more. During summer and holidays, Adventure Science classes are conducted by specially trained science staff. The program blends science with entertainment—rockets, slime, and bubbling potions included.

Royal Caribbean operates what is claimed as the world's largest passenger cruise terminal at its home base in Miami. The building has to be large; on turnaround day as many as 8,400 guests may be getting off or on the ship, at more or less the same time. The roof sports a replica of Royal Caribbean's signature Viking Crown Lounge as an observation point.

■ ITINERARIES

Royal Caribbean has a major presence in the Caribbean, with seven ships sailing year-round to eastern, western, and southern ports: *Adventure of the Seas, Enchantment of the Seas, Explorer of the Seas, Mariner of the Seas, Navigator of the Seas, Rhapsody of the Seas,* and *Voyager of the Seas.*

Seasonal service in the Caribbean is offered by *Brilliance of the Seas, Monarch of the Seas, Nordic Empress, Radiance of the Seas,* and *Splendour of the Seas.*

Majesty of the Seas sails three- and four-day trips to the Bahamas year-round from Miami; *Sovereign of the Seas* sails a similar schedule from Port Canaveral.

Ships that move seasonally between the Caribbean and Europe include *Brilliance of the Seas, Grandeur of the Seas,* and *Splendour of the Seas.*

Alaskan voyages are offered on *Legend of the Seas, Radiance of the Seas,* and *Vision of the Seas.*

Seasonally, Royal Caribbean ships also pass through the Panama Canal and make visits to the Mexican Riviera, Hawaii, and Australia. Seasonal service is offered in New England and Canada.

The new 3,114-passenger *Mariner of the Seas* will sail regularly from Port Canaveral, joining *Sovereign of the Seas* in sailing from that port.

■ WEB SITE

Royal Caribbean's Web site allows selection of a cruise and browsing specific available staterooms. Visitors can also learn about and book more than 1,500 shore excursions in 260 ports of call. *Ease of use: excellent.*

Adventure of the Seas, Explorer of the Seas, Mariner of the Seas, Navigator of the Seas, Voyager of the Seas (VOYAGER CLASS)	
Econoguide rating:	★★★★ 84 points
Ship size:	Gargantuan
Category:	Top of the Line
Price range:	Premium $$$
Registry:	Liberia
Year built:	*Adventure of the Seas,* 2001; *Explorer of the Seas,* 2000; *Mariner of the Seas,* 2003; *Navigator of the Seas,* 2003; *Voyager of the Seas,* 1999
Information:	(305) 539–6000, (800) 327–6700
Web site:	www.royalcaribbean.com
Passenger capacity:	3,114 (double occupancy)
Crew:	1,181
Passenger-to-crew ratio:	2.6:1
Tonnage:	142,000
Passenger-space ratio:	45.6
Length:	1,021 feet
Beam:	157.5 feet
Draft:	29 feet
Cruising speed:	22 knots
Guest decks:	14
Total cabins:	1,557
Outside:	939
Inside:	618, including 138 Promenade View staterooms
Suites:	119
Wheelchair cabins:	Call (305) 539–4440 for special assistance
Cuisine:	International
Style:	Resort casual, with occasional formal nights
Price notes:	Single-occupancy premium, 150 to 200 percent; Single Guarantee Program guests add $250 or $500; Special Share Program pairs people of same gender and smoking prefer-ence
Tipping suggestions:	$7.50 pp/pd

The *Voyager of the Seas* took the mantle as the largest cruise ship when she debuted in November 1999 at 1,019 feet long, 157.5 feet wide, and 206.5 feet above the waterline. The behemoth is thus about 20 feet too long and 50 feet too wide to fit through the Panama Canal. It has to be that big, you see, to fit the

Explorer of the Seas backs out of her berth in St. Thomas, USVI. *Photo by Corey Sandler*

skating rink, twin eleven-story atria, and the Royal Promenade shopping district with its own version of Mardi Gras onboard.

On its May 28, 2000, cruise, *Voyager of the Seas* set a world record, carrying 3,608 guests, including 380 honeymooners. The theoretical limit for the vessel, if all of its third and fourth berths were filled, is 3,838.

These are not your typical cruise ships: They include an ice-skating rink with its own Zamboni machine, a rock-climbing wall, and a wedding chapel in the sky. The Peek-a-Boo Bridge above the wheelhouse allows guests to watch the team that is "driving" and navigating the ship.

The Royal Promenade runs most of the length of each of the ships, four decks high, punctuated by two atria (the Centrums). The promenade offers shops, restaurants, and entertainment areas fronting on a winding "street." Special lighting effects allow the promenade to change in ambience from day to night.

On *Voyager*, the Royal Promenade has street festivities and performers, including *Voyager*'s own version of Mardi Gras. Arching over the promenade is the Captain's Balcony, a podium the captain uses to welcome guests on formal nights.

The Royal Promenade also features inside staterooms that offer a view of the atrium and street scene. The cabins, which represent about 10 percent of the staterooms on the ship, have bay windows—the first such inside views on a cruise ship. Almost half the cabins offer balconies, and rooms are generally larger than those on other ships.

Voyager of the Seas includes a three-level main dining room with separate and distinct themed dining areas—Carmen, La Boheme, and Magic Flute—all connected by a dramatic three-deck grand staircase. Smaller dining rooms, Seville and Granada, adjoin the Carmen area. Casual eateries include the SeaSide Diner, a 1950s-style, twenty-four-hour spot; Island Grill, a casual restaurant; and Portofino, an upscale Euro-Italian restaurant.

Entertainment areas include the La Scala Theater, a 1,350-seat theater that spans five decks and offers a hydraulic orchestra pit and stage area and abovestage fly space for full productions.

Studio B is a 900-seat arena for variety shows, ice shows, game shows, and rock and roll performances. The seating and floor can be retracted, allowing the area to be used as an ice-skating rink for guests.

The *Voyager*'s outdoor sports deck includes a golf course, driving range, and golf simulator. Also onboard is a rock-climbing wall, an in-line skating track, and regulation-size basketball, paddleball, and volleyball courts.

A full range of youth facilities for Aquanauts (ages three to five), Explorers (six to eight), and Voyagers (nine to twelve) include Mission Control, with interactive virtual rockets and a space theater. A computer lab has games and educational software, and there's a large arcade. Optix is a clubhouse for teens that has computers, a soda bar, and a dance area with a DJ.

Explorer of the Seas is the first cruise ship to boast a state-of-the-art atmospheric and marine laboratory, with an interactive environmental classroom.

Navigator of the Seas introduced the company's first wine bar, a Latin jazz bar, the Royal Caribbean's Chops Grille steakhouse, and a new Asian fusion restaurant, Jade. In addition, *Navigator* features expanded kids activities areas, with three new teen-only hangouts: an ultrahip nightclub, a laid-back lounge, and a private sundeck. *Navigator* also has a slightly different look than her sister ships, with more exterior glass offering even grander views from balcony staterooms.

The fifth and final member of the Voyager class, ***Mariner of the Seas,*** was due to join the fleet by the end of 2003 and sail year-round from Port Canaveral to the Caribbean.

***Radiance of the Seas, Brilliance of the Seas, Serenade of the Seas, Jewel of the Seas* (2004) (RADIANCE CLASS)**	

Econoguide rating:	★★★★ 85 points
Ship size:	Megaship
Category:	Top of the Line
Price range:	Premium $$$
Registry:	Liberia
Year built:	*Radiance of the Seas,* 2001; *Brilliance of the Seas,* 2002; *Serenade of the Seas,* 2003; *Jewel of the Seas,* November 2004
Information:	(305) 539–6000, (800) 327–6700
Web site:	www.royalcaribbean.com

Passenger capacity:	2,100 (double occupancy)
Crew:	859
Passenger-to-crew ratio:	2.4:1
Tonnage:	88,000
Passenger-space ratio:	41.9 (estimated)
Length:	961 feet
Beam:	105 feet
Draft:	26.7 feet
Cruising speed:	24 knots
Guest decks:	12
Total cabins:	1,050
Outside:	813
Inside:	237
Suites:	80
Wheelchair cabins:	Call (305) 539–4440 for special assistance
Cuisine:	International
Style:	Resort casual with occasional formal nights
Price notes:	Single-occupancy premium, 150 to 200 percent; Single Guarantee Program guests add $250 or $500; Special Share Program pairs people of same gender and smoking preference.
Tipping suggestions:	$7.50 pp/pd

On **Radiance of the Seas,** the indoor-outdoor Windjammer Cafe provides sweeping views of the ocean from floor-to-ceiling windows, a sail-like tent roof, and a yachting decor that includes scale models of famed yachts. At pool's edge, a bronze statue of a lion cub dips its paw into the water; nearby, an elephant waterfall is surrounded by live jungle vegetation.

Active sports include a rock-climbing wall, in-line skating track, basketball and volleyball courts, a miniature golf course, a jogging track, and a golf simulator. In the gymnasium, a bank of treadmills faces a wall of windows overlooking the sea.

Brilliance of the Seas includes similar sports and recreation facilities. After you've worked up an appetite, five dining venues await you: the Chops Grille steakhouse, Portofino Italian restaurant, Minstrels main dining room, the casual Windjammer and Seaview cafes, and pizza, cappuccino, and pastry offerings at Books Books & Coffee.

Royal Caribbean has options to purchase a fifth and sixth ship in the class.

Rhapsody of the Seas, Vision of the Seas

Econoguide rating:	★★★★ 84 points
Ship size:	Megaship
Category:	Top of the Line
Price range:	Moderate to Premium $$$–$$$$

Registry:	Norway
Year built:	*Rhapsody of the Seas,* 1997; *Vision of the Seas,* 1998
Information:	(305) 539–6000, (800) 327–6700
Web site:	www.royalcaribbean.com
Passenger capacity:	2,000 (double occupancy)
Crew:	765
Passenger-to-crew ratio:	2.6:1
Tonnage:	78,491
Passenger-space ratio:	39.2
Length:	915 feet
Beam:	105.6 feet
Draft:	25 feet
Cruising speed:	22 knots
Guest decks:	11
Total cabins:	1,000
Outside:	496
Inside:	407
Suites:	97
Wheelchair cabins:	14
Cuisine:	International
Style:	Resort casual, with occasional formal nights
Price notes:	Single-occupancy premium, 150 to 200 percent; Single Guarantee Program guests add $250 or $500; Special Share Program pairs people of same gender and smoking preference
Tipping suggestions:	$7.50 pp/pd

Rhapsody of the Seas and **Vision of the Seas** are twins, close sisters to *Enchantment, Grandeur, Legend,* and *Splendour of the Seas.*

Enchantment of the Seas, Grandeur of the Seas

Econoguide rating:	★★★★ 84 points
Ship size:	Megaship
Category:	Top of the Line
Price range:	Premium $$$
Registry:	Norway
Year built:	*Enchantment of the Seas,* 1997; *Grandeur of the Seas,* 1996
Information:	(305) 539–6000, (800) 327–6700
Web site:	www.royalcaribbean.com
Passenger capacity:	1,950 (double occupancy)
Crew:	760
Passenger-to-crew ratio:	2.6:1
Tonnage:	74,140
Passenger-space ratio:	38

Royal Caribbean's *Grandeur of the Seas* arrives in Charlotte Amalie, Saint Thomas. *Photo by Corey Sandler*

Length:	916 feet
Beam:	105.6 feet
Draft:	25 feet
Cruising speed:	22 knots
Guest decks:	11
Total cabins:	975
Outside:	554
Inside:	399
Suites:	22
Wheelchair cabins:	14
Cuisine:	International
Style:	Resort casual, with occasional formal nights
Price notes:	Single-occupancy premium, 150 to 200 percent; Single Guarantee Program guests add $250 or $500; Special Share Program pairs people of same gender and smoking preference
Tipping suggestions:	$7.50 pp/pd

Enchantment of the Seas and her near-identical older sister, **Grandeur of the Seas,** are members of Royal Caribbean's six-ship Project Vision series, a group of vessels that are aflood with light from acres of windows. Their seven-deck-high central atrium is topped off with a glass skylight, and nearly every other public room is open to the sunsets, sunrises, daylight, and moonlight of a voyage at sea.

In April 2000 *Enchantment of the Seas* moved her base to Port Everglades near Fort Lauderdale, sailing alternating eastern and western Caribbean itineraries. The move opened space at the Port of Miami for Royal Caribbean's two new 142,000-ton Eagle-class vessels.

The Vision series, which also includes the *Legend of the Seas, Rhapsody of the Seas, Splendour of the Seas,* and the namesake *Vision of the Seas* are big ships, but well below the size of the Megaships and Colossuses that are now becoming common.

Royal Caribbean is known for its shipboard entertainment as well, presenting Broadway-style revues, musicals, comedians, movies, discos, limbo competitions, country line dancing, and just about anything to draw a crowd.

The free Adventure Ocean program for children from ages three through seventeen includes a professional staff, play facilities, science demonstrations, a video game room, arts and crafts, and a teen disco.

Majesty of the Seas, Monarch of the Seas, Sovereign of the Seas

Econoguide rating:	★★★ 76 points
Ship size:	Megaship
Category:	Top of the Line
Price range:	Moderate $$
Registry:	Norway
Year built:	*Majesty of the Seas,* 1992; *Monarch of the Seas,* 1991; *Sovereign of the Seas,* 1988
Information:	(305) 539–6000, (800) 327–6700
Web site:	www.royalcaribbean.com
Passenger capacity:	2,744 (double occupancy)
Crew:	822
Passenger-to-crew ratio:	2.9:1
Tonnage:	*Majesty of the Seas, Monarch of the Seas,* 73,941; *Sovereign of the Seas,* 73,192
Passenger-space ratio:	31.5
Length:	880 feet
Beam:	106 feet
Draft:	25 feet
Cruising speed:	22 knots
Guest decks:	14
Total cabins:	1,177
Outside:	669
Inside:	445
Suites:	63
Wheelchair cabins:	4
Cuisine:	International

Style:	Resort casual, with occasional formal nights
Price notes:	Single-occupancy premium, 150 to 200 percent; Single Guarantee Program guests add $250 or $500; Special Share Program pairs people of same gender and smoking preference
Tipping suggestions:	$7.50 pp/pd

The design of **Majesty of the Seas, Monarch of the Seas,** and **Sovereign of the Seas** puts most of the cabins forward and the public rooms aft, allowing passengers to move vertically by elevator or stairs from lounge to restaurant or show room without having to traverse hallways of cabins. On the five lowest decks—Tween, Showtime, Main, A, and B—there are as many as nine cabins shoehorned across the beam of the ship. There is a pair of outside cabins, of course, with five or more cross-width hallways serving rows of seven inside cabins. Put another way, on this class of ship, some inside cabins are as far as four cabins away from the nearest outside window; that's *really* inside.

The *Monarch of the Seas* suffered an unpleasant encounter with an underwater shoal off the coast of Saint Martin in December 1998 and began taking on water. Her captain was able to steer the ship back to port where it was beached; all 2,557 passengers were evacuated from the ship in the middle of the night without injury. After a few weeks of repairs, the ship was returned to service.

The *Sovereign of the Seas* is an older, slightly smaller sister.

In 2003 *Monarch of the Seas* underwent major renovations in preparation for reassignment to her new homeport of Los Angeles to sail three- and four-night cruises year-round to Baja California in Mexico.

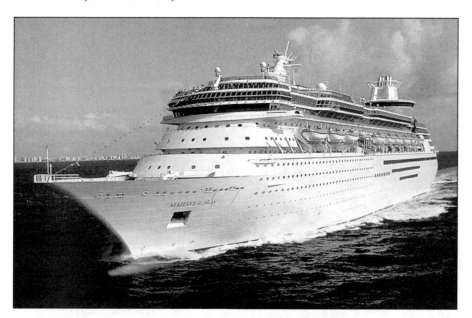

Royal Caribbean's *Majesty of the Seas* under way. *Courtesy Royal Caribbean International*

The first floor of the casual two-story Windjammer Cafe gained an Asian fusion restaurant; the eatery was also reconfigured with buffet "islands" for better traffic flow. Upstairs, guests can try the exotic offerings at the upscale sushi bar, Jade Sushi, or check out the creations at the gourmet pizza station.

The ship's main dining rooms were renamed and refurbished with new carpet, chairs, tables, and decor. The dining rooms—now called Claude's and Vincent's—feature color palettes inspired by the works of Monet and Van Gogh. Between meals, guests can enjoy specialty drinks from Seattle's Best Coffee or indulge their sweet tooth with Ben & Jerry's ice cream.

The midship lounge on Deck 7 now offers Boleros, a Latin-themed bar that dispenses specialty tequilas and cocktail favorites like mojitos, as well as live entertainment that includes jazz bands and dueling pianos. The secondary lounge on Deck 8 was transformed into a disco, The Circuit.

The renovations also tripled the space dedicated to Monarch's Adventure Ocean Youth Program, including a video arcade; the Living Room coffee bar and hangout, complete with Club Cafe Internet center; Fuel nightclub; and the Back Deck, a private outdoor area.

Other refurbishments include updates to all staterooms. Up top, the ship gained a rock-climbing wall, part of the line's fleetwide program.

Legend of the Seas, Splendour of the Seas

Econoguide rating:	★★★★ 83 points
Ship size:	Large
Category:	Top of the Line
Price range:	Moderate to Premium $$–$$$
Registry:	Liberia
Year built:	*Legend of the Seas,* 1995; *Splendour of the Seas,* 1996
Information:	(305) 539–6000, (800) 327–6700
Web site:	www.royalcaribbean.com
Passenger capacity:	1,800 (double occupancy)
Crew:	720
Passenger-to-crew ratio:	2.5:1
Tonnage:	69,130
Passenger-space ratio:	38.4
Length:	867 feet
Beam:	105 feet
Draft:	24 feet
Cruising speed:	24 knots
Guest decks:	11
Total cabins:	902
Outside:	488
Inside:	327

Suites:	87
Wheelchair cabins:	17
Cuisine:	International
Style:	Resort casual, with occasional formal nights
Price notes:	Single-occupancy premium, 150 to 200 percent; Single Guarantee Program guests add $250 or $500; Special Share Program pairs people of same gender and smoking preference
Tipping suggestions:	$7.50 pp/pd

Among the *Legend of the Seas'* claims to fame is the first miniature golf course at sea, a nine-hole challenge ten decks up on the Compass Deck, just below the cruise line's signature Viking Crown Lounge.

In recent years, *Legend of the Seas* has pioneered Royal Caribbean's Exotic Destinations itineraries in Australasia, the Middle East, India, Asia, and the South Pacific.

Splendour of the Seas offers a nine-hole miniature golf course, circled by the jogging track on the Compass Deck.

Nordic Empress

Econoguide rating:	★★★ 72 points
Ship size:	Large
Category:	Top of the Line
Price range:	Moderate $$
Registry:	Liberia
Year built:	1990
Information:	(305) 539–6000, (800) 327–6700
Web site:	www.royalcaribbean.com
Passenger capacity:	1,600 (double occupancy)
Crew:	671
Passenger-to-crew ratio:	2.4:1
Tonnage:	48,563
Passenger-space ratio:	30.4
Length:	692 feet
Beam:	100 feet
Draft:	25 feet
Cruising speed:	19 knots
Guest decks:	12
Total cabins:	800
Outside:	467
Inside:	329
Suites:	4

Wheelchair cabins:	4
Cuisine:	International
Style:	Resort casual, with occasional formal nights
Price notes:	Single-occupancy premium, 150 to 200 percent; Single Guarantee Program guests add $250 or $500; Special Share Program pairs people of same gender and smoking preference
Tipping suggestions:	$7.50 pp/pd

The **Nordic Empress** is a classy, younger version of the short-cruise ship, a segment of the market usually delegated to golden oldies and vintage ships serving out their final days. The ship is organized around the dramatic Centrum atrium, with most other parts of the ship branching off from there.

CHAPTER FOURTEEN

ECONOGUIDE'S BEST LUXURY CRUISE LINES

✿✿✿✿✿✿	Crystal Cruises	✿✿✿✿✿✿	Seabourn Cruise Line
✿✿✿✿✿	Radisson Seven Seas Cruises	✿✿✿✿✿	Silversea Cruises

CRYSTAL CRUISES

Address: 2049 Century Park East, Suite 1400
Los Angeles, CA 90067
Information: (800) 820–6663, (310) 785–9300
www.crystalcruises.com
Econoguide's Best Luxury Cruise Lines

✿ ✿ ✿ ✿ ✿ ✿

The Crystal Cruises Fleet

Crystal Serenity	2003	1,080 passengers	68,000 tons
Crystal Symphony	1995	940 passengers	51,044 tons
Crystal Harmony	1990	940 passengers	49,400 tons

Crystal Cruises is a luxury cruise line that has a most unusual pedigree. Founded in 1988, Crystal offers a world of attendants in white gloves, leaded crystal wineglasses filled with the contents of a world-class wine cellar at sea, Wedgwood bone china, teak deck furniture, goose down pillows, and mohair lap blankets.

The line's newest ship, *Crystal Serenity,* entered the fleet in June 2003. The 1,080-guest, 68,000-ton cruise ship is a large ship by any measure; it joins a set of 50,000-ton twins. But these ships are less than half the size of the current heavyweight champions, and they carry only about one-third the number of passengers, resulting in a very large amount of space per passenger. On the new ship, 635 crew members serve about 1,080 passengers; the *Crystal Harmony* and

Crystal Symphony carry a crew of about 545 for about 940 passengers. (It's an unusual mix for the crew, too: A Norwegian captain commands Norwegian and Japanese officers, a European hotel and dining staff, and an international crew.)

All this from a company that is much more used to hauling around grain and auto parts. Crystal Cruises is owned by the Japanese company Nippon Yupen Kaiska (NYK), the largest freighter shipping company in the world, with more than 500 vessels in its fleet.

■ ITINERARIES

In 2004 Crystal Cruises operated for the first time with three vessels, charting a course for visits to 178 ports in fifty-six countries on six continents, including a 106-day World Cruise from Los Angeles to New York aboard the new *Crystal Serenity*. Destinations include the Mediterranean, the Caribbean, Canada/New England, Alaska, and the Hawaiian islands. In the light of international tensions, Crystal boosted its sailings from homeland ports, with twenty-eight cruises sailing round-trip from domestic ports and thirty-three cruises beginning or ending at domestic ports.

In distant waters, cruises will include visits to the Cannes Film Festival in France, the Military Tattoo during two summer calls in Edinburgh, and Cutty Sark's Tall Ship parade in Antwerp. Among the maiden calls scheduled for Crystal's 2004 worldwide program were visits to Christmas Island in the Republic of Kiribati, Nuuk in Greenland, Calvi on France's island of Corsica, and Zadar in Croatia.

Crystal Serenity's World Cruise will circumnavigate the globe beginning and ending in North America via Hawaii, Japan, China, Southeast Asia, the exotic islands of the Indian Ocean, east and South Africa, South America, and the Caribbean. The cruise departs Los Angeles in January 2004 and concludes on May 5 in New York City. Port calls include Honolulu, Hiroshima, Kobe, Yokohama, Shanghai, Hong Kong, Ho Chi Minh City, Bangkok, Singapore, Yangon, Mombasa, Cape Town, and Rio de Janeiro. The World Cruise will also be offered in segments ranging from twenty-two to twenty-nine days.

In addition to the World Cruise, *Crystal Serenity*'s schedule includes a fourteen-day round-trip Mexican Riviera cruise from Los Angeles, with a rare embarkation and disembarkation call in San Diego in order to allow guests to sail round-trip San Diego for a twelve-day cruise. The ship will also offer two transatlantic voyages in 2004, from New York to London and Lisbon to Ft. Lauderdale.

Crystal Serenity will feature sixteen sailings in the Mediterranean, including London to Athens, Athens to Rome, Rome to Athens, Athens to Venice, Venice to Athens, and Athens to Rome. Other visits include ports in Italy, France, Spain, the Dalmatian coast, and the Greek and Turkish Isles.

After crossing the Atlantic, *Crystal Serenity* will offer a seven-day Caribbean cruise sailing round-trip from Fort Lauderdale, followed by a ten-day round-trip Caribbean sailing from Fort Lauderdale and a fifteen-day Panama Canal cruise from Fort Lauderdale to Los Angeles.

Crystal Harmony is scheduled to begin 2004 from New Orleans with a transit of the Panama Canal and then a crossing of the Pacific Ocean to Honolulu. The ship will then sail three round-trip cruises from Honolulu, with visits to Kauai, Hawaii, Christmas Island, and Maui.

The ship will next sail an eighteen-day exotic voyage from Honolulu to Auckland, featuring calls in Tahiti, the Cook Islands, and Fiji; a thirteen-day Auckland to Sydney and a fourteen-day Sydney to Singapore sailing; and a fourteen-day Southeast Asia itinerary from Singapore to Hong Kong, including overnight calls in Bangkok and Ho Chi Minh City and Hong Kong. Continuing in Asia, *Crystal Harmony* will offer a fifteen-day Hong Kong to Beijing cruise with calls in Taiwan and Japan and a three-night postcruise land program in Beijing. A fourteen-day Beijing to Tokyo cruise features an overnight call in Shanghai and calls at three Japanese ports plus a three-night precruise land program in Beijing. The Orient season concludes with a fifteen-day transpacific crossing from Tokyo to San Francisco with a stop in Honolulu.

In summer and fall 2004, *Crystal Harmony* will sail ten round-trip San Francisco Alaska/Canada cruises in summer and fall. Calls include Victoria, Vancouver, Sitka, Juneau, Skagway, spectacular Glacier Bay or Hubbard Glacier, and Ketchikan. Following that, the ship will transition from Los Angeles to the Mexican Riviera, and then through the Panama Canal to Fort Lauderdale to begin winter operations in the Caribbean.

Crystal Symphony is set to open 2004 with four Panama Canal sailings between Fort Lauderdale and Caldera, Costa Rica. Other trips from Fort Lauderdale include seven-day round-trips in the Gulf of Mexico and the Bahamas.

Crystal Symphony begins her European season with a nine-day Mediterranean cruise from Lisbon to Rome, followed by a twelve-day Mediterranean sailing from Rome to London, with an overnight call at Cannes, allowing guests the opportunity to visit the acclaimed Cannes Film Festival in May 2004. *Crystal Symphony* will offer two Baltic Sea and Russia cruises sailing from London to Stockholm and Stockholm to London. Also offered will be a North Cape cruise from London to Copenhagen, with calls in Stavanger, Flaam, Gudvangen, Tromsoe, Honningvaag, Trondheim, Hellesylt, and Geiranger. A Baltic Sea and Russia cruise will sail from Copenhagen to London, followed by three more twelve-day Baltic cruises from Rouen, France, to Stockholm; from Stockholm to Copenhagen, including the Cutty Sark's Tall Ships regatta in Stavanger; and from Copenhagen to London.

At the end of the summer, *Crystal Symphony* begins her sixteen-day grand crossing following the Arctic Circle, beginning in London and calling at Leith (Edinburgh), Torshavn, Reykjavik (Iceland), a maiden call to Nuuk (Greenland), St. John's, Sydney (Nova Scotia), Newport, and concluding in New York. Next, Crystal will offer three eleven-day New England and Canada cruises between New York and Montreal and a new seven-day round-trip New York sailing calling at Newport, Boston, Bar Harbor, Halifax, and Martha's Vineyard. At the end of October, *Crystal Symphony* sails down the U.S. East Coast from Montreal to Ft. Lauderdale to position for the fall South America season.

In November *Crystal Symphony* makes a pair of seventeen-day cruises along the east coast of South America from Fort Lauderdale to Buenos Aires, and Buenos Aires to Fort Lauderdale.

■ THE CRYSTAL EXPERIENCE

Crystal's two older ships are very similar, although they were built oceans apart: the *Crystal Harmony* in Nagasaki, Japan, in 1990 and the *Crystal Symphony* in Turku, Finland, in 1995. They shared the same lead designer. The newer *Crystal Symphony* includes a larger atrium and restaurants.

The *Crystal Serenity* was built at Chantiers de l'Atlantique in France. About 85 percent of the staterooms on the new ship offer private verandas. Other features include a full outside promenade, a grand observation lounge, a variation of Crystal's popular Palm Court lounge, multiple dining rooms, and a state-of-the-art theater.

On all three ships, most of the cabins have private verandas, and the most spectacular suites are, well, spectacular. The Penthouse Suites are nearly a thousand square feet in size, including a private Jacuzzi with an ocean view. The *Crystal Harmony* has a small number of inside cabins, while the *Crystal Symphony* offers outside accommodations for all. The lobby of each ship showcases a "crystal" piano (made of lucite, actually, but still an impressive objet d'art).

Shipboard dining is a high priority. The elegant Crystal Dining Room never repeats a menu, even on three-month world cruises, although guests can order past favorites. The *Crystal Harmony* offers Japanese cuisine in the Kyoto dining room, and *Crystal Symphony* offers Asian specialties at Jade Garden. A third choice, the Italian bistro Prego, is offered on both ships. The small alternative restaurants can accommodate only a portion of the total number of guests, though.

While *Crystal Harmony* and *Crystal Symphony* have two alternative specialty restaurants, *Crystal Serenity* has three: the Italian restaurant Prego, reminiscent of northern Italy and offering a seasonally changing "Valentino at Prego" menu alongside its own, featuring the cuisine and wine offerings of the revered Los Angeles Valentino restaurant; Silk Road, an elegant pan-Asian restaurant, and the Sushi Bar, which will exclusively feature menu selections by chef Nobu Matsuhisa.

On *Crystal Serenity,* casual international fare is offered throughout the day at Tastes, a hot food counter aft of the second pool.

On select evenings during a cruise, Crystal offers casual dining on deck at the Trident Grill around the Neptune Pool, which features a retractable roof. Unusual for Crystal, the dress code at the grill is casual.

Onboard entertainment ranges from *Some Enchanted Evening,* the first licensed shipboard production show of Rodgers and Hammerstein music, to a performance by a concert pianist, to a nightclub comedian. And if you haven't spent enough money already, you can go to a Caesars Palace casino at sea.

The Crystal Visions Enrichment Program features authors, journalists, historians, and famed chefs.

A handful of cruises each year are designated as Value Collection offerings, with discounts of as much as 50 percent. Membership in the Crystal Society (for previous customers) brings with it a 5 percent discount on future sailings.

■ WEB SITE

Crystal's Web site presents an attractive and detailed view of the line's ships, itineraries, and activities. Once you register, you can request a booking by telephoning Crystal, requesting a callback through the Web site or going through a travel agent. *Ease of use: very good.*

Crystal Serenity

Econoguide rating:	★★★★★★ 95 points
Ship size:	Large
Category:	Ultraluxury
Price range:	Beyond Opulent $$$$$
Registry:	Bahamas
Year built:	2003
Information:	(800) 820–6663
Web site:	www.crystalcruises.com
Passenger capacity:	1,080 (double occupancy)
Crew:	635; Norwegian and Japanese officers
Passenger-to-crew ratio:	1.7:1
Tonnage:	68,000
Passenger-space ratio:	63.0
Length:	820 feet
Beam:	106 feet
Draft:	24.9 feet
Cruising speed:	22 knots
Guest decks:	9
Total cabins:	548
Outside:	550 (468 with verandas)
Inside:	0
Suites:	100
Wheelchair cabins:	8
Cuisine:	Continental and American; two specialty restaurants: Japanese, Italian
Style:	Casual, with at least three formal evenings per cruise
Price notes:	Single-occupancy supplement, 125 to 200 percent of advance-booking fares; discounts available for bookings made six months or more in advance, and cruises booked onboard a previous cruise; an adult or child age twelve or older in a third berth pays minimum fare, children ages eleven and younger pay 50 percent of the minimum fare when accompanied by two full-fare adults
Tipping suggestions:	$10.50 pp/pd
Best deal:	Value Collection cruises discounted as much as 50 percent

Crystal Serenity boasts an even greater space-per-guest ratio than her sister ships *Crystal Harmony* and *Crystal Symphony,* two of the most spacious ships afloat. The ship's one hundred penthouse accommodations include four 1,345 square-foot Crystal Penthouses, thirty-two Penthouse Suites, and sixty-four penthouses. All but 80 of the ship's 548 cabins offer verendas.

Guests have five evening dining choices, beginning with the Crystal Dining Room and extending to Italian and Asian specialty restaurants, a casual evening deck menu, and a sushi bar. Other new features on Crystal's third ship are a pair of paddle tennis courts, a Creative Learning Center for interactive educational classes, and an expanded Computer University@Sea classroom with an Internet center and private area for computer use.

Additional daytime dining venues, which have been favorites on *Crystal Harmony* and *Crystal Symphony,* include the Bistro, a popular social coffee and wine bar, for morning and afternoon snacks; the Trident Grill, for casual poolside lunches throughout the afternoon; plus lavish themed luncheon buffets on selected days by the ship's second pool.

Entertainment venues include the Galaxy Lounge, with improved sight lines for the Broadway-style production shows; the Stardust Club for dancing and cabaret; the Caesars Palace at Sea casino; the Hollywood Theatre cinema and conference center; a Bridge Lounge for card players; and the line's signature Avenue Saloon cocktail and piano bar. Young passengers can visit the Fantasia children's playroom or the Waves teen center.

The Caesars Palace at Sea Casino continues the exclusive alliance between Crystal Cruises and the Las Vegas gaming establishment and is one of the largest luxury casinos afloat. Fantasia is home to the supervised Junior Activities Program, while Waves offers a teen center and video arcade.

The ship's second pool is covered by a sliding dome for inclement weather. A full promenade extends around the exterior of the ship, and the sports deck offers a golf driving range, shuffleboard court, and table tennis area.

Crystal Harmony

Econoguide rating:	★★★★★★ 95 points
Ship size:	Large
Category:	Ultraluxury
Price range:	Beyond Opulent $$$$$
Registry:	Bahamas
Year built:	1988
Information:	(800) 820–6663
Web site:	www.crystalcruises.com
Passenger capacity:	940 (double occupancy)
Crew:	545; Norwegian and Japanese officers

Passenger-to-crew ratio:	1.7:1
Tonnage:	49,400
Passenger-space ratio:	52.6
Length:	790 feet
Beam:	105 feet
Draft:	24.6 feet
Cruising speed:	22 knots
Guest decks:	8
Total cabins:	480
Outside:	461 (260 with verandas)
Inside:	19
Suites:	62
Wheelchair cabins:	4
Cuisine:	Continental and American; two specialty restaurants: Japanese, Italian
Style:	Casual, with at least three formal evenings per cruise
Price notes:	Single-occupancy supplement, 125 to 200 percent of advance-booking fares; discounts available for bookings made six months or more in advance, and cruises booked onboard a previous cruise; an adult or child age twelve or older in a third berth pays minimum fare, ages eleven and younger pay 50 percent of the minimum fare when accompanied by two full-fare adults
Tipping suggestions:	$10.50 pp/pd
Best deal:	Value Collection cruises discounted as much as 50 percent

Offering high-tone elegance and service on one of the largest of the luxury ships, the **Crystal Harmony** has eight guest decks; cabins with verandas include four 948-square-foot Crystal Penthouses, fifty-eight other suites, and 198 outside deluxe staterooms. The smallest cabins are nineteen inside staterooms, a not-too-tiny 183 square feet in size.

Entertainment includes the Caesars Palace at Sea casino with 115 slot machines, seven tables, and a roulette wheel. The domed Vista Observation Lounge up forward offers three levels of seating and a 270-degree view.

The Crystal Dining Room serves international cuisine and a world-class wine list. Crystal also offers a pair of alternative restaurants: The Kyoto restaurant features a Japanese menu, not surprising for a ship line owned by a Japanese freight line. Typical menu items include tempura, Pacific salmon with shiitake mushrooms, and traditional sukiyaki dinner with filet mignon. The Prego restaurant offers intimate Italian dining.

Recreation facilities include a full-length lap pool and an indoor/outdoor pool, a paddle tennis court, golf driving ranges and putting greens, and a sumptuous spa.

The ship underwent a multimillion dollar renovation at the end of 2003. The Connoisseur Club, modeled after a similar improvement to *Crystal Symphony,*

Crystal Symphony under way. *Courtesy Crystal Cruises*

brings an intimate cigar and cognac lounge with private club atmosphere. Located adjacent to the ship's existing Avenue Saloon, the club features a dedicated ventilation system and a well-stocked island humidor complete with imported cigars and individual compartments for guest's cigar storage during a cruise.

The 450-seat Galaxy Lounge was redesigned with ceiling and wall finishes, window treatments, carpet, seating, and cocktail tables. The Crystal Spa & Salon and Fitness Center was completely reconstructed, recast in accordance with the principles of Feng Shui, the ancient philosophy of balance and harmony.

Crystal Symphony

Econoguide rating:	★★★★★★ 95 points
Ship size:	Large
Category:	Ultraluxury
Price range:	Beyond Opulent $$$$$
Registry:	Bahamas
Year built:	1992

Information:	(800) 820–6663
Web site:	www.crystalcruises.com
Passenger capacity:	940 (double occupancy)
Crew:	545; Norwegian and Japanese officers
Passenger-to-crew ratio:	1.7:1
Tonnage:	51,044
Passenger-space ratio:	54.3
Length:	781 feet
Beam:	99 feet
Draft:	24.9 feet
Cruising speed:	22 knots
Guest decks:	8
Total cabins:	480
Outside:	416 (278 with verandas)
Inside:	0
Suites:	64
Wheelchair cabins:	7
Cuisine:	International; two specialty restaurants: Italian, Asian
Style:	Casual, with three formal nights per cruise
Price notes:	Single-occupancy supplement, 125 to 200 percent of advance-booking fares; reduced rates for third in cabin
Tipping suggestions:	$10.50 pp/pd
Best deal:	Value Collection cruises discounted as much as 50 percent

Crystal Symphony, the younger and near-identical sister to the *Crystal Harmony,* includes a larger Caesars Palace at Sea casino and a different alternative restaurant in addition to the Crystal Dining Room. The Jade Garden restaurant features a broad Asian menu and offers such items as Peking duck with plum sauce; spicy coconut chicken with eggplant, lemongrass, and basil; and orange-glazed beef with red chilies and basil. There's also the Prego restaurant for classic Italian cuisine served in a Venetian atmosphere.

On both of these Crystal ships, dance concerts and lessons are presented regularly in the Club 2100. Each ship's library has more than 2,000 books, plus a collection of videotapes that can be borrowed for play on VCRs in the staterooms.

In December 2001 *Crystal Symphony* emerged from a major renovation project. The ship's Asian specialty restaurant, Jade Garden, was remodeled from floor to ceiling with new paneling, carpet, furniture, framed artwork, and lighting. The Crystal Cove and Plaza, the central lobby area and gathering place aboard *Crystal Symphony,* was completely outfitted with new furnishings. Each of *Crystal Symphony*'s two Crystal Penthouses, the luxury line's most lavish accommodations on its coveted Penthouse Deck, were completely renovated to replicate the drawing room, master suite, and bath of a discerning world traveler's private residence.

RADISSON SEVEN SEAS CRUISES

RADISSON SEVEN SEAS
CRUISES

Address: 600 Corporate Drive, Suite 410
Fort Lauderdale, FL 33334
Information: (800) 333–3333, (800) 285–1835
www.rssc.com
Econoguide's Best Luxury Cruise Lines
Econoguide's Best Dining at Sea

The Radisson Seven Seas Fleet

Radisson Seven Seas Voyager	2003	700 passengers	50,000 tons
Radisson Seven Seas Mariner	2001	700 passengers	50,000 tons
Radisson Seven Seas Navigator	1999	490 passengers	33,000 tons
Radisson Diamond	1992	350 passengers	20,295 tons
Paul Gauguin	1998	320 passengers	18,800 tons
Song of Flower	1986	180 passengers	8,282 tons

Radisson Seven Seas Cruises has an eclectic collection of small luxury cruise ships and a pair of sybaritic adventure ships. The tony ships are managed by the upscale hotel chain of the same name; plans call for the gradual removal of the "Radisson" label in coming years in favor of "Seven Seas Cruises." Radisson claims to be the only cruise line whose vessels reach all seven continents, as well as the polar regions.

The line's largest ships, the *Radisson Seven Seas Mariner* and the *Radisson Seven Seas Voyager,* are home to the first permanent Le Cordon Bleu restaurant at sea, the 110-seat reservations-only Signatures. The all-suite, all-balcony ships accommodate 700 passengers and offer four dining venues, including a main dining room that is capable of seating the entire passenger load at once.

Also in the fleet are *Radisson Seven Seas Navigator, Radisson Diamond, Song of Flower,* and *Paul Gauguin.*

The company is part of Carlson Hospitality Worldwide, which includes among its holdings the Radisson and Regent hotel chains, Country Inns and Suites by Carlson, and TGI Friday's.

The ship's staff is made up of Norwegian officers and Scandinavian stewardesses, and gratuities are neither expected nor accepted.

The cruise line has moved away from its previous position, which ignored and sometimes banned children. Radisson has brought the Club Mariner children's program to selected Alaskan and European sailings of the *Seven Seas Mariner, Seven Seas Voyager,* and *Seven Seas Navigator.* Club Mariner offers a program of events in two tiers: for ages six to eleven and ages twelve to seventeen. Counselor-supervised activities are organized onboard and ashore, focusing on the destination's nature, heritage, and crafts.

ITINERARIES

The new *Seven Seas Voyager* began its service in Europe, crossing over to the Caribbean in winter 2003–04 for sailings from Fort Lauderdale. In January 2004 the ship is due to begin Radisson's first-ever Grand Asia Pacific Voyage, sailing round-trip from Los Angeles and stopping at forty-one ports in eighteen countries. The voyage is available in its ninety-four-night entirety or in five shorter, combinable segments of fifteen to twenty-three nights. The ship will call at the Marquesas Islands, French Polynesia, Tonga, New Caledonia, Australia, New Zealand, Singapore, Thailand, Vietnam, China, Taiwan, Japan, and Hawaii, with extended overnight calls in Sydney, Melbourne, Fremantle (Perth), Singapore, Laem Chabang (Bangkok), Hong Kong, Shanghai, Tianjin (for Beijing), Kobe, and Tokyo.

Seven Seas Navigator sailed the season from April to October to Bermuda, including eleven seven-night round-trip voyages from New York with a call in Norfolk, Virginia, on the return. Those trips will be followed by New England and Canada fall foliage cruises and then Caribbean cruises from Palm Beach.

After a summer of Alaska sailings, *Seven Seas Mariner* will depart San Francisco in September 2003 for a twenty-six-night round-trip Grand South Pacific Voyage, followed in October by a fifty-six-night Grand Circle South America Voyage that concludes in Fort Lauderdale.

In 2003 Radisson Seven Seas deployed four ships in European waters. Joining the *Seven Seas Voyager* for full seasons were the *Radisson Diamond* and *Song of Flower*. The *Seven Seas Navigator* cruised from New York to Copenhagen in June to spend July in the Baltic, returning to New York in August via Edinburgh.

In 2003 the *Radisson Diamond*'s Mediterranean season was cut by thirteen weeks, with most of its sailings moved to the Caribbean. The ship's Mediterranean sailings in 2003 included calls in Turkey and Greece on voyages between Rome, Istanbul, and Athens. As we went to press, Radisson announced the sale of *Song of Flower* to a European operator.

Paul Gauguin continued to sail in the South Pacific, adding voyages to the remote Marquesas Islands, including an "Homage to Gauguin" cruise to commemorate the centenary of post-Impressionist artist Paul Gauguin's death.

WEB SITE

Radisson Seven Seas' Web site provides good information about cruises and itineraries. All bookings are directed to travel agents—either one you specify or one that the cruise line suggests in your area. *Ease of use: very good.*

Radisson Seven Seas Mariner
Radisson Seven Seas Voyager

Econoguide rating:	★★★★★★ 94 points
Ship size:	Large
Category:	Ultraluxury

Price range:	Beyond Opulent $$$$$
Registry:	France
Year built:	*Radisson Seven Seas Mariner,* 2001; *Radisson Seven Seas Voyager,* 2003
Information:	(800) 333–3333
Web site:	www.rssc.com
Passenger capacity:	700
Crew:	445
Passenger-to-crew ratio:	1.6:1
Tonnage:	50,000
Passenger-space ratio:	71.4
Length:	670 feet
Beam:	90 feet
Draft:	21 feet
Cruising speed:	20 knots
Guest decks:	8
Total cabins:	350
Outside:	350
Inside:	0
Suites:	All
Cuisine:	Inventive international cuisine; open, single-seating dining in main restaurant
Style:	Jackets required for men on occasion; suitable resort wear or dresses for women
Price notes:	Single-occupancy premium, expected to be up to 200 percent
Tipping suggestions:	Gratuities included in cruise fare; no tips expected onboard
Best deal:	Advance-booking discounts and onboard credits

The **Seven Seas Mariner** was Radisson's first all-balcony, all-suite vessel and the first in the line with a pod propulsion system. Slung below the ship are a pair of pods with forward-facing propellers that can be turned 360 degrees to drive the ship in any direction.

The main dining room is the Compass Rose, where guests are free to come at any time that suits them. Latitudes is the smallest restaurant onboard, a reservations-only hideaway featuring tableside preparation. By night, the ship's breakfast and lunch buffet eatery becomes La Veranda, a Mediterranean bistro. Finally, there is Signatures, where chefs wear the white toque and blue riband of the Cordon Bleu of Paris. In addition to reservations-only dining at Signatures, passengers may enroll in intensive cooking classes on selected cruises.

The nearly identical sister ship, **Radisson Seven Seas Voyager,** features the same single-corridor design, with standard ocean-view suites offering more than 300 square feet of living space (including balconies), with separate living areas, walk-in closets, and full bathrooms that have separate showers and full bathtubs.

Paul Gaugin

Econoguide rating:	★★★★★ 90 points
Ship size:	Medium
Category:	Ultraluxury
Price range:	Beyond Opulent $$$$$
Registry:	France
Year built:	1998
Information:	(800) 333–3333
Web site:	www.rssc.com
Passenger capacity:	320 (double occupancy)
Crew:	206; European officers
Passenger-to-crew ratio:	1.6:1
Tonnage:	18,800
Passenger-space ratio:	58.8
Length:	513 feet
Beam:	71 feet
Draft:	17 feet
Cruising speed:	18 knots
Guest decks:	7
Total cabins:	161
Outside:	142
Inside:	0
Suites:	19
Wheelchair cabins:	1
Cuisine:	Inventive international cuisine by two-star Michelin chef Jean-Pierre Vigato
Style:	Resort casual, with occasional semiformal nights
Price notes:	Single-occupancy premium, up to 200 percent
Tipping suggestions:	Gratuities included
Best deal:	Advance-booking discounts and onboard credits

An elegant resident of Polynesia, among **Paul Gauguin**'s recreational facilities is a retractable platform that brings guests to sea level for windsurfing, kayaking, waterskiing, snorkeling, and more. Original works by Gauguin from the 1890s and a gallery of vintage black-and-white photographs of French Polynesia are part of the ship's decor.

Radisson Diamond

Econoguide rating:	★★★★ 87 points
Ship size:	Medium
Category:	Ultraluxury

Price range:	Opulent and Beyond $$$$–$$$$$
Registry:	Bahamas
Year built:	1992
Information:	(800) 333–3333
Web site:	www.rssc.com
Passenger capacity:	354 (double occupancy)
Crew:	192
Passenger-to-crew ratio:	1.8:1
Tonnage:	20,295
Passenger-space ratio:	57.3
Length:	420 feet
Beam:	103 feet
Draft:	23 feet
Cruising speed:	12.5 knots
Guest decks:	12
Total cabins:	177
Outside:	177
Inside:	0
Suites:	2 master suites
Wheelchair cabins:	2
Cuisine:	Inventive international cuisine; single, open-seating dining; indoor/outdoor specialty restaurant and lounge offering Northern Italian cuisine
Style:	Resort casual, with occasional semiformal evenings
Price notes:	Single-occupancy premium, 125 to 200 percent
Tipping suggestions:	Gratuities included
Best deal:	Advance-booking discounts and onboard credits

The 20,295-ton **Radisson Diamond** is one of the most readily identifiable ships afloat, with its one-of-a-kind twin-hull design intended to cut down on pitch and roll movements. Of her 177 outside staterooms, 123 have private balconies, and her space ratio of 57.3 is among the highest of any cruise ship in its class.

A luxury hotel afloat, the *Radisson Diamond* is the world's first major cruise ship to use a submerged twin hull; there are only a handful of other passenger-carrying twin-hull vessels, all considerably smaller.

The SWATH (Small Waterplane Area Twin Hull) design utilizes a narrow hull area in contact with the waves and computer-controlled fins to counteract the effects of the sea. According to the company, the resulting degree of vessel roll is only one-fifth that of a monohull cruise vessel, and the vibration level is one-tenth that of a conventional ship.

In a traditional single-hull ship, stabilizers are only effective in reducing side-to-side rolling. By contrast, the *Radisson Diamond* has stabilizer fins on the front and back of each submerged hull, thus reducing both pitching and rolling.

By placing the propulsion machinery in the hulls beneath the waterline, the ship's 26-foot draft adds to the stability and greatly reduces engine noise and vibration. The ship has a wind-resistant nose cone on the bow and a computerized control center.

About the only downside to the design (besides its most untraditional profile, which makes it look like an overgrown houseboat) is the relatively poky speed of the ship. The *Diamond* can eke out a top speed of approximately 12.5 knots.

The five-story entry atrium contains a grand staircase and glass-enclosed elevators. The 230-seat Windows Lounge, located at the bow of the ship on Deck 8, provides a breathtaking view. The elegant Grand Dining Room offers individualized seating at times convenient to passengers.

Recreational facilities include a jogging track, swimming pool, a golf driving range with nets and a putting green, and a hydraulic marina for such activities as windsurfing and personal watercraft.

(You can read a cruise diary about the Radisson Diamond in Chapter 11.)

Radisson Seven Seas Navigator

Econoguide rating:	★★★★★ 91 points
Ship size:	Medium
Category:	Ultraluxury
Price range:	Beyond Opulent $$$$$
Registry:	Bahamas
Year built:	1999
Information:	(800) 333–3333
Web site:	www.rssc.com
Passenger capacity:	490
Crew:	325; Italian officers
Passenger-to-crew ratio:	1.5:1
Tonnage:	33,000
Passenger-space ratio:	67.3
Length:	560 feet
Beam:	81 feet
Draft:	21 feet
Cruising speed:	20 knots
Guest decks:	12
Total cabins:	245
Outside:	245
Inside:	0
Suites:	All
Cuisine:	International; open single-seating dining in main restaurant
Style:	Jackets required for men on occasion; suitable resort wear or dresses for women
Price notes:	Single-occupancy premium, expected to be up to 200 percent

Tipping suggestions:	Gratuities included in cruise fare; no tips expected onboard
Best deal:	Advance-booking discounts and onboard credits

The **Seven Seas Navigator** gives 490 passengers an all-suite 33,000-ton luxury cruise ship with 245 ocean-view suites, 90 percent of which have private balconies. The ship cruises the world, with a regular circuit including the Americas and a series of Panama Canal transits. The ship's ice-strengthened hull permits operation around the world.

The smallest accommodations on the ship comprise a spacious 301 square feet, about twice the size of a typical small cabin on a cruise ship. The passenger-space ratio is 67.3, among the highest of any cruise ship afloat.

There is open seating in the main restaurant, which has sufficient space for the entire passenger complement. There is also an alternative Italian restaurant.

The ship was finished at the renowned Fincantieri yard in Italy; the hull was built in Saint Petersburg, Russia, but never completed there.

Song of Flower

Econoguide rating:	★★★★ 89 points
Ship size:	Small
Category:	Ultraluxury
Price range:	Beyond Opulent $$$$$
Registry:	Bahamas
Year built:	1986
Information:	(800) 333–3333
Web site:	www.rssc.com
Passenger capacity:	180
Crew:	157
Passenger-to-crew ratio:	1.1:1
Tonnage:	8,282
Passenger-space ratio:	46.1
Length:	409 feet
Beam:	52.5 feet
Draft:	15 feet
Cruising speed:	17 knots
Guest decks:	6
Total cabins:	100
Outside:	100
Inside:	0
Suites:	All
Cuisine:	Inventive international cuisine; open, single-seating dining in main restaurant

Style:	Jackets required for men on occasion; suitable resort wear or dresses for women
Price notes:	Single-occupancy premium, expected to be up to 200 percent
Tipping suggestions:	Gratuities included; no tips expected onboard
Best deal:	Advance-booking discounts and onboard credits

As we went to press, Radisson announced that it had sold *Song of Flower* to a European company that planned to rename the vessel and operate it in Mediterranean and nearby waters beginning in 2004.

SEABOURN CRUISE LINE

Address: 6100 Blue Lagoon Drive, Suite 400
Miami, FL 33126
Information: (800) 929–9391
www.seabourn.com
Econoguide's Best Luxury Cruise Lines

Seabourn Cruise Line Fleet

Seabourn Legend	1993	200 passengers	10,000 tons
Seabourn Spirit	1989	200 passengers	10,000 tons
Seabourn Pride	1988	200 passengers	10,000 tons

Seabourn is a floating home for the rich and famous, the rich and private, and others for whom price is of little object. The only real question is whether these are very large yachts or relatively small cruise ships. There are ways, though, to save big dollars on Seabourn cruises: Look for repositioning cruises, advance booking, and last-minute deals.

Seabourn, with its sister operation Cunard line, is one of the anchors of the luxury cruise ship business. Seabourn operates three sister ships: the *Seabourn Pride, Seabourn Spirit,* and *Seabourn Legend.* Each is a 200-passenger all-suite vessel, with a crew of 150. All three of the ships were refurbished in 2000 to replace picture windows with French balconies—sliding doors and minibalconies—in forty-four suites.

The company's first vessel, the *Seabourn Pride,* set sail in 1988 and today includes itineraries that enter North American waters and the Caribbean. The other ships cruise the Mediterranean, western Europe, Scandinavia, the British Isles, South America, Southeast Asia, India, Africa, and the Red Sea.

In mid-2001, the line unloaded the *Seabourn Goddess I* and *Seabourn Goddess II* to a start-up cruise line, SeaDream Yacht Club; the ships were renamed *Sea Dream I* and *Sea Dream II.* The new venture was started by some of the founders and former executives of Seabourn and Cunard.

■ THE SEABOURN EXPERIENCE

The basic idea of Seabourn can be summed up quite simply: This is about as close as you can get to owning your own luxury yacht without having to go out and hire yourself a captain and crew.

The three Seabourn sisters, cut from the same pattern and nearly identical inside, feature large outside suites with all the amenities. Passengers can dine when they please, with whom they please, and pretty much where they please: in the formal dining room, the indoor/outdoor Veranda Cafe, the Sky Grill on deck, or in their cabins. Where appropriate, you can even pick up some takeout to bring with you to shore. You'll travel in no ordinary tender, either; guests are chauffeured from anchorage to shore in a mahogany-paneled water taxi. Somewhere on the beach, the staff will also set up a catered barbecue, served on fine china and crystal.

The 440-foot-long vessels carry about half the number of passengers of comparably sized ships. Standard suites offer 277 square feet of space, with walk-in closets, marble-clad bathrooms, and large picture windows.

The cuisine on the ships is described as a mixture of classic and eclectic offerings. Dishes are prepared "a la minute" (as they are ordered) as they would be in a fine restaurant. The Veranda Cafe offers alternative casual dining. A selection of wines and spirits is included in the fare, but the ship also carries a more specialized wine cellar for those who just have to spend more.

The crew is drilled to learn the names of all passengers and keep up to speed on their preferences in food, entertainment, and comfort.

Each ship has a marina at the stern that opens out into the ocean to provide a dock for water sports. An enclosed steel mesh pool allows passengers to swim without fear of interruption by unpleasant marine creatures.

All this comes at a price, of course. Per person rates for Seabourn's suites average about $761 per day; there is a strict no-tipping policy aboard ship. According to the company, on any cruise as many as half the passengers are repeat customers, which says a lot about satisfaction with the product. If you become a regular, the Seabourn Club offers a complimentary cruise of up to 14 days after you have sailed 140 days.

In 1998 Seabourn became a division of Cunard Line Limited, which also owns and operates Cunard Line. Cunard is, in turn, owned by Carnival Corporation and a consortium of Norwegian investors.

In 2002 Seabourn secured the services of renowned American chef-restaurateur Charlie Palmer to develop more than 200 new recipes to be served in the exclusive, single-seating restaurants aboard the line's ships. Palmer's Progressive American Cuisine is featured at his restaurants: Aureole, Alva, and Métrazur in New York City; Aureole at Mandalay Bay Resort and Casino and Charlie Palmer Steak at The Four Seasons Hotel in Las Vegas; and Dry Creek Kitchen, located in the Palmer-owned boutique Hotel Healdsburg in Sonoma, California. The three-year agreement calls for Palmer to create a wide array of signature dishes consisting of hot and cold appetizers, soups, and entrees, as well as vegetarian entrees, low-fat low-calorie options for the line's celebrated Simplicity offerings, and desserts. These signature dishes will supplement the existing favorites to provide dinner menus rich with variety. The ship's chefs will be trained in Palmer's shoreside restaurants, and Palmer will then provide shipboard training on each of Seabourn's three ships.

Among the Charlie Palmer recipes that will be added to the Seabourn repertoire are butter braised lobster and sweet pea leaf ravioli with carrot-ginger emulsion; herb grilled quail and French green lentils; roasted Vidalia onion consommé with sherry-braised oxtail and bone marrow; olive-oil-poached rock shrimp gazpacho with lime, avocado, and cumin; sautéed pheasant with crisp spring rolls and red onion marmalade; rabbit saddle with truffle sauce, snap peas, and pea shoots; grilled venison chops with fifty-year-old balsamic vinegar and foie gras sauce; and grilled lamb loin with roasted morels, Parmesan flan, and sweet peas.

Beginning in 2002, in one port of call on each cruise, guests enjoy insights into local culture, art, history, cuisine, and other aspects specific to the destination on complimentary shoreside experiences designed and reserved especially for them. Fine wines and spirits are complimentary in all bars, lounges, and dining areas throughout each of the yachtlike ships. Guests' in-suite bars are stocked with their choice of internationally known wines and spirits as well.

ITINERARIES

Voyages range from four to seventy-two days to the Mediterranean and Atlantic Isles; northern Europe; Asia and India; South America; Costa Rica; Belize and Panama; the Caribbean; New England and Canada; and transoceanic cruises, including transatlantic and transpacific voyages and the South Pacific.

In 2004 cruises include exotic voyages exploring Australia, New Zealand, Fiji, Papua New Guinea, Vietnam, and Thailand aboard *Seabourn Spirit*. Also offered are Seabourn Journeys combining luxury land extensions in India with cruises of Myanmar and the Red Sea.

Seabourn Pride will sail a seventy-two-day circumnavigation of South America, exploring the continent's various regions from the Inca Coast, Patagonia, the Amazon, and Cape Horn to the vibrant cities of Buenos Aires and Rio de Janeiro.

Seabourn Legend's season will include fourteen-day cruises in Central America, featuring the natural wonders of Costa Rica, Belize, and Panama. The ship also offers one-week cruises to less-known corners of the Caribbean.

Transatlantic sailings carry *Seabourn Pride* and *Seabourn Legend* guests to Europe in spring 2004, returning in the fall.

WEB SITE

The Seabourn Web site includes basic information about the cruise line and ships. Booking requests are forwarded to a telephone callback service or a travel agent. *Ease of use: good.*

Seabourn Legend, Seabourn Pride, Seabourn Spirit

Econoguide rating:	★★★★★★ 97 points
Ship size:	Medium
Category:	Ultraluxury
Price range:	Beyond Opulent $$$$$
Registry:	Norway
Year built:	*Seabourn Legend,* 1993; *Seabourn Pride,* 1988; *Seabourn Spirit,* 1988
Information:	(800) 929–9391
Web site:	www.seabourn.com
Passenger capacity:	208 (double occupancy)
Crew:	150
Passenger-to-crew ratio:	1.3:1
Tonnage:	10,000
Passenger-space ratio:	50
Length:	440 feet
Beam:	63 feet
Draft:	16.4 feet
Cruising speed:	18 knots
Guest decks:	4
Total cabins:	104
Outside:	104
Inside:	0
Suites:	104
Wheelchair cabins:	4
Cuisine:	International cuisine and eclectic offerings; alternative casual dining in Veranda Cafe; the onboard wine cellar with boutique wines from the vineyards of Italy, France, and the United States
Style:	Semiformal to formal
Price notes:	Single-occupancy premium, 175 to 200 percent, some special offers available
Tipping suggestions:	Strict no-tipping policy

After a renovation, the ***Seabourn Legend, Seabourn Pride,*** and ***Seabourn Spirit*** now feature thirty-six suites per vessel with step-out French balconies, each with floor-to-ceiling glass doors, in addition to the six full verandas on each ship's premium category suites.

Every stateroom is a suite, each with a large picture window that has an electrically operated blackout curtain. A marina opens out into the ocean from the stern of the ship, providing a launch for water sports. An enclosed steel mesh pool allows for swimming right in the ocean (weather permitting).

SILVERSEA CRUISES

Address: 110 East Broward Boulevard
Fort Lauderdale, FL 33301
Information: (800) 722–9955, (954) 522–4477
www.silversea.com
Econoguide's Best Luxury Cruise Lines

The Silversea Cruises Fleet

Silver Shadow	2000	396 passengers	25,000 tons
Silver Whisper	2001	396 passengers	25,000 tons
Silver Cloud	1994	296 passengers	16,800 tons
Silver Wind	1994	296 passengers	16,800 tons

Guests are greeted by white-gloved attendants offering perfectly chilled flutes of champagne; they are then escorted to their suites where a private bottle awaits. Need we say more?

Life aboard the *Silver Cloud* and *Silver Wind* or the younger and slightly larger *Silver Shadow* and *Silver Whisper,* two pairs of near-identical luxury twins, is pretty rarified: Limoges china, Christofle silverware, Frette linens, and soft down pillows.

Silversea also makes a big deal about wine onboard its vessels, offering selected wines as part of a cruise package and carrying a seagoing wine cellar and a staff of sommeliers for guests who insist on spending even more. So, too, with caviar and other gastronomic specialties.

The dining room is simply called The Restaurant, although it is less than simple. There's a single sitting with open seating. On formal nights the ship's orchestra provides dance music. If gentlemen don't feel like wearing a tuxedo, dinner jacket, or suit, you can have dinner served in your cabin, course by course.

In coming years, Silversea intends to emphasize headliner concerts, local performers, and guest artists on each cruise. In 2003 renowned Italian mezzo-soprano Cecilia Bartoli sailed on four voyages in the Mediterranean and Black Sea, giving intimate recitals for the guests and conducting discussions of music and opera.

■ PERSONALIZED VOYAGES

You say you'd rather not fly to Barbados to pick up a Caribbean cruise that ends in Fort Lauderdale but would rather catch up with the ship after it passes Morro Castle in San Juan harbor? And while you're at it, you'd rather stay on board past Fort Lauderdale and disembark in Virgin Gorda? No problem . . . with Silversea's unusual Personalized Voyages plan.

In 2003 Silversea extended the plan to all four of its ships, permitting guests to choose the length of their voyage and to embark and disembark from their choice of a wide selection of ports.

The Silversea Cruise Atlas lists available ports and daily rates. Guests can cruise for as long as they want, with a minimum of five consecutive nights.

■ THE SILVERSEA STORY

Silversea is owned by the Lefebvre family of Rome, former owners of Sitmar Cruises. The company was founded in the early 1990s with a concept for "ultraluxury" ships with the largest passenger-space ratio of any ship at sea. All cabins are outside, and most have private verandas. There's an open, single-seating dining room and a show lounge for nightly entertainment.

Silver Shadow and *Silver Whisper* joined the fleet in 2000 and mid-2001, and the company has an option for two additional ships in following years. The younger 25,000-ton vessels have 194 outside suites for 388 passengers. The resulting passenger-space ratio of 63 places the ships among the most spacious afloat.

Cruise fares include all gratuities, all beverages including select wines and spirits, and port charges. Passengers can make their own air reservations to connect with the ships or use Silversea's travel department to arrange for flights and pre- or postcruise hotel stays.

Guests who have sailed for one hundred days or more are eligible for membership in the Silversea Venetian Society; they are also eligible to receive a 5 percent discount. At 250 days or more the discount rises to 10 percent, and guests will also receive a free 7-day cruise; at the 500-day milestone, the company offers a complimentary 14-day cruise.

■ ITINERARIES

The core of Silversea's itineraries in 2004 are in the Mediterranean, with seasonal forays into the Baltic, to Australia and New Zealand, and across the Atlantic to the Caribbean, South America, and the West Coast of the United States.

Like many other lines, the 2004 schedule is expected to pull back from cruises in the Middle East, the Far East, and Africa because of the political situation. The company hopes to move at least one of its ships north to Alaska for summer cruises in coming years.

The newly refurbished *Silver Wind* returned to the fleet in mid-2003, with voyages to the Caribbean and South America. Sister ship *Silver Cloud* entered into an extended refurbishment and is due to return to service in mid-April 2003 with Mediterranean sailings.

Silver Shadow,
Silver Whisper

Econoguide rating:	★★★★★★ 97 points
Ship size:	Medium
Category:	Ultraluxury
Price range:	Beyond Opulent $$$$$
Registry:	Bahamas
Year built:	*Silver Shadow,* 2000; *Silver Whisper,* 2001

Information:	(800) 722–9955
Web site:	www.silversea.com
Passenger capacity:	388 (double occupancy)
Crew:	295; Italian officers
Passenger-to-crew ratio:	1.3:1
Tonnage:	25,000
Passenger-space ratio:	64.4
Length:	597 feet
Beam:	81.8 feet
Draft:	19.6 feet
Cruising speed:	21 knots
Guest decks:	11
Total cabins:	194
Outside:	194
Inside:	0
Suites:	194
Wheelchair cabins:	4
Cuisine:	Regional, American, continental; select wines, spirits, and champagnes from around the world included
Style:	Casual to formal; two formal nights on sailings of eight days or less, three or four formal nights on longer cruises
Price notes:	Single-occupancy premium, 110 to 200 percent
Tipping suggestions:	All gratuities included
Best deal:	Special promotions on some cruises

Silver Shadow was christened in Civitavecchia, Italy, in September 2000, using a salmanazar of Moët & Chandon champagne. (A salmanazar is the equivalent of twelve bottles, or six magnums.)

The restaurant on the fourth deck is appropriately sumptuous. Beneath three grand chandeliers, Frette tablecloths are set with Christofle silverware and European stemware.

(See Chapter 11 for a cruise diary about a *Silver Shadow* voyage from Iceland to New York.)

Silver Whisper joined the fleet in mid-2001; during its construction Silversea changed its name from *Silver Mirage*.

**Silver Cloud,
Silver Wind**

Econoguide rating:	★★★★★★ 96 points
Ship size:	Medium
Category:	Ultraluxury
Price range:	Beyond Opulent $$$$$
Registry:	Bahamas

Year built:	*Silver Cloud,* 1994; *Silver Wind,* 1994
Information:	(800) 722–9955
Web site:	www.silversea.com
Passenger capacity:	296 (double occupancy)
Crew:	209; Italian officers
Passenger-to-crew ratio:	1.4:1
Tonnage:	16,800
Passenger-space ratio:	56.8
Length:	514 feet
Beam:	70 feet
Draft:	18 feet
Cruising speed:	20.5 knots
Guest decks:	6
Total cabins:	148
Outside:	148
Inside:	0
Suites:	148
Wheelchair cabins:	2
Cuisine:	Regional, American, continental; select wines, spirits, and champagnes from around the world included
Style:	Casual to formal; two formal nights on sailings of eight days or less, three or four formal nights on longer cruises

Silver Wind arrives in London. *Courtesy of Silversea Cruises*

Price notes:	Single-occupancy premium, 110 to 200 percent; Venetian Society discounts of 5 to 15 percent for past customers
Tipping suggestions:	All gratuities included
Best deal:	Special promotions on some cruises

Silver Cloud and *Silver Wind* provide a luxurious cruising experience, with opulent appointments and service within and a wide range of interesting ports of call without, helped by the shallow draft of the yachtlike ships.

This is a classy, pricey world of Limoges china, Christofle silverware, Frette bed linens monogrammed with the Silversea logo, down pillows, and brand-name bath amenities.

The restaurant offers open seating for the entire passenger complement; on select formal nights, there's an orchestra for dancing. Terrace Cafe offers alternative dining with Italian regional specialties on a reservation basis. Items from the restaurant menu can be delivered to your suite. On select sailings, visiting chefs from Le Cordon Bleu Culinary Academy prepare delicacies to complement the menu selections, including regional, American, and continental cuisine.

Silver Wind entered its scheduled dry dock in October 2001 for a comprehensive refurbishment and sat out the 2002 calendar year until its return in mid-2003. *Silver Cloud* was taken out of service in October 2003 and was to be brought back to the fleet in April 2004.

Upgrades to *Silver Cloud* include new furniture, linens, and artwork in all suites. The ship will also feature an intimate new wine bar, echoing the innovative and highly popular Le Champagne wine bars aboard Silversea's newer ships. Guests will also find an expanded spa facility featuring a new Tranquility Room—a blissful, between-treatment sanctuary. The ship will also receive a new Internet cafe, and an expanded fitness center, relocated to the observation deck and providing a panoramic view of the ocean.

Econoguide Ship Classifications

Gargantuan	130,000 or more tons
Colossus	100,000 to 130,000 tons
Megaship	70,000 to 100,000 tons
Large	40,000 to 70,000 tons
Medium	10,000 to 40,000 tons
Small	Less than 10,000 tons

CHAPTER FIFTEEN

OTHER CRUISE LINES

♛♛ Imperial Majesty Cruise
Line
♛♛♛ MSC Italian Cruises

♛♛♛ Oceania Cruises
♛♛♛ Royal Olympia Cruises

IMPERIAL MAJESTY CRUISE LINE

Address: 2950 Gateway Boulevard
Pompano Beach, FL 33069
Information: (954) 956–9505
www.imperialmajesty.com

The Imperial Majesty Cruise Line Fleet

Regal Empress	1953	900 passengers	21,909 tons

Imperial Majesty retired the venerable *Ocean Breeze* in June 2003, replacing her with the slightly older but more technologically current *Regal Empress*. That ship, built in 1953 as the flagship of the Greek Line, offers a very similar classic design and accommodations.

Per person rates run from as low as $150 for a minimal inside cabin to $400 for a suite for two nights. Prices more than double for peak-season cruises in holiday periods.

This is a party ship, with all the basic trappings of the early days of cruising: happy hours, karaoke bars, late night buffets, a casino, and bingo. You can try skeet shooting off the stern of the ship, play shuffleboard, and enter a table tennis tournament.

■ ITINERARY

The ship leaves Fort Lauderdale at 5:00 P.M. and sails overnight directly to Nassau. She stays in port there from about 9:00 A.M. to 6:00 P.M. before heading back to home port. The short cruises are marketed to first-time cruisers, families, and those looking for a quick getaway.

■ WEB SITE

Visitors to the Imperial Majesty Web site find a very detailed description of the ship and her history. The site includes an on-line request for booking but no prices. Travelers will be contacted by phone to book a voyage. *Ease of use: very good.*

Regal Empress	
Econoguide rating:	★★ 61 points
Ship size:	Medium
Category:	Vintage
Price range:	Budget $
Registry:	Bahamas
Year built:	1953 (formerly *Olympia, Caribe I*; refurbished 1993, 1999)
Information:	(800) 511–5737
Web site:	www.imperialmajesty.com
Passenger capacity:	900 (double occupancy)
Crew:	396
Passenger-to-crew ratio:	2.3:1
Tonnage:	21,909
Passenger-space ratio:	24.3
Length:	612 feet
Beam:	79 feet
Draft:	27.5 feet
Cruising speed:	17 knots
Guest decks:	8
Total cabins:	457
Outside:	201
Inside:	227
Suites:	29
Wheelchair cabins:	2
Cuisine:	International
Style:	Semiformal and casual
Price notes:	Single-occupancy premium, 150 percent
Tipping suggestions:	$9.00 pp/pd
Best deal:	Early-booking discounts reduce rates by almost 50 percent

The *Regal Empress* is a fine old ship, a bit worn around the edges, but very appropriate for cruise virgins and travelers looking for an excellent deal and some less-visited ports of call. A renovation in 1999 added a new small and casual restaurant, a computer cafe, and other amenities. The ship has been brought up to date with most SOLAS regulations, including fire safety sprinklers.

Note that, as with many older liners, many of the "outside" cabins actually look out on an open or enclosed promenade along the rail.

MSC ITALIAN CRUISES

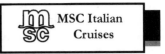

MSC Italian Cruises

Address: 250 Moonachie Road
   Moonachie, NJ 07074
Information: (800) 666–9333
   www.msccruises.com

🏵 🏵 🏵

The MSC Italian Cruises Fleet

Lirica	2003	1,530 passengers	58,600 tons
Melody	1982	1,076 passengers	36,500 tons
Monterey	1952	576 passengers	20,040 tons
Rhapsody	1977	768 passengers	16,852 tons

FUTURE SHIPS
Opera	2004	1,530 passengers	58,600 tons

MSC Italian Cruises (formerly Mediterranean Shipping Cruises) operates a small fleet of cruise ships around the world.

The company will more than double in capacity in 2003 and 2004 with the arrival of two new Megaships. In spring 2003 the company added *Lirica,* a new 1,590-passenger ship. The 58,600-ton vessel has 795 cabins, including 132 suites with private verandas. A sister ship, *Opera,* is due in spring 2004. Both vessels will sail Mediterranean itineraries.

MSC's older fleet includes *Melody,* which sails in the Caribbean in winter and in Europe for the remainder of the year. *Melody* is the former *Star/Ship Atlantic,* one of the Big Red Boats of the former Premier Cruise Line.

Also in the fleet are the *Rhapsody,* formerly the *Cunard Princess,* and the *Monterey,* formerly the U.S. flag freighter the *Free State Mariner.* They serve European, South American, and South African ports.

The line began as Flotta Lauro, an Italian carrier little known outside its home waters until the 1985 terrorist attack on its cruise ship *Achille Lauro* off Egypt. The *Achille Lauro* later sank off Africa in 1994.

The company was purchased in 1990 by Mediterranean Shipping Cruises, part of the Swiss-based Mediterranean Shipping Company, which is one of the world's largest container carrier companies, with a fleet of 140 container ships serving 166 ports on five continents.

■ ITINERARIES

Lirica crosses the Atlantic for the first time in late 2003 from Genoa through to the Caribbean to Fort Lauderdale. She is due to sail a winter cruise season that includes port calls in San Juan, Antigua, Grenada, St. Lucia, St. Barthelemy, Tortola, and Nassau. *Lirica* will also offer a Panama Canal partial transit and South America cruise. The ship will return to Portugal, Spain, and Italy in mid-May for summer 2004.

The other ships in the fleet sailed primarily in Europe. In recent years, *Rhapsody* sailed from Genoa or Venice on trips in the Mediterranean—to Greece, Croatia, Turkey, Corsica, and other ports. The ship wintered with cruises in South America.

Melody sailed from Fort Lauderdale to the southern Caribbean and into the Panama Canal in winter, crossing the Atlantic to Genoa in late April to sail in the Mediterranean, with destinations including Marseille, Malta, Turkey, and Greece.

In recent seasons *Monterey* sailed most of the year from Genoa, with cruises to the Mediterranean plus a half dozen forays to the Middle East, with visits to Port Said and Alexandria, Egypt; Beirut; and Athens. In past years the ship has spent the winter sailing South African waters.

■ WEB SITE

The MSC Web site presents basic information about ships and detailed itineraries. You can research prices for cruises and request that a reservations agent call you to book a trip. ***Ease of use: good.***

Lirica, Opera (2004)

Econoguide rating:	★★★★ 83 points (estimated)
Ship size:	Large
Category:	Top of the Line
Price range:	Premium $$$
Registry:	Panama
Year built:	*Lirica,* 2003; *Opera,* 2004
Information:	(800) 666–9333
Web site:	www.msccruisesusa.com
Passenger capacity:	1,590 (double occupancy)
Crew:	750
Passenger-to-crew ratio:	2:1
Tonnage:	58,600
Passenger-space ratio:	36.9
Length:	824 feet
Beam:	94.5 feet
Draft:	N/A
Cruising speed:	21 knots
Guest decks:	14
Total cabins:	795
Outside:	523

Inside:	272
Suites:	132
Wheelchair cabins:	4
Cuisine:	Italian, international
Style:	Casual, with two or more semiformal evenings
Price notes:	Single-occupancy premium, 150 percent
Tipping suggestions:	$8.00 pp/pd
Best deals:	Advance-booking discounts

These two modern ships offer all the amenities contemporary cruisers expect. Spread over the fourteen decks are two swimming pools, a spa with a Turkish bath and sauna, and an Internet cafe. The main dining rooms are La Bussola and Ippocampo; informal eateries include La Pergola and La Canzone del Mare on the pool deck plus a pizzeria. Entertainment offerings include the Blue Disco, the Rossini Music Hall, the Puccini Theatre, and the Broadway Theatre.

(During construction, the ships had been expected to bear different names: *Symphony* and *Harmony*. Italian actress Sophia Loren christened *Lirica* in April 2003.)

Melody

Econoguide rating:	★★★ 69 points
Ship size:	Medium
Category:	Vintage
Price range:	Budget $
Registry:	Panama
Year built:	1982 (formerly Star/Ship *Atlantic;* refurbished 1996)
Information:	(800) 666–9333
Web site:	www.msccruisesusa.com
Passenger capacity:	1,076 (double occupancy)
Crew:	535
Passenger-to-crew ratio:	2:1
Tonnage:	36,500
Passenger-space ratio:	33.9
Length:	671 feet
Beam:	90 feet
Draft:	25.5 feet
Cruising speed:	21 knots
Guest decks:	8
Total cabins:	627
Outside:	392
Inside:	157
Suites:	78
Wheelchair cabins:	4, but not up to modern standards for handicapped access

Cuisine:	Italian, international
Style:	Casual, with two or more semiformal evenings
Price notes:	Single-occupancy premium, 150 percent
Tipping suggestions:	$8.00 pp/pd
Best deals:	Advance-booking discounts

The **Melody** is a sturdy but undistinguished vessel that manages to pack a large number of guests onboard. There's a nice pool area with a retractable cover that allows use in any weather.

There are only three of the lowest-price staterooms on the ship, two on the bottommost Bahamas Deck and one on the Restaurant Deck. The most plentiful outside cabins are Class 8 staterooms, primarily on the Oceanic Deck, with some additional cabins scattered about the ship.

Monterey

Econoguide rating:	★★ 61 points
Ship size:	Medium
Category:	Vintage
Price range:	Budget $
Registry:	Panama
Year built:	1952 (formerly *Free State Mariner*; refurbished 1997)
Information:	(800) 666–9333
Web site:	www.msccruisesusa.com
Passenger capacity:	576 (double occupancy)
Crew:	200; Italian
Passenger-to-crew ratio:	2.9:1
Tonnage:	20,040
Passenger-space ratio:	34.8
Length:	563 feet
Beam:	80 feet
Draft:	29.5 feet
Cruising speed:	20 knots
Guest decks:	8
Total cabins:	294
Outside:	163
Inside:	127
Suites:	4
Cuisine:	Italian, international
Style:	Casual, with two or more semiformal evenings
Price notes:	Single-occupancy premium, 150 percent
Tipping suggestions:	$8.00 pp/pd
Best deals:	Advance-booking discounts

Monterey is a sturdy old ship, built as the fast freighter *Free State Mariner* during the Korean War. After the war, the ship was converted for use as a passenger liner, sailing for many years from the West Coast to Australia, New Zealand, and Hawaii. Although most cabins are relatively small and simple, there's a lot of space per passenger throughout.

Rhapsody

Econoguide rating:	★★★ 65 points
Ship size:	Medium
Category:	Vintage
Price range:	Budget $
Registry:	Panama
Year built:	1977 (formerly *Cunard Princess, Cunard Conquest*)
Information:	(800) 666–9333
Web site:	www.msccruisesusa.com
Passenger capacity:	768 (double occupancy)
Crew:	250; Italian
Passenger-to-crew ratio:	3:1
Tonnage:	16,852
Passenger-space ratio:	21.9
Length:	541 feet
Beam:	76 feet
Draft:	18.5 feet
Cruising speed:	19 knots
Guest decks:	8
Total cabins:	406
Outside:	257
Inside:	127
Suites:	22
Cuisine:	Italian, international
Style:	Casual, with two or more semiformal evenings
Price notes:	Single-occupancy premium, 150 percent
Tipping suggestions:	$8.00 pp/pd
Best deals:	Advance-booking discounts

A relatively simple ship, *Rhapsody* is one of the last two ships built for the original Cunard Line. The ship sailed mostly in the Caribbean from San Juan in her early years, moving on to the Mediterranean. During the Persian Gulf War she was chartered by the U.S. government to serve as a troop recreation vessel in Bahrain.

Cabins are on the small side. Her twin sister, the former *Cunard Countess*, now operates as the *Olympia Countess* for Royal Olympia Cruise Lines.

OCEANIA CRUISES

Address: 8120 Northwest 53rd Street
  Miami, FL 33166
Information: (800) 531–5658, (305) 514–2300
  www.oceaniacruises.com

The Oceania Cruises Fleet

Insignia	1997	680 passengers	30,277 tons
Regatta	1997	680 passengers	30,277 tons

Renaissance Cruise Lines is dead, but some of its many fans now hope: "Long live Oceania."

Two of Renaissance's nearly identical sister ships, *R3* and *R4,* along with several former top executives of the bankrupt line, returned to service in mid-2003 and early 2004 with a new company. The elegant midsize vessels, which bridge the gap between the top end of the mass market and the ultraluxury cruise lines, have been spruced up a bit and their formerly black hulls repainted white—but former customers will recognize them immediately. (Two other former Renaissance ships are now in the fleet of Princess Cruises, and another now sails for Swan Hellenic.)

The formal central stairs of *Insignia. Photo by Corey Sandler*

Aside from the appeal of the ships themselves, Renaissance also prided itself on its itineraries, which put the emphasis on extended port calls. In previous editions of *Econoguide Cruises,* we described the operation as providing a floating five-star hotel that delivers pampered guests from one spectacular destination to another, while delivering one of the best deals in the cruise industry.

Oceania Cruises hopes to continue the same cruise philosophy. *Regatta* began service in July 2003, and *Insignia* was due to return to service in April 2004. The company has an option to lease a third former Renaissance vessel in coming years.

■ ITINERARIES

On most European itineraries, Oceania Cruises calls on a minimum of eight ports. The initial schedule for *Regatta* included ten- to sixteen-day sailings from Barcelona to London (with stops in France, Portugal, and Mallorca), London to Stockholm (including visits to Denmark, Estonia, Russia, and Finland); Barcelona to Venice, Barcelona to Istanbul, Istanbul to Rome, and Rome to Barcelona.

Regatta was due to make visits to the Caribbean, South America, and the Panama Canal in winter 2003–04 before returning to Europe.

■ WEB SITE

Oceania's Web site includes all the necessary information for researching the ships and itineraries. Would-be travelers are asked to contact a travel agent to book passage. *Ease of use: very good.*

Regatta, Insignia

Econoguide rating:	★★★★ 81 points
Ship size:	Medium
Category:	Top of the Line
Price range:	Premium $$$
Registry:	Marshall Islands
Year built:	1997 (as *R3* and *R4;* refurbished 2003)
Information:	(800) 531–5658
Web site:	www.oceaniacruises.com
Passenger capacity:	680
Crew:	386
Passenger-to-crew ratio:	1.8:1
Tonnage:	30,277
Passenger space ratio:	44.1
Length:	594 feet
Beam:	83.5 feet
Draft:	19.5 feet
Cruising speed:	18 knots
Guest decks:	9
Total cabins:	342
Outside:	317
Inside:	25
Suites:	10
Wheelchair cabins:	14
Cuisine:	International
Style:	Country club casual
Price notes:	Advance booking discounts
Tipping suggestions:	$10.50 pp/pd

The main restaurant on both ships is the Grand Dining Room, offering continental cuisine designed by celebrity French chef Jacques Pepin.

Up top is a pair of intimate ninety-seat reservations-only restaurants: Toscana offers gourmet Italian fare; the Polo Grill serves beef, chops, and fresh seafood. (There is no extra charge for reservations.)

The Tides Cafe offers casual buffet breakfast or lunch. In the evening the same room is transformed into "Tapas at Tides" for cocktails, live entertainment, and a menu featuring a wide array of tapas and authentic dishes from Spain and around the world.

Oceania has upgraded the bedding, carpeting, and upholstery throughout the ships and added new teak decking on all 233 verandas.

ROYAL OLYMPIA CRUISES

Address: 805 Third Avenue
New York, NY 10022
Information: (800) 872–6400
www.royalolympiacruises.com

The Royal Olympia Cruises Fleet

Olympia Explorer	2002	836 passengers	25,000 tons
Olympia Voyager	2000	836 passengers	25,000 tons
Stella Solaris	1953	628 passengers	18,000 tons
Olympia Countess	1976	814 passengers	18,000 tons
Triton	1953	676 passengers	14,155 tons
World Renaissance	1966	474 passengers	12,000 tons

Royal Olympia Cruises puts the emphasis on its destinations, delivering guests from port to port on comfortable and well-appointed ships; don't expect rock-climbing walls or in-line skating courses aboard ship.

The company is a leading cruise line in the eastern Mediterranean, born in 1995 with the merger of SunLine and Epirotiki. Until 2000 the line had a fleet of older, more modest ships; that changed with the introduction of the ultramodern twins *Olympia Voyager* and *Olympia Explorer*. (The company changed its name from Royal Olympic Cruises to Royal Olympia Cruises in 2003 in response to objections from officials of a certain well-known international sporting event.)

With the ability to travel comfortably at speeds as high as 30 knots, the *Olympia Voyager* and *Olympia Explorer* hold the current record as the fastest cruise ships in the world. The ship's high speed, attributed to its fast monohull design—originally conceived for naval frigates—enables the vessels to spend more time in port or reach more distant ports.

(You can read a cruise diary about the *Olympia Voyager* in Chapter 11.)

■ ITINERARIES

The 2003-2004 schedule for *Olympia Explorer* begins with a transatlantic repositioning from Piraeus, Greece, in November. The eighteen-day itinerary includes stops in Nice, Barcelona, Las Palmas, Cape Verde, an entry into the Amazon River in Brazil, Devil's Island, Barbados, Guadeloupe, and Nassau before terminating at Port Canaveral, Florida.

Olympia Explorer next travels from Port Canaveral through the Panama Canal to Mexico and Los Angeles. In December the ship sails a pair of two-week Aloha Odyssey cruises from Los Angeles to Ensenada, Mexico, and on to Hawaii, Maui, Kauai, and Oahu before returning to Los Angeles. The ship next repositions north to San Francisco for a similar Aloha Odyseey cruise in late January.

In February the ship sails from San Francisco down the west coast of the Americas, with calls in Mexico, Costa Rica, and Ecuador and ending in Callao, Peru. From Callao, the Magellan Straits Cruise ventures farther south to Chile, Patagonia, Punta Arenas, and ends in Ushuaia, Argentina.

In March the ship continues southward to Cape Horn; the South Shetland Islands; Anvers Island, Antarctica; the Falklands; and Buenos Aires. In mid-March *Olympia Explorer* begins her northward passage from Buenos Aires with a twenty-day itinerary that includes calls at Rio de Janeiro, the Amazon River, Devil's Island in French Guiana, and the Orinoco River; on into the Caribbean with stops at Trinidad, Dominica, St. Thomas; and ending in Fort Lauderdale.

In April 2004 the ship departs Fort Lauderdale for a repositioning to Venice, Italy, with intermediate stops in Nassau, St. Bart's, St. Martin, Îles des Saintes, Barbados, Lisbon, Palma de Mallorca, Barcelona, Nice, Civitavecchia, Messina, Piraeus, and Corfu.

Sister ship *Olympia Voyager* crosses from Piraeus to Fort Lauderdale in mid-November 2003 on a cruise that includes entry into the Amazon River. In December the ship makes a seventeen-day cruise from Fort Lauderdale to the Orinoco and Amazon Rivers, plus other stops in South America and the Caribbean before returning to Fort Lauderdale.

The seventeen-day Christmas–New Year's cruise sails round-trip from Fort Lauderdale through the Panama Canal to Acapulco and then back through the canal to Belize and Cozumel. A second seventeen-day cruise to the Orinoco and Amazon Rivers takes place in early January.

At the end of January, *Olympia Voyager* sails from Fort Lauderdale through the Panama Canal to Los Angeles. In February and March the ship sails from Los Angeles to the Hawaiian islands and back. In mid-March the ship departs San Francisco for a transit of the Panama Canal and a return to Fort Lauderdale.

The ship ends her American visit in April, departing Fort Lauderdale for Genoa, Italy, with stops in the Caribbean and at Madeira, Tangier, Barcelona, Marseille, Nice, Messina, Istanbul, and Piraeus.

In August 2004 three of the line's ships, *Olympia Voyager, Olympia Explorer,* and *Olympia Countess,* will serve as floating hotels for as many as 2,500 visitors to the 2004 Athens Summer Olympic Games. For the duration of the Olympics, the three ships will be docked at the port of Piraeus, located just outside Athens

The yachtlike *Olympia Voyager* tied up in Progreso, Mexico. *Photo by Corey Sandler*

and the departure point for many cruises to the Greek Islands. Bookings on the ships can be made through travel agents.

Odysseus sails most of the year in the Mediterranean from Genoa or Barcelona, with visits to Marseille, France; Palma de Mallorca, Spain; Tangier, Morocco; and Gilbraltar. *World Renaissance* sailed from Istanbul or Athens to the Greek Islands and Turkey for the same period. These ships and *Triton* also offered a number of four-day Aegean cruises from Athens.

Olympia Explorer, Olympia Voyager

Econoguide rating:	★★★ 79 points
Ship size:	Medium
Category:	Top of the Line
Price range:	Moderate $$
Registry:	Greece
Year built:	*Olympia Explorer,* 2002; *Olympia Voyager,* 2001
Information:	(800) 872–6400
Web site:	www.royalolympiacruises.com
Passenger capacity:	836 (double occupancy)
Crew:	360
Passenger-to-crew ratio:	2.3:1
Tonnage:	25,000
Passenger-space ratio:	29.9
Length:	590 feet
Beam:	84 feet
Draft:	24 feet
Cruising speed:	28 knots
Guest decks:	6
Total cabins:	418
Outside:	296
Inside:	122
Suites:	52
Wheelchair cabins:	4

Cuisine:	Greek and continental
Style:	Casual, informal, and formal nights
Price notes:	Single-cabin supplement, 150 to 200 percent
Tipping suggestions:	$9.00 pp/pd
Best deal:	Early-booking discounts

Olympia Voyager was the pride of Greece—the first new cruise ship sailing under the country's flag in more than a decade—when it was christened by the president in late 2000. That ship and her near-identical sister **Olympia Explorer** are neat and trim ships, more like a superyacht in appearance than a small version of a Megaship.

The national flavor of Greece runs through the ships, with decks and public rooms named after Greek gods and goddesses and epic Greek poetry inscribed on the two main staircases.

Cabins are on the small side, and onboard amenities are very good but limited; these ships are aimed at delivering adventurous guests to destinations in Mexico, Central America, and the Mediterranean.

Stella Solaris

Econoguide rating:	★★★ 65 points
Ship size:	Medium
Category:	Top of the Line
Price range:	Moderate $$
Registry:	Greece
Year built:	1953 (formerly *Cambodge*)
Information:	(800) 872–6400
Web site:	www.royalolympiacruises.com
Passenger capacity:	628 (double occupancy)
Crew:	320
Passenger-to-crew ratio:	2:1
Tonnage:	18,000
Passenger-space ratio:	28.7
Length:	544 feet
Beam:	72 feet
Draft:	29 feet
Cruising speed:	22 knots
Guest decks:	8
Total cabins:	314
Outside:	264
Inside:	50
Suites:	66
Cuisine:	Greek and continental
Style:	Casual, informal, and formal nights

Price notes:	Single-cabin supplement, 150 to 200 percent
Tipping suggestions:	$9.00 pp/pd
Best deal:	Early-booking discounts

Stella Solaris is a proud old lady, a steam-turbine ship with touches of her original French Colonial interior design. Built as the *Cambodge*, she sailed in Asia for most of her early life.

In 2003 rising fuel costs led Royal Olympia Cruises to mothball *Stella Solaris*. Her Baltic itineraries were taken over by *Triton* and her proposed 2004 world cruise postponed to 2005.

Olympia Countess

Econoguide rating:	★★★ 68 points
Ship size:	Medium
Category:	Top of the Line
Price range:	Moderate $$
Registry:	Greece
Year built:	1976 (formerly *Awani Dream I, Cunard Countess*)
Information:	(800) 872–6400
Web site:	www.royalolympiacruises.com
Passenger capacity:	814 (double occupancy)
Crew:	350
Passenger-to-crew ratio:	2.3:1
Tonnage:	18,000
Passenger-space ratio:	22.1
Length:	537 feet
Beam:	75 feet
Draft:	19 feet
Cruising speed:	18.5 knots
Guest decks:	7
Total cabins:	407
Outside:	272
Inside:	135
Suites:	26
Cuisine:	Greek and continental
Style:	Casual, informal, and formal nights
Price notes:	Single-cabin supplement, 150 to 200 percent
Tipping suggestions:	$9.00 pp/pd
Best deal:	Early-booking discounts

Olympia Countess is the sister ship of the *Rhapsody* of MSC Italian Cruises, one of the last two ships built for the original Cunard Line.

Triton

Econoguide rating:	★★ 57 points
Ship size:	Medium
Category:	Top of the Line
Price range:	Moderate $$
Registry:	Greece
Year built:	1971 (formerly *Cunard Adventurer, Sunward II*)
Information:	(800) 872–6400
Web site:	www.royalolympiacruises.com
Passenger capacity:	676 (double occupancy)
Crew:	300
Passenger-to-crew ratio:	2.3:1
Tonnage:	14,000
Passenger-space ratio:	20.7
Length:	486 feet
Beam:	71 feet
Draft:	21 feet
Cruising speed:	22 knots
Guest decks:	7
Total cabins:	338
Outside:	277
Inside:	61
Suites:	26
Cuisine:	Greek and continental
Style:	Casual, informal, and formal nights
Price notes:	Single-cabin supplement, 150 to 200 percent
Tipping suggestions:	$9.00 pp/pd
Best deal:	Early-booking discounts

Triton sailed in 2002 in the Mediterranean on seven-day itineraries from Civitavecchia (Rome) with calls at Messina, Italy; Corfu, Piraeus (Athens), and Olympia, Greece; Lipari and Genoa, Italy, and back to Civitavecchia. The same trip can be boarded in Genoa or Piraeus.

World Renaissance

Econoguide rating:	★★ 61 points
Ship size:	Medium
Category:	Top of the Line
Price range:	Moderate $$

Registry:	Greece
Year built:	1966 (formerly *Awani Dream, Renaissance, Homeric Renaissance*)
Information:	(800) 872–6400
Web site:	www.royalolympiacruises.com
Passenger capacity:	474 (double occupancy)
Crew:	230
Passenger-to-crew ratio:	2:1
Tonnage:	12,000
Passenger-space ratio:	25.3
Length:	492 feet
Beam:	69 feet
Draft:	23 feet
Cruising speed:	16 knots
Guest decks:	7
Total cabins:	237
Outside:	207
Inside:	30
Suites:	15
Cuisine:	Greek and continental
Style:	Casual, informal, and formal nights
Price notes:	Single-cabin supplement, 150 to 200 percent
Tipping suggestions:	$9.00 pp/pd
Best deal:	Early booking discounts

A well-traveled 1960s-era ship of classic design, small but adequate cabins, and limited onboard facilities, **World Renaissance** is a fine way to travel from port to port.

Econoguide Ship Classifications

Gargantuan	130,000 or more tons
Colossus	100,000 to 130,000 tons
Megaship	70,000 to 100,000 tons
Large	40,000 to 70,000 tons
Medium	10,000 to 40,000 tons
Small	Less than 10,000 tons

CHAPTER SIXTEEN

ADVENTURE CRUISE LINES

♀♀♀ American Canadian
Caribbean Line
♀♀♀ American Cruise Lines
♀♀♀ Clipper Cruise Lines
♀♀♀ Cruise West
♀♀♀ Delta Queen Steamboat
Company

♀♀♀ Glacier Bay Cruise Line
♀♀♀ Lindblad Special
Expeditions
♀♀♀ RiverBarge Excursion Line
♀♀♀ Society Expeditions

AMERICAN CANADIAN CARIBBEAN LINE

Address: 461 Water Street
Warren, RI 02885
Information: (800) 556–7450
www.accl-smallships.com

♀ ♀ ♀

The American Canadian Caribbean Line Fleet

Grande Caribe	1997	100 passengers	761 tons
Grande Mariner	1998	100 passengers	781 tons
Niagara Prince	1994	84 passengers	687 tons

American Canadian Caribbean Line is a multinational name for a small but ambitious American-flagged cruise line. The line's three vessels sail a grand tour of the Americas, including the Mississippi, Great Lakes, Erie Canal, Newfoundland, and Labrador, as well as the Caribbean and Central America to ports including the Virgin Islands, Antigua, Nassau, Trinidad and Tobago, Panama, Venezuela, Belize, Guatemala, and Honduras. Another interesting itinerary travels from Rhode Island to Buffalo, through New York City and Albany, and across the Erie Canal.

The twin flagships of the line are the *Grande Mariner* and the *Grande Caribe,* each having a capacity of one hundred passengers. The third ship is the slightly smaller *Niagara Prince,* which carries eighty-four passengers.

■ THE ACCL STORY

ACCL was founded in 1966 by shipbuilder Luther Blount; all the vessels are constructed at Blount Industries in Warren, Rhode Island. The company is one of the last working shipyards in New England building midsize metal boats; it has produced more than 300 ships since it began in 1949. Blount finally retired in 2001 at the age of eighty-four and was succeeded by his daughter, Nancy.

One of the goals of ACCL is to explore smaller waterways and ports. The vessels are custom designed for that purpose, with shallow drafts and other features, such as bow ramps for easy unloading of passengers directly to shore, an innovative retractable pilot house that permits the ships to sail under low bridges on waterways such as the Erie Canal, and glass-bottom launches on most trips. According to the company, Blount "seeks out unusual places and then builds the ships to take us there."

Cabins and public areas are simple and functional. There's no room service, no frills, no glitz, and a bring-your-own-bottle bar policy. The company's emphasis is much more on the destinations sailed by its ships than on the ships themselves.

■ ITINERARIES

In 2003 ACCL ships sailed in Belize and Roatan early in the year, in the Intracoastal Waterway along the U.S. East Coast, and from New Orleans to Chicago. Later in spring, ships expanded north to Baltimore to sail to Chesapeake Bay and Alexandria.

In June cruises began on the Erie Canal and the Saguenay River. Other summer cruises include visits to Lake Michigan, Lake Superior, the Finger Lakes, and New England islands. Erie Canal and fall foliage cruises begin in late September. Cruises on the Intracoastal Waterway return in November, setting the stage for a return to the Caribbean for the winter.

■ WEB SITE

ACCL's site provides only basic information and a clumsy listing of itineraries. There is no provision to check availability on-line. Visitors can request a callback from the cruise line for booking or can telephone directly. *Ease of use: good.*

Grande Caribe

Econoguide rating:	★★ 60 points
Ship size:	Small
Category:	Adventure
Price range:	Premium $$$
Registry:	United States
Year built:	1997
Information:	(800) 556–7450, (401) 247–0955
Web site:	www.accl-smallships.com
Passenger capacity:	100 (double occupancy)
Crew:	17
Passenger-to-crew ratio:	6:1
Tonnage:	761
Length:	183 feet
Beam:	40 feet
Draft:	6.6 feet
Cruising speed:	10 knots
Guest decks:	3
Total cabins:	50
Outside:	50
Inside:	0
Suites:	0
Wheelchair cabins:	None indicated
Cuisine:	American
Style:	Always casual
Price notes:	Single-occupancy premium, 175 percent in certain cabin classifications; certain cabins on each vessel accommodate a third passenger at a 15 percent discount for each occupant
Tipping suggestions:	Gratuities are left to the discretion of guests

A comfortable soft-adventure ship, *Grande Caribe* has some special features that are well suited to small harbors and landings. The ship's small draft enables access to shallow rivers, canals, and waterways; a retractable pilot house allows ships to maneuver under low bridges and locks. By using its bow ramp, the ship can make its own landings on beaches and river banks.

ACCL brings along experts on wildlife, marine biology, flora and fauna, and local indigenous cultures. Like the other vessels in the ACCL fleet, this is a no-frills operation. You will not find room service, casinos, swimming pools, or formal dinners. One dining room on main deck accommodates all passengers for single-seating dining. The Vista View Lounge has a bring-your-own-bottle policy.

Grande Mariner

Econoguide rating:	★★ 60 points
Ship size:	Small
Category:	Adventure
Price range:	Premium $$$
Registry:	United States
Year built:	1998
Information:	(800) 556–7450, (401) 247–0955
Web site:	www.accl-smallships.com
Passenger capacity:	100 (double occupancy)
Crew:	17
Passenger-to-crew ratio:	6:1
Tonnage:	781
Length:	183 feet
Beam:	40 feet
Draft:	6.6 feet
Cruising speed:	10 knots
Guest decks:	3
Total cabins:	50
Outside:	50
Inside:	0
Suites:	0
Wheelchair cabins:	None indicated
Cuisine:	American
Style:	Always casual
Price notes:	Single-occupancy premium, 175 percent in certain cabin classifications; certain cabins on each vessel accommodate a third passenger at a 15 percent discount for each occupant
Tipping suggestions:	Gratuities are left to the discretion of guests

The **Grande Mariner**'s philosophy and set of offerings are similar to those of the *Grande Caribe*.

Niagara Prince

Econoguide rating:	★★ 60 points
Ship size:	Small
Category:	Adventure
Price range:	Premium $$$
Registry:	United States

Year built:	1994
Information:	(800) 556–7450, (401) 247–0955
Web site:	www.accl-smallships.com
Passenger capacity:	84 (double occupancy)
Crew:	17
Passenger-to-crew ratio:	5:1
Tonnage:	687
Length:	175 feet
Beam:	40 feet
Draft:	6.3 feet
Cruising speed:	10 knots
Guest decks:	3
Total cabins:	42
Outside:	42
Inside:	0
Suites:	0
Wheelchair cabins:	None indicated
Cuisine:	American
Style:	Always casual
Price notes:	Single-occupancy premium, 175 percent; certain cabins accommodate a third passenger at a 15 percent discount for each occupant
Tipping suggestions:	Gratuities are left to discretion of guests

The oldest, simplest, and most casual of the ACCL fleet, the **Niagara Prince** is still a favorite with passengers who find their entertainment as they move along.

AMERICAN CRUISE LINES

Address: One Marine Park
Haddam, CT 06438
Information: (860) 345–3311
www.americancruiselines.com

The American Cruise Lines Fleet

American Eagle	2000	49 passengers	1,200 tons
American Glory	2002	49 passengers	1,200 tons

American Eagle began her coastal cruiser career in April 2000, journeying up and down the eastern seaboard. Sister ship *American Glory* joined the fleet in July 2002.

■ ITINERARIES

American Eagle offers a New England islands cruise to Block Island, Nantucket, Martha's Vineyard, New Bedford, and Newport. The Maine Coast and Harbors cruise stops at Camden, Bar Harbor, Rockland, Bath, and Portland, Maine. The Antebellum South cruise extends up or down the inside passage from Amelia Island, Florida, to Charleston, South Carolina, with stops in Saint Simons Island and Savannah, Georgia; and Hilton Head Island and Beaufort, South Carolina. Some trips explore from Connecticut to New York, and then up the Hudson to Albany.

American Glory sailed from Baltimore, Maryland; New London, Connecticut; and Charleston, South Carolina, and spent the winter operating on Florida inland waterway cruises, returning to the Northeast in June.

■ WEB SITE

Basic information on the ships and itineraries of the line is presented on the Web site. Visitors must call the cruise line or a travel agent to book a trip. There is no provision to check availability on-line. *Ease of use: good.*

American Eagle, American Glory

Econoguide rating:	★★ 50 points
Ship size:	Small
Category:	Adventure
Price range:	Premium $$$
Registry:	United States
Year built:	*American Eagle,* 2000; *American Glory,* 2002
Information:	(860) 345–3311
Web site:	www.americancruiselines.com
Passenger capacity:	49 (double occupancy)
Crew:	22
Passenger-to-crew ratio:	2.2:1
Tonnage:	1,200
Passenger-space ratio:	24.5
Length:	*American Eagle,* 162 feet; *American Glory,* 168 feet
Beam:	*American Eagle,* 39 feet; *American Glory,* 43 feet
Draft:	7 feet
Cruising speed:	11 knots
Guest decks:	3 passenger decks, 1 sundeck
Total cabins:	31
Outside:	31
Inside:	0
Suites:	1
Wheelchair cabins:	0

Cuisine:	American
Style:	Casual
Tipping suggestions:	$14.25 pp/pd
Best deal:	Savings up to $1,000 for bookings five months or more in advance

Each of American Cruise Lines' young sister ships has thirty-one outside cabins. The newer **American Glory** offers fourteen staterooms with private balconies; **American Eagle** has six with balconies. Both have a glass-enclosed dining room that accommodates all passengers in one seating.

CLIPPER CRUISE LINE

❖ *CLIPPER*

Address: 7711 Bonhomme Avenue
　Saint Louis, MO 63105
Information: (800) 325–0010, (314) 727–2929
　www.clippercruise.com

The Clipper Cruise Line Fleet

Clipper Adventurer	1975	122 passengers	4,364 tons
Clipper Odyssey	1989	120 passengers	5,050 tons
Nantucket Clipper	1984	102 passengers	1,471 tons
Yorktown Clipper	1988	138 passengers	2,354 tons

The Clipper ships emphasize expeditions to unusual destinations; there are no casinos, Las Vegas–type shows, or glitzy gift shops aboard. The accommodations and public rooms are comfortable but hardly posh.

The small ships travel to places as diverse as the hidden fjords of Alaska, Caribbean coves, the Intracoastal Waterway of the U.S. South, the coast of New England, the Guadalquivir River of Spain, and the icescapes of Antarctica.

The line's two U.S.-flagged ships, the *Nantucket Clipper* and the *Yorktown Clipper,* were designed with shallow drafts and easy maneuverability for coastal trips along the mainland United States, Alaska, Canada, Mexico, the Caribbean, and Central and South America.

The *Clipper Adventurer* was built in 1975 as the Russian research vessel *Alla Tarasova;* it has a hardened hull that allows her to navigate in rugged natural environments, including ice fields. It was completely converted in 1998 for use as a small oceangoing cruise ship, with a remake of all of the cabins and public rooms; stabilizers were added later in the year. She includes a fleet of ten Zodiac landing craft.

■ ITINERARIES

In 2003 *Nantucket Clipper* and *Yorktown Clipper* continued their domestic cruising along the eastern and western coastlines of North America and the Caribbean

Islands. *Nantucket Clipper* sailed as far north as Prince Edward Island in eastern Canada and all along the Atlantic seaboard and made inland voyages via the St. Lawrence Seaway into the Great Lakes. In winter months the ship continued south to Belize and Honduras.

Yorktown Clipper traveled from the Inside Passage of Alaska south along the west coast of the Americas to the Panama Canal, with voyages in the Pacific Northwest, Northern California, the Sea of Cortez, Costa Rica, and the Caribbean Sea.

The expedition-capable *Clipper Adventurer* followed the path of the sun with voyages south to Antarctica and as far south as the High Arctic. In the early part of the year, voyages were offered in South America and to the Antarctic Peninsula. From there the ship visited South America for cruises along the eastern coast of Brazil and into the Amazon River. After crossing the Atlantic Ocean, the *Clipper Adventurer* spent the summer in Europe, from the Western Mediterranean to the Arctic Circle, before returning for cruises along the east coast of North America and the west coast of South America.

Clipper Odyssey's 2003 itineraries visited New Zealand and Australia, including the Great Barrier Reef. In March the ship sailed in the South China Sea and Japan, moving on to remote Alaska and Russia for the summer. In fall *Clipper Odyssey* navigated the islands of the South Pacific with itineraries in Hawaii, the Line Islands, French Polynesia, and Melanesia. In December the ship returned to Antarctica and the Falkland Islands.

■ THE CLIPPER STORY

Clipper Cruise Line was founded in 1982 in Saint Louis. In 1996 Clipper was purchased by Intrav, a deluxe-tour operator that was a sister company. In 1999 Clipper and Intrav were, in turn, purchased by a Swiss company, Kuoni Travel Holding Ltd.

All of Clipper's voyages feature guest speakers, including naturalists, historians, and other experts. On cruises through the South, a Civil War historian gives lectures. On Alaskan cruises, guests are accompanied by a park ranger and naturalist.

■ WEB SITE

The Web site presents basic information about the cruise line and itineraries. There is no on-line provision to check availability. Visitors can either request a callback to book a cruise or go through a travel agent. ***Ease of use: good.***

Clipper Adventurer

Econoguide rating:	★★ 64 points
Ship size:	Small
Category:	Adventure

Price range:	Premium $$$
Registry:	Bahamas
Year built:	1991 (formerly Russian research vessel *Alla Tarasova;* rebuilt 1997–98)
Information:	(800) 325–0010
Web site:	www.clippercruise.com
Passenger capacity:	122 (double occupancy)
Crew:	72
Passenger-to-crew ratio:	1.7:1
Tonnage:	4,364
Passenger-space ratio:	35.8
Length:	330 feet
Beam:	53.5 feet
Draft:	16 feet
Cruising speed:	14 knots
Guest decks:	4
Total cabins:	61
Outside:	61
Inside:	0
Suites:	3
Cuisine:	American regional
Style:	Casual and comfortable; no formal clothing or evening wear required
Price notes:	Single-occupancy premium, approximately 150 percent
Tipping suggestions:	$9.00 pp/pd

A relatively new vessel, especially after its 1998 conversion from its former life as a Russian research ship, the *Clipper Adventurer* in some ways harks back in style to the heyday of the steamship era in the 1930s and 1940s.

Public rooms are small and clublike, including the Clipper Club and Bar, and an intimate library/card room. The ship includes a covered promenade, sheltered from the weather. The windowed dining room accommodates all passengers at a single seating. The Main Lounge and Bar will accommodate a full passenger load.

I toured the ship soon after her arrival in America when she set anchor outside the harbor of Nantucket Island. Most of her load of passengers clambered onto the ship's ten Zodiacs for a choppy ride through October seas into town; others stayed onboard to listen to a lecture by a local artist. The bridge was open to visitors.

An important part of the entertainment is educational: Historians, naturalists, and other experts are often on the cruises or come aboard in port. They replace variety shows and bingo. There's no gambling and no disco, and there are no television sets in the staterooms.

The cabins and public rooms are airy and well appointed with Scandinavian furnishings. An attractive dining room has windows on three sides.

In March 2002 the ship, with 118 passengers aboard, ran aground on a sandbank in the Essequibo River in Guyana. No injuries were reported, and the ship was freed several days later. *Clipper Adventurer* was on a tour to Brazil, French Guiana, and Suriname.

Clipper Odyssey

Econoguide rating:	★★★★ 80 points
Ship size:	Small
Category:	Adventure
Price range:	Premium $$$
Registry:	Bahamas
Year built:	1989
Information:	(800) 325–0010
Web site:	www.clippercruise.com
Passenger capacity:	128 (double occupancy)
Crew:	72
Passenger-to-crew ratio:	1.8:1
Tonnage:	5,218
Passenger-space ratio:	40.8
Length:	338 feet
Beam:	51 feet
Draft:	15 feet
Cruising speed:	15 knots
Guest decks:	5
Total cabins:	64
Outside:	64
Inside:	1
Suites:	1
Wheelchair cabins:	None listed
Cuisine:	American regional
Style:	Casual and comfortable; no formal clothing or evening wear required
Price notes:	Single-occupancy premium, approximately 150 percent
Tipping suggestions:	$9.00 pp/pd

The **Clipper Odyssey** was built in Japan to the specifications of a master Dutch yacht designer specifically for year-round itineraries in the Pacific that range from New Zealand and Australia's Great Barrier Reef to Japan, the Kuril Islands, and the Russian Far East, including the Kamchatka Peninsula.

Unusual for a smaller ship, amenities include an outdoor swimming pool, dedicated jogging track, and two sundecks.

Clipper Cruise Line's *Nantucket Clipper.* *Photo by Wolfgang Kaehler, courtesy of Clipper Cruise Line*

Nantucket Clipper

Econoguide rating:	★★★ 67 points
Ship size:	Small
Category:	Adventure
Price range:	Premium $$$
Registry:	United States
Year built:	1984
Information:	(800) 325–0010
Web site:	www.clippercruise.com
Passenger capacity:	102 (double occupancy)
Crew:	32
Passenger-to-crew ratio:	3.2:1
Tonnage:	1,471
Length:	207 feet
Beam:	37 feet
Draft:	8 feet
Cruising speed:	8 knots
Guest decks:	4
Total cabins:	51
Outside:	51

Inside:	0
Suites:	0
Wheelchair cabins:	0
Cuisine:	American
Style:	Casual and comfortable; no formal clothing or evening wear required
Price notes:	Single-occupancy premium, 150 percent of category 2
Tipping suggestions:	$9.00 pp/pd

Nantucket Clipper is a basic small ship for a cruise line that focuses more on ports of call and sights along the way than on interior flash. Historians, naturalists, and other experts often are on the cruises, replacing variety shows, disco dancing, bingo, and gambling. In some ports, local musicians or artisans come aboard.

The young chefs are recruited from the Culinary Institute of America in upstate New York; the cabin and restaurant staff are bright-faced young (mostly) Americans who serve with casual friendliness.

Yorktown Clipper

Econoguide rating:	★★★ 68 points
Ship size:	Small
Category:	Adventure
Price range:	Premium $$$
Registry:	United States
Year built:	1988
Information:	(800) 325–0010
Web site:	www.clippercruise.com
Passenger capacity:	138 (double occupancy)
Crew:	40
Passenger-to-crew ratio:	3.4:1
Tonnage:	2,354
Length:	257 feet
Beam:	43 feet
Draft:	8 feet
Cruising speed:	10 knots
Guest decks:	4
Total cabins:	69
Outside:	69
Inside:	0
Suites:	0
Wheelchair cabins:	0
Cuisine:	American regional

Style:	Casual and comfortable; no formal clothing or evening wear required
Price notes:	Single-occupancy premium, 150 percent
Tipping suggestions:	$9.00 pp/pd

The **Yorktown Clipper** provides a relaxed country-club atmosphere on an unpretentious small ship. The excitement comes from the ports of call and waterways. Again, historians, naturalists, and other experts often are on the cruises, and local musicians, artisans, and representatives come aboard in some ports.

CRUISE WEST

Alaska Sightseeing
Cruise West

Address: 2401 Fourth Avenue, Suite 700
Seattle, WA 98121
Information: (206) 441–8687, (800) 888–9378
www.cruisewest.com

The Cruise West Fleet

Spirit of Oceanus	1990	114 passengers	4,200 tons
Spirit of '98	1984	96 passengers	1,472 tons
Spirit of Alaska	1980	78 passengers	529 tons
Spirit of Columbia	1979	78 passengers	514 tons
Spirit of Discovery	1976	84 passengers	910 tons
Spirit of Endeavour	1983	102 passengers	1,425 tons
Pacific Explorer	1995	100 passengers	438 tons

Chuck West, a World War II pilot who returned home to start a bush flying service in Alaska, founded a small cruise company that eventually became Westours. That company was sold to Holland America Line, and he later began Alaska Sightseeing/Cruise West.

The company began with day cruises in the Inside Passage and by 1990 had added overnight cruises on the *Spirit of Glacier Bay*. In 1991 the company introduced cruises from Seattle to Alaska, restoring a long-suspended U.S.-flagged route.

Today the company is run by West's son and has seven small cruise ships. It has a legitimate claim to knowing Alaska from the insider's point of view, and the small vessels allow guests to get up close and personal with whales and other aquatic life and the occasional bear on shore.

■ ITINERARIES

Cruise West ships are small enough to be allowed unrestricted access to Glacier Bay; larger vessels must vie for a limited number of permits. As American-flagged vessels, they can sail from Seattle to Alaska without making a stop in Canada.

Other journeys include Tracy Arm for an up-close visit with South Sawyer Glacier, LeConte Bay, and narrow inlets off Glacier Bay. The line claims it has the only ships that regularly sail through Wrangell Narrows, rarely visited El Capitan, and Sea Otter Sound.

The company's longer tours—fourteen to nineteen days—begin in Fairbanks or Anchorage and include rail, bus, and boat tours in central Alaska, then a flight to Juneau for a five-day cruise in the southeast portion of the state.

Alaska itineraries generally run from about April through October, after which time the ships migrate south to California and down to Mexico for explorations of Baja California. California trips include San Francisco to the Napa-Carneros-Sonoma wine region and a visit to Old Sacramento.

In recent winters, the company has based the *Spirit of Endeavour* in Cabo San Lucas to explore the Sea of Cortés in Mexico, home to many species of wildlife, including visits to remote desert beaches. Available shore excursions include a visit to Copper Canyon with a trip on the South Orient Express; the railroad, which took almost a century to build, travels from sea level to almost 8,000 feet, across thirty-six bridges and through eighty-six tunnels, including a 360-degree spiral through a mile-long tunnel.

Cruise West's *Spirit of Discovery* passes through a glacier-filled fjord in Alaska. *Courtesy of Cruise West*

The latest addition to the fleet, *Temptress Explorer,* sails year-round in Central America.

■ THE CRUISE WEST EXPERIENCE

Four vessels have bow landing platforms, permitting the ships to offload passengers in many locations without having to use tenders. (This harks back to the stern-wheeler riverboats of the American heartland.)

Passengers are generally permitted to visit the bridge while the ships are under way, which allows guests to chat with the captain and consult charts and radar screens.

The dining room emphasizes the cuisine of the Pacific Northwest. Orders for dinner entrees are often taken the night before the meal; special requests can often be met.

These are decidedly casual cruises, with an open seating for meals and little in the way of entertainment—except for the spectacular passing scenery. And aside from your cabin, there are not many quiet hideaways away from the other guests. When the ship overnights in a port, the concierge will make dinner reservations and provide transportation to shore points.

One interesting plus on some Cruise West trips: a Kodak Ambassador to assist guests in getting the perfect photo. The ambassadors are retired photo professionals with a wide range of technical backgrounds.

Cruise West has introduced a program that reduces the cost of single supplements; the plan guarantees double-occupancy rates for single cruise guests who agree to share a cabin with another single traveler. If a roommate is unavailable, there is no extra charge for a single cabin.

■ WEB SITE

The Web site presents basic information about the cruise line and itineraries. There is no on-line provision to check availability. Visitors can either request a callback to book a cruise or go through a travel agent. *Ease of use: good.*

Spirit of Oceanus

Econoguide rating:	★★★ 67 points
Ship size:	Small
Category:	Adventure
Price range:	Opulent $$$$
Registry:	Bahamas
Year built:	1990 (formerly *Megastar Sagittarius, Renaissance V*)
Information:	(800) 888–9378
Web site:	www.cruisewest.com
Passenger capacity:	114 (double occupancy)
Crew:	65
Passenger-to-crew ratio:	1.75:1
Tonnage:	1,263
Length:	295 feet
Beam:	50 feet
Draft:	13 feet
Cruising speed:	15.5 knots
Guest decks:	5
Total cabins:	57

Outside:	57
Inside:	0
Suites:	0
Wheelchair cabins:	None indicated
Cuisine:	Regional American
Style:	Casual
Price notes:	Single supplement, 125 to 175 percent
Tipping suggestions:	$10 pp/pd
Best deal:	Early-booking discount

Launched in 1990, **Spirit of Oceanus** has fifty-seven oversize staterooms ranging in size from 215 to 353 square feet, as much as twice the size of standard cabins on other ships. Twelve cabins have private teak verandas.

The ship, originally built for Star Cruises, sailed as *Megastar Sagittarius* and was later renamed *Renaissance V* for upscale Renaissance Cruises. *Spirit of Oceanus* splits its time between Alaska in summer and the South Pacific in winter, with forays into Asia between seasons.

Renovations by Cruise West included the removal of the casino and hair salon; both have been replaced with more public and lounge space. The ship flies the Bahamas flag and has a predominantly foreign crew.

Spirit of '98

Econoguide rating:	★★ 56 points
Ship size:	Small
Category:	Adventure
Price range:	Opulent $$$$
Registry:	United States
Year built:	1984 (formerly *Pilgrim Belle, Colonial Explorer,* and *Victorian Empress*; refurbished 1995)
Information:	(800) 888–9378
Web site:	www.cruisewest.com
Passenger capacity:	96 (double occupancy)
Crew:	26
Passenger-to-crew ratio:	3.7:1
Tonnage:	96
Length:	192 feet
Beam:	40 feet
Draft:	9.3 feet
Cruising speed:	13 knots
Guest decks:	4
Total cabins:	49
Outside:	48

Inside:	0
Suites:	1
Wheelchair cabins:	1
Cuisine:	Regional American; single, open seating
Style:	Casual
Price notes:	Two single cabins available, 125 to 175 percent supplement
Tipping suggestions:	$10 pp/pd
Best deal:	Early-booking discount

A modern-day re-creation of a Victorian-era riverboat, with nice attention to detail, the ***Spirit of '98*** was built to resemble old-time coastal cruising vessels; her Gay Nineties interior includes carved cabinetry, etched glass, and plush upholstery.

The *Spirit of '98* travels the Inside Passage between Seattle and Juneau in the summer, moving to the California Wine Country in the fall. In 1997 the ship helped lead a centennial celebration of the Klondike Gold Rush.

In the summer of 1999 the *Spirit of '98* suffered an unpleasant encounter with a rock about 16 miles into Tracy Arm in Alaska's Inside Passage. There were no reports of injuries or fuel spills, and all ninety-three passengers were transferred to another boat by inflatable rafts. The ship was about 100 yards from shore in the passage when it struck the rock and began taking on water. Some of the ship's crew members remained aboard to operate pumps, and with the aid of the U.S. Coast Guard and another cruise ship, the *Regal Princess*, the flooding was controlled and the ship was rescued.

Spirit of Alaska

Econoguide rating:	★★ 52 points
Ship size:	Small
Category:	Adventure
Price range:	Opulent $$$$
Registry:	United States
Year built:	1980 (formerly *Pacific Northwest Explorer*)
Information:	(800) 888–9378
Web site:	www.cruisewest.com
Passenger capacity:	78 (double occupancy)
Crew:	21
Passenger-to-crew ratio:	3.7:1
Tonnage:	97
Length:	143 feet
Beam:	28 feet
Draft:	7.5 feet
Cruising speed:	12 knots

Guest decks:	4
Total cabins:	39
Outside:	27
Inside:	12
Suites:	3
Wheelchair cabins:	0
Cuisine:	American; single, open seating
Style:	Casual
Tipping suggestions:	$10 pp/pd
Best deal:	Early-booking discount

The **Spirit of Alaska** cruises Prince William Sound in summer and the Columbia and Snake Rivers in spring and fall. Guests are accommodated in staterooms that range from lower-deck inside cabins that have two single beds to upper-deck cabins that have double beds or two single beds, as well as windows. *Spirit of Alaska* is the near-twin sister to the *Spirit of Columbia.*

Spirit of Columbia

Econoguide rating:	★★ 52 points
Ship size:	Small
Category:	Adventure
Price range:	Opulent $$$$
Registry:	United States
Year built:	1979 (formerly *New Shoreham II*; refurbished 1995)
Information:	(800) 888–9378
Web site:	www.cruisewest.com
Passenger capacity:	78 (double occupancy)
Crew:	21
Passenger-to-crew ratio:	3.7:1
Tonnage:	98
Length:	143 feet
Beam:	28 feet
Draft:	6.5 feet
Cruising speed:	9 knots
Guest decks:	3
Total cabins:	38
Outside:	27
Inside:	11
Suites:	4
Wheelchair cabins:	0
Cuisine:	American; single, open seating
Style:	Casual

Tipping suggestions:	$10 pp/pd
Best deal:	Early-booking discount

The **Spirit of Columbia** sails weekly in the summer between Ketchikan and Juneau. In spring and fall, the ship cruises Canada's Inside Passage round-trip from Seattle.

The ship, sister to the *Spirit of Alaska*, carries seventy-eight guests.

Spirit of Discovery

Econoguide rating:	★★ 52 points
Ship size:	Small
Category:	Adventure
Price range:	Opulent $$$$
Registry:	United States
Year built:	1976 (formerly *Independence, Columbia*; refurbished 1992)
Information:	(800) 888–9378
Web site:	www.cruisewest.com
Passenger capacity:	84 (double occupancy)
Crew:	21
Passenger-to-crew ratio:	4:1
Tonnage:	94
Length:	166 feet
Beam:	37 feet
Draft:	7.5 feet
Cruising speed:	13 knots
Guest decks:	3
Total cabins:	43
Outside:	43
Inside:	0
Suites:	0
Wheelchair cabins:	0
Cuisine:	American; single, open seating
Style:	Casual
Price notes:	Two single cabins available, 125 to 175 percent premium
Tipping suggestions:	$10 pp/pd
Best deal:	Early-booking discount

The **Spirit of Discovery** sails within Alaska between Ketchikan and Juneau in summer and in fall cruises the Columbia and Snake Rivers.

Spirit of Endeavour

Econoguide rating:	★★ 52 points
Ship size:	Small
Category:	Adventure
Price range:	Opulent $$$$
Registry:	United States
Year built:	1983 (formerly *Newport Clipper, Sea Spirit*; refurbished 1996, 1999)
Information:	(800) 888–9378
Web site:	www.cruisewest.com
Passenger capacity:	102 (double occupancy)
Crew:	28
Passenger-to-crew ratio:	3.6:1
Tonnage:	95
Length:	217 feet
Beam:	37 feet
Draft:	8.5 feet
Cruising speed:	12 knots
Guest decks:	4
Total cabins:	51
Outside:	51
Inside:	0
Suites:	0
Wheelchair cabins:	0
Cuisine:	American; single, open seating
Style:	Casual
Price notes:	Single supplement, 125 to 175 percent
Tipping suggestions:	$10 pp/pd
Best deal:	Early-booking discount

The **Spirit of Endeavour** cruises the Inside Passage between Seattle and Juneau in summer, moving to California Wine Country in fall, and on to Baja Mexico's Sea of Cortés in winter.

Pacific Explorer

Econoguide rating:	★★ 53 points
Ship size:	Small
Category:	Adventure
Price range:	Premium $$$
Registry:	Panama

Year built:	1995 (as *Temptress Explorer*); remodeled 1998
Information:	(800) 888–9378
Web site:	www.cruisewest.com
Passenger capacity:	100 (double occupancy)
Crew:	25; Costa Rican
Passenger-to-crew ratio:	4:1
Tonnage:	438
Length:	185 feet
Beam:	40 feet
Draft:	12.5 feet
Cruising speed:	12 knots
Guest decks:	4
Total cabins:	50
Outside:	50
Inside:	0
Suites:	4
Wheelchair cabins:	0
Cuisine:	International; with Central American specialties
Style:	Casual
Price notes:	Single cabins, 125 to 175 percent premium
Tipping suggestions:	$10 pp/pd
Best deal:	Early-booking discount

The neat *Pacific Explorer* looks like a pocket version of a major cruise ship, with fifty outside cabins and an open top deck for sight-seeing. The ship visits Panama, Belize, Honduras, Guatemala, and Costa Rica year-round.

DELTA QUEEN STEAMBOAT COMPANY

THE DELTA QUEEN STEAMBOAT CO.

Address: Robin Street Wharf
1380 Port of New Orleans Place
New Orleans, LA 70130-1890
Information: (800) 543–1949
www.deltaqueen.com
Econoguide's Best Adventure Cruise Lines

The Delta Queen Steamboat Fleet

American Queen	1995	436 passengers	3,707 tons
Delta Queen	1927	174 passengers	3,360 tons
Mississippi Queen	1976, refurbished 1996	414 passengers	3,364 tons

The Delta Queen Steamboat Company, the oldest U.S. flag cruise line, returned to the rivers of America in summer 2002, a season after it went aground when an overly ambitious expansion program foundered.

New owner Delaware North Companies bought the company in a bankruptcy sale and has returned its three ships—the *Delta Queen,* the *Mississippi Queen,* and the *American Queen*—to year-round schedules on the rivers of America.

American Classic Voyages Company, the former parent company of the Delta Queen Steamboat Company, had attempted to expand in three other directions in 2001: American Hawaii Cruises, operating the *Independence* and the *Patriot* (the reflagged *Nieuw Amsterdam* of Holland) on cruises in Hawaii; the new Delta Queen Coastal Voyages, which built a pair of small coastwise packet boats, the *Cape Cod Light* and the *Cape May Light;* and the new United States Line, which commissioned the first new American-built cruise ships in forty years—a pair of 1,900-passenger, 72,000-ton ships, one of which was about half-finished when the company went under.

Delaware North, a hospitality and food service provider, is one of the largest privately held companies in the United States with more than $1.6 billion in annual revenue.

■ THE DELTA QUEEN STEAMBOAT COMPANY STORY

The cruise line traces its lineage back to 1890 when a young riverboat captain bought his first paddle wheeler. The fleet, founded by Captain Gordon Greene and his wife, Mary Becker Greene, also a licensed steamboat captain, eventually included thirty boats.

The flagship of the current fleet is the *Delta Queen,* a National Historic Landmark. She was launched in 1927, built with the finest woods available, including teak, oak, birch, and Oregon cedar; within she features Tiffany-style stained-glass windows and gleaming brass fixtures. The larger *Mississippi Queen* was launched in 1976.

These are real paddle wheelers; the main source of propulsion is that large red contraption at the stern. (They are updated a bit, with bow thrusters located below the waterline for maneuvering, and modern navigational devices.)

■ STEAMBOATIN'

At the peak of the steamboat era, from about 1811 to the early 1900s, there were more than 10,000 of these vessels on U.S. rivers. Onboard an old-style steamboat, the master of ceremonies is the "Interlocutor"; on the ships in the Delta Queen fleet, he oversees a cast of musicians and singers that pays tribute to American music, from Stephen Foster to Dixieland jazz to bluegrass to Broadway.

For many, the meal service onboard the steamboats is worth the trip, even though it would not qualify as haute cuisine. The boats feature regional American specialties such as bayou stuffed catfish, Cincinnati five-way chili, Minnesota wild rice soup, fried green tomatoes, and other down-home cooking.

The line also has an interesting mix of theme cruises, from Big Band to '50s rock to Elvis and Mark Twain (not together). Several voyages are "tramping" itineraries; on these, the boat will stop at the whim of the captain.

The annual Great Steamboat Race between the *Delta Queen* and *Mississippi Queen,* a most casual event, is usually scheduled for the last week of June, finishing on or about the Fourth of July.

Lewis & Clark Vacations take travelers to areas of interest to aficionados of Meriwether Lewis, William Clark and their stalwart Corps of Discovery in the early 1800s. Guest historians provide lectures on cruises in the upper Mississippi River.

ITINERARIES

Today the Delta Queen Steamboat Company's boats explore the inner passage of America on ten major waterways. The main road is the Mississippi, which meanders some 2,350 miles from its mouth below New Orleans to Saint Paul in Minnesota.

In 2003 cruises traveled the lower Mississippi from Galveston and New Orleans to Memphis; the upper Mississippi from Memphis through St. Louis to Minneapolis/St. Paul; and Wilderness Rivers from Chatanooga and Nashville to Louisville, Cincinnati, and Pittsburgh.

Steamboat race fans could also ride along for a number of special events. The *Mississippi Queen* and *American Queen* squared off for the Southern Steamboat Scramble between New Orleans and Memphis. Later, the *Delta Queen* renewed her decades-old rivalry with the venerable *Belle of Louisville* during the Kentucky Derby Great Steamboat Race. The final racing event had the *Delta Queen* and the *Mississippi Queen* shoving off from New Orleans for the Great Steamboat Race to St. Louis, a time-honored tradition retracing the route of the 1870 contest between the *Natchez* and the *Rob't E. Lee.*

WEB SITE

Delta Queen's Web site presents basic information about the cruise line and itineraries. There is no on-line provision to check availability. Visitors must call the cruise line to book a cruise or go through a travel agent. ***Ease of use: good.***

American Queen

Econoguide rating:	★★★ 75 points
Ship size:	Small
Category:	Adventure
Price range:	Premium $$$
Registry:	United States
Year built:	1995
Information:	(800) 543-1949

Web site:	www.deltaqueen.com
Passenger capacity:	436 (double occupancy)
Crew:	180
Passenger-to-crew ratio:	2.4:1
Tonnage:	3,707
Passenger-space ratio:	19.3
Length:	418 feet
Beam:	89.4 feet
Draft:	8.6 feet
Cruising speed:	13 knots
Guest decks:	6
Total cabins:	222
Outside:	72
Inside:	150
Suites:	24
Wheelchair cabins:	9
Cuisine:	American regional
Style:	Casual by day, semiformal at night
Price notes:	Single-occupancy premium, 150 to 175 percent
Tipping suggestions:	$11.50 pp/pd
Best deal:	Early-booking incentives

This re-creation of an opulent nineteenth-century floating palace is the largest steamboat ever built. The **American Queen** stands 97 feet tall when her

American Queen. Photo courtesy of Delta Queen Steamboat Company

twin fluted stacks are fully extended; the stacks and the pilot house can be lowered to 55 feet to pass beneath low bridges.

The ship is furnished largely with antique furniture, vintage artwork, photographs, and books. Her J. M. White Dining Room has filigree woodwork, stunning chandeliers, and a full view of the riverside. The two-story Grand Saloon has private box seats in the mezzanine, in the style of an 1890s opera house. Other public rooms include the delicate Ladies' Parlor, the leather-upholstered Gentlemen's Card Room, and the Engine Room Bar. The ship's library has more than 600 volumes, including many classic, late-nineteenth-century accounts of river lore.

The *American Queen* still uses steam to propel its 30-foot-wide, forty-five ton paddle wheel; the builders refurbished a pair of 1930s-era steam engines that once drove a U.S. Army Corps of Engineers dredge.

Nearly every cruise has a theme; examples include Dixie Fest, Gardens of the River, the Civil War, Rockin' on the River, Fall Foliage, and Southern Christmas.

"Riverlorians" and naturalists present talks about the history, culture, and lore of the river.

Delta Queen

Econoguide rating:	★★★ 75 points
Ship size:	Small
Category:	Adventure
Price range:	Premium $$$
Registry:	United States
Year built:	1927
Information:	(800) 543–1949
Web site:	www.deltaqueen.com
Passenger capacity:	174 (double occupancy)
Crew:	75
Passenger-to-crew ratio:	2.32:1
Tonnage:	3,360
Passenger-space ratio:	19.3
Length:	285 feet
Beam:	60 feet
Draft:	9 feet
Cruising speed:	9 knots
Guest decks:	4
Total cabins:	87
Outside:	87
Inside:	0
Suites:	4

Wheelchair cabins:	0
Cuisine:	American regional
Style:	Casual by day, semiformal at night
Price notes:	Single-occupancy premium, 150 to 175 percent
Tipping suggestions:	$11.50 pp/pd
Best deal:	Early-booking incentives

Here's a chance to sail aboard a floating National Historic Landmark. The **Delta Queen** was launched in Stockton, California, in 1928 at a then impressive cost of $1 million. She boasts a fully welded steel hull; her superstructure and paddle wheel are made of various woods, reinforced with steel. The plates for the hull were fabricated in Scotland and then shipped to California for assembly.

The ship operated as a coastal steamboat between San Francisco and Sacramento from 1927 through 1940. During World War II, painted Navy gray, the *Delta Queen* was operated as a U.S. Navy ferry in San Francisco Bay. After the war, the *Delta Queen* was auctioned off for $46,250 (a fraction of its original cost) by the government and purchased by Tom Greene, president of the Cincinnati-based Greene Line Steamers.

The next problem: getting the ship from California to the inland rivers. A huge watertight crate was constructed to protect the *Delta Queen* from the ocean, and she set off on a 5,000-mile voyage from San Francisco—under tow through the Panama Canal, north into the Gulf of Mexico, and finally up the Mississippi River to New Orleans—arriving May 21, 1947. There she was uncrated before setting off to Pittsburgh under steam for a major face-lift.

The interior was restored and reconfigured for new staterooms and dining rooms. The *Delta Queen*'s steam calliope was recovered from the sunken showboat *Water Queen* and installed on the paddle wheeler in 1947.

The forty-four-ton paddle wheel is driven by a pair of steam engines with a combined 2,000 horsepower, capable of producing a top speed of nearly 10 miles per hour.

The ship's wooden superstructure was almost her undoing in the late 1960s, but the steamboat was granted an exemption from federal safety legislation by Congress. The boat also does not have elevators and is not especially easy to navigate for mobility-impaired passengers; the *Mississippi Queen* and *American Queen* are more accommodating in this regard.

Most cruises include a historian, "riverlorian," or naturalist. Theme cruises in recent years have included Mardi Gras, Spring Pilgrimage, Kentucky Derby, Cajun Culture, Mark Twain, Dickens on the Strand, and Old-Fashioned Holidays. There are no childrens' programs on the steamboats.

The *Delta Queen*'s twin, the *Delta King,* is a floating hotel in Sacramento.

Mississippi Queen

Econoguide rating:	★★★ 75 points
Ship size:	Small
Category:	Adventure
Price range:	Premium $$$
Registry:	United States
Year built:	1976 (refurbished 1996)
Information:	(800) 543–1949
Web site:	www.deltaqueen.com
Passenger capacity:	416 (double occupancy)
Crew:	156
Passenger-to-crew ratio:	2.6:1
Tonnage:	3,364
Passenger-space ratio:	8.0
Length:	382 feet
Beam:	68 feet
Draft:	9 feet
Cruising speed:	9.5 knots
Guest decks:	7
Total cabins:	208
Outside:	135
Inside:	73
Suites:	26
Wheelchair cabins:	1
Cuisine:	American regional
Style:	Casual by day, semiformal at night
Tipping suggestions:	$11.50 pp/pd
Best deal:	Early-booking incentives

The **Mississippi Queen** is a modern re-creation of a classic steamboat, built in 1976 and refurbished in 1996 in Victorian style. The boat was built at the former Howard Shipyard in Jeffersonville, Illinois, where, beginning in 1834, more than 4,800 steamboats were built, including the famous *J. M. White* in 1878.

Half the 208 staterooms offer a private veranda. All the cabins are named after river towns, old riverboats, and historic Civil War sites.

The *Mississippi Queen*'s calliope, with forty-four whistles, is the world's largest. The two-story Paddlewheel Lounge, decorated as an 1890s saloon, offers ragtime, Dixieland, and banjo music. In the Forward Cabin Lounge is a grand silver water cooler of the style of the Reed and Barton cooler that adorned the *J. M. White*. At midship, the grand staircase is topped with a trompe l'oeil ceiling of cherubs frolicking among the clouds.

Historians, "riverlorians," and naturalists accompany most cruises. In recent years theme cruises have included Big Band, Mardi Gras, Spring Pilgrimage, Kentucky Derby, Korean War Years, the Great Steamboat Race, Old-Fashioned Thanksgiving, and Southern Christmas holidays. There are no childrens' programs on the steamboats.

GLACIER BAY CRUISE LINE

Address: 107 West Denny Way, Suite 303
Seattle, WA 98119
Information: (800) 451–5952, (206) 623–7110
www.glacierbaytours.com

The Glacier Bay Fleet

Wilderness Adventurer	1983	72 passengers	98 tons
Wilderness Discoverer	1993	88 passengers	95 tons
Wilderness Explorer	1969	36 passengers	98 tons

With a small fleet of intimate soft-adventure ships owned by an Alaskan company, Glacier Bay makes the most of its shallow-draft vessels to explore some of the more remote inlets of our most isolated state. The ships visit Alaska's Inside Passage, Glacier Bay National Park, Tracy Arm fjord, and Admiralty Island National Monument. All voyages include the option for sea kayaking and onshore hiking.

Glacier Bay has in the past offered various discounts for preseason advance bookings and in 2002 also offered free air transportation between Juneau and Seattle or reverse for spring and fall repositioning cruises.

■ WEB SITE

Glacier Bay's Web site presents basic information about the cruise line and itineraries. There is no on-line provision to check availability. Visitors must call the cruise line to book a cruise or go through a travel agent. ***Ease of use: good.***

Wilderness Adventurer

Econoguide rating:	★★ 52 points
Ship size:	Small
Category:	Adventure
Price range:	Premium $$$
Registry:	United States
Year built:	1983 (formerly *Caribbean Prince*)
Information:	(800) 451–5952

Web site:	www.glacierbaytours.com
Passenger capacity:	72 (double occupancy)
Crew:	19
Passenger-to-crew ratio:	3.8:1
Tonnage:	89
Length:	156.6 feet
Beam:	38 feet
Draft:	6.5 feet
Cruising speed:	10 knots
Guest decks:	4
Total cabins:	34
Outside:	34 (B cabins have no windows)
Inside:	0
Suites:	0
Cuisine:	Alaskan
Style:	Casual
Price notes:	Single supplement, 175 percent of cabin category chosen; triple rates (three in a room) on request
Tipping suggestions:	$10 pp/pd

The **Wilderness Adventurer** carries a fleet of stable two-person sea kayaks for up-close exploration of southeast Alaska's spectacular shoreline. The ship also has a bow ramp for easy access to the shore.

The vessel was given a makeover for the 2001 season. Four new suites were added to the observation deck, and all of the cabins were refurbished. Glacier Bay also brought aboard twenty two-person sea kayaks and a launching platform. Other important work included updates to the vessel to meet strict new emission requirements, and improved fire protection systems throughout the vessel.

The ship had a minor mishap in June 1999 in Glacier Bay National Park and Reserve, going aground and spilling some of its fuel.

Wilderness Discoverer

Econoguide rating:	★★ 52 points
Ship size:	Small
Category:	Adventure
Price range:	Premium $$$
Registry:	United States
Year built:	1993 (formerly Mayan Prince)
Information:	(800) 451–5952
Web site:	www.glacierbaytours.com
Passenger capacity:	88 (double occupancy)
Crew:	19
Passenger-to-crew ratio:	4.6:1

Tonnage:	95
Draft:	6.6 feet
Length:	169 feet
Beam:	38 feet
Cruising speed:	12 knots
Guest decks:	4
Total cabins:	44
Outside:	44 (category B staterooms have no windows)
Inside:	0
Suites:	0
Cuisine:	Alaskan specialties
Style:	Casual
Price notes:	Single supplement, 175 percent; triple rate (three in a room) on request
Tipping suggestions:	$10 pp/pd

The largest ship in the Glacier Bay fleet, **Wilderness Discoverer** is still intimate, with just forty-four cabins on four decks. She sails one-way between Juneau and Sitka or reverse.

Wilderness Explorer

Econoguide rating:	★★ 50 points
Ship size:	Small
Category:	Adventure
Price range:	Premium $$$
Registry:	United States
Year built:	1969
Information:	(800) 451–5952
Web site:	www.glacierbaytours.com
Passenger capacity:	34 (double occupancy)
Crew:	13
Passenger-to-crew ratio:	2.6:1
Tonnage:	98
Draft:	6.6 feet
Length:	112 feet
Beam:	22 feet
Cruising speed:	9 knots
Guest decks:	3
Total cabins:	17
Outside:	17
Inside:	0
Suites:	0
Cuisine:	Alaskan

Style:	Casual
Price notes:	Single supplement, 175 percent
Tipping suggestions:	$10 pp/pd

Luxury lies beyond the windows of the **Wilderness Explorer,** not in the small but comfortable cabins and public rooms. The vessel is the only cruise to regularly begin and end in Glacier Bay National Park.

Wilderness Explorer ran aground in an inlet 70 miles west of Juneau in 1999; there were no injuries and the ship was repaired.

LINDBLAD SPECIAL EXPEDITIONS

SVEN·OLOF·LINDBLAD'S

SPECIAL⊙EXPEDITIONS

Address: 720 Fifth Avenue
New York, NY 10019
Information: (800) 397–3348
www.expeditions.com

🏵 🏵 🏵

The Lindblad Special Expeditions Fleet

Endeavour	1966	110 passengers	3,132 tons
Polaris	1959	80 passengers	2,214 tons
Sea Voyager	1982	64 passengers	1,195 tons
Sea Bird	1981	70 passengers	100 tons
Sea Lion	1982	70 passengers	100 tons

The Lindblad family has been taking travelers to extraordinary destinations since 1979, visiting Alaska, the Pacific Northwest, Baja California, Central and South America, the Galapagos Islands, Western Europe, Egypt, the Baltics, Antarctica, the Mediterranean, Australia, and New Zealand.

The company traces its roots to Lars-Eric Lindblad, who began a travel agency in 1958, specializing in visits to far-flung places such as Antarctica, the Galapagos, China, Mongolia, Tibet, and Africa. Today the company is run by his son, Sven-Olof.

The company's fleet of oceangoing vessels carries between 64 and 110 passengers. The ships are equipped with Zodiac landing craft; some also carry sea kayaks. These are tours for active travelers—swimmers, kayakers, snorkelers, hikers—and observers of all sorts. The onboard entertainment consists of naturalists and scientists who explain the views all around.

On these small ships, the accommodations and public areas can best be described as casual and intimate. There are open sundecks for observation, a dining room, and a lounge. Don't look for a casino, hydrotherapy pool, or a virtual-reality/multimedia entertainment center; the excitement is outside.

The line also offers a series of special photo expeditions conducted by naturalists and professional photographers who help guests record their journeys.

■ ITINERARIES

Sea Voyager is stationed year-round in Central America, sailing in the waters off Belize, Costa Rica, Guatemala, Honduras, Nicaragua, and Panama.

Sea Lion and *Sea Bird* sail in Alaska's coastal waters for the summer; in May and August the ships venture into Alaska, British Columbia, and the San Juan Islands. The same ships sail in Baja California and the Sea of Cortés from January through April.

Polaris sails year-round in the Galapagos Islands, with excurions to Peru and Ecuador.

Endeavour sails the world, visiting South America in October, and moving on to the Falkland Islands and Antarctica from November through February. Crossing the Atlantic in March, the ship sails in Europe from April through September, including visits to Scandinavia and the Mediterranean.

■ WEB SITE

The Lindblad Web site presents basic information about the cruise line and itineraries. There is no on-line provision to check availability. Visitors must call the cruise line to book a cruise or go through a travel agent. ***Ease of use: fair.***

Sea Bird

Econoguide rating:	★★ 52 points
Ship size:	Small
Category:	Adventure
Price range:	Premium $$$
Registry:	United States
Year built:	1982 (formerly *Majestic Explorer;* refurbished 1995)
Information:	(800) 397–3348
Web site:	www.expeditions.com
Passenger capacity:	70 (double occupancy)
Crew:	21
Passenger-to-crew ratio:	2.5:1
Tonnage:	100
Length:	152 feet
Beam:	31 feet
Draft:	8 feet
Cruising speed:	12 knots
Guest decks:	4
Total cabins:	35
Outside:	35
Inside:	0
Suites:	0

Wheelchair cabins:	Main deck, category 3 cabins; no elevators onboard
Cuisine:	American
Style:	Informal
Price notes:	Single-occupancy premium, about 150 percent
Tipping suggestions:	$9.00 pp/pd

Sea Bird is a comfortable transport to some of the most remote places on earth. Guests venture out in Zodiac landing craft to view whales and explore on-shore happenings. Most voyages carry naturalists and other lecturers.

Sea Lion

Econoguide rating:	★★ 52 points
Ship size:	Small
Category:	Adventure
Price range:	Premium $$$
Registry:	United States
Year built:	1981 (formerly *Great Rivers Explorer*, refurbished 1995)
Information:	(800) 397–3348
Web site:	www.expeditions.com
Passenger capacity:	70 (double occupancy)
Crew:	21
Passenger-to-crew ratio:	3.3:1
Tonnage:	100
Length:	152 feet
Beam:	31 feet
Draft:	8 feet
Cruising speed:	12 knots
Guest decks:	4
Total cabins:	37
Outside:	37
Inside:	0
Suites:	0
Wheelchair cabins:	Main deck, category 3 cabins; no elevators onboard
Cuisine:	American
Style:	Informal
Price notes:	Single-occupancy premium, about 150 percent
Tipping suggestions:	$9.00 pp/pd

Sea Lion is designed top to bottom for her role as an expedition vessel to exotic and remote ports in search of wildlife in the sea, the sky, and shore; much of her public areas are geared to serve as observation platforms.

Sea Voyager

Econoguide rating:	★★ 52 points
Ship size:	Small
Category:	Adventure
Price range:	Premium $$$
Registry:	United States
Year built:	1982 (formerly *Temptress Voyager*; refurbished 2001)
Information:	(800) 397–3348
Web site:	www.expeditions.com
Passenger capacity:	64 (double occupancy)
Crew:	25
Passenger-to-crew ratio:	2.6:1
Tonnage:	1,195
Length:	175 feet
Beam:	40 feet
Draft:	12 feet
Cruising speed:	12 knots
Guest decks:	3
Total cabins:	33
Outside:	33
Inside:	0
Suites:	0
Cuisine:	Regional
Style:	Informal
Tipping suggestions:	$9.00 pp/pd

The **Sea Voyager** was added to the Lindblad fleet in 2001 after a major refitting. Stationed full-time in Central America, the ship includes a full-time undersea specialist and carries a variety of equipment for exploring the area waters, including underwater cameras and video microscopes. A fleet of Zodiacs, inflatable kayaks, and snorkeling gear are offered to guests.

Endeavour

Econoguide rating:	★★★ 68 points
Ship size:	Small
Category:	Adventure
Price range:	Premium $$$
Registry:	Bahamas
Year built:	1966 (formerly *Caledonian Star*, renamed in 2001; refurbished 1998)

Information:	(800) 397–3348
Web site:	www.expeditions.com
Passenger capacity:	110 (double occupancy)
Crew:	45
Passenger-to-crew ratio:	2.4:1
Tonnage:	3,132
Length:	295 feet
Beam:	46 feet
Draft:	21 feet
Cruising speed:	12 knots
Guest decks:	5
Total cabins:	61
Outside:	61
Inside:	0
Cuisine:	International
Style:	Informal
Tipping suggestions:	$9.00 pp/pd

Lindblad Expeditions renamed the *Caledonian Star* as **Endeavour** in honor of famed explorer Captain James Cook's ship at a ceremony in Whitby, England, in 2001. Three of Cook's ships—*Endeavour, Resolution,* and *Adventure*—were built in Whitby in the second half of the eighteenth century.

Cook made discoveries and charted coastlines from the Arctic to the Antarctic, gaining Australia and New Zealand for Britain. The original *Endeavour* was built to transport coal; the *Caledonian Star* first went to sea as a trawler.

The modern ship includes an array of scientific equipment for exploration above and below the water, including a remotely operated vehicle with a video camera that can be piloted from the surface in areas not suitable for a diver, such as under unstable icebergs. Diving and underwater filming by a naturalist take place when conditions permit. Hydrophones allow guests to hear vocalizations from marine mammals such as whales and dolphins. The ship is also equipped with sea kayaks to allow guests of all skill levels to explore the Arctic and Antarctic.

Polaris

Econoguide rating:	★★ 61 points
Ship size:	Small
Category:	Adventure
Price range:	Premium $$$
Registry:	Ecuador
Year built:	1959 (formerly *Oresund;* refurbished 1987)
Information:	(800) 397–3348
Web site:	www.expeditions.com
Passenger capacity:	80 (double occupancy)

Crew:	34
Passenger-to-crew ratio:	2.3:1
Tonnage:	2,214
Length:	238 feet
Beam:	42.7 feet
Draft:	20 feet
Cruising speed:	12 knots
Guest decks:	3
Total cabins:	41
Outside:	41
Inside:	0
Cuisine:	International
Style:	Informal
Tipping suggestions:	$9.00 pp/pd

Polaris was built as a small ferry but was refurbished by Lindblad to serve as an expedition vessel. The Lookout Point on the Sky Deck is a favorite spot, along with the bridge, which is open to guests.

RIVERBARGE EXCURSIONS LINE

RiverBarge Excursions

Address: 201 Opelousas Avenue
New Orleans, LA 70114
Information: (888) 462–2743
www.riverbarge.com

The RiverBarge Fleet

River Explorer	1998	198 passengers	8,864 tons

River Explorer is the only hotel barge traveling America's rivers and inland waterways. The vessel is made up of two 295-foot-long river barges, pushed along by the *Miss Nari*, a 3,000-horsepower towboat.

The company is the brainchild of Eddie Conrad, a native of New Orleans who has devoted his life to the rivers; he founded a successful towing company in Louisiana. In 1990 he began carrying recreational vehicles along the bayous and backwaters of Southern Louisiana and the Mississippi River, expanding his offerings in 1998 with the launch of the *River Explorer*.

■ ITINERARIES

The company offers four- to ten-day excursions on the lower and upper Mississippi River, the Cumberland River Valley, the Atchafalaya River Basin, Ohio River Valley, Missouri River, and along the Texas-Louisiana Gulf Intracoastal Waterway.

Ports of embarkation include New Orleans, Memphis, Saint Louis, Kansas City, Nashville, Cincinnati, and Galveston. Fares include all scheduled shore excursions.

In 2003 RiverBarge added four "America's Junction" trips along the Ohio and upper Mississippi Rivers to replace its summer Missouri River itineraries—the result of permitting issues raised by the U.S. Army Corps of Engineers and the U.S. Fish and Wildlife Services working to protect nests of forty-one endangered piping plovers and least terns on the river. Plans call for a return to the Missouri in 2004 if permitted. The replacement cruises sailed from St. Louis to Cincinnati: a pair of round-trips from Cincinnati to West Virginia and a return from Cincinnati to St. Louis with stops in the river towns of Madison, Indiana, and Paducah, Kentucky, on the Ohio River and Cape Girardeau, Missouri, on the Mississippi.

■ WEB SITE

The Web site presents basic information about the cruise line and itineraries. There is no on-line provision to check availability. Visitors must call the cruise line to book a cruise or go through a travel agent. *Ease of use: good.*

River Explorer

Econoguide rating:	★★★ 65 points
Ship size:	Small
Category:	Adventure
Price range:	Premium $$$
Registry:	United States
Year built:	1998
Information:	(888) 462–2743
Web site:	www.riverbarge.com
Passenger capacity:	198 (double occupancy)
Crew:	40
Passenger-to-crew ratio:	5:1
Tonnage:	8,864
Length:	730 feet
Beam:	54 feet
Draft:	8.5 feet
Cruising speed:	9 knots
Guest decks:	3
Total cabins:	98
Outside:	98
Inside:	0
Suites:	0
Wheelchair cabins:	3
Cuisine:	American regional

Style:	Casual
Tipping suggestions:	Included
Best deal:	Advance-booking onboard credits; discounts for active or retired teachers

The *River Explorer*'s forward barge, DeSoto, holds public rooms; the aft barge, LaSalle, is home to ninety-eight identical staterooms. Cabins on the upper Platinum Deck include verandas; Royal Deck staterooms have a picture window.

The Galley features home-style cooking and is able to accommodate all passengers in a single open seating. Just like at home, the kitchen is always open, allowing guests to raid the fridge anytime.

The Guest Pilot House is a replica of the real pilot house; open to guests, it features radar displays and radios with actual transmissions from the bridge.

(A cruise diary about a trip on the *River Explorer* is included in Chapter 11.)

SOCIETY EXPEDITIONS

Address: 2001 Western Avenue, Suite 300
Seattle, WA 98121
Information: (800) 548–8669
www.societyexpeditions.com

The Society Expeditions Fleet

World Discoverer	1989	160 passengers	6,000 tons

Society Expeditions was one of the pioneers of expedition-style cruising. The company was founded in 1974 as the Society for the Preservation of Archaeological Monuments to escort five small groups of adventurers to Easter Island. The profits were donated to aid the restoration of the gigantic stone moai statues. The company's name was changed to Society Expeditions in 1976 when more destinations were added. It is now owned by a German firm.

The original *World Discoverer* was chartered in 1980 to conduct a series of Amazon expedition cruises. One of only two of the world's expedition cruise ships, the vessel embarked on a long career of explorations to Indonesia, Myanmar, Singapore, Seychelles, Iceland, Greenland, West Africa, Saudi Arabia, Yemen, Polynesia, Melanesia, Micronesia, Korea, Japan, Alaska, the Northwest Passage, Hudson Bay, the Saint Lawrence Seaway, and the Galapagos Islands. The ship went aground in the Solomon Islands in 2000, ending its service.

Society Expeditions' "new" ship replaced the company's original vessel. The new *World Discoverer* was built in 1989 in Finland as a Baltic ferry; it was later purchased by Samsung Industries and refitted for educational seminars.

■ ITINERARIES

The *World Discoverer* lives up to its name with an eclectic collection of cruises mostly in the South Pacific, with summer forays north into Russia and Alaska.

In 2003 the ship sailed to Papua New Guinea in May and September, followed by the Pearls of the South Pacific itinerary that visited Fiji, Tonga, Niue, and the Cook Islands. In October the ship departed from Rarotonga, Cook Islands, for an exploration of the Cook and Society Islands.

At the end of October the ship left Tahiti on a twenty-three-night expedition to the easternmost island of Polynesia, Easter Island. The Wake of the *Bounty* tour visited four coral isles of the Tuamotu Archipelago: the Marquesas Islands; farther eastward to remote Gambiers, made famous in James Michener's *Return to Paradise;* Pitcairn Islands, famed for the mutiny on the *Bounty;* and finally Easter Island.

Other itineraries include Lost Islands of Micronesia and Melanesia, which departed Guam to sail the atolls and islands of Yap, Chuck, Pohnpei, and Papua New Guinea. Treasures of the Coral Seas focused on four Papua New Guinea destinations before cruising on to Vanuatu and Fiji.

From November to February the ship sailed south to Antarctica and the Scotia Sea.

■ WEB SITE

The Society Expeditions Web site presents basic information about the cruise line and itineraries. There is no on-line provision to check availability. Visitors must call the cruise line to book a cruise or go through a travel agent. *Ease of use: good.*

World Discoverer

Econoguide rating:	★★★ 69 points
Ship size:	Small
Category:	Adventure
Price range:	Opulent $$$$
Registry:	Bahamas
Year built:	1989 (formerly *Delphin Star, Dream 21*)
Information:	(800) 548–8669
Web site:	www.societyexpeditions.com
Passenger capacity:	160 (double occupancy)
Crew:	90
Passenger-to-crew ratio:	1.8:1
Tonnage:	6,000
Length:	354 feet
Beam:	52 feet
Draft:	14 feet
Cruising speed:	16 knots
Guest decks:	5
Total cabins:	86
Outside:	86

Inside:	0
Suites:	2
Wheelchair cabins:	2
Cuisine:	Continental
Style:	Casual
Price notes:	Single-occupancy premium, 175 percent of cabin category chosen; triple and quad rates upon request
Tipping suggestions:	Included

Built specifically for expedition cruising, ***World Discoverer*** features an ice-hardened hull and is fully equipped for kayaking, scuba diving, snorkeling, and other sports and transport.

Econoguide Ship Classifications

Gargantuan	130,000 or more tons
Colossus	100,000 to 130,000 tons
Megaship	70,000 to 100,000 tons
Large	40,000 to 70,000 tons
Medium	10,000 to 40,000 tons
Small	Less than 10,000 tons

CHAPTER SEVENTEEN

SAILING VESSELS

𝕏𝕏𝕏𝕏𝕏	Sea Cloud Cruises	𝕏𝕏𝕏	Windjammer Barefoot
𝕏𝕏𝕏	Star Clippers		Cruises
		𝕏𝕏𝕏𝕏	Windstar Cruises

SEA CLOUD CRUISES

Address: 32-40 North Dean Street
Englewood Cliffs, NJ 07631
Information: (888) 732–2568, (201) 227–9404
www.seacloud.com
Econoguide's Best Luxury Cruise Lines
Econoguide's Best Dining at Sea

The Sea Cloud Cruises Fleet

Sea Cloud II	2000	96 passengers	3,000 tons
Sea Cloud	1931	69 passengers	2,532 tons

The four-masted bark *Sea Cloud* was built in 1931 for cereal food heiress Marjorie Merriweather Post by her husband, Wall Street broker Edward F. Hutton. Post, famous for her parties and social events, turned the ship into a gathering place for royalty, heads of state, and society hobnobbers.

After a half century of various adventures, including a stint as a weather observation and submarine spotting ship during World War II and as a notorious party boat for a Panamanian dictator and his son, *Sea Cloud* was restored to her former glory within and without.

More than a football field long, the ship is a place of marble and teak and gold-plated fixtures; several of the original owners' cabins have fireplaces. Dining includes fine wine and beer at lunch, often served beneath a canopy on deck, and dinner in the elegant dining parlor.

The ship was rescued from oblivion by a group of German businessmen who bankrolled her restoration. Modern updates include air-conditioning, some additional cabins, and the latest radar, satellite, and communications gear. But lucky guests are very much at sea in a classic with the feel of the 1930s and earlier. (You can read about a cruise on the *Sea Cloud* in Chapter 11.)

In 2001 a new close cousin was added to the line. *Sea Cloud II* has all of the romance of the original, with many modern touches within.

ITINERARIES

Sea Cloud winters in the Caribbean, sailing mostly fron Antigua. In spring she repositions across the Atlantic to sail in the western Mediterranean from Civitavecchia, Italy, and other ports. In fall the ship sails in the eastern Mediterranean from Turkey and Greece, returning to the Caribbean in December.

Sea Cloud II sails in the Caribbean in winter, mostly from Barbados and Antigua, followed by a repositioning cruise to Lisbon in late April. In May and again from September through October, *Sea Cloud II* usually sails in the western Mediterranean from ports including Barcelona; Monte Carlo; Piraeus, Greece; and Valletta, Malta. In summer 2003 the ship sailed in northern Europe, from ports including Dublin; Edinburgh; Copenhagen; Saint Petersburg, Russia; and Hamburg, Germany. In November the ship was due to return across the Atlantic from Las Palmas to Barbados for winter in the Caribbean.

The classic *Sea Cloud* under full sail. *Courtesy of Sea Cloud Cruises*

■ WEB SITE

The company Web site provides basic information about the ships and itineraries. There is no way to check availability of cabins on specific trips. Reservations must be made by telephone or through a travel agent; visitors can also request a callback from the line. *Ease of use: good.*

Sea Cloud

Econoguide rating:	★★★★★ 94 points
Ship size:	Small
Category:	Adventure
Price range:	Opulent $$$$
Registry:	Malta
Year built:	1931 (formerly SV *Hussar;* refurbished 1979, 1993)
Information:	(888) 732–2568
Web site:	www.seacloud.com
Passenger capacity:	69
Crew:	60
Passenger-to-crew ratio:	1.15:1
Tonnage:	2,532
Length:	360 feet
Beam:	50 feet
Draft:	17 feet
Cruising speed:	12 knots under power
Guest decks:	3
Total cabins:	34
Outside:	34
Inside:	0
Suites:	8
Wheelchair cabins:	0
Cuisine:	Nouvelle; wines included
Style:	Informal
Tipping suggestions:	$10–$12 pp/pd
Best deal:	Various promotions posted on the Web site through the year

If you're very lucky, you'll find yourself in *Sea Cloud*'s Cabin 1, Marjorie Post's own cabin, a seagoing palace complete with a fireplace and bathroom of Carrara marble, mahogany furniture, Louis Philippe chairs, and an antique French bed. But even most of the lesser cabins are rather grand, outfitted in marble and fine furniture. (A few newer cabins, up top, are attractive but simple.) The restaurant, created from the ship's original saloon, is like a fine private club. Passengers receive rotating invitations to sit at the captain's table.

Sea Cloud II

Econoguide rating:	★★★★★ 94 points
Ship size:	Small
Category:	Adventure
Price range:	Opulent $$$$
Registry:	Malta
Year built:	2000
Information:	(888) 732–2568
Web site:	www.seacloud.com
Passenger capacity:	96
Crew:	60
Passenger-to-crew ratio:	1.6:1
Tonnage:	3,000
Length:	384
Beam:	53 feet
Draft:	18 feet
Cruising speed:	14 knots under power
Guest decks:	4
Total cabins:	48
Outside:	48
Inside:	0
Suites:	0
Wheelchair cabins:	0
Cuisine:	Nouvelle; wines included
Style:	Informal
Tipping suggestions:	$10–$12 pp/pd

The *Sea Cloud* gained a new cousin, the ***Sea Cloud II,*** in 2001. The new ship offers forty-eight cabins under a set of rigging with twenty-four sails on masts reaching 174 feet into the sky. Public rooms include an elegant restaurant, lounge, fitness room, and sauna. *Sea Cloud II* also has a water sports platform.

STAR CLIPPERS

STAR CLIPPERS

Address: 4101 Salzedo Street
    Coral Gables, FL 33146
Information: (800) 442–0551
    www.starclippers.com
Econoguide's Best Adventure Cruise Lines

The Star Clippers Fleet

Royal Clipper	2000	228 passengers	5,000 tons
Star Clipper	1992	170 passengers	2,298 tons
Star Flyer	1991	170 passengers	2,298 tons

The ships in the Star Clipper fleet are modern re-creations of the classic clipper sailing ships that were the wonders of the nineteenth century. The clippers were called the greyhounds of the sea in their heyday; the largest of the ships was the *Great Republic*, built in 1853, at 308 feet. Many of the ships sailed from Great Britain or the United States to Asia; the end of the clipper age arrived with the opening of the Suez Canal in 1869, which made the steamboat more cost-effective.

Swedish businessman Mikael Krafft brought the clipper ship back from extinction in 1991 when construction began in Belgium on what would be the largest clipper ship in history, the 360-foot-long *Star Flyer*, later joined by an identical twin, *Star Clipper*. In 2000 the even larger and more opulent 439-foot *Royal Clipper* joined the fleet.

Royal Clipper is the world's largest sailing ship, outsizing the Russian *Sedov* by about 39 feet. Her 226-foot-high mainmast is taller than almost any cruise liner on the seas, holding a suit of forty-two sails. The first five-masted sailing ship constructed in nearly a century, *Royal Clipper* is based on the classic German five-master *Preussen*.

Although the ships are quite modern in their appointments, these are not computerized cruise ships with a sail on top for old-time's sake. The crew—and the passengers—are pressed into service to handle 40,000 square feet of sails on four masts on the *Star Clipper* and *Star Flyer* and 56,000 square feet on five masts on the *Royal Clipper*. Under a strong wind astern, the ships have reached speeds of as much as 17 knots, about the same as a modern cruise ship.

Rooms are attractive and tidy, most with small portholes; a few of the upper deck cabins have doors that open directly onto the main deck. The best views are found up on the large sundecks of the ships, outfitted with deck chairs and lounging spaces alongside several pools. The captain meets with guests every morning to discuss the day's schedule and tell stories of sailing lore and technique.

One of the real treats of these ships is posing for pictures for passengers along the rails of modern Megaships in the harbor; the Star Clippers are among the prettiest sights they're likely to find at sea.

■ ITINERARIES

Royal Clipper sailed out of Barbados in early 2003, cruising to the Windward Islands (Saint Lucia, Îles des Saintes, Antigua, Saint Kitts, Dominica, and Martinique) and the Grenadines (Grenada, Tobago Cays, Saint Vincent, Bequia). The ship crossed the Atlantic to Italy to sail in the western Mediterranean for the summer, returning to the Caribbean in mid-October.

Star Clipper sailed in 2003 in the Caribbean and the Gulf of Mexico through the end of April, when she crossed the Atlantic to cruise the western Mediterranean. In October she returned to Barbados for Caribbean cruises.

In 2003 *Star Flyer* was positioned in the Far East for most of the year, sailing from Phuket, Thailand, to other ports in Thailand and Malaysia. In April she sailed across the Indian Ocean to sail the Greek Islands until October, when she returned to Thailand.

◼ WEB SITE

The Star Clippers Web site provides basic information about the ships and itineraries. There is no way to check availability of cabins on specific trips. Reservations must be made by telephone or through a travel agent; visitors can also request a callback from the line. *Ease of use: very good.*

Royal Clipper

Econoguide rating:	★★★★ 83 points
Ship size:	Small
Category:	Adventure
Price range:	Moderate $$
Registry:	Luxembourg
Year built:	2000
Information:	(800) 442–0551
Web site:	www.star-clippers.com
Passenger capacity:	227
Crew:	105
Passenger-to-crew ratio:	2.2:1
Tonnage:	5,000
Length:	439 feet
Beam:	54 feet
Draft:	18.5 feet
Cruising speed:	Approximately 11 knots under sail
Guest decks:	5
Total cabins:	114
Outside:	108
Inside:	6
Suites:	16
Wheelchair cabins:	0
Cuisine:	International and regional
Style:	Informal
Price notes:	Single-occupancy premium, 150 percent
Tipping suggestions:	$8.00 pp/pd

This is not your basic little sailboat. In fact, **Royal Clipper** is the world's largest sailing ship. Her dimensions follow those of the famed clipper ship *Preussen,* which dominated the world's sail cargo routes from 1902 to 1908. Five steel masts hold forty-two sails aloft, a total area of 56,000 square feet, more than an acre of sail. (For the record, there are twenty-six square sails, eleven staysails, four jibs, and one gaff-rigged spanker.) Under full sail, the *Royal Clipper* is capable of speeds of as much as 20 knots.

The 197-foot-tall mainmast includes a 19-foot hinged top section that can be folded down to allow passage under bridges and other obstructions.

The ship is under sail most of the time, with twin 2,500-horsepower diesel engines in reserve when necessary. Stabilizing tanks are used to reduce roll, and heeling is usually held to less than 6 percent.

Cabins are trimmed in mahogany and brass, with marble bathrooms and color televisions. The three-level dining room is a step back into the Edwardian age. The ceiling above the Piano Bar is the glass bottom of the largest of three swimming pools. The lounge also offers submarine portholes, illuminated after dusk by underwater floodlights.

Each of the five masts includes a passenger lookout platform part of the way up; there's a settee in place, and stewards will deliver refreshments to the perch on call.

A small fleet of boats is available to passengers from the water sports platform that is lowered into the sea from the stern.

Star Clipper, Star Flyer

Econoguide rating:	★★★ 77 points
Ship size:	Small
Category:	Adventure
Price range:	Moderate $$
Registry:	Luxembourg
Year built:	Star Clipper, 1992; Star Flyer, 1991
Information:	(800) 442–0551
Web site:	www.star-clippers.com
Passenger capacity:	170
Crew:	72
Passenger-to-crew ratio:	2.4:1
Tonnage:	2,298
Length:	360 feet
Beam:	50 feet
Draft:	18.5 feet
Cruising speed:	11 knots under sail
Guest decks:	4

Total cabins:	85
Outside:	81
Inside:	4
Suites:	0
Wheelchair cabins:	0
Cuisine:	International and regional
Style:	Informal
Price notes:	Single-occupancy premium, 150 percent
Tipping suggestions:	$8.00 pp/pd

Launched in Ghent, Belgium, the **Star Clipper** and **Star Flyer** are four-masted, square-rigged barkentines with 36,000 square feet of sail. Although they are shorter in length than the *Royal Clipper,* the ships hold the record for the tallest mast in the world, at 226 feet above the waterline.

There are teak decks and a pair of swimming pools. Passenger amenities include an indoor-outdoor bar with a piano lounge and an Edwardian-style library with fireplace.

WINDJAMMER BAREFOOT CRUISES

Address: P.O. Box 190-200
　Miami, FL 33119-0120
Information: (800) 327–2601
　www.windjammer.com

The Windjammer Barefoot Cruises Fleet

Legacy	1959	122 passengers	1,740 tons
Mandalay	1923	72 passengers	420 tons
Polynesia	1938	126 passengers	430 tons
Yankee Clipper	1927	64 passengers	327 tons
Amazing Grace	1955	94 passengers	1,585 tons (motorship)

Windjammer is the largest operator of Tall Ships in the world. The five ships in its fleet have passenger capacities of 64 to 126, sailing year-round in the Caribbean.

According to company lore, Mike Burke woke up in Miami in 1947 with a headache and a 19-foot sloop, purchased sometime during the night with $600 in Navy pay. The boat, christened *Hangover,* became the basis for the Windjammer empire.

Each of the ships has an interesting story of its own, the oldest dating back more than seventy-five years. The vessels have been refurbished and accommodations brought up to modern standards.

The fleet includes some true classics. *Mandalay* was considered one of the most luxurious yachts in the world when she was built in 1923 as a three-masted barkentine for financier E. F. Hutton and his wife, Marjorie Merriweather Post. (The ship was a predecessor to the even more opulent *Sea Cloud,* covered earlier in this chapter.)

Legacy, the flagship of the fleet, was built in 1959 as a meteorological research and exploration ship for the French government.

Polynesia, a four-masted schooner, was built in Holland in 1938 for the Portuguese Grand Banks cod fishing fleet. *Yankee Clipper,* the only armor-plated private yacht in the world, was built in 1927 for German arms maker Alfred Krupp. She was confiscated by the United States after World War II and later acquired by the Vanderbilt family and raced off California.

Amazing Grace is a former Scottish service ship, built in 1955, that provided supplies to North Sea lighthouses. The motorized vessel today supplies the five sailing vessels in the Windjammer fleet, carrying passengers on a full itinerary of Caribbean stops.

Windjammer suffered a major loss in 1998 with the destruction of the *Fantome* during Hurricane Mitch off Central America; the ship's passengers had been safely deposited in port, but the crew of thirty-one perished when the ship headed out to sea to attempt to outrun the storm. The handsome ship was built in 1927 as a destroyer for the Italian navy and was later reconstructed as a private floating palace for the Duke of Westminster.

In early 2003 the venerable *Flying Cloud* was pulled from the fleet, with its future uncertain. Built in 1935 as a cadet training ship for the French navy, it later served as a decoy and spy ship for the Allied Forces, participating in the sinking of two Japanese submarines during World War II.

In 2001 Windjammer purchased *Discover,* a 303-foot former oceanographic research vessel, and began converting it to carry 160 to 180 passengers. No plans have been announced for addition of the ship to the Windjammer fleet.

■ THE WINDJAMMER EXPERIENCE

None of the Windjammer ships could qualify as a luxury liner, and cabins and public rooms are small and simple. The atmosphere is decidedly relaxed, sometimes verging on nonstop partying. Some cruises have lifestyle themes, such as nudism, singles, swingers, and gays. Be sure to inquire whether any such gathering is planned on the cruise you might select.

Windjammer has been experiencing increasing bookings in recent years, and before the loss of the *Fantome* had announced plans to add three ships in the next decade and as many as five during the next fifteen years.

One interesting offering is a "stowaway" onboard the ship the night before departure. For a reasonable fee, guests can spend the night onboard the ship and partake of dinner, rum swizzles, a steel drum band party, and breakfast.

■ ITINERARIES

Legacy sailed in summer from Miami and Nassau to Bimini, Great Abaco, the Barry Islands, and New Providence. In fall she sails from Aruba to Bonaire,

Curacao, and Klein Curacao. Winter and spring itineraries depart St. Thomas to Water Island, Jost van Dyke, St. John, Norman Island, Tortola, and Virgin Gorda.

Mandalay sailed in June from the Caribbean coast of Panama to Playa Francis, Isla Grande, Isla Verde, Cayos Hollandes, Porvenir, and Portobello. In winter and spring the ship alternated between departures from Grenada or Antigua, sailing the Windward and Leeward Islands.

Polynesia sailed in summer and fall from St. Lucia to Grenada, St. Vincent, and Union Island in the Grenadines. In winter and spring *Polynesia*'s home port was St. Martin, sailing to Anguilla, Nevis, Saba, St. Bart's, Tintamarre, and St. Eustasius (Statia).

Yankee Clipper sails year-round from Grenada to Carriacou, Bequia, Saint Vincent, Union Island, and Tobago Cays.

The motor vessel *Amazing Grace* makes provisioning trips among the Caribbean islands to meet up with the company's fleet of sailing vessels. The home port alternates every two weeks between Grand Bahama and Trinidad, with calls to Antigua, Barbados, Bequia, Cooper, Dominica, the Dominican Republic, Grand Turk, Great Iguana, Grenada, Guadeloupe, Îles des Saintes, Jost Van Dyke, Marie-Galante, Martinique, Nevis, Norman, Saint Bart's, Saint Kitts, Saint Lucia, Saint Martin, Tobago, Tortola, and Virgin Gorda.

■ WEB SITE

The Windjammer Web site provides basic information about the ships and itineraries. There is no way to check availability of cabins on specific trips. Reservations must be made by telephone or through a travel agent; visitors can also fill out a reservation request on-line and receive a callback from the line. *Ease of use: very good.*

Legacy

Econoguide rating:	★★ 57 points
Ship size:	Small
Category:	Adventure
Price range:	Moderate $$
Registry:	Equatorial Guinea
Year built:	1959 (refurbished 1989)
Information:	(800) 327–2601
Web site:	www.windjammer.com
Passenger capacity:	122 (double occupancy)
Crew:	43
Passenger-to-crew ratio:	2.8:1
Tonnage:	1,740
Length:	294 feet
Beam:	40 feet
Draft:	23 feet

Cruising speed:	12 knots
Guest decks:	4
Total cabins:	61
Outside:	61
Inside:	0
Suites:	0
Wheelchair cabins:	0
Cuisine:	Island/continental, served family-style
Style:	Informal
Price notes:	Single-occupancy, premium 175 percent; reduced rates for children younger than twelve sharing cabin; stowaway aboard ship the night before sailing for $55 pp including meals
Tipping suggestions:	$8.50 pp/pd

The youngest antique in the Windjammer fleet, *Legacy* is a four-masted barkentine built in 1959. Originally named *France II*, she served as a meteorological research and exploration vessel for the French government. The ship was acquired in 1989 by Windjammer and converted into a traditional Tall Ship. She spends the year in the Caribbean.

Mandalay

Econoguide rating:	★★ 50 points
Ship size:	Small
Category:	Adventure
Price range:	Budget $
Registry:	Equatorial Guinea
Year built:	1923 (formerly *Hussar*, *Vema*; refurbished 1982)
Information:	(800) 327–2601
Web site:	www.windjammer.com
Passenger capacity:	72 (double occupancy)
Crew:	28
Passenger-to-crew ratio:	2.6:1
Tonnage:	420
Length:	236 feet
Beam:	33 feet
Draft:	15 feet
Cruising speed:	10 knots
Guest decks:	3
Total cabins:	36
Outside:	30
Inside:	0
Suites:	6

Wheelchair cabins:	0
Cuisine:	Island/continental; family-style
Style:	Informal
Price notes:	Single occupancy, premium 175 percent; reduced rates for children under twelve sharing cabin; stowaway aboard ship the night before sailing for $55 pp including meals
Tipping suggestions:	$8.50 pp/pd

Mandalay was built in 1923 as *Hussar,* a three-masted barkentine, for financier E. F. Hutton and his wife, Marjorie Merriweather Post. The wealthy couple traded up to a new vessel, now sailing for Sea Cloud Cruises as *Sea Cloud.*

In the 1930s the ship was sold to shipping magnate George Vettlesen and renamed *Vema.* Beginning in 1953 she took on a new role as a floating laboratory for Columbia University's Lamont-Doherty Geological Observatory, sailing more than a million miles while studying the ocean floor and gathering important research in confirmation of the continental drift theory.

The ship joined the Windjammer fleet in 1982; it was renamed *Mandalay* and renovated throughout. All cabins are outside and have a porthole or window; two deck cabins have private verandas.

Polynesia

Econoguide rating:	★★ 50 points
Ship size:	Small
Category:	Adventure
Price range:	Budget $
Registry:	Equatorial Guinea
Year built:	1938 (formerly *Argus,* refurbished 1975)
Information:	(800) 327–2601
Web site:	www.windjammer.com
Passenger capacity:	126 (double occupancy)
Crew:	45
Passenger-to-crew ratio:	2.8:1
Tonnage:	430
Length:	248 feet
Beam:	36 feet
Draft:	18 feet
Cruising speed:	8 knots
Guest decks:	4
Total cabins:	57
Outside:	55
Inside:	0
Suites:	2
Wheelchair cabins:	0
Cuisine:	Island/continental; usually family-style, occasionally buffet

Style:	Informal
Price notes:	Single occupancy, premium 175 percent; reduced rates for children under twelve sharing cabin; stowaway aboard ship the night before sailing for $55 pp including meals
Tipping suggestions:	$8.50 pp/pd

Built in Holland in 1938, **Polynesia** is a four-masted schooner. Originally named *Argus*, she was at one time the swiftest and most profitable of the Portuguese cod fishing fleet on the Grand Banks. The ship was purchased and brought out of retirement in 1975. Renamed *Polynesia*, renovations have included the installation of a teak deck, exotic wood paneling, and a dining salon with each table depicting one of the islands on the ship's itinerary.

Polynesia is one of Windjammer's most popular vessels, hosting special singles' and theme cruises.

Yankee Clipper

Econoguide rating:	★★ 50 points
Ship size:	Small
Category:	Adventure
Price range:	Budget $
Registry:	Equatorial Guinea
Year built:	1927 (formerly *Cressida, Pioneer*; refurbished 1965)
Information:	(800) 327–2601
Web site:	www.windjammer.com
Passenger capacity:	64 (double occupancy)
Crew:	24
Passenger-to-crew ratio:	2.7:1
Tonnage:	327
Length:	197 feet
Beam:	30 feet
Draft:	17 feet
Cruising speed:	14 knots
Guest decks:	3
Total cabins:	32
Outside:	32
Inside:	0
Suites:	0
Wheelchair cabins:	0
Cuisine:	Island/continental; usually family-style
Style:	Informal
Price notes:	Single occupancy, premium 175 percent; reduced rates for children under twelve sharing cabin; stowaway aboard ship the night before sailing for $55 pp including meals
Tipping suggestions:	$8.50 pp/pd

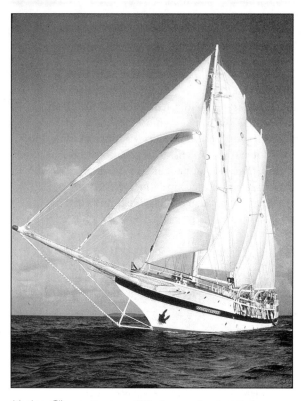

Yankee Clipper. Courtesy of Windjammer Barefoot Cruises

The *Yankee Clipper* is an updated antique, one of the fastest Tall Ships at sea, often sailing at 14 knots. The only armor-plated private yacht in the world, the former *Cressida* was built in Kiel, Germany, in 1927 by German industrialist and manufacturer Alfred Krupp. After World War II the U.S. Coast Guard confiscated the schooner as a war prize.

Acquired by the Vanderbilts and renamed *Pioneer,* she was raced off Newport Beach, California, where she was considered one of the fastest Tall Ships on the West Coast. *Pioneer* was purchased by Windjammer's Mike Burke in 1965 and, following extensive renovations, renamed *Yankee Clipper.* In 1984 she was completely restored to her former majesty, with refurbishments totaling $4 million. The work included a new set of three masts and a new engine room with custom-designed navigation, communication, and weather-monitoring devices.

Amazing Grace

Econoguide rating:	★★ 55 points
Ship size:	Small
Category:	Adventure
Price range:	Budget $
Registry:	Equatorial Guinea
Year built:	1955 (formerly *Pharos,* a British navy motor vessel)
Information:	(800) 327–2601
Web site:	www.windjammer.com
Passenger capacity:	94 (double occupancy)
Crew:	40

Passenger-to-crew ratio:	2.3:1
Tonnage:	1,585
Length:	257 feet
Beam:	40 feet
Draft:	17 feet
Cruising speed:	14 knots
Guest decks:	5
Total cabins:	48
Outside:	46
Inside:	1
Suites:	1
Wheelchair cabins:	0
Cuisine:	Island/continental; usually family-style, occasionally buffet
Style:	Very informal
Price notes:	Single occupancy, premium 175 percent
Tipping suggestions:	$8.50 pp/pd

The motorized supply ship for the Windjammer fleet, ***Amazing Grace*** permits passengers to hitch a ride on her circuit through the Caribbean and the Bahamas. She sails from Trinidad to Grand Bahama, reversing course every two weeks.

Built in 1955 as the Scottish lighthouse service ship *Pharos,* she has hosted Queen Elizabeth II and other members of the Royal Family. Acquired by Windjammer in 1985, *Amazing Grace* delivers provisions to the four Tall Ships in the fleet on thirteen-day tours.

Restored to her original British charm, the ship has a smoking lounge, antique fireplaces, and a piano room. Only the top-priced cabins have private bathrooms; other cabins share facilities on the same level. The owner's suite, named Burke's Berth, has a large sitting room separated from the stateroom by a set of aquariums. The bath, which includes a hot tub, is built with marble and teak.

WINDSTAR CRUISES

Address: 300 Elliott Avenue West
Seattle, WA 98119
Information: (800) 258–7245, (206) 281–3535
www.windstarcruises.com
Econoguide's Best Adventure Cruise Lines

The Windstar Cruises Fleet

Wind Surf	1990	312 passengers	14,745 tons
Wind Spirit	1988	148 passengers	5,350 tons
Wind Star	1986	148 passengers	5,350 tons

In November 1986 the first commercial sailing vessel built in sixty years left the dock in Le Havre, France. Although the *Wind Star* had the appearance of a classic sailing schooner, the ship, along with the two others in the Windstar fleet, is a decidedly modern-day creation. Computers control the rigging; the huge booms are motor-controlled, with high-tech sensors to trim the angle of the sail. Some 21,000 square feet of white sail unfurls at the push of a button. The angle of heel is kept at a maximum of 6 degrees by a computerized stabilizing system that pumps thousands of gallons of water from side to side with changes in the wind.

Today the *Wind Star* is joined by sister *Wind Spirit* and the larger *Wind Surf,* a five-masted cruise ship. Originally the *Club Med I,* it was rebuilt for Windstar in mid-1998.

The ships have auxiliary engines that are used when wind conditions are not favorable and for maneuvering in some harbors. Windstar says, though, that almost half the time at sea is spent under sail.

In late 2002 *Wind Song*—another sister to *Wind Star*—suffered a serious fire while sailing 10 miles off the coast of Tahaa, French Polynesia. All 127 passengers and 92 crew were safely evacuated to the nearby island of Raiatea by a passenger ferry, but the ship was destroyed.

■ ITINERARIES

Windstar was forced to rejigger its itineraries in 2003 after the loss of *Wind Song.* The company maintained its year-round presence in Tahiti by repositioning *Wind Star* from Europe to those waters.

Windstar's 2004 schedule offers 143 cruises to more than one hundred ports of call. *Wind Surf* and *Wind Spirit* winter in the Caribbean and summer in Europe; *Wind Star* sails year-round in South Pacific Seas of Tahiti and her islands.

Tahiti. *Wind Star* explores the islands of Tahiti; forty-five weekly cruises depart from Papeete, Tahiti, to visit the Society Islands of Huahine, Raiatea, Bora Bora, and Moorea. Two fourteen-day cruises travel from Tahiti round-trip to the Marquesas Islands of Fatu Hiva, Hiva Oa, Ua Pou, and Nuku Hiva and to Rangiroa in the Tuamotus, as well as visiting Bora Bora and Moorea. Two Christmas holiday cruises feature visits to the islands of Rangiroa, Huahine, Raiatea, Bora Bora, Moorea, and Tahiti.

Caribbean. A total of thirty-four cruises on eight itineraries explore the Caribbean from January through March and late November through December 2004. New for 2004, the *Wind Surf* makes its home port in St. Thomas. The *Wind Spirit* offers twelve journeys round-trip from St. Thomas to the Virgin Islands, plus six more one-way trips between St. Thomas and Barbados that can be combined for a fourteen-day cruise without repeating any ports.

Transatlantic. Sailing aficionados are offered a choice of three transatlantic crossings between St. Thomas and Lisbon, Portugal. The fourteen-day trips depart from the Caribbean in April 3 and 4 on *Wind Spirit* and *Wind Surf.* In November *Wind Spirit* returns from Europe.

Greek Isles. *Windstar* will sail eighteen times on two different itineraries aboard *Wind Spirit.* Most of the cruises sail between Athens, Greece, and Istanbul, Turkey, in May and June and mid-September to mid-October. Four cruises between Athens and Rome call at little-known Ermoupolis, Navplion, and Gythion, Greece; as well as Messina and Capri, Italy.

Mediterranean. From mid-April through mid-November, two ships offer trips that can be combined to create tours of six to thirty-five days in length without any repeated ports. *Wind Surf* makes nineteen journeys in the Mediterranean, with cruises departing from Lisbon, Portugal; Barcelona, Spain; Nice, France; Rome and Venice, Italy; and Grand Harbour, Malta. *Wind Spirit* sails twelve cruises from Lisbon, Barcelona, Rome, and Nice.

Baltic and northern Europe. From mid-June through early September, *Wind Surf* heads to the Baltic and northern Europe. Four ten-day cruises from Copenhagen, Denmark, feature a two-day stay in St. Petersburg, Russia, and an optional shore tour to Berlin at the port of Rostock, Germany. While repositioning to and from the Baltic Sea, *Wind Surf* makes two ten-day cruises between Lisbon, Portugal, and London (Dover), England, and two twelve-day cruises between London (Dover) and Copenhagen.

■ THE WINDSTAR EXPERIENCE

These are not the ships that Charles Dickens or Herman Melville wrote about. Cabin amenities include a color television and video player, CD player, refrigerator, and direct-dial telephones. Cuisine onboard the ships is directed by Joachim Splichal, chef and owner of Patina Restaurant in Los Angeles, with regional specialties and fine wines. Splichal created 180 signature dishes for Windstar vessels, ranging from rich continental fare to light menus.

Windstar shops local markets for native foods, including cheeses, fruits, spices, and fish. Ambience is casual, with no assigned seating or dress codes.

The ships offer waterskiing, sailboarding, kayaking, and snorkeling. Scuba diving is available for an additional charge.

Windstar cruises include a wide range of shore excursions, from the ordinary to the extraordinary, including an exploration of Costa Rica's rain forests where guests will "zip-line" on a pulley and cable from tree to tree way above the forest floor. Other onshore activities include sea kayaking, cultural odysseys, and river float expeditions.

Transatlantic repositioning cruises are unusual treats for sailing aficionados. On past ocean crossings, *Wind Spirit* guests had the luck of witnessing more than five consecutive days of strong winds and straight sailing unassisted by motor power. On another crossing, *Wind Surf* encountered a woman in a 22-foot rowboat, midway on her ultimately successful solo crossing. The ship and guests provided her with fresh food, reading material, a CD player, and a world-band radio.

Children—especially infants and toddlers—are not encouraged aboard the cruises. Windstar ships have no elevators, and therefore are not suitable for people in wheelchairs.

Windstar was purchased by Holland America in 1988; Holland America was in turn purchased by Carnival Corporation in 1989.

■ WEB SITE

Windstar's Web site provides basic information about the ships and itineraries. There is no way to check availability of cabins on specific trips. Reservations must be made by telephone or through a travel agent; visitors can also request a callback from the line. *Ease of use: very good.*

Wind Spirit, Wind Star

Econoguide rating:	★★★★ 84 points
Ship size:	Small
Category:	Adventure
Price range:	Opulent $$$$
Registry:	Bahamas
Year built:	*Wind Spirit,* 1988; *Wind Star,* 1986 (ships refurbished 1999)
Information:	(800) 258–7245
Web site:	www.windstarcruises.com
Passenger capacity:	148 (double occupancy)
Crew:	88
Passenger-to-crew ratio:	1.7:1
Tonnage:	5,350
Passenger-space ratio:	36.1
Length:	360 feet (waterline); 440 including bowsprit
Beam:	52.1 feet
Draft:	14 feet
Cruising speed:	8.5 to 14 knots, depending on wind; 8.5 to 10 knots with engines only
Guest decks:	4, plus flying bridge
Total cabins:	74
Outside:	74
Inside:	0
Suites:	1 owner's suite
Wheelchair cabins:	0
Cuisine:	Includes Sail Light and vegetarian menus
Style:	Casually elegant
Price notes:	Single-occupancy premium, 175 to 200 percent
Tipping suggestions:	Tipping not required
Best deals:	As much as 50 percent discount through A.S.A.P. early-booking program

A pair of football-field-size sailboats, **Wind Spirit** and **Wind Star** have four 204-foot-tall masts and six self-furling, computer-operated Dacron sails. Modern amenities include a restaurant that accommodates all passengers at one seating, a disco, CD and video libraries, a water sports platform, a saltwater pool, a hot tub, a casino, and a fitness center.

Wind Spirit broke its own record on a transatlantic crossing in December 2001 when it completed 103 consecutive hours under sail propulsion, covering 690 nautical miles at an average speed of 6.7 knots, with northeast winds ranging from 10 to 25 knots.

Sister ship *Wind Song* caught fire and was destroyed in a December 2001 fire in Polynesia; all passengers and crew were successfully evacuated.

Wind Surf

Econoguide rating:	★★★★ 84 points
Ship size:	Medium
Category:	Adventure
Price range:	Opulent $$$$
Registry:	Bahamas
Year built:	1990 (formerly *Club Med I*; refurbished 1999)
Information:	(800) 258–7245
Web site:	www.windstarcruises.com
Passenger capacity:	312 (double occupancy)
Crew:	163
Passenger-to-crew ratio:	1.9:1
Tonnage:	14,745
Passenger space ratio:	47.3
Length:	535 feet; 617 feet including bowsprit
Beam:	66 feet
Draft:	16.5 feet
Cruising speed:	10 to 15 knots, depending on wind; 12 knots under power
Guest decks:	7
Total cabins:	156
Outside:	125
Inside:	0
Suites:	31
Wheelchair cabins:	0
Cuisine:	Sail Light and vegetarian menus
Style:	Casually elegant
Price notes:	Single-occupancy premium, 175 to 200 percent
Tipping suggestions:	Tipping not required
Best deals:	As much as 50 percent discount through A.S.A.P. early-booking program

The seven-deck **Wind Surf** was born as the *Club Med I,* a thoroughly modern sailing and party vessel. The ship includes two restaurants, able to accommodate all passengers at one seating without assigned tables. Windstar refurbished the *Club Med* to reduce the number of cabins, adding a deck of 400-square-foot suites.

Seven self-furling, computer-operated triangular Dacron sails offer 26,881 square feet of surface area. Depending on destination and wind conditions, the ship is typically under sail about half the time.

CHAPTER EIGHTEEN

A HISTORY OF CRUISING

TODAY'S CRUISE INDUSTRY can trace its lineage back to the nineteenth century, when passenger ships were a means of transportation, primarily from Europe to the United States and between Europe and its far-flung colonies in Asia and Africa.

The arrival of commercial jet airplanes in the late 1950s marked the beginning of the end for the transatlantic and transpacific liners. Many of the big ships went to the breakers to be cut up for salvage. But not that long afterward, a new concept took hold: the cruise ship. Here the ship itself took center stage as a floating resort hotel.

THE ATLANTIC FERRY

By the middle of the nineteenth century, the traffic from Europe to America (and to a lesser extent, the other direction) was so steady that the route across the North Atlantic became known as the "Atlantic Ferry."

The race was on, literally, as shipbuilders pushed for larger and faster ships. The queens of the line also became more and more opulent within, at least for the relatively few wealthy first-class passengers; at the same time, builders crammed more and more low-fare travelers into "steerage" areas, which were often more like bunkhouses than staterooms. (Steerage, though, was the source of much of the shipping lines' profits because of the sheer number of those passengers.)

The first commercial steamship to cross the Atlantic was the *Savannah*, an American coastal packet ship designed as a sailing vessel in 1818 but refitted with an engine during construction. The ship made its first crossing in 1819, a twenty-eight-day voyage from Savannah, Georgia, to Ireland and Liverpool; the ship was never a commercial success.

The real beginnings of the Atlantic Ferry can be traced to Isambard Kingdom Brunel, chief engineer of the Great Western Railway in Great Britain. The rail line between Bristol and London was nearly finished in the 1830s, and Brunel decided to extend his company's reach across the pond. The ship he designed, the *Great Western*, left England for New York on April 8, 1838.

THE EARLY CUNARD LINERS

In 1840 the Cunard Line began mail service across the Atlantic with a quartet of paddle-wheel steamers that had auxiliary sails: the *Britannia, Acadia, Columbia,* and *Caledonia.* In 1858 Brunel's company launched the *Great Eastern,* an iron-hulled vessel that approached in size many of today's cruise ships, with a length of 692 feet.

For the next two decades, British and American interests competed for supremacy as merchant marine powers. During the U.S. Civil War, however, much of the American fleet was destroyed, and Britain regained its leading role, a position it held for the rest of the nineteenth century.

German shipping lines held size and speed records near the end of the nineteenth century, with vessels such as the 1,749-passenger *Kaiser Wilhelm der Grosse.* By 1898 the North German Lloyd line was carrying 28 percent of the passengers from Europe to New York.

The speed of the liners was limited because of the piston design of the steam engines. But by the 1890s, new technology using steam turbine engines began to be used. These systems were more powerful and reliable.

The British, led by the Cunard Line, sought to recapture preeminence with a set of superliners of the day. Cunard's *Lusitania* and *Mauretania* were launched in 1906. The *Mauretania* captured the Blue Riband for the fastest crossing in 1907, holding on to the honor until 1929. The *Lusitania* was sunk by a German submarine in 1915, an action that helped lead to the United States' entry into World War I.

THE *TITANIC* AND THE GREAT WAR

About this same time, the White Star Line, direct competitor of Cunard, also commissioned a pair of superliners. The 45,324-ton *Olympic,* launched in 1911, was for a short period of time the largest ship ever built. That title was taken over by White Star's slightly larger *Titanic* in 1912. The *Titanic,* of course, came to an unhappy end on her maiden voyage in 1912.

After the end of World War I, Germany was removed from competition, with the three surviving German liners confiscated as war reparations. In the postwar boom of the early 1920s, tourism grew markedly. Leaders included the French Line's *Île de France* and the return of the German lines. The Great Depression, though, slowed most new construction, but not all of it.

In 1930 the French Line planned and launched the gigantic *Normandie,* considered one of the most beautiful ships ever built. She was also the first large ship to be built in accordance with the 1929 Convention for Safety of Life at Sea rules. The *Normandie,* which included 1,975 berths, used turboelectric engines that reached a speed of 32.1 knots during trials in 1935. The ship caught fire and sank at a New York dock in 1942 while being refitted as a troopship.

Cunard struck back with the *Queen Mary,* a 975-foot-long classic that was launched in 1934. A sister ship, the 83,673-ton *Queen Elizabeth,* was launched in 1938 but served first as a troopship during World War II, along with most other civilian liners. After the war, it was completed as a luxury liner.

THE TRUE TALE OF THE *TITANIC*

The *Titanic* was big, all right . . . although in today's terms she would merely be one of many large ships, not exactly a Colossus. The *Titanic* was the new flagship of the White Star Line. Work began in 1909, with the launch of the uncompleted hull two years later.

Titanic was 883 feet long, 92 feet wide, and 104 feet tall from keel to bridge. Her gross tonnage was 46,328 tons. She was, at the time, the largest movable object ever made, standing taller than most buildings of the time.

The ship's construction featured a double hull of inch-thick steel plates. Below the waterline, the ship was divided into sixteen supposedly watertight compartments that could be sealed off with massive doors by the closing of a switch on the bridge. The *Titanic* also included an early Marconi radio system, allowing communication with other ships similarly equipped, as well as occasional connection with land-based stations.

Within, the *Titanic*'s accommodations were among the most luxurious afloat, at least for those passengers booked into first class. She was among the first ships with electric lighting in every room, as well as an indoor swimming pool, a squash court, and a gymnasium that had a mechanical horse and camel for exercise.

In an example of how everything old is someday considered a new idea, the *Titanic* offered two alternative restaurants in addition to the formal first-class dining salon.

Down below, hundreds of immigrants were packed into steerage-class accommodations, which were nevertheless described as being of better quality than full-rate cabins on some other ships of the time.

The ship's designers had specified thirty-two lifeboats, which was probably not adequate for the ship's total capacity of 3,500 passengers and crew. White Star made the situation even worse by reducing the number of lifeboats to twenty for appearance's sake. As the *Titanic* left on her maiden voyage, her lifeboats had a capacity of just 1,178 persons.

Titanic departed Southampton, England, on April 10, 1912, stopping across the channel in Cherbourg, France, to pick up some additional passengers and calling the next day in Queenstown, Ireland, for one more group. She headed out into the Atlantic on April 11, reaching her top speed of 22 knots; the *Titanic* was among the fastest ships of her time, but not expected to be the record holder.

The weather on the crossing was good. The winter of 1912 had been unusually moderate, making for good conditions at sea but also contributing to an unusually large amount of icebergs and floes breaking off the Arctic pack. In fact, the *Titanic* may have received a half dozen or more warnings of ice in the North

Atlantic. The captain, perhaps under pressure by executives of the ship line, continued to travel under full steam through the night of April 14.

At 11:40 that night, lookouts spotted a large iceberg ahead of the ship. The first officer ordered the ship hard to port and the engines put into reverse, but the big ship was moving too fast and was too slow to turn; she struck a glancing blow against the side of the berg.

Five of the ship's watertight compartments were ruptured, and water spilled over the top of the other compartment doors—the *Titanic* was doomed.

Investigations claimed that the liner *Californian* was less than 20 miles away from the disaster and could have been on the scene in less than an hour, but its radio cabin was not staffed during the night. Cunard's *Carpathia* finally arrived more than an hour after the ship went down, picking up most of the survivors in lifeboats.

In 1985 the wreck of the *Titanic* was located, split into two large pieces at a depth of about 13,000 feet. Surprisingly, no sign of the expected lengthwise gash in the side of the ship was found; scientists now believe the glancing blow against the iceberg popped open seams in the riveted hull plates of the ship and made a series of smaller gashes.

THE LAST HURRAH OF THE LINERS

The last great American liner was the *United States,* launched in 1952; the ship had a top speed of 35.6 knots and captured the coveted Blue Riband from the *Queen Mary.*

Not long afterward, the arrival of commercial air traffic across the Atlantic spelled the beginning of the end of the great liners. The propeller-driven DC-7 made the crossing at approximately 300 miles per hour, with a range of nearly 3,000 miles. By 1957 there were more passengers crossing the Atlantic by air than by sea. About 1958, commercial jet planes began regular service, and regular transatlantic traffic by liner was entering its final days.

Of course, today the industry is booming. The difference is that nearly all passenger vessels are cruise ships rather than liners.

The increasingly more fabulous ships and their ports of call are the lures, not mere transportation across an ocean or from continent to continent. On some cruises a significant number of passengers don't get off the ship when it ties up at the dock: Their entertainment, dining, and sports activities all take place on board.

GLOSSARY OF CRUISING

―――

OK, LET'S GET ONE THING STRAIGHT: It's a ship, not a boat. A boat is something you row across the pond or sail across the river. A ship is a big vessel that has lots of cabins, many levels, a bingo parlor, a health club, and a rotating disco at the top of its massive funnel. You get the idea: Boat is little, ship is big.

If you really want to sound like a swabbie (the opposite of a landlubber), here is a guide to some nautical terms for the cruise vacationer.

Abeam. To the side of the ship, at a right angle to the keel that runs the length of the vessel.

Aft. At the stern (rear) of the ship, or rearward from your present location.

Amidships. At or near the middle of the ship.

Astern. Behind the stern of the ship.

Beam. The width of the ship at its broadest point, usually amidships.

Bearing. The compass direction of the ship in motion, or the direction toward a specified point.

Below. Any area beneath the main deck of the ship.

Berth. A dock or pier for the ship, or a bed for a passenger or crewman.

Bilge. The lowest interior space of the ship.

Boat station. The assigned assembly place for passengers and crew in a lifeboat drill or a true emergency.

Bow. The front of the ship.

Bridge. The principal navigation and control station.

Bulkhead. A vertical wall used to divide sections of the ship into waterproof and fire-resistant compartments.

Bunkers. Fuel storage areas.

Colors. The national flag or emblem flown by a particular vessel.

Companionway. An interior stairway.

Course. The bearing of the ship as underway, expressed in degrees.

Davit. The rope and pulley or motor system used to lower and raise lifeboats.

Draft. The distance from the ship's waterline to the lowest part of the keel; a ship cannot safely enter waters shallower than its draft.

Fantail. An overhang at the stern of the ship.

Fathom. A measurement of water depth equal to 6 feet. The measure was derived from the average distance from fingertip to fingertip of the outstretched arms of a man.

Galley. The ship's kitchen.

Gangway. A walkway extended to connect the ship to shore.

Gross registered tons (GRT). A measurement of the total permanently enclosed spaces of the ship, excluding certain essential areas such as the bridge and galleys, developed as a means of taxing vessels based on their cargo-carrying capacity; 1 GRT = 100 cubic feet of enclosed space.

Helm. The steering mechanism. As a verb, to take the control of the steering mechanism.

Hull. The body of the ship.

Knot. One nautical mile. This is based on a measure of one-sixtieth of a degree of the earth's circumference, which works out to 6,080.2 feet, or about 800 feet longer than a land-based mile. The term knot as a measure of speed refers to distance per hour; 20 knots means 20 knots per hour. (Only a landlubber says "per hour.") To convert knots to miles per hour, add about 15 percent. For example, 20 knots is equal to just over 23 miles per hour.

Leeward. The side of the ship or a body of land that is sheltered from the wind. The opposite is windward.

Nautical mile. A measurement of distance equal to one-sixtieth of a degree of the circumference of the earth, or about 6,080.2 feet.

Pilot. A specially trained guide to local waters sometimes taken aboard when a ship enters an unfamiliar or tricky harbor or area.

Pitch. The rise and fall of the ship's bow when it is under way.

Plimsoll mark. A set of marks on the side of a vessel that shows at least three depths indicating the maximum safe draft (the lowest the ship can safely sit in the water). One line is for summer when seas are generally calm in most parts of the world, another for winter when seas are usually rougher, and a third is a freshwater line to account for the fact that fresh water is significantly less buoyant than salt water. The mark was named for nineteenth-century social reformer Samuel Plimsoll, who was concerned about ship disasters blamed on overloading by greedy owners.

Port. The left side of the ship when facing forward. On old Viking ships, the steering board was on the right side, so the left side was used as the side to tie up in port.

Quay. A berth or dock.

Rudder. A movable part of the ship that extends into the water and is used to steer the vessel.

Screw. A ship's propeller.

Stabilizer. An adjustable finlike structure that extends from the side of a ship to minimize roll.

Starboard. The right side of the ship when facing forward. On Viking ships, the steering board (the star board) was placed on the right side.

Stern. The rearmost part of the ship.

Tender. A small boat used to transport passengers or crew to shore when the ship is anchored away from a dock.

Veranda. A private balcony for a passenger cabin, a feature of some of the most modern and luxurious vessels and generally located on the upper decks.

Wake. The track of disturbed water left behind a ship in motion.

Watches. Assigned duties for the crew. On a naval ship, the twenty-four-hour day was divided into seven watches: the midwatch from midnight to 4:00 A.M., the morning watch from 4:00 to 8:00 A.M., the forenoon watch from 8:00 A.M. to noon, the afternoon watch from noon to 4:00 P.M., the first dog watch from 4:00 to 6:00 P.M., the second dog watch from 6:00 to 8:00 P.M., and the evening watch from 8:00 P.M. to midnight. Traditionally, because few sailors could afford a timepiece, the passage of time aboard Navy ships was indicated by the striking of bells during each four-hour watch. One bell was struck after the first half hour, two bells after one hour, three bells after an hour and a half, four bells after two hours, and so on up to eight bells at the completion of the four-hour watch.

Windward. The side of the ship or a body of land that is exposed to the wind.

And while I'm on the subject, here are a few terms from nautical sources that have become part of our common language.

Between the devil and the deep blue sea. On an old wooden ship, the longest seam, which ran from the bow to the stern, was called the "devil." The seam needed to be caulked regularly to keep it watertight, and to do so a sailor was suspended in a boatswain's chair—between the devil and the deep blue sea. The caulking was an asphalt pitch, also known as "pay." Sailors were sometimes assigned to this unpleasant task as punishment for infractions of the rules. The threat was to behave, or there would be the "devil to pay."

The cat is out of the bag. The cat-o'-nine-tails was used to whip sailors as punishment; when it was removed from its cloth bag, everyone knew what came next.

Chewing the fat. Salted beef was one of the staples aboard nineteenth-century ships, not much more edible than shoe leather. It sometimes required hours of chewing to make it soft enough to swallow.

Crow's nest. Vikings carried ravens or crows as part of their navigation equipment. In poor weather, the birds—carried in a cage at the top of the mast—were released. Sailors observed the direction the birds headed and plotted a course toward land. The platform at the top of the mast, or the uppermost place on a motor ship, is now known as the crow's nest.

Cup of Joe. Josephus Daniels, the U.S. Secretary of the Navy under President Woodrow Wilson, introduced a number of changes in the early part of the twentieth century, among them the end of the wine mess for officers; thereafter, the strongest available drink aboard Navy ships was coffee, which became known as a "cup of Joe."

Feeling blue. A ship that lost its captain or principal officer during a voyage would paint a blue band around the hull and fly blue flags from the rigging.

Hunky-dory. Derived from the name of a street in the port of Yokohama, Japan, where residents catered to the carnal pleasures of sailors, the term means that everything is satisfactory.

Jury-rig. Meaning to put something together in a makeshift way, the term comes from "jury mast," a temporary mast constructed from any available spar.

Log book. Early ship's records were kept on shingles cut from logs, hinged into a log book.

Mayday. The international radio phrase for ships in trouble is an anglicized version of the French phrase *m'aidez,* meaning "help me." It was officially adopted as a signal in 1948.

Minding your p's and q's. The careful and neat sailor took care that his pigtail, or queue, which was kept in shape with a mousse of tar, did not soil his pea jacket.

Portholes. Ships that were equipped with large cannons in the fifteenth century were held behind large doors that could be opened when needed; the French word for door is *porte.*

S.O.S. The letters S.O.S. were selected for a Morse code signal of distress because the combination of sounds—dot-dot-dot, dash-dash-dash, dot-dot-dot—was easily recognized. It is not an acronym for "save our ship" or "save our souls," a mere coincidence.

Three sheets to the wind. On a small sailing vessel, three sheets (ropes) controlled the sails; if the sheets were loose, the sails were out of control. Today we apply the term to a sailor or a landlubber who is out of control with the assistance of drink.

The whole nine yards. A square-rigger sailing vessel had three masts with three yards (or sails) on each; if the captain was sailing hard, he was giving the vessel the whole nine yards.

Beaufort Scale

If you're lucky enough to experience the excitement of a storm at sea (all right, not all cruisegoers are thrilled) your captain is likely to describe the conditions using the thirteen-step Beaufort Scale. The numbers correspond as follows:

Force	Wind speed (mph)	Wind description	Ocean conditions
0	0	Calm	Glassy smooth, mirrorlike
1	1–3	Light wind	Rippled surface
2	4–7	Light breeze	Small wavelets
3	8–12	Gentle breeze	Large wavelets, scattered whitecaps
4	13–18	Moderate breeze	Small waves, frequent whitecaps
5	19–24	Fresh breeze	Moderate waves, many whitecaps
6	25–31	Strong breeze	Large waves, white foam crests
7	32–38	Near-gale	Streaky white foam
8	39–46	Fresh gale	Moderately high waves
9	47–54	Strong gale	High waves
10	55–63	Storm	Very high waves, curling crests
11	64–73	Violent storm	Extremely high waves, poor visibility
12	73+	Hurricane	High waves, thundering spray

CRUISE LINES IN THIS BOOK

American Canadian Caribbean Line 🎗🎗🎗
(800) 556–7450; www.accl-small ships.com
American Cruise Lines 🎗🎗🎗
(860) 345–3311; www.americancruiselines.com
Carnival Cruise Lines 🎗🎗🎗
(800) 227–6482, (305) 599–2600; www.carnival.com
Celebrity Cruises 🎗🎗🎗🎗
(800) 437–3111, (305) 262–6677; www.celebrity-cruises.com
Clipper Cruise Line 🎗🎗🎗
(800) 325–0010, (314) 727–2929; www.clippercruise.com
Costa Cruise Lines 🎗🎗🎗
(800) 332–6782, (305) 358–7325; www. costacruises.com
Cruise West 🎗🎗🎗
(800) 888–9378, (206) 441–8687; www.cruisewest.com
Crystal Cruises 🎗🎗🎗🎗🎗🎗
(800) 820–6663, (310) 785–9300; www.crystalcruises.com
Cunard Line 🎗🎗🎗🎗🎗
(800) 528–6273, (305) 463–3000; www.cunard.com
Delta Queen Steamboat Company 🎗🎗🎗
(800) 543–7637; www.deltaqueen.com
Disney Cruise Line 🎗🎗🎗🎗
(800) 326–0620; www.disneycruise.com
Glacier Bay Cruiseline 🎗🎗🎗
(800) 451–5952, (206) 623–7110; www.glacierbaytours.com
Holland America Line 🎗🎗🎗🎗
(800) 227–6482, (800) 426–0327; www.hollandamerica.com
Imperial Majesty Cruise Line 🎗🎗
(800) 511–5737; www.oceanbreezecruise.com
Lindblad Special Expeditions 🎗🎗🎗
(800) 397–3348; www.expeditions.com
MSC Italian Cruises 🎗🎗🎗
(800) 666–9333; www.msccruisesusa.com
Norwegian Cruise Line 🎗🎗🎗🎗
(800) 327–7030; www.ncl.com

Oceania Cruises ♥♥♥
Princess Cruises ♥♥♥♥
(800) 421–0522, (800) 774–6237; www.princess.com
Radisson Seven Seas Cruises ♥♥♥♥♥
(800) 333–3333, (800) 285–1835; www.rssc.com
RiverBarge Excursion Lines ♥♥♥
(888) 462–2743; www.riverbarge.com
Royal Caribbean International ♥♥♥
(800) 327–6700; www.royalcaribbean.com
Royal Olympia Cruises ♥♥♥
(800) 872–6400; www.royalolympiacruises.com
Seabourn Cruise Line ♥♥♥♥♥♥
(800) 929–9391; www.seabourn.com
Sea Cloud Cruises ♥♥♥♥♥
(888) 732–2568, (201) 227–9404; www.seacloud.com
Silversea Cruises ♥♥♥♥♥♥
(800) 722–9955, (954) 522–4477; www.silversea.com
Society Expeditions ♥♥♥
(800) 548–8669; www.societyexpeditions.com
Star Clippers ♥♥♥
(800) 442–0551; www.star-clippers.com
Windjammer Barefoot Cruises ♥♥♥
(800) 327–2601; www.windjammer.com
Windstar Cruises ♥♥♥♥
(800) 258–7245, (206) 281–3535; www.windstarcruises.com

OTHER CRUISE LINES AND PACKAGERS

Abercrombie and Kent International
(800) 323–7308; www.abercrombiekent.com
Club Med
(800) 258–2633, (305) 925–9000; www.clubmed.com
Eurocruises
(800) 688–3876, (212) 691–2099; www.eurocruises.com
First European Cruises
(212) 779–7168; www.first-european.com
Norwegian Coastal Voyages
(800) 666–2374, (212) 319–1300; www.coastalvoyage.com
Peter Deilmann Cruises
(800) 348–8287, (703) 549–1741; www.deilmann-cruises.com
Star Cruises
(305) 436 4694; www.starcruises.com
Swan Hellenic
(877) 219–4239; www.swanhellenic.com

QUICK-FIND INDEX

ABOUT THE AUTHOR

Corey Sandler is a former newsman and editor for the Associated Press, Gannett Newspapers, Ziff-Davis Publishing, and IDG. He has written more than 160 books on travel, video games, and computers; his titles have been translated into French, Spanish, German, Italian, Portuguese, Polish, Bulgarian, Hebrew, and Chinese. When he's not traveling, he hides out with his wife and two children on Nantucket, an island 30 miles off the coast of Massachusetts.

ECONOGUIDE® 2004 ECONOGUIDE® 2004
ECONOGUIDE® 2004 ECONOGUIDE® 2004
ECONOGUIDE® 2004 ECONOGUIDE® 2004
ECONOGUIDE® 2004 ECONOGUIDE® 2004
ECONOGUIDE® 2004 ECONOGUIDE® 2004
ECONOGUIDE® 2004 ECONOGUIDE® 2004
ECONOGUIDE® 2004 ECONOGUIDE® 2004
ECONOGUIDE® 2004 ECONOGUIDE® 2004
ECONOGUIDE® 2004 ECONOGUIDE® 2004
ECONOGUIDE® 2004 ECONOGUIDE® 2004
ECONOGUIDE® 2004 ECONOGUIDE® 2004
ECONOGUIDE® 2004 ECONOGUIDE® 2004
ECONOGUIDE® 2004 ECONOGUIDE® 2004
ECONOGUIDE® 2004 ECONOGUIDE® 2004
ECONOGUIDE® 2004 ECONOGUIDE® 2004
ECONOGUIDE® 2004 ECONOGUIDE® 2004
ECONOGUIDE® 2004 ECONOGUIDE® 2004
ECONOGUIDE® 2004 ECONOGUIDE® 2004
ECONOGUIDE® 2004 ECONOGUIDE® 2004
ECONOGUIDE® 2004 ECONOGUIDE® 2004
ECONOGUIDE® 2004 ECONOGUIDE® 2004
ECONOGUIDE® 2004 ECONOGUIDE® 2004
ECONOGUIDE® 2004 ECONOGUIDE® 2004
ECONOGUIDE® 2004 ECONOGUIDE® 2004
ECONOGUIDE® 2004 ECONOGUIDE® 2004
ECONOGUIDE® 2004 ECONOGUIDE® 2004

EXPERIENCE THE QUEEN MARY

SPEND THE DAY, SPEND THE NIGHT

QUEEN MARY TOURS

THE HAUNTED SHIP
GHOSTS AND LEGENDS SPECIAL
EFFECTS ADVENTURE

SEE MORE OF THE SHIP
ALL NEW SELF-GUIDED OR
GUIDED TOURS OF THE SHIP

COLD WAR
RUSSIAN SUBMARINE

ART DECO
OBSERVATION BAR

ALL NEW TOURS

Come explore the elegance and adventure that is the Queen Mary. Tour this magnificent floating palace and discover its secrets. Your tour will take you through the entire ship from its impressive engine room to its newly restored decks. Stroll through Art Deco Ballrooms, be captivated by the Treasures from the Queen Mary Archive. Your admission also includes the New Ghosts & Legends Show and our New WWII Exhibit which brings the Queen's rich history to life. So bring the entire family for a fun-filled, affordable adventure to the past.

THE QUEEN MARY.

HOTEL QUEEN MARY

365-STATEROOM
ART DECO HOTEL

AWARD-WINNING
CASUAL TO ELEGANT
RESTAURANTS

SIXTEEN ORIGINAL
SALONS FOR
MEETING AND BANQUETS

ELEGANT
CHAMPAGNE SUNDAY BRUNCH

For information or reservations 562.435.3511 or online at: www.queenmary.com

BUY ONE GENERAL ADMISSION,
GET ONE FREE!

Present this coupon at the Queen Mary Box Office and receive one (1) complimentary General Admission when one (1) General Admission of the same or greater value is purchased. Additional charge for guided tours, special events, and submarine attraction. This coupon has no cash value. This is not a ticket and is not for resale and cannot be combined with any other offer. Valid for (1) one ticket. Expires December 31, 2004.

Located at the end of the 710 freeway, on the water in Long Beach. There is a charge for parking. © 2003 RMS Foundation, Inc./The Queen Mary

ECONOGUIDE® 2004 ECONOGUIDE® 2004
ECONOGUIDE® 2004 ECONOGUIDE® 2004
ECONOGUIDE® 2004 ECONOGUIDE® 2004
ECONOGUIDE® 2004 ECONOGUIDE® 2004
ECONOGUIDE® 2004 ECONOGUIDE® 2004
ECONOGUIDE® 2004 ECONOGUIDE® 2004
ECONOGUIDE® 2004 ECONOGUIDE® 2004
ECONOGUIDE® 2004 ECONOGUIDE® 2004
ECONOGUIDE® 2004 ECONOGUIDE® 2004
ECONOGUIDE® 2004 ECONOGUIDE® 2004
ECONOGUIDE® 2004 ECONOGUIDE® 2004
ECONOGUIDE® 2004 ECONOGUIDE® 2004
ECONOGUIDE® 2004 ECONOGUIDE® 2004
ECONOGUIDE® 2004 ECONOGUIDE® 2004
ECONOGUIDE® 2004 ECONOGUIDE® 2004
ECONOGUIDE® 2004 ECONOGUIDE® 2004
ECONOGUIDE® 2004 ECONOGUIDE® 2004
ECONOGUIDE® 2004 ECONOGUIDE® 2004
ECONOGUIDE® 2004 ECONOGUIDE® 2004
ECONOGUIDE® 2004 ECONOGUIDE® 2004
ECONOGUIDE® 2004 ECONOGUIDE® 2004
ECONOGUIDE® 2004 ECONOGUIDE® 2004
ECONOGUIDE® 2004 ECONOGUIDE® 2004
ECONOGUIDE® 2004 ECONOGUIDE® 2004
ECONOGUIDE® 2004 ECONOGUIDE® 2004

Where moments
become memories

SeaWorld®
ADVENTURE PARK
Orlando

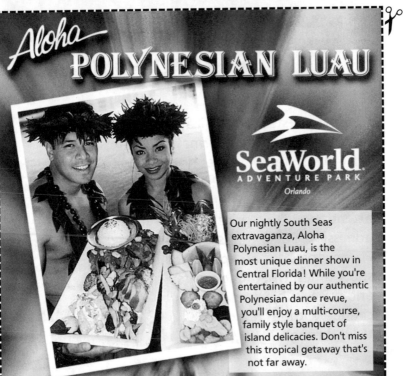

Aloha
POLYNESIAN LUAU

SeaWorld®
ADVENTURE PARK
Orlando

Our nightly South Seas extravaganza, Aloha Polynesian Luau, is the most unique dinner show in Central Florida! While you're entertained by our authentic Polynesian dance revue, you'll enjoy a multi-course, family style banquet of island delicacies. Don't miss this tropical getaway that's not far away.

$2⁰⁰ OFF ADMISSION

Limit six guests per certificate. Reservations not valid with other discounts, special events or on purchase of multi-park/multi-visit passes or tickets. Present certificates at Front Gate before bill is totaled. Redeemable only at time of ticket purchase. Photocopies not accepted. Operating hours and general admission price subject to change without notice. Certificate has no cash value. Valid through 12/31/04.

PLU 4354/4353

SeaWorld.
ADVENTURE PARK
Orlando

$5⁰⁰ OFF ADULT & JUNIOR LUAU ADMISSION

Limit six guests per certificate. Reservations required. Inquire at Information Center or call (407) 351-3600. Offer not valid with other discounts. Present certificate before bill is totaled. Redeemable only at time of Luau attendance. Luau price separate from park admission. Park admission not required. Photocopies not accepted. Call for show times. Operating hours and prices subject to change without notice. Valid through 12/31/04 only.

SeaWorld.
ADVENTURE PARK
Orlando

$1⁰⁰ OFF

SeaWorld.
ADVENTURE PARK
Orlando

BEHIND-THE-SCENES TOURS

Present this coupon at the Information Counter inside SeaWorld Orlando and receive $1 off a **Behind-the-Scenes Tour**. Choose from To the Rescue, Predators and Polar Expedition— or take all three! These one-hour adventures are filled with animal interactions, adventure and fun!

Discount valid for up to six people. Not valid with any other offer. Tour availability and components subject to change. Park admission not included and is required. Expires 12/31/04.

$5⁰⁰ OFF ADVENTURE EXPRESS

Adventure Express is a 6-hour exclusive adventure and includes front-of-the-line access to rides, reserved seats at select shows, animal interaction and feeding opportunities, lunch and an expert guide to help make your day a great adventure.

Sign up at the Information Counter inside SeaWorld Orlando or call **800-406-2244** for advance reservations. Discount valid for up to six people. Not valid with any other offer. Tour availability and components subject to change. Park admission is not included and is required. Expires 12/31/04.

SeaWorld.
ADVENTURE PARK
Orlando

ECONOGUIDE® 2004 ECONOGUIDE® 2004
ECONOGUIDE® 2004 ECONOGUIDE® 2004
ECONOGUIDE® 2004 ECONOGUIDE® 2004
ECONOGUIDE® 2004 ECONOGUIDE® 2004
ECONOGUIDE® 2004 ECONOGUIDE® 2004
ECONOGUIDE® 2004 ECONOGUIDE® 2004
ECONOGUIDE® 2004 ECONOGUIDE® 2004
ECONOGUIDE® 2004 ECONOGUIDE® 2004
ECONOGUIDE® 2004 ECONOGUIDE® 2004
ECONOGUIDE® 2004 ECONOGUIDE® 2004
ECONOGUIDE® 2004 ECONOGUIDE® 2004
ECONOGUIDE® 2004 ECONOGUIDE® 2004
ECONOGUIDE® 2004 ECONOGUIDE® 2004
ECONOGUIDE® 2004 ECONOGUIDE® 2004
ECONOGUIDE® 2004 ECONOGUIDE® 2004
ECONOGUIDE® 2004 ECONOGUIDE® 2004
ECONOGUIDE® 2004 ECONOGUIDE® 2004
ECONOGUIDE® 2004 ECONOGUIDE® 2004
ECONOGUIDE® 2004 ECONOGUIDE® 2004
ECONOGUIDE® 2004 ECONOGUIDE® 2004
ECONOGUIDE® 2004 ECONOGUIDE® 2004
ECONOGUIDE® 2004 ECONOGUIDE® 2004
ECONOGUIDE® 2004 ECONOGUIDE® 2004
ECONOGUIDE® 2004 ECONOGUIDE® 2004

ECONOGUIDE® 2004 ECONOGUIDE® 2004
ECONOGUIDE® 2004 ECONOGUIDE® 2004
ECONOGUIDE® 2004 ECONOGUIDE® 2004
ECONOGUIDE® 2004 ECONOGUIDE® 2004
ECONOGUIDE® 2004 ECONOGUIDE® 2004
ECONOGUIDE® 2004 ECONOGUIDE® 2004
ECONOGUIDE® 2004 ECONOGUIDE® 2004
ECONOGUIDE® 2004 ECONOGUIDE® 2004
ECONOGUIDE® 2004 ECONOGUIDE® 2004
ECONOGUIDE® 2004 ECONOGUIDE® 2004
ECONOGUIDE® 2004 ECONOGUIDE® 2004
ECONOGUIDE® 2004 ECONOGUIDE® 2004
ECONOGUIDE® 2004 ECONOGUIDE® 2004
ECONOGUIDE® 2004 ECONOGUIDE® 2004
ECONOGUIDE® 2004 ECONOGUIDE® 2004
ECONOGUIDE® 2004 ECONOGUIDE® 2004
ECONOGUIDE® 2004 ECONOGUIDE® 2004
ECONOGUIDE® 2004 ECONOGUIDE® 2004
ECONOGUIDE® 2004 ECONOGUIDE® 2004
ECONOGUIDE® 2004 ECONOGUIDE® 2004
ECONOGUIDE® 2004 ECONOGUIDE® 2004
ECONOGUIDE® 2004 ECONOGUIDE® 2004
ECONOGUIDE® 2004 ECONOGUIDE® 2004
ECONOGUIDE® 2004 ECONOGUIDE® 2004
ECONOGUIDE® 2004 ECONOGUIDE® 2004
ECONOGUIDE® 2004 ECONOGUIDE® 2004
ECONOGUIDE® 2004 ECONOGUIDE® 2004

MOSI
4801 East Fowler Avenue
Tampa, FL 33617-2099
(813) 987-6300
www.mosi.org

One free child admission with paid adult.
Not valid with any other coupons,
special offers, or special events.
Expires 12/31/04

World's Greatest Aircraft Collection®

1400 Broadway Blvd SE (I–4 Exit 44)
Polk City, FL 33868
www.fantasyofflight.com
863–984–3500, ext. 233
Fax: 863–984–9506

$3.00 off General Admission
Present coupon at time of purchase.
Not valid with any other discount,
special event or annual pass.
Limit 6 persons per coupon

SKU 521322 - Adult
521323 - Child
521324 - Senior

Expires 12/31/04

ECONOGUIDE® 2004 ECONOGUIDE® 2004
ECONOGUIDE® 2004 ECONOGUIDE® 2004
ECONOGUIDE® 2004 ECONOGUIDE® 2004
ECONOGUIDE® 2004 ECONOGUIDE® 2004
ECONOGUIDE® 2004 ECONOGUIDE® 2004
ECONOGUIDE® 2004 ECONOGUIDE® 2004
ECONOGUIDE® 2004 ECONOGUIDE® 2004
ECONOGUIDE® 2004 ECONOGUIDE® 2004
ECONOGUIDE® 2004 ECONOGUIDE® 2004
ECONOGUIDE® 2004 ECONOGUIDE® 2004
ECONOGUIDE® 2004 ECONOGUIDE® 2004
ECONOGUIDE® 2004 ECONOGUIDE® 2004
ECONOGUIDE® 2004 ECONOGUIDE® 2004
ECONOGUIDE® 2004 ECONOGUIDE® 2004
ECONOGUIDE® 2004 ECONOGUIDE® 2004
ECONOGUIDE® 2004 ECONOGUIDE® 2004
ECONOGUIDE® 2004 ECONOGUIDE® 2004
ECONOGUIDE® 2004 ECONOGUIDE® 2004
ECONOGUIDE® 2004 ECONOGUIDE® 2004
ECONOGUIDE® 2004 ECONOGUIDE® 2004
ECONOGUIDE® 2004 ECONOGUIDE® 2004
ECONOGUIDE® 2004 ECONOGUIDE® 2004
ECONOGUIDE® 2004 ECONOGUIDE® 2004
ECONOGUIDE® 2004 ECONOGUIDE® 2004
ECONOGUIDE® 2004 ECONOGUIDE® 2004
ECONOGUIDE® 2004 ECONOGUIDE® 2004